The Probate Manual

Waterlow Law Books

Waterlow Practitioner's Library
Estate Conveyancing *by P. M. A'Court*
The Law of Co-operatives *by Ian Snaith*
A Practical Introduction to Trade Marks *by Brian C. Reid*
Consumer Credit Agreements *by Jan Karpinski and Stephen Fielding*
Handling Criminal Cases, A Guide to Preparation and Defence *by James Morton*
Copyright through the Cases *by Gavin McFarlane*
Cases on Patents—a New Anthology *by Brian C. Reid*
Challenging Delegated Legislation *by Keith Puttick*
Confidentiality and the Law *by Brian C. Reid*
Police Powers and the Rights of the Individual *by J. B. Hill and Karen E. Fletcher-Rogers*
Weapons Law *by J. B. Hill*

Procedure Notes
Insolvency Procedure Notes *by Paul Gordon-Saker and Michael Stubbs*
Probate Procedure Notes *by Kevin Donnelly*

For further information write to Waterlow Publishers,
Oyez House, 27 Crimscott Street, London SE1 5TS
Tel. 01-232 1000

The Probate Manual

Twenty-Third (completely revised) Edition

by

R. F. YELDHAM
Principal of the Probate Department,
Principal Registry of the Family Division

and

ANGELA PLUMB
Chief Examiner in the Capital Taxes Office,
Inland Revenue

WATERLOW PUBLISHERS

Twenty-Third Edition 1988

Waterlow Publishers
Oyez House, PO Box 55,
27 Crimscott Street,
London SE1 5TS
A division of Hollis Financial and Professional Services PLC

ISBN 0 08 033109 2

British Library Cataloguing in Publication Data
Yeldham, R. F.
The probate manual.—23rd (completely rev.) ed.—(Waterlow practitioner's library)
1. England. Probate. Law
I. Title II. Plumb, Angela
344.2065'2 KD1518

Printed and bound in Great Britain by
A. Wheaton & Co Ltd, Exeter

Preface to the 23rd Edition

Numerous changes have again been necessary in this edition of the *Probate Manual*. Perhaps the most significant have followed from the new Non-Contentious Probate Rules, the Family Law Act 1986 and the Family Law Reform Act 1987 (in particular, the reform whereby illegitimacy is not taken into consideration for succession to property on intestacies happening on or after 4 April 1988) and these are fully incorporated into the text. The introduction of Inheritance Tax, while welcome to the taxpayer, has involved considerable difficulties for the practitioner, and readers should find the sections on this new tax helpful.

This book deals with non-contentious probate practice only and references to a "Rule" or "Rules" are to the Non-Contentious Probate Rules 1987. The full current text of the Rules is set out in Appendix 1.

The following abbreviations are used in Chapter 6:

I.H.T.A.	Inheritance Tax Act
F.A.	Finance Act

and section references are to the Inheritance Tax Act 1984 unless otherwise mentioned.

The law is stated as at 1 October 1988.

Contents

Table of Cases

Table of Statutes

Statutory Instruments

Table of Forms and Precedents

CHAPTER 1

Introduction: General Procedure and Copies

FUNCTIONS OF THE COURT

1.01 The functions of the Family Division of the High Court of Justice in England and Wales include the issuing and revocation of grants of probate and administration and the determination of what documents may be admitted to proof as testamentary, and who is entitled to be constituted the legal and personal representative of a deceased person.

1.02 Although not bound to do so, the Family Division has power, after considering the terms of a testamentary document, to determine a question of its construction for the limited purpose of making a grant of representation (*In the Estate of Frogley* [1905] P. 137; *In the Estate of Lupton* [1905] P. 321; *In the Estate of Fawcett* [1941] P. 85; [1941] 2 All E.R. 341).

1.03 Section 116 of the Supreme Court Act 1981 provides the Court with discretionary powers to make a grant to any suitable person or body, leaving the question of construction to be decided by the Chancery Division.

1.04 The decision of the Court regarding the title to a grant of probate or the title to administration is conclusive in all courts in England and Wales, and when a document has been admitted to probate all courts in England and Wales must regard it as being testamentary.

1.05 Section 128 of the Supreme Court Act 1981 defines "non-contentious or common form probate business" as

> "the business of obtaining probate and administration where there is no contention as to the right thereto, including
> (*a*) the passing of probates and administrations through the High Court in contentious cases where the contest has been terminated,
> (*b*) all business of a non-contentious nature in matters of testacy and intestacy not being proceedings in any action, and
> (*c*) the business of lodging caveats against the grant of probate or administration."

APPLICATIONS FOR GRANTS

1.06 Application for a grant of probate or administration may be made at the Principal Registry of the Family Division or at any one of the district probate registries or sub-registries. When application is made to a sub-registry, the grant is issued from the parent registry. The names and addresses of the registries are set out blow:

Registry	Sub-registry	Address (and British Document Exchange number, where a member)
The Principal Registry		Somerset House, Strand, London WC2A 1LP. (DX 396 Chancery Lane)
Birmingham		3rd Floor, Cavendish House, Waterloo Street, Birmingham B2 5PS
	Stoke-on-Trent	2nd Floor, Town Hall, Albion Street, Hanley, Stoke-on-Trent ST1 1QL
Brighton		William Street, Brighton BN2 2LG (DX 2734 Brighton (1))
	Maidstone	The Law Courts, Barker Road, Maidstone ME18 8EW (DX 4846 Maidstone)
Bristol		The Crescent Centre Temple Back, Bristol BS1 6EP
	Bodmin	Market Street, Bodmin PL31 2JW.
	Exeter	Eastgate House, High Street, Exeter EX4 3JZ
Ipswich		Level 3, Haven House, 17 Lower Brook Street, Ipswich IP4 1DN (DX 3279 Ipswich)
	Norwich	The Law Courts, Bishopgate, Norwich NR3 1UR (DX 5202 Norwich)

Registry	**Sub-registry**	**Address (and British Document Exchange number, where a member)**
	Peterborough	Clifton House, Broadway, Peterborough PE1 1SL. (DX 12327 Peterborough (1))
Leeds		3rd Floor, Coronet House, Queen Street, Leeds LS1 2BA. (DX 26451 Leeds Park Square)
	Lincoln	Mill House, Brayford Side North, Lincoln LN1 1YW. (DX 17701 Lincoln (2))
	Sheffield	4th Floor, The Court House, Castle Street, Sheffield S3 8LW. (DX 26054 Sheffield (2))
Liverpool		3rd Floor, India Buildings, Water Street, Liverpool L2 0QR
	Chester	5th Floor, Hamilton House, Hamilton Place, Chester CH1 2DA.
	Lancaster	Mitre House, Church Street, Lancaster LA1 1HE.
Llandaff		Probate Registry of Wales, 49 Cardiff Road, Llandaff, Cardiff CF5 2YW.
	Bangor	1st Floor, Bron Castell, Bangor High Street, LL57 1YS.
	Carmarthen	14 King Street, Carmarthen SA31 1BL.
	Gloucester	3 Pitt Street, Gloucester GL1 2BJ. (DX 7537 Gloucester)

Registry	**Sub-registry**	**Address (and British Document Exchange number, where a member)**
Manchester		9th Floor, Astley House, 23 Quay Street, Manchester M3 4AT. (DX 14387 Manchester)
	Nottingham	Upper Ground Floor, Lambert House, Talbot Street, Nottingham NG1 5NR. (DX 10055 Nottingham)
Newcastle-upon-Tyne		2nd Floor, Plummer House, Croft Street, Newcastle-upon-Tyne, NE1 6ND. (DX 61081 Newcastle-upon-Tyne)
	Carlisle	2 Victoria Place, Carlisle CA1 1ER. (DX 63034 Carlisle)
	Middlesbrough	12/16 Woodlands Road, Middlesbrough, TS1 3BE.
	York	Duncombe Place, York YO1 2EA. (DX 61543 York)
Oxford		10a New Road, Oxford OX1 1LY. (DX 4337 Oxford)
	Leicester	Government Buildings, Newarke Street, Leicester LE1 5SE. (DX 10870 Leicester)
Winchester		4th Floor, Cromwell House, Andover Road, Winchester, SO23 7EW. (DX 2528 Winchester)

LODGING PAPERS FOR GRANT

1.07 Whether application for a grant is to be made to the Principal Registry or to a district probate registry, the papers to lead to the grant may be taken or posted to the appropriate registry. In order to avoid delay in obtaining the grant all the necessary papers should be lodged at the time of making the application. Care should be taken to see that the oath to lead to the grant has been duly sworn by the applicants and that testamentary documents, if any, have been marked by the signatures of the applicants and the person who administered the oath.

1.08 In addition to the oath and any testamentary documents, an Inland Revenue account must be lodged, unless it is an "excepted estate" (see paras. 6.06ff). Where it is necessary for the Inland Revenue account to be assessed before the grant is issued, this must be done before the papers are lodged at court. If Inheritance Tax is payable, and the application is to proceed in the Principal Registry, the account and a cheque for the tax payable to the Inland Revenue should be sent to:

Finance Division,
Inland Revenue, (A),
Barrington Road,
Worthing,
West Sussex BN12 4XH

and on its return the account should be sent to the Principal Registry with the other papers to lead to the grant. Alternatively, payment of the tax may be made in person at the Inland Revenue Department at Somerset House.

1.09 Where an application is to proceed in a district probate registry, the Inland Revenue account and a cheque made payable to the Inland Revenue in respect of Inheritance Tax, may be sent to the Finance Division, Worthing or direct to the registry with the other papers to lead to the grant. If lodged at court with the other papers, the district probate registry then forward the account and cheque to the Finance Division at Worthing.

1.10 For payment of tax and the preparation and delivery of the Inland Revenue account, where necessary, see paras. 6.01 ff.

Court fees should normally be paid by crossed cheque made payable to "H.M. Paymaster General".

Duty of registrar on receiving application for grant

1.11 Rule 6 provides—

"(1) A registrar shall not allow any grant to issue until all inquiries which he may see fit to make have been answered to his satisfaction.

(2) Except with the leave of a registrar, no grant of probate or of administration with the will annexed shall issue within seven days of the death of the deceased and no grant of administration shall issue within fourteen days thereof."

DIRECTIONS ON MARKING PAPERS AND SWEARING OATHS AND AFFIDAVITS

1.12 Rule 10 must be observed with regard to the marking of testamentary documents. The registrar may allow a facsimile copy to be marked or exhibited in lieu of the original document.

1.13 It is generally sufficient that the applicants for the grant and persons administering the oath to lead to the grant mark the testamentary documents to be proved with their signatures in this form:

A.B. C.D. }	Executors	E. F., Commissioner for Oaths. (Solicitor)

No exhibit clause is required. The testamentary documents should not be attached to the oath. The signatures should not be written near the signatures of the testator and witnesses. If the will and codicil(s) are on one sheet of paper, only one marking is necessary. When a copy of a foreign will which has been translated is presented for proof it is the foreign copy and not the translation of it which must be marked. Where any additional affidavit is to be filed the following form should be written on the will:

"This is the will marked "A" referred to in the affidavit of .... sworn on the .... day of ....19..............., before me, ... Commissioner for Oaths/Solicitor". The affidavit should identify the will as: "now produced to me and marked "A", and bearing date ....".

1.14 The oath or affidavit must be signed by the deponent with his usual signature, and particular care should be taken that the signature agrees with the name of the deponent in the body of, and in the jurat to, the oath or affidavit. If the deponent is illiterate, blind or otherwise unable to sign his name and therefore makes his mark, such mark must be made in the presence of the person who administers the oath. The jurat must contain a statement that the oath was previously read over to the deponent and that he understood the same and made his mark "before me", (*i.e.* the person who administers the oath). The words "the mark of A.B.," must appear above the mark.

1.15 Where there are alterations in the oath or affidavit, care should be taken that the person who administers the oath initials them all, and where two alterations occur in the same line the person who administers the oath must initial each alteration.

1.16 If the oath is returned by the registrar for additions or amendments, it should be re-sworn and a fresh jurat added (the will need not be re-marked). When it is necessary to prepare a fresh form, the form which had been previously examined must be returned to the registrar for comparison.

1.17 If several separate jurats are necessary, the back of the oath may be used if there is insufficient room at the foot of the front page thereof.

1.18 The oath must not be administered by the extracting solicitor or his partner or his clerk. In any part of the British Commonwealth, it may be sworn before any judge, notary public or other person lawfully appointed to administer oaths, who must show that he is qualified to administer the oath. Oaths sworn elsewhere abroad should be taken before a British consular official, a judge of the High Court of such country under the seal of such court, or before any person authorised by the law of such country to administer oaths in that country. An affidavit sworn in a foreign country before a notary public and duly signed and sealed by him is acceptable, but any other person administering an oath or affidavit must annex a certificate to it to the effect that he has such authority, and the certificate must be signed by a British Consul or Vice-Consul, or verified by the seal of the High Court of such country.

1.19 An officer of the regular forces of a rank of or above that of Lieutenant-Commander or equivalent or relative rank may, at a place outside the United Kingdom, take affidavits and declarations from persons subject to military law and persons not so subject who are employed by, or are in the service of, or accompany, Her Majesty's Forces in an official capacity. The jurat or attestation must state the date on which, and the place at which, the affidavit or declaration was taken and the full name and rank of the officer.

TRANSLATIONS

1.20 If a will lodged for proof, or any other document relative to an application for a grant, is in a foreign language, it must be accompanied by a translation. The translation should be certified as being complete and accurate by, and under the seal of, an English notary public or a British Consul or Vice-Consul; but where such a translation cannot be obtained, the matter should be referred to a registrar for directions as to who may make and verify a translation, and in such a case the registrar may accept a translation made by some other competent person. A translation verified as correct by a British Consul or Vice-Consul is acceptable, but a translation by a Consul General of a foreign country must be submitted to a registrar for a decision as to whether it will suffice. Where the competency of the translator cannot be assumed from the official position he holds, the registrar will normally require him to file an affidavit setting out his qualifications and experience and verifying the completeness and accuracy of the translation. The foreign will, not the translation, must be marked by the signatures of the applicant for the grant and the person who administers the oath to lead to the grant.

COPIES

1.21 The testamentary documents and other papers leading to the making of a grant of probate or administration (except the Inland Revenue account, which is forwarded to the Capital Taxes Office) are filed in the registry from which the grant is issued. Copies of any such testamentary document or other paper which is available for public inspection and copies of the record of the grant may be obtained from that registry upon payment of the prescribed fee. Copies of testamentary documents and copies of grants in District Probate Registry cases may also be obtained from the Principal Registry upon payment of the prescribed fee. When applying for copies, it is necessary to give the full name of the deceased, the date of the death, the date of grant (if possible) and the address of the deceased.

Types of copies

1.22 The type of copy made depends upon the nature of the document and the purpose for which the copy is needed. The various types of copies obtainable are:

(1) *Sealed office copies.* Where practicable, all copies are made by photocopying or other process which produces a facsimile copy and those bearing the seal of the registry are issued and marked as office copies. Photocopies of the record of a grant which are sealed with the seal of the registry are accepted as evidence of the grant in all parts of the United Kingdom without further proof (Section 132, Supreme Court Act 1981). Office copies of the record of resealing a colonial grant are obtainable at the Principal Registry, or at the district probate registry if the colonial grant was resealed there.

(2) *Sealed and certified copies.* A copy bearing the seal of the registry and certified under the hand of a registrar to be a true copy of the original, is obtainable from the registry in which the original document is filed or from the Principal Registry. Sealed copies of proved testamentary documents must include all documents admitted to proof, whether proved together or separately. A sealed and certified copy of an original document in a foreign language which is filed in the registry may be obtained and the English translation will be excluded if so desired.

(3) *Exemplification.* An exemplification is a special type of sealed copy which may be required by a foreign court. It contains a recitation of the fact of search having been made of the record of grants, a summary of the grant and a copy of the testamentary documents (if any) admitted to proof. Application for an exemplification must be made in the registry from which the grant issued.

(4) *Special copy for use abroad.* The laws of certain foreign countries may call for the production of this special type of copy. It comprises a copy of the grant and testamentary documents (if any) and bears special forms of certificate signed by the district probate registrar and/or a registrar of the Principal Registry, also a certificate given by the President of the Division, and bears the seal of the registry or registries concerned. Application for this type of copy must be made to the Record Keeper at the Principal Registry, or to the district probate registrar where the grant issued from a district probate registry.

(5) *Plain (unofficial) copies.* Plain, unsealed copies are obtainable, including copies of documents of a testamentary nature filed in the registry but not admitted to proof (*e.g.* wills marked "probate refused"). Copies of any testamentary document which has not been admitted to proof in its original form, (*e.g.* a valid will containing unauthenticated alterations or additions) are also obtainable.

Fees

1.23 Fees are payable for inspecting documents, for obtaining copies of documents and for handling postal applications (see Appendix 2).

CHAPTER 2

Wills

WHAT DOCUMENTS MAY BE PROVED

2.01 Any formally valid testamentary document which deals with estate situated in England or Wales, or which affects a testamentary document which deals with such estate, or which appoints an executor, is capable of proof in the English courts (see also *In the Estate of Wayland* [1951] 2 All E.R. 1041 in which it was held that a will which did not deal with estate in England was admissible to proof).

2.02 Although a will may have become inoperative (*e.g.* where all the executors are dead and all the beneficiaries have predeceased the testator), it must still be submitted for proof if a grant of representation is sought in the estate of the deceased. It cannot be sworn that the deceased died intestate.

Documents not admissible to proof

2.03 A document duly executed in the same manner as a will, but merely revoking all testamentary dispositions and effective to create an intestacy, is not admissible to proof (*In the Goods of Fraser* (1869) L.R. 2 P. & D. 40; *Toomer v. Sobinska* [1907] P. 106; *Re Spracklan's Estate* [1938] 2 All E.R. 345), but must be filed with the papers to lead to a grant of administration. A document merely appointing a guardian has been held to be not entitled to proof (*In the Goods of Morton* (1864) 3 Sw. & Tr. 422).

FORMAL VALIDITY OF TESTAMENTARY DOCUMENTS

2.04 Before a testamentary document can be admitted to proof the appropriate system of law must be applied in order to test its validity. The system of law to be chosen is dependant upon the date of death of the testator.

2.05 The Wills Act 1963 applies only to wills where the testator has died on or after 1st January 1964, the date on which the Act came into force, irrespective of whether the will was made before, or on, or after that date. (see para. 2.101).

2.06 The Wills Act 1861 (Lord Kingsdown's Act) (which is not discussed in this book) is repealed as from 1st January 1964, but the repeal does not invalidate a will executed before that date which can only be set up under that Act (Section 7, Wills Act 1963).

EXECUTION OF WILLS

2.07 The internal law of England and Wales requires that a will must be executed in accordance with the provisions of the Wills Act 1837 unless it can be shown to be a privileged will.

2.08 Where the deceased died *before 1st January 1983,* Section 9 of the Wills Act 1837 provides that:

> "No will shall be valid unless it shall be in writing and executed in manner hereinafter mentioned; (that is to say) it shall be signed at the foot or end thereof by the testator, or by some other person in his presence and by his direction; and such signature shall be made or acknowledged by the testator in the presence of two or more witnesses present at the same time, and such witnesses shall attest and shall subscribe the will in the presence of the testator, but no form of attestation shall be necessary."

The Wills Act Amendment Act 1852 amended the requirements as to the position of the signature in execution of a will but not to the extent that any disposition or direction underneath or following the signature was effective.

2.09 Where the deceased died *on or after 1st January 1983,* Section 9 of the Wills Act 1837 as amended by Section 17 of the Administration of Justice Act 1982 provides that:

> "No will shall be valid unless—
> (*a*) it is in writing, and signed by the testator, or by some other person in his presence and by his direction; and
> (*b*) it appears that the testator intended by his signature to give effect to the will; and
> (*c*) the signature is made or acknowledged by the testator in the presence of two or more witnesses present at the same time; and
> (*d*) each witness either—
> (i) attests and signs the will; or
> (ii) acknowledges his signature,
> in the presence of the testator (but not necessarily in the presence of any other witness),
> but no form of attestation shall be necessary."

It should be noted, in particular, that in respect of deaths on or after 1st January 1983 words below the testator's signature may be included as part of his will, if it is established that the testator intended by his signature to give effect to them as part of his will. It should also be noted that in respect of deaths on or after 1st January 1983 an acknowledgement of his own signature by a witness to a will, in the presence of the testator, will be sufficent.

2.10 The testator must have attained the age of 18 years in relation to wills executed on or after 1st January 1970 (Section 7, Wills Act 1837 as amended by Section 3(1), Family Law Reform Act 1969), except that a member of a class of persons entitled to make a privileged will may make a valid will if of the age of 14 years and upwards (for privileged wills see paras. 2.87 ff).

Wills to be "in writing"

2.11 Writing, in relation to wills (and codicils), includes typing, printing, lithography, photography and other modes of representing or reproducing words in a visible form (see Sch. 1, Interpretation Act 1978). A will written in shorthand has been accepted (*Orrin v. Orrin,* "The Times", 20th December 1921). The writing may be wholly or partly by pencil. An oral testamentary statement (nuncupative will) may be accepted if made in circumstances which entitled the testator to make a privileged will (see paras. 2.87 ff).

Signature of testator:

2.12 A will or codicil may be signed by the testator with his name, initials (*In the Goods of Blewitt* (1880) 5 P.D. 116), or mark. Re-execution of a will or codicil by the testator going over his signature with a dry pen is held to be sufficient if in the joint presence of two or more witnesses who then attest the re-execution by signing in the presence of the testator or, where the testator died on or after 1st January 1983, by either signing or acknowledging their signatures in the testator's presence.

Testator signs by mark or initials:

2.13 The mark is usually made by a cross, but a mark by thumb-print has been accepted (*Re Finn* (1935) 154 L.T. 242). When a will or codicil is signed by mark or initials, the attestation clause should state that the testator either read the document himself or that it was read over to him prior to execution, and that he perfectly understood and approved its contents. If the attestation clause does not include such statements, an affidavit speaking as to how the testator had knowledge of the contents (and as to due execution) may be required to be made by a subscribing witness, or failing a witness, by some other person competent to speak to the fact that the testator had knowledge of the contents of the document (Rule 13) (Form of affidavit after para. 2.151 No. (1)).

Signature by another person by direction of testator

2.14 When a will or codicil is signed by another person on behalf of and at the direction of the testator, such other person may sign his own or the testator's name. In this case the attestation clause should state that the signature was made by such person in the presence of and by the direction of the testator; that the contents of the document were read over to, and approved by, the testator; and that the testator duly acknowledged such signature in the presence of the subscribing witnesses as being that in final execution of the document. If these facts are not shown in the attestation clause, an affidavit as to the circumstances in which the will or codicil was executed is required to be made, preferably by a subscribing witness, or by some other person who was present at the time of execution and is able to speak to the facts.

2.15 The signature on behalf of the testator may be made by one of the attesting witnesses (*In the Goods of Bailey* (1838) 1 Curt. 914; *Smith v. Harris* (1845), 1 Rob. 262). It should be noted that when a signature in execution of his will or codicil is made on behalf of, and is acknowledged by, the testator, the signatures of the witnesses must be subscribed after such signature and acknowledgement (*Wyatt v. Berry* [1893] P. 5 and *White v. Jones,* "The Times", 19th February 1932) or, where the testator died on or after 1st January 1983, the witnesses' signatures must be either subscribed or acknowledged after the signature in execution is made and acknowledged.

Execution by acknowledgment of signature

2.16 The testator may acknowledge his signature in execution of his will or codicil expressly by words or by implication or signs (*Re Hadler*, "The Times", 20th October 1960), *e.g.* by producing the document with his signature thereon, or by assenting to some other person producing it in his presence with his signature thereon, and with his signature visibly apparent on the face of it, in the joint presence of the witnesses, and requesting them to subscribe it.

2.17 Provided that the testator's signature was there and that the witnesses had opportunity to see it if they had looked, it does not matter if they did not actually see it (*Re Macdonald* (1942) I.R. 201), but if there is no evidence as to the existence of the signature at the time of execution, proof of the will may be refused (*Fischer v. Popham* (1875) L.R. 3 P. & D. 246). If the signature was covered so that the witnesses could not see it if they had looked, there is not sufficient acknowledgment (*Re Gunstan, Blake v. Blake* (1882) 7 P.D. 102). The acknowledgment must be in the joint presence of the witnesses and before either of them has subscribed as a witness (*Re Davies* [1951] 1 All E.R. 920) but see the substituted Section 9 of the Wills Act 1837 (para. 2.09) in respect of testators who have died on or after 1st January 1983, and the sufficiency of an acknowledged witness's signature. The acknowledgment of his signature by the testator may be sufficient even though the witnesses were unaware of the nature of the document (*Daintree v. Butcher and Fasulo* (1888) 13 P.D. 67, 102).

Position of testator's signature where testator died before 1st January 1983

2.18 Section 9 of the Wills Act 1837, in respect of testators who died before 1st January 1983, required that a will or codicil must be signed by the testator "at the foot or end thereof". Section 1 of the Wills Act Amendment Act 1852, which still applies to the wills of testators who died before 1st January 1983, provides that a will or codicil shall not be invalidated for the reason that the testator's signature does not appear in that position.

2.19 In each case the court must decide from the position of the signature whether it is so placed as to show on the face of the document that it was the testator's intention to give effect by such signature to the contents of the document (*Re Long* [1936] P. 166 *In the Goods of Hornby* [1946] 2 All E.R. 150). A signature in the testimonium clause or attestation clause is not necessarily sufficent without affidavit evidence to show that the testator intended such signature to be in execution of the document (*Re Pearn* (1875) 1 P.D. 70).

2.20 Under the Wills Act Amendment Act 1852, "no signature . . . shall be operative to give effect to any disposition or direction which is underneath or which follows it" (see also *Re Gee, deceased* (1898) 78 L.T. 843) even if the signature of the testator appears at the extreme top of the will (*In Re Stalman, Stalman v. Jones* (1931) W.N. 143). Where a will has been signed at the foot of the first page only (or as the case may be) and for some reason, such as lack of space, has been continued on the next page, such continuation will not be admitted to proof as part of the will, unless there is a reference, above the signature on the first page (or as the case may be) which effects incorporation. In the case of *Re Evans* (1923) 128 L.T. 669 it was decided that a clause written after the signature, although written on the will before execution, could not be admitted to probate. A signature in the margin of the will has been held to be sufficent execution (*Re Roberts* [1934] P. 102).

2.21 A signature made in completion of the form of endorsement which appears on the back of most printed will forms is not accepted as a signature to a will, unless it is shown by evidence that the testator intended such signature to be in execution of the will and that it was duly attested. It has been held that a will could be admitted to proof as duly executed where the testator wrote on an envelope in which the paper on which the will was written was afterwards enclosed, "This is my last Will and Testament" and then signed on the envelope in the joint presence of the witnesses, intending such signature to be in execution of the will, and the witnesses afterwards and in the presence of the testator signed the paper on which the will was written (*Re Mann* [1942] P. 146).

Position of testator's signature (death on or after 1st January 1983)

2.22 Section 9 of the Wills Act 1837 as substituted in respect of testators who die on or after 1st January 1983 makes no requirement as to the position of the testator's signature. The testator's signature may appear anywhere on the will or codicil provided that it appears that the testator intended by his signature to give effect to the will or codicil. As in cases where the testator died before 1st January 1983, evidence as to due execution, speaking to the testator's signature being made or acknowledged with the intention of givng effect to the will or codicil, and to the content of the same at the time of execution, will normally be required where the testator's signature is not at the end of the will or is in the attestation clause.

Two or more signatures

2.23 If the testator has signed more than once, it may be necessary to furnish an affidavit by one of the attesting witnesses in explanation. The affidavit should state, by a reference to its position, which signature was made by the testator in due and final execution of the will or codicil. Evidence of a similar nature is required if it appears that the testator made more than one attempt to sign, and in such a case the affidavit should also speak as to whether the document was read over to the testator prior to execution, and as to his approval of the contents of it. (Form of affidavit after para. 2.151 No. (2)).

Testator's signature below signatures of witnesses

2.24 If the signature of the testator appears below the signatures of the witnesses, there is a presumption that he signed after the witnesses. The presumption can only be rebutted by an affidavit of due execution.

Attestation clause

2.25 Except when the registrar so requires (Rule 12(1)), it is not necessary to adduce any evidence as to the due execution of a will or codicil if there is an attestation clause stating that it was signed by the testator, that such signature was made or acknowledged by the testator in the joint presence of two or more witnesses, and that such witnesses attested and subscribed their signatures to the document (or, where the testator died on or after 1st January 1983 that such witnesses either made or acknowledged their signatures) in the presence of the testator after he had signed or acknowledged his signature.

2.26 No form of attestation is necessary (Section 9, Wills Act 1837), but an affidavit of due execution will be called for in accordance with Rule 12(1), if there is no attestation clause, or if there is an attestation clause which does not clearly show due execution according to the statute unless the registrar exercises his discretion and dispenses with such evidence where he is satisfied that the distribution of the estate is not affected by the will (Rule 12(3)). Where there is no attestation clause, or a defective attestation clause, and there is a later testamentary document bearing a sufficent attestation clause and which confirms or refers to the earlier document by date or in some other specific way, evidence of due execution of the earlier document is not required. If the will or codicil has been made on a printed form, evidence of due execution is not required solely because the words "his/her" or "his or her" or the incompleted word "h   " appear in the attestation clause.

Competency of witnesses

2.27 Section 14 of the Wills Act 1837 provides that if a witness, at the time of the execution of the will or at any time thereafter, is incompetent to be admitted as a witness, the will is not invalid on that account alone. Although it is inadvisable that a minor should be a witness, there is no rule or enactment to prevent this. A blind person is not a competent witness (*Re Gibson* [1949] P. 434). Under Section 15 of the Wills Act 1837, a beneficial gift to a witness, or to the husband or wife of a witness, is void (but see para. 4.24 as to when this does not apply). However this does not affect the competency of the witness. A person appointed as an executor by the will or codicil is a competent witness.

Presence of attesting and subscribing witnesses

2.28 It is not necessary that the witnesses should be aware of the nature of the document (*Re Benjamin* (1934) 150 L.T. 417).

2.29 The testator must subscribe his signature (or mark) in execution of the document, or acknowledge it, in the actual visual presence of two or more witnesses, present at the same time, and (where the testator died before 1st January 1983) before any witness subscribes his signature. Where he dies on or after 1st January 1983, he must subscribe or acknowledge before the witnesses subscribe or acknowledge their signatures. The witnesses must sign (or sign or acknowledge where the testator dies on or after 1st January 1983) in the presence of the testator.

2.30 It is essential that the witnesses must have seen, or have had the opportunity of seeing, the testator's signature (or mark) in execution of the document (*Re Gunstan, Blake v. Blake* (1882) 7 P.D. 102; and *Groffman and Block v. Groffman* [1969] 2 All E.R. 108, where the will was in the testator's pocket).

Attestation and subscription by witnesses

2.31 The witnesses must, after the testator has made or acknowledged his signature in their joint presence, subscribe their signatures to the will or codicil in the presence of the testator (or, where the testator dies on or after 1st January 1983, subscribe or acknowledge their signatures in the testator's presence). The testator must have had the opportunity of seeing the witnesses subscribe their signatures if he had chosen to look (*Jenner v. Ffinch* (1879) 5 P.D. 106). Presumably, where the testator dies on or after 1st January 1983, he must have had the opportunity of seeing the already written signature (or signatures), had he chosen to look, when the acknowledgment of a witness's signature is relied on.

2.32 It is not essential that the witnesses should sign or acknowledge in the presence of each other. Although it is preferable that their signatures should be written immediately below the final signature of the testator, the witnesses may sign on any part of the will or codicil provided they intended to attest the testator's execution thereof. If their signatures appear on a separate sheet, it must be shown by affidavit that such sheet was physically connected (*e.g.* with a pin) to the sheet on which the testator signed.

2.33 Witnesses may subscribe their names, initials or marks. The signature of a witness may not be made by another person on his behalf (*Re Duggins* (1870) 39 L.J.P. & M. 24), nor, where the testator died before 1st January 1983, may a witness acknowledge a signature that he has previously written (*Re Maddock* (1874), 3 P. & D. 169). The addresses and descriptions of the witnesses are not essential.

2.34 If there is an unnecessary signature on the will or codicil it may be omitted from the probate provided that it is proved that it was not subscribed in attestation of the testator's signature (*Kitcat v. King* [1930] P. 266; but doubted in *Re Bravada, Bravada v. Bravada,* [1968] 2 All E.R. 217).

Date of will or codicil

2.35 If a will or codicil bears no date, or where there is a doubt as to the date on which it was executed, an affidavit as to due execution, particularly referring to the date of execution, will be called for (Rule 14(4)). The affidavit should, if possible, be made by an attesting witness or by some other person present at the time of execution. Whenever it is possible, the affidavit should speak to the actual date on which the document was executed, and it should recite the facts which enable the deponent to recollect the date.

2.36 If evidence as to the actual date of execution cannot be obtained, the attesting witnesses or other deponent to the affidavit should speak as to execution between two definite dates (*e.g.* in a certain week or month). When there is a considerable period of time between the two dates, the applicant for the grant is usually required to file an affidavit of search for other documents of a testamentary nature. (Form of affidavit of search after para. 2.151 No. (6)). Affidavit evidence is required when a will or codicil:

(1) bears no date;
(2) bears more than one date (but see para. 2.37);
(3) was executed on a date other than that which it bears;
(4) bears a date on the endorsement later than that shown in the document as the date of execution. (In such a case evidence may be dispensed with if there is only a slight difference in the dates.)

2.37 Where a document bears one date as its commencement and a later date at the foot thereof, the later date is usually accepted as the true date without affidavit evidence. An affidavit will, however, be called for if the later date is in the attestation clause or is not in close connection with the testator's signature, or conflicts with a date on the endorsement, or if the applicant's title to the grant depends on the later date being the true one.

Misrecital of date of will in codicil

2.38 Where a codicil misquotes the date of the will or the date of a previous codicil, the registrar will require an explanatory affidavit from the person who prepared the codicil and may also call for an affidavit as to search having been made for any other document of a testamentary nature. The registrar may require an application to be made for an order that the codicil be rectified to show the correct date of the earlier document (see paras. 2.58–62).

Affidavit of due execution

2.39 Where it appears to the registrar that there is some doubt about the due execution of a testamentary document, he will call for an affidavit of due execution from one or more of the attesting witnesses or, if no attesting witness is conveniently available, from any other person who was present at the time the will or codicil was executed, unless the registrar exercises his discretion where he is satisfied that the distribution of the estate is not affected by the will and dispenses with such evidence (Rule 12). In every case where, for any purpose, an affidavit is made by an attesting witness or other person present at the time of execution, the deponent must depose to the manner in which the document was executed (Rule 16). When such an affidavit is made by an attesting witness to a will who was also a witness to a codicil to that will, the affidavit should speak to the due execution of both documents, even if the codicil shows that it was properly executed. This also applies conversely.

2.40 The affidavit must show that the will or codicil was produced to the deponent at the time of his being sworn to the affidavit, and the original will or codicil must normally be marked as an exhibit to the affidavit (see Rule 10(1)). The registrar may allow a facsimile copy of it to be exhibited in lieu of the original document (Forms of affidavit after para. 2.151 Nos. (1)–(4)).

Evidence of due execution unobtainable

2.41 Where an affidavit of due execution cannot be obtained, the registrar may accept evidence on affidavit from any person he may think fit, to show that the signature on the document is in the handwriting of the deceased, or of any other matter which may raise a presumption in favour of the due execution of the document and he may, if he thinks fit, require that notice of the application be given to any person who may be prejudiced by the will (Rule 12(2)). (Form of affidavit of handwriting after para. 2.151 No. (12)). The registrar has a discretion to dispense with such evidence if he is satisfied that the distribution of the estate is not affected by the will (Rule 12(3)).

2.42 If the attesting witnesses are dead, or there is evidence showing that they cannot be traced, and it cannot be ascertained whether any other person was present at the time of execution of the document, the consents of all persons who would be prejudiced if the document were admitted to proof will usually be required. There must be affidavit evidence showing the names of such persons, how they would be entitled in the event of an intestacy or under an earlier will (if such exists) and stating that they are all *sui juris.* If such persons are not all *sui juris,* or do not all consent, the matter must be referred to a registrar for his directions.

2.43 If an affidavit of due execution cannot be obtained, evidence by affidavit as to the handwriting of the testator should be obtained. The directions of a registrar must be sought if evidence of the handwriting of the testator cannot be obtained.

Attesting witnesses unable to remember circumstances in which they subscribed their signatures

2.44 Where the witnesses identify their signatures but are unable to recollect the exact circumstances in which they subscribed their names to the document, affidavits should be obtained from them to that effect. If any other person was present at the time of execution, an affidavit should, if possible, also be obtained from such person. In the absence of evidence as to due execution, an affidavit as to the handwriting of the testator will also be required.

Recalcitrant witnesses

2.45 Under Section 122(1) of the Supreme Court Act 1981, where it appears that there are reasonable grounds for believing that any person has knowledge of any document which is, or purports to be, a testamentary document, the High Court may, whether or not any legal proceedings are pending, order him or her to attend for the purpose of being examined in open court. Under Section 122(2)(*a*) of the Act, the court may require any person who is before it in compliance with an order under subsection (1) to answer any question relating to the document concerned. A person who fails to attend for such examination or who fails to answer any such question is guilty of contempt of court—Section 122(3). An application under Section 122 for an order requiring a person to attend for examination may, unless a probate action has been commenced, be made to a registrar by summons, which must be served on the person concerned—Rule 50(1).

Will or codicil not duly executed

2.46 Where there is definite evidence that a will or codicil was not duly executed, probate will be refused.

2.47 When in the case of a testator who has died on or since 1st January 1964, the evidence shows that the will or codicil was not duly executed according to English law, and it appears that the testator may have been connected with a foreign country, the possibility of establishing the validity of the document by some other system of law must be considered (see para. 2.101). Before refusing probate in such a case, the registrar may require to be satisfied that all reasonable enquiries for this purpose have been made.

2.48 A will which is not duly executed is admissible to proof by incorporation where the testator has duly executed a codicil which refers to the will. Similarly, a codicil which is not duly executed is admissible to proof by incorporation if it is refered to in a later codicil which is duly executed (see paras 2.65–75).

Draft of will or codicil executed

2.49 When it is sought to prove a will or a codicil which bears evidence (*e.g.* is endorsed "draft" or "instructions") that the document which has been executed was intended to be a draft only or instructions for a will or codicil, it is necessary to file an affidavit setting out the circumstances in which the draft or instructions were executed; and such affidavit should state particularly that no engrossment from the draft or instructions was made, or if made, was not executed. The affidavit may be made by any person having knowledge of the facts, but is best made by the solicitor or person who prepared the draft or put the instructions in writing. If the affidavit is made by a person who is an attesting witness to the will or codicil, the affidavit must have the usual clause setting up due execution according to the Act. In addition, the applicant for the grant is required to swear an affidavit as to search (Form of affidavit after para. 2.151 No. (8) and of affidavit of search at No. (6)).

Will executed in duplicate

2.50 If a will has been executed in duplicate, only one part is proved, but both parts should be lodged with the papers to lead to the grant, the duplicate being returned to the practitioner after examination. If only one part is produced, the absence of the other part must be satisfactorily accounted for by affidavit. If one part was destroyed by the testator, with intention to revoke it, the will is revoked, and the duplicate is not entitled to proof (*Boughey v. Moreton* (1758) 3 Hagg. Ecc. 191). There is a *prima facie* presumption of revocation if the duplicate has been in the testator's possession but cannot be found at his death (*Jones v. Harding* (1887) 58 L.T. 60). Every circumstance leading to a presumption of revocation must be accounted for to the registrar's satisfaction (Rule 15).

Damaged will

2.51 A damaged will or other testamentary document should first be submitted to the registrar for his directions, accompanied if possible by an examined copy of it. If the registrar decides that it is too badly damaged to be admitted, he will accept an application for an order to prove a copy or reconstruction of it.

Will in the Welsh language

2.52 The translation into English of a will in the Welsh language is considered the registry's responsibility and normally the translation will be made by one of the officers of the probate registry concerned. However, if the applicant wishes, he may lodge a translation which must be verified by the certificate of a notary public or by the affidavit of a private individual setting out his qualifications. The registry from which the grant is to issue will reimburse the applicant for notarial charges not exceeding 85p per folio of 72 words.

2.53 The *original* will must be marked by the applicant for the grant and the person who administers the oath. The engrossment for probate must be headed "Translation from the Welsh". The translation will be photocopied and registered and a photocopy of the original will may be included in the probate copy in addition to the translation if the solicitor so requests. If for any reason a photocopy of the original document cannot be used, or the original is not suitable for photocopying, the request must be refused.

OMISSION OF WORDS FROM PROBATE WHERE TESTATOR DIED BEFORE 1st JANUARY 1983

2.54 Contested applications for omission of words from probate must be made to a registrar of the Principal Registry on summons.

2.55 Uncontested applications for the omission of words should be made to the registrar of the registry to which application for the grant will be made. The application is made *ex parte,* by lodging affidavit evidence (exhibiting the will or codicil in question) together with any consents in writing of persons not under disability who might be prejudiced by the order. If the registrar is satisfied on the facts, and in the absence of consent, that there is no substantial interest unprotected, he will make the order. Alternatively, the registrar may require the application to be made by summons to a judge in chambers or open court (Rule 61(1)).

2.56 If an order is made for the omission of words from probate, a copy of the order should be lodged when application is made for the grant and it will be filed with the original will. A typewritten copy or (where a complete page or pages are to be excluded, or where words on the same page below the testator's signature can be excluded by masking out, or where the original has been altered but not re-executed or republished and there exists a photocopy of the original executed document) a photocopy of the will omitting such part must be lodged at the appropriate registry for the fiat of the probate officer or the district probate registrar to be written in the margin before photocopying.

2.57 The court has power to exclude from probate words included in a will or codicil by mistake or without the instructions or knowledge of the testator, where the testator died before 1st January 1983. The court also has power to exclude from probate words of an offensive, libellous or blasphemous nature.

RECTIFICATION OF A WILL WHERE TESTATOR DIED ON OR AFTER 1st JANUARY 1983

2.58 Under Section 20(1) of the Administration of Justice Act 1982, which applies to a will made by a testator who dies on or after 1st January 1983,

> "If a court is satisfied that a will is so expressed that it fails to carry out the testator's intentions, in consequence–
> (*a*) of a clerical error; or
> (*b*) of a failure to understand his instructions,
> it may order that the will shall be rectified so as to carry out his intentions."

Under Section 20(2) of the Administration of Justice Act 1982 an application for an order under Section 20(1) cannot, except with the permission of the court, be made after the end of the period of six months from the date on which representation with respect to the estate of the deceased is first taken out.

2.59 Section 20(3) of the Act provides that personal representatives shall not be rendered liable for having distributed any part of the estate after the end of the six-month period from the date on which representation was first taken out, and Section 20(4) states which limited grants shall be left out of account in deciding when representation was first taken out.

2.60 Unless a probate action has been commenced, application for an order that a will be rectified by virtue of Section 20(1) of the Act may be made to a registrar. The application must be supported by an affidavit setting out the grounds for the application, together with such evidence as can be adduced as to the testator's intentions and whichever of the following matters are in issue:

(a) in what respects the testator's intentions were not understood; or
(b) the nature of any alleged clerical error.

Unless the registrar directs otherwise, notice of the application must be given to every person having an interest under the will whose interest might be prejudiced by the rectification applied for. Any comments in writing by any such person must be exhibited to the affidavit in support of the application. If the registrar is satisfied that, subject to any direction to the contrary, notice has been given to every person having an interest which might be prejudiced, and that the application is unopposed, he may order that the will be rectified accordingly (Rule 55).

2.61 If the application for an order for rectification is opposed, or if it is connected with a construction application to the Chancery Division, it should be made to the Chancery Division under Order 76 of the Rules of the Supreme Court.

2.62 Where an order for rectification is made prior to the will being proved, an engrossment of the will in the form in which it is to be proved must be lodged (Rule 11(2). Where an order for rectification is made after the will has been proved, a note of the order is made on the grant in the registry.

INTERPRETATION OF WILL WHERE TESTATOR DIED ON OR AFTER 1st JANUARY 1983

2.63 Although not bound to do so, the probate registries may determine a point of construction for the limited purpose of making a grant of representation (see para. 1.02). When interpreting for such a purpose a will made by a testator who died on or after 1st January 1983, recourse may be had to Section 21 of the Adminstration of Justice Act 1982. The section states:

"(1) This section applies to a will—
(*a*) in so far as any part of it is meaningless;
(*b*) in so far as the language used in any part of it is ambiguous on the face of it;

(*c*) in so far as evidence, other than evidence of the testator's intention, shows that the language used in any part of it is ambiguous in the light of surrounding circumstances.

(2) In so far as this section applies to a will extrinsic evidence, including evidence of the testator's intention, may be admitted to assist in its interpretation."

This section is of particular use where the appointment of an executor is, on the face of it, void for uncertainty. If evidence of the testator's intention can be produced to resolve the uncertainty, an effective appointment of executor may be established. Evidence on affidavit is required, normally by the person who took the instructions and drafted the will, giving details of the intention expressed by the testator and exhibiting any written instructions, attendance note or any other relevant document. The affidavit should also give any explanation there may be why the engrossed and executed will was worded in the way it was, in the light of the testator's expressed intention. The consent of any person who might be prejudiced by the proposed interpretation, and who is *sui juris,* should also be lodged with the application. An application under Section 21 of the Act may be preferable to, and avoid the need for, an order for rectification under Section 20, although under Section 20 the Court can only deal with the ambiguity and not go any further (see *Re Williams* [1985] 1 All E.R. 964).

PRESUMPTION AS TO EFFECT OF GIFTS TO SPOUSES

2.64 Section 22 of the Administration of Justice Act 1982 provides that, in relation to a will of a testator who *dies on or after 1st January 1983:*

> "Except where a contrary intention is shown it shall be presumed that if a testator devises or bequeaths property to his spouse in terms which in themselves would give an absolute interest to the spouse, but by the same instrument purports to give his issue an interest in the same property, the gift to the spouse is absolute notwithstanding the purported gift to the issue."

This section is of particular value with "home-made" wills where the testator has expressed himself unclearly.

INCORPORATION OF PAPERS BY REFERENCE

2.65 When a testator in his will or codicil expressly refers to any other document or written wishes as containing disposition of or directions as to the disposition of any part of his property, the production of such document or written wishes is required in order that it may be ascertained whether it should be incorporated in the will or codicil and included in the probate. If the document or written wishes cannot be produced, the reason for non-production must be accounted for normally by affidavit. (Rule 14(3)).

2.66 A document or written wishes will not be incorporated unless:
(1) The wishes are referred to in the will or codicil as being in the form of a written document (*Goodman* (1944) Motion.)
(2) The document or written wishes are clearly referred to in the will or codicil as being then in existence (*Re Bateman's Will Trusts, Brierley v. Perry,* [1970] 3 All E.R. 817; *Smart* [1902] P. 238; *Durham v. Northern* [1895] P. 66).
(3) The document or written wishes are clearly described in the will or codicil without any expression capable of covering a possible substitution (*University College of N. Wales v. Taylor* [1908] P. 140, 144).
Before the oath leading to the grant is sworn the directions of the Principal of the Probate Department or the district probate registrar should be obtained if there is doubt as to whether a document is incorporated by reference.

2.67 Where there is no trace of the document, the applicant for the grant should make an affidavit of search setting out all documents of a testamentary nature found among the papers of the testator or deposited by him with his solicitor, or as the case may be, and it must be shown that no testamentary writing other than those set out has been discovered (Form of affidavit of search after para. 2.151 No. (6)).

2.68 A document not definitely identified as that mentioned in the will (or codicil) or which is not identified as having been in existence prior to execution of the will (or codicil) will not be incorporated.

2.69 Where the testator declares that a document refered to is not to have testamentary force, or that it is not binding, it is not the practice to include the document in the probate and no affidavit is necessary with reference to it. The trusts of such a document would not be effective (*Re Louis, Louis v. Treloar* (1916) 32 T.L.R. 313).

2.70 In the estate of *Joseph Jones* (1920) 123 L.T. 202, there was at the end of the will below the attestation clause and signatures the words "schedule over" and on the other side was a list of shares, etc. and a memorandum of a sum due to the testator. The list and memorandum were mentioned in the body of the will and it was held that the schedule was incorporated by reference and should be admitted to probate.

2.71 A document referred to in a will as existing but which was not in existence at the date of the will, may be incorporated if evidence is produced showing that it was in existence at the date of execution of a codicil to the will. A document referred to in like manner in a codicil, although not in existence at the date of the codicil, may be incorporated if the making thereof is proved to have preceded a later codicil.

2.72 If the will is contained in two separate documents, both documents are admitted to probate.

2.73 If the will or codicil refers in error to some other testamentary disposition (*e.g.* a codicil referring to the three previous codicils when in fact there were only two), the applicant for the grant will be required to swear an affidavit of search.

2.74 A will or codicil which is not duly executed is entitled to proof by incorporation where the testator has duly executed a later codicil which refers to it.

2.75 The oath to lead to the grant should not be sworn before any question of incorporation has been decided. A will and a document to be incorporated should be referred to in the oath as, "the will as contained in paper writings marked A and B". The will and document to be incorporated must be so marked and must both be marked by the applicant for the grant and by the person who administers the oath with their signatures.

REVOCATION OF WILLS

2.76 There are a number of ways by which a testamentary document may be revoked but any act of revocation must clearly show the intention to revoke all previous testamentary documents or a particular testamentary document, as the case may be. Section 20 of the Wills Act 1837 provides that:

> "No will or codicil, or any part thereof, shall be revoked otherwise than as aforesaid, or by another will or codicil executed in manner hereinbefore required, or by some writing declaring an intention to revoke the same and executed in the manner in which a will is hereinbefore required to be executed, or by the burning, tearing, or otherwise destroying the same by the testator, or by some person in his presence and by his direction, with the intention of revoking the same."

Where there is a document executed in the same manner as a will, but merely revoking all testamentary dispositions, it is not entitled to proof.

The grant of letters of administration will bear a note that it was so made in consequence of the execution of the revoking document (*Toomer v. Sobinska* [1907] P. 106). Although it may lack a revocatory clause, a duly executed testamentary document which clearly disposes of the whole of the estate is held to revoke any previous testamentary document (*Henfrey v. Henfrey* (1840) 4 Moore P.C.C. 29).

Wills made in contemplation of marriage

Wills made before 1st January 1983

2.77 Section 18 of the Wills Act 1837 and Section 177 of the Law of Property Act 1925 continue to apply to wills made on or after 1st January 1926 and before 1st January 1983. Section 18 of the Wills Act 1837 provides that a will is revoked by the subsequent marriage of the testator save in respect of certain wills made in exercise of a power of appointment; a voidable marriage is also effective to revoke a previously made will (*Roberts v. Roberts,* [1978] 3 All E.R. 225) but a will made on or after the 1st January 1926, in contemplation of an intended marriage with a specified person and expressed so to be, is not revoked by the solemnisation of the marriage contemplated (Section 177, Law of Property Act 1925; *Sallis v. Jones* [1936] P. 43; *Pilot v. Gainfort* [1931] P. 103; *In the Estate of Langston* [1953] P. 100). The oath filed on application for proof of such a will should, if the contemplated marriage was solemnised, state the facts and the date of the marriage.

2.78 If the testator dies before the marriage is solemnised, the will is capable of proof unless the whole of the will is conditional upon the solemnisation of the marriage. In this case the oath should include a statement that the testator did not marry subsequently to the date of making the will.

2.79 Although the will may not expressly state that it is made in contemplation of marriage, it is sufficient if the testator gives a practical expression regarding his contemplated marriage to a specified person. The will as a whole has to be expressed to be in contemplation of the marriage (*Re Coleman* [1975] 1 All E.R. 675).

Wills made on or after 1st January 1983

2.80 Section 18 of the Administration of Justice Act 1982 replaces the old form of Section 18 of the Wills Act 1837 and Section 177 of the Law of Property Act 1925 (repealed by the 1982 Act), in respect of wills made on or after 1st January 1983. The new form of Section 18 of the Wills Act 1837 is in the following terms:

"(1) Subject to subsections (2) to (4) below, a will shall be revoked by the testator's marriage.
(2) A disposition in a will in exercise of a power of appointment shall take effect notwithstanding the testator's subsequent marriage unless the property so appointed would in default of appointment pass to his personal representatives.
(3) Where it appears from a will that at the time it was made the testator was expecting to be married to a particular person and that he intended that the will should not be revoked by the marriage, the will shall not be revoked by his marriage to that person.
(4)Where it appears from a will that at the time it was made the testator was expecting to be married to a particular person and that he intended that a disposition in the will should not be revoked by his marriage to that person—
(*a*) that disposition shall take effect notwithstanding the marriage; and
(*b*) any other disposition in the will shall take effect also, unless it appears from the will that the testator intended the disposition to be revoked by the marriage."

The main change made in respect of wills made on or after 1st January 1983 is that the will as a whole need not be expressed to be in contemplation of the marriage for it (or part of it) not to be revoked by the marriage.

Effect of dissolution or annulment of marriage on wills

2.81 Section 18A of the Wills Act 1837, inserted by Section 18(2) of the Administration of Justice Act 1982 (and as amended by Section 53 of the Family Law Act 1986 on 4th April 1988), provides that, in respect of deaths on or after 1st January 1983:

"(1) Where, after a testator has made a will, a decree of a court of civil jurisdiction in England and Wales dissolves or annuls his marriage or his marriage is dissolved or annulled and the divorce or annulment is entitled to recognition in England and Wales by virtue of Part II of the Family Law Act 1986—
(*a*) The will shall take effect as if any appointment of the former spouse as an executor or as the executor and trustee of the will were omitted; and
(*b*) any devise or bequest to the former spouse shall lapse,

except in so far as a contrary intention appears by the will.

(2) Subsection (1)(*b*) above is without prejudice to any right of the former spouse to apply for financial provision under the Inheritance (Provision for Family and Dependants) Act 1975.

(3) Where—
(*a*) by the terms of a will an interest in remainder is subject to a life interest; and
(*b*) the life interest lapses by virtue of subsection (1)(*b*) above,

the interest in remainder shall be treated as if it had not been subject to the life interest and, if it was contingent upon the termination of the life interest, as if it had not been so contingent."

Where a will takes effect as if the appointment of the former spouse as an executor were omitted, any other executor named in the will may apply for probate. If there is no other executor appointed, letters of administration (with will annexed) may be applied for by the persons entitled in order of priority under Rule 20.

2.82 It should be noted that as regards any devise or bequest to the former spouse in the will the word used in Section 18A(1)(*b*) is "lapse". It was decided by the Court of Appeal in *Re Sinclair dec., Lloyds Bank PLC v. Imperial Cancer Research Fund and Another* [1985] 1 All E.R. 1066 that "lapse" in Section 18A(1)(*b*) means fails in a general sense and not in the restricted sense of failing on the basis as if the former spouse had predeceased the testator. Consequently if a will has a gift over upon the (former) spouse predeceasing the testator it will not take effect because the marriage is dissolved or annulled. Such a gift over would only take effect if the specific event had occurred, *i.e.* if the (former) spouse had died before the testator.

Written declaration of intention to revoke

2.83 A statement written at the foot of an obliterated testamentary document "We are witnesses to the erasure of the above" signed by the testator and attested by witnesses has been held to be an effective revocation (*Re Gosling* (1886) 11 P.D. 79). A letter, signed by the testator and attested, requesting a third person to destroy a testamentary document made by the testator, is sufficient to revoke it (*Re Spracklan's Estate* [1938] 2 All E.R. 345). A statement in the attestation clause of a codicil to the effect that a previous codicil is revoked does not revoke such previous codicil (*Re Atkinson* (1883) 8 P.D. 165).

Revocation by destruction

2.84 The question of intention arises in all cases of revocation by destruction. Destruction of a testamentary document on the erroneous supposition that it is invalid (*Re Thornton* (1889) 14 P.D. 82), or that it has been revoked, or that it is useless (*Stamford v. White* [1901] P. 46), or that another testamentary document is valid (*In the Estate of Davies* [1951] 1 All E.R. 920; *In the Estate of Botting* [1951] 2 All E.R. 997) or that the beneficiaries named in the document will be entitled on an intestacy (*Re Southerden* [1925] P. 177), will not revoke the document.

Dependent relative revocation

2.85 A revocation made with the intention to make or to revive another testamentary document is only effective if such other testamentary document is duly executed or revived (*Dixon v. Treasury Solicitor* [1905] P. 42; *Re Irvine* (1919) 2 Ir. 485). To bring a case within the doctrine of dependent relative revocation, the evidence must show that at the time of the revocation the testator considered the substitution or revival of a valid testamentary document as part of the act of revocation, but that no such other document was effectually made or revived. The doctrine of dependent relative revocation may also be involved to restore parts of a testamentary document which have been obliterated but not where the testator did not intend the disposition to take effect in any circumstances (*Re Jones* [1976] 1 Ch. 200).

Revocation under some other system of law

2.86 It should not be forgotten that a will or codicil may, in appropriate circumstances, be revoked in accordance with some other system of law which can be properly applied, under Section 6 of the Wills Act 1963 (see para. 2.113).

PRIVILEGED WILLS

(Informal Wills and Codicils of Members of H.M. Forces, Mariners and Seamen)

2.87 By Section 11 of the Wills Act 1837 it is provided that a soldier or airman in actual military service, or a member of the Royal Naval or Marine Forces at sea or so circumstanced that if he were a soldier he would be in actual military service, or a mariner or seaman at sea, may dispose of his personal estate as he might have done before the passing of the Act (*i.e.* without observing the formalities as to the execution of his will or codicil as required by Section 9 of the Act). The Wills (Soldiers and Sailors) Act 1918 extends this provision to real estate in the case of a testator dying after 6th February 1918.

2.88 A testator can exercise the privilege only if it is at the time allowed him by the law of his domicile. If the testator was domiciled outside England and Wales at the date of the will or codicil, it must be proved by affidavit as to the law of the country where he was domiciled at that time that such law allows a similar privilege. Where the testator has died on or since 1st January 1964, reference may be made to any system of law which is relevant under the Wills Act 1963, and not only to the law of the country where he was domiciled at the time of making the will or codicil.

Age of testator

2.89 It is generally accepted that a person entitled to make a privileged will may do so from the age of 14 years (*Re Wernher* [1918] 2 Ch. 82). Where the testator was under the age of 18 years at the time of making the will, his age at that time must be sworn to in the oath leading to the grant.

"Actual military service"

2.90 A sailor, marine, soldier or airman must, at the date of the privileged will, be actually serving with the armed forces of the Crown in connection with military operations which are, or have been, taking place, or are believed to be imminent. The privilege of making a will without any formalities is extended to all those who serve in the Forces (*e.g.* doctors, nurses, chaplains, WRNS) whether they are in the field, in billets, or sleeping at home or have been captured by the enemy or interned by neutrals (see also *Re Wingham, Andrews v. Wingham* [1949] P. 187; [1948] 2 All E.R. 908, which gives a much wider meaning to the words "military service" and *Re Jones* [1981] Fam. 7; [1981] 1 All E.R. 1 where an oral declaration by a soldier serving in Northern Ireland during terrorist activities was admitted to proof).

Mariner or seaman "at sea"

2.91 The term "at sea" has been held to mean "on maritime service", and in addition to persons actually serving on the high seas has been held to apply to persons serving in vessels permanently engaged on harbour duties, and in vessels engaged on service in a river. A female typist on board ship is a "seaman" and entitled to make a privileged will (*Re Hale* [1915] 2 I.R. 362).

Form of privileged will or codicil

2.92 Any written or oral statement of testamentary intentions may be accepted provided that it is clear that the testator intended it to be testamentary. A written document need not be signed or witnessed, and may even be in the form of a memorandum written by some other person as to testamentary statements made by the testator (*In the Goods of Scott* [1903] P. 243).

Nuncupative will (oral statement)

2.93 A nuncupative will must be made in circumstances showing that it was intended to be testamentary (see *Re Spark* [1941] P. 115).

Will contained in a letter

2.94 Where a will is contained in a letter, the registrar may direct that the whole of the letter or only the testamentary portions thereof be admitted to proof (*Re M. Heywood* [1916] P. 47).

Evidence of handwriting of testator

2.95 The will may be admitted to proof if the registrar is satisfied that it is signed by the testator or, if unsigned, that it is in the testator's handwriting (Rule 18): affidavit evidence identifying the signature or handwriting as that of the testator is usually required. If there is only one attesting witness, or no attesting witnesses, to the will the registrar may require more than one affidavit as to handwriting (see after para. 2.151 No. (12) for form of affidavit).

Alterations in will

2.96 If a privileged will contains unattested alterations or interlineations in the testator's handwriting, they must, if possible, be proved by affidavit identifying his handwriting. If in the handwriting of another person, affidavit evidence is required to show that they were known to and approved by the testator (Rule 17).

Gift to an attesting witness

2.97 As attesting witnesses are not essential, a gift in a privileged will to such a witness is held to be valid (*Re Limond* [1915] 2 Ch. 240).

Revocation

2.98 The revocation of a previous will, whether a privileged will or not, may be effected by a privileged will (*Re Gossage, Wood v. Gossage* [1921] P. 194); a privileged will is revoked by the subsequent marriage of the testator (*Re Wardrop* [1917] P. 54).

Practice

2.99 In order to prove a privileged will an affidavit is required setting out the facts relied upon to establish that the will is entitled to privilege. The domicile of the testator at the time of the will must also be sworn to in all cases.

2.100 It must be shown in the case of:

(1) *A soldier or airman:* that at the date of the making of the will he was serving as a soldier or airman in actual military service.

(2) *A sailor, marine, seaman or mariner at sea:* that at the date of the making of the will he was actually in naval service, or was serving on the

high seas, or was serving in a port at which his ship had called during its voyage, or as the case may be.

In the case of a nuncupative will (oral statement), the court must be satisfied that the testator intended it to be testamentary (*Re Donner* (1917) 34 T.L.R. 138). Affidavits by persons present when the statement was made are required, and should set out the facts and circumstances and recite the words used by the testator. Where all persons prejudiced are *sui juris* and consent, the registrar will usually, in a clear case, make an order and the usual papers will be filed. The words of the oral statement will be recorded on a separate sheet of paper and it must be marked by the applicant for the grant and person who administers the oath with their signatures.

WILLS ACT 1963

2.101 The rules for determining the validity of testamentary documents in cases where the testator has died on or after 1st January 1964 are contained in the Wills Act 1963, regardless of the date upon which the testamentary document was executed. The Act is applicable to all persons whatever their nationality or domicile, and it enables a testamentary document to be accepted as formally valid if in the execution thereof the testator had complied with the formal requirements of any system of internal law which was, in the circumstances, applicable.

General rules as to formal validity

2.102 Section 1 of the Act provides that:

> "A will shall be treated as properly executed if its execution conformed to the internal law in force in the territory where it was executed, or in the territory where, at the time of its execution or of the testator's death, he was domiciled or had his habitual residence, or in a state of which, at either of those times, he was a national."

When applying this Act, any question regarding the domicile of the testator must be determined by English law. Before it can be accepted that a person had acquired a domicile of choice in a particular state, English law requires it to be evidenced that he had taken up residence in that particular state with the intention of remaining there permanently. Where the rules of English law give rise to difficulty in proving that a testator was domiciled in a particular state so as to enable the validity of his will to be established by the law of that state, Section 1 allows recourse to be had to the law of that state if the testator had his habitual residence there.

2.103 When a testator had dual nationality, this Section allows the law of any state of which he was a national at the time of execution of his will, or at the time of his death, to be invoked for the purpose of establishing the validity of his will.

Additional rules

2.104 Section 2 of the Act provides that:

"(1) Without prejudice to the preceding section, the following shall be treated as properly executed—

(*a*) a will executed on board a vessel or aircraft of any description, if the execution of the will conformed to the internal law in force in the territory with which, having regard to its registration (if any) and other relevant circumstances, the vessel or aircraft may be taken to have been most closely connected;

(*b*) a will so far as it disposes of immovable property, if its execution conformed to the internal law in force in the territory where the property was situated;

(*c*) a will so far as it revokes a will which under this Act would be treated as properly executed or revokes a provision which under this Act would be treated as comprised in a properly executed will, if the execution of the later will conformed to any law by reference to which the revoked will or provision would be so treated;

(*d*) a will so far as it exercises a power of appointment, if the execution of the will conformed to the law governing the essential validity of the power.

(2) A will so far as it exercises a power of appointment shall not be treated as improperly executed by reason only that its execution was not in accordance with any formal requirements contained in the instrument creating the power."

The reference in Section 2(1)(*a*) to a vessel also includes a hovercraft.

2.105 It should be observed that Section 2(1)(*b*) is without prejudice to Section 1 of the Act; a will which is established as valid under Section 1 is effective to pass both movable and immovable estate; but even if the validity of the will cannot be established under Section 1, it will still be admitted to proof so far as it disposes of immovable estate, provided that its execution conformed to the internal law of the country where such estate was situated.

Certain requirements to be treated as formal

2.106 Section 3 of the Act provides that:

"Where (whether in pursuance of this Act or not) a law in force outside the United Kingdom falls to be applied in relation to a will, any requirement of that law whereby special formalities are to be observed by testators answering a particular description, or witnesses to the execution of the will are to possess certain qualifications, shall be treated, notwithstanding any rule of that law to the contrary, as a formal requirement only."

Construction of wills

2.107 Section 4 of the Act provides that:

"The construction of a will shall not be altered by reason of any change in the testator's domicil after the execution of the will."

Interpretation

2.108 Section 6 of the Act provides that:

"—(1) In this Act:

'internal law' in relation to any territory or state means the law which would apply in a case where no question of the law in force in any other territory or state arose;

'state' means a territory or group of territories having its own law of nationality;

'will' includes any testamentary instrument or act, and 'testator' shall be construed accordingly.

(2) Where under this Act the internal law in force in any territory or state is to be applied in the case of a will, but there are in force in that territory or state two or more systems of internal law relating to the formal validity of wills, the system to be applied shall be ascertained as follows—

(*a*) if there is in force throughout the territory or state a rule indicating which of those systems can properly be applied in the case in question, that rule shall be followed; or

(*b*) if there is no such rule, the system shall be that with which the testator was most closely connected at the relevant time, and for this purpose the relevant time is the time of the testator's death where the matter is to be determined by reference to circumstances prevailing at his death, and the time of execution of the will in any other case.

(3) In determining for the purposes of this Act whether or not the execution of a will conformed to a particular law, regard shall be had to the formal requirements of that law at the time of execution, but this shall not prevent account being taken of an alteration of law affecting wills executed at that time if the alteration enables the will to be treated as properly executed."

2.109 The definition of "internal law" excludes any question of reference to the law system of any other place, or of the doctrine of *renvoi*. Nevertheless, the Act does not appear to take away the existing right to prove in this country a will which has already been accepted as valid by the court of the country in which the testator died domiciled, even if that court accepted the will on some basis other than the internal law of that country.

2.110 Some states have two or more concurrent but different systems of internal law, each of which is applied to different communities within the state (e.g. on a religious or tribal basis). In the absence of any rule throughout the territory or state indicating which system of law should be applied to the case in question, affidavit evidence is required setting out the facts relied upon to establish that the testator was at the date of execution of the will or at the date of his death, as the case may require, most closely connected with a particular system of law as to the validity of wills.

2.111 The definition of the term "will" applies not only to written wills and codicils, but also to oral testamentary dispositions and any form of deliberate revocation of a will or codicil. Section 6 allows a revocation (wholly or partial) of a will or codicil, either by document or physical act (*e.g.* destruction *animo revocandi*), to be accepted as effective if executed in accordance with the requirements of any system of law to which, in the circumstances of the case, reference may be made under the provisions of the Act. Although a will containing a revocatory clause as to a previous will may not have been duly executed according to any system of law to which reference may be made under the provisions of the Act, provided that the will is validly executed in accordance with any system of law by which validity of the previous will could have been set up under the said provisions, the revocatory clause will be treated as an effective revocation of the previous will, or relevant part thereof as the case may be. In such a case the revoking instrument is not proved where the previous will is wholly revoked, but it must be lodged with the papers to lead to the grant. Where there is only partial revocation of the previous will, both documents are admitted to proof as together constituting the will of the testator. Affidavit evidence as to the validity of the revocatory provisions is required.

Wills valid as to part only

2.112 Where a will, which is otherwise invalid, is entitled to proof so far as it contains a disposition of immovable estate in England and Wales, the exercise of a power of appointment or revocatory provisions, it may be necessary for such part of the will only to be admitted to proof. In such cases it is advisable to obtain the directions of the Principal of the Probate Department of the Principal Registry or of the district probate registrar before preparing the papers to lead to the grant.

Evidence required to establish validity of a testamentary document under the Wills Act 1963

2.113 Affidavit evidence of the relevant facts is necessary (Form of affidavit after para. 2.151 No. (13)). Where the internal law of any territory other than England and Wales, Northern Ireland, the Republic of Ireland, Australia, Canada or New Zealand is relied upon to establish validity, then, unless the document has been accepted as valid by the court of such territory, being also the territory where the testator was domiciled at the time of his death, evidence showing that the execution of the document complied with the internal law of such territory must also be furnished. The evidence of foreign law is given by affidavit of an expert in the law in question or by a certificate by a notary practising in the country or territory concerned (Rule 19) (see form of affidavit as to foreign law after para. 7.29).

2.114 If the document has been proved in a territory other than that in which the testator was domiciled at the time of his death, evidence of law may still be required because the court which admitted the document to proof may have applied a system of law other than its own internal law in accepting the validity of the document. The affidavit (or notary's certificate) of law should speak only to the internal law of the territory or state concerned, and (in order to comply with Section 6(2) of the Act) should show whether a single system of law as to the validity of testamentary documents is in force throughout the territory or state, or whether there is more than one system. If there is more than one system of law, the affidavit (or notary's certificate) should state whether there is a rule in force throughout the territory or state indicating which system is applicable to the case in question; if so, such rule should be the basis upon which the expert gives his opinion as to the validity of the execution of the document. In the absence of such rule, the expert should specify the system of law upon which his opinion as to the validity of the execution of the document is based. In the latter case, the deponent to the affidavit of facts must state the grounds upon which it is claimed that the testator was most closely connected, at the time of execution of the document or at the time of his death (whichever is the relevant time: see Section 6(2)(*b*) of the Act), with the system of law specified in the affidavit or certificate of law.

2.115 For the practice as to the obtaining of grants in cases where the testator died domiciled outside England and Wales, see "Foreign Domicile", Chapter 7.

PROBATE REFUSED

2.116 If the registrar, after considering the evidence, is satisfied that the will or codicil was not duly executed, he will refuse probate and mark the document accordingly; but if he is doubtful whether it was duly executed he may refer the matter to a judge in chambers or open court (Rule 61(1). A document marked "Probate refused" and its relative affidavits will be retained in the registry and filed with the papers to lead to any subsequent grant in the estate of the deceased.

ALTERATIONS

(*Note:* The followng paragraphs deal with the internal law of England and Wales. Where the testator has died on or after 1st January 1964, the provisions of the Wills Act 1963 should also be considered in connection with unattested alterations, interlineations, etc., in the will or codicil.)

2.117 If it appears to the registrar that any obliteration, interlineation, or other alteration is of no practical importance he will not require evidence in respect of it (Rule 14(2)).

2.118 When a will or codicil contains alterations which are not specifically referred to in the attestation clause as having been made prior to execution, the *prima facie* presumption is that they were made after execution. The initials of the testator and attesting witnesses written near to the alteration are usually accepted as sufficient to rebut that presumption.

2.119 Alterations made in a will or codicil may be set up by a codicil made subsequently (*Tyler v. Merchant Taylor's Co.* (1890) 15 P.D. 216). The codicil may refer to the alterations either expressly or by implication only (*In the Goods of Heath* [1892] P. 253).

2.120 The fact that an alteration bears a date prior to that on which the document was executed does not alone entitle such alteration to probate (*Re Adamson* (1875) L.R. 3 P. & D. 253).

2.121 If the testator has erased, obliterated, cut out, or has completely covered by paper pasted over it, the whole of a provision or bequest in a testamentary document so that the wording cannot be made out on the face of the document, the revocation is complete under Section 21 of the Wills Act 1837, and probate is granted with a blank where the obliteration was (*Re Horsford* (1874) L.R. 3 P. & D. 211). The use of artificial means to decipher the original words is allowed but the court will not permit physical interference with the document (*Re Itter* [1950] P. 130). Where the amount of a bequest or the name of the beneficiary has been obliterated after execution of the document and the amount of the bequest or the name of the beneficiary is substituted, the inference is that it was the testator's intention to revoke the original amount or name only in the event of his having effectually substituted another, and where it is possible to restore them the court will grant probate of the original figures or words (*Brooke v. Kent* (1841) 3 Moore P.C. 334; *Re Itter* [1950] P. 130). The doctrine of dependent relative revocation applies only where other words have been substituted. If there is merely an obliteration the position is different; in such a case if the obliterated words cannot be made out probate will issue with a blank where the obliteration occurs in the original (*In the Goods of Ibbetson* (1839) 2 Curt 337).

2.122 Affidavit evidence will be accepted from:

(1) An attesting witness to the document or a person who was present at the time of the execution of the will or codicil and who observed the alterations.
(2) The person who made the alterations (*e.g.* the draftsman of the document).
(3) Any other person who can depose to the alterations having been made prior to execution.

If the affidavit is made by an attesting witness, he must also depose to the due execution of the document (Form of affidavit after para 2.151 No. (7)). Where the document contains more than one alteration, the deponent to the affidavit should, so far as he is able, speak as to whether all or which of them were made before or after execution. The affidavit should specifically set out the nature of each alteration.

2.123 Alterations etc. which are not established as having been made prior to execution are not admitted to proof (except when the registrar considers that they are of no practical importance) and are ignored for the purpose of making the grant. A copy of the document as it was at the time of execution, and bearing the fiat of the registrar, will be annexed to the grant (see Rule 11(2)).

CODICILS

2.124 The rules as to wills (validity, execution, alterations, revocation) are equally applicable to codicils. Where no contrary intention is shown, a duly executed codicil which confirms a will has the effect of republishing the latter and of bringing it down to the time of execution of the codicil. Although there may not be any actual expression of confirmation of the will, it is republished by the codicil provided there is sufficient identification. Where a codicil has been revoked by a later codicil, the revoked codicil must be proved if it alters the terms of the will or of a preceding codicil. If in existence, a revoked codicil must be lodged with the papers to lead to the grant, but if the codicil has been revoked by destruction it may be ordered that a copy or reconstruction of it be proved. In such a case it is advisable to obtain the directions of the registrar before the papers to lead to the grant are prepared. Where a revoked will or codicil is revived by a later will or codicil, the documents will be proved in chronological order as will and codicil, or as the case may be.

Codicil found after probate of will

2.125 If a codicil to a will has been found after probate of the will has been granted, a separate grant of probate of the codicil will be made to the executor provided that it does not make any change in the appointment of the executor. If the executor who proved the will has died, the proving executor of his will, if any, must prove the codicil, being the executor of the will and codicil by chain of executorship. Should, however, the codicil effect a change in the executorship, or operate as a complete revocation of the preceding testamentary disposition or dispositions, then the grant of probate issued in the first instance must be revoked (see paras. 14.17 ff.) and a new grant applied for in respect of the effective testamentary disposition or dispositions. Where an Inland Revenue Account is necessary it should be made on the form appropriate to the circumstances (see paras. 6.10 ff.).

REPUBLICATION AND REVIVAL OF WILLS AND CODICILS

Republication

2.126 Provided that no contrary intention is shown, a duly executed codicil which expressly confirms or otherwise sufficiently identifies a will has the effect of republishing the will and of bringing it down to the date of the codicil (Section 34, Wills Act 1837, and see *Re Smith, Bilke v. Roper* (1890) 45 Ch. D. 632). Such republication gives effect to the same dispositions of estate as if the testator had, at the date of the codicil, executed a new will containing the same dispositions as the original will but with the alterations effected by the codicil.

Revival of revoked will or codicil

2.127 No will or codicil, or any part thereof, which has been revoked can be revived otherwise than by the re-execution thereof, or by a duly executed codicil showing an intention to revive the same. Where a will or codicil which has been partly revoked, and afterwards wholly revoked, is revived, such revival does not extend to the part first revoked unless an intention to that effect is shown (Section 22, Wills Act 1837).

2.128 A testamentary document revoked by destruction cannot be revived (*In the Goods of Reade* [1902] P. 75). Where a will or codicil is revived by a later will or codicil, the documents will be proved in chronological order as will and codicil, or as the case may be.

TWO OR MORE WILLS

2.129 A will may be contained in two or more testamentary documents (*Lemage v. Goodban* (1865) L.R. 1 P. & D. 57). There may be a number of duly executed testamentary papers which, being read together, contain the aggregate of a person's testamentary intentions and constitute one will, not a will and codicils. If the second of two testamentary documents purports to be a will and not a codicil, in order to decide whether one or both documents are entitled to proof the court is guided by the tenor of both documents as to what dispositions of his estate the testator wished to effect. Where a testator executes on the same day two wills which are inconsistent, both containing revocatory clauses as to all previous wills, and there is no evidence regarding the order in which they were executed, neither document can be admitted to proof, the effect of the revocatory clauses being an intestacy (*Re Howard, Howard v. Treasury Solicitor* [1944] P. 39).

2.130 Where the order of execution of two testamentary documents is uncertain and there are no express words of revocation in either document and the provisions are inconsistent, the court will endeavour to construe the contents of both documents so that, if possible, they may both be admitted to proof as together containing the whole of the testator's testamentary intentions (*Townsend v. Moore* [1905] P. 66 C.A.; *Jones v. Treasury Solicitor* (1932) 49 T.L.R. 75 C.A.).

2.131 If the testator has made two wills, in one of which he declares that he is dealing with his English estate only and in the other he disposes of his foreign estate only and it is the clear intention that they should take effect separately, the will relating to the English estate alone is admitted to probate but an authenticated copy of the will dealing only with the foreign estate should be lodged (*In the Goods of Astor* (1876) 1 P.D. 150; *In the Goods of Callaway* (1890) 15 P.D. 147; *In the Goods of*

De la Rue (1890) 15 P.D. 185). In cases of doubt both wills should be submitted to the Principal of the Probate Department of the Principal Registry or to the district probate registrar before papers to lead to the grant are completed. If, however, by the will purporting to deal with the foreign estate the testator, nevertheless, disposes of English estate also, or if the other will otherwise affects the contents of the will relating to the English estate, both wills must be proved.

2.132 Although it may lack a revocatory clause, a duly executed testamentary document which clearly disposes of the whole of the estate is held to revoke any previous testamentary document (*Henfrey v. Henfrey* (1840), 4 Moore P.C.C. 29). If the will to be admitted to proof is contained in more than one document, the oath should refer to it as being "contained in paper writings marked A and B" and each document must be so marked and be marked by the applicant for the grant and the person who administers the oath with their signatures.

CONDITIONAL WILLS

2.133 Whether a testamentary document is conditional or not depends upon the intention of the testator, as definitely expressed in or as indicated by the tenor of the document. In doubtful cases the surrounding circumstances of its execution must also be considered (*Re Spratt* [1897] P. 28).

2.134 Where the wording indicates that the document is operative only on the happening of a specified event, that event must happen before the document can become effective; but where the testator has mentioned the possibility of an event occurring as his reason for executing the document, the document is operative whether the event occurs or not. For example: if a testator writes, "Should I die tomorrow, my will is . . .", his death must occur on the morrow for the document to take effect; but if he writes, "Lest I die tomorrow, my will is . . .", the document is operative whether he dies on the morrow or not (*Vines v. Vines* [1910] P. 147).

2.135 When a question arises as to whether a testamentary document is conditional, or as to its admissibility to proof, it must be referred to a registrar for decision. Affidavit evidence as to the fulfilment or non-fulfulment of the condition will be required, unless it is apparent from the application for the grant that the condition is inoperative. A conditional document which is not admitted to proof and the affidavit evidence, if any, should be filed with the papers to lead to a grant in the estate of the deceased.

JOINT WILLS—MUTUAL WILLS

Joint wills

2.136 A joint will made by two persons disposing of their separate property may be proved on the death of the first to die. On the first application for proof of the will, for identification purposes and to avoid any difficulty at a later date, the practitioner should (preferably by a marginal note on the oath to lead to the grant) supply the date of birth of the other testator, or the date of death if already deceased. On the death of the survivor of the testators, the will may be proved again as the will of that testator, and application for the grant should be made at the same registry as on the first death. If affidavit evidence is required regarding the execution of a joint will such evidence should, where practicable, deal with execution by both testators. A joint will disposing of joint property only cannot be proved until the death of the survivor of the testators. A separate codicil made by one of the testators of a joint will would only be proved with the joint will on the death of that testator.

Mutual wills

2.137 A mutual will is one or two separate testamentary documents made respectively by two testators giving each other similar rights in each other's estate.

Revocation of mutual and joint wills

2.138 A mutual or joint will is revocable by either of the testators, but a revocation by one of them may not be fully effective unless it is done during the lifetime of both of them, either jointly, or by one testator only with notice of the revocation being given to the other. Where such a will is revoked by the survivor of the testators the revocation is operative, but if he executes a fresh will his legal personal representatives may be directed to hold the estate on trust to carry out the terms of the contract, actual or implied (if any), made between the testators by their mutual or joint wills (*Re Green, Linder v. Green* [1951] Ch. 148; *Re Cleaver, Cleaver v. Insley* [1981] 2 All E.R. 1018).

WILL IN EXERCISE OF POWER OF APPOINTMENT

2.139 The exercise of a power of appointment by a will has no legal effect unless the will is proved in England and Wales.

2.140 Where a testator has died on or after 1st January 1964, Section 1 of the Wills Act 1963 provides a number of alternative systems of law to which, in specified circumstances, reference may be made in order to establish the validity of testamentary documents, and the exercise of a power of appointment in a will or codicil set up as valid under this Section is accepted as properly exercised.

2.141 Section 2(1)(*d*) of the Act, without prejudice to Section 1, provides that a will so far as it exercises a power of appointment is to be treated as properly executed if its execution conformed to the law governing the essential validity of the power. If valid execution of the will cannot be established under any of the alternatives available under Section 1 of the Act, Section 2(1)(*d*) enables only that portion of the will which exercises the power to be admitted to proof, if its execution conformed to the law governing the essential validity of the power.

ENGROSSMENTS (RULE 11)

2.142 If the will or codicil is not suitable to be photographed or if there are unauthenticated alterations, additions or obliterations which, by reason of their having been made, or (in the absence of evidence to the contrary) are presumed to have been made, after execution, the practitioner is required to furnish a typed or written engrossment of the document, omitting the alterations and additions, and restoring any obliteration where the original words or figures can be deciphered. Where obliteration is so complete that the original words or figures cannot be deciphered, a blank space must be left in the engrossment. The engrossment should contain all the features of the original document, and, although a strict facsimile copy is not necessary, the punctuation, spacing and paragraphing of the original must be reproduced. The engrossment must be written or typed bookwise on durable paper and on both sides of the paper.

2.143 Where there is a will with one or more codicils and some only (but not all) of the documents contain alterations etc. as above or are not suitable for photography, the registrar may direct that only those documents be engrossed and not the whole set. Where an order has been made that a will be rectified before it is proved, an engrossment of the will in the form in which it is to be proved must be lodged (Rule 11(2)).

ORIGINAL WILL (OR CODICIL) LOST, DESTROYED, OR NOT AVAILABLE (RULE 54)

2.144 Where an original will or other testamentary document has been lost, mislaid or inadvertently destroyed, application may be made for an order admitting to proof a copy or reconstruction of the contents of the missing document. If the original testamentary document is not available by reason that it is retained by a foreign court or official, an order is not required where a copy of the document authenticated by the foreign court or official holding the original can be submitted for proof.

2.145 Where it is known that the missing document was last in the possession of the testator and it cannot be found on his death, there is a presumption that he destroyed it with intent to revoke, and, in these circumstances, the person seeking to prove the contents of the document must furnish affidavit evidence to rebut that presumption. Where a copy or reconstruction of the contents of a testamentary document has been admitted to proof limited until the original or a more authentic copy shall be proved, the grantee should extract a cessate grant upon the original document or more authentic copy being discovered.

Application for order

2.146 The application may be made *ex parte* at the Principal Registry, or, if application for the grant is to be made at a district probate registry, application for the order should be made to the registrar of that district probate registry.

Evidence required in support of application

2.147 A normal application requires an affidavit sworn by the person seeking to establish the contents of the missing document, setting out:

(1) The facts as to the loss or destruction of the document, and, if lost, what efforts have been made to find it. Copies of advertisements, if any, should be exhibited and it should be stated whether there has been any reply to the advertisements.
(2) Whether the original document was whole and unrevoked and in existence after the death of the testator. If it cannot be proved that the document was in existence after the death, the presumption as to revocation by destruction must be rebutted. Corroborative affidavit evidence should, if possible, be obtained from other persons.
(3) If it is sought to prove the contents of the missing document as contained in a copy, the latter must be exhibited to the affidavit

and the deponent must state that he believes it to be a true copy of the original. In these circumstances, the copy should also be exhibited to an affidavit, sworn by the person who prepared it, stating whether it was prepared before or after execution of the original document and whether it was examined with the original and found to be correct.

(4) If there is no copy and it is desired to prove a reconstruction of the contents of the missing document, the paper containing the reconstruction must be exhibited to the affidavit. An affidavit is also required from the person able to make a declaration of the contents of the original document, exhibiting the paper containing the reconstruction and stating whether the latter contains the exact words of the original document or whether it merely shows the main features of it.

(5) The names, and relationships to the testator, of all persons who would be prejudiced by the proof of the contents of the missing document (*i.e.* all persons who would be entitled to share in the estate on an intestacy and under any earlier testamentary document) and whether they are *sui juris*. If any of such persons are dead, it must be stated whether or not they have legal personal representatives. The signed and witnessed consents of all such persons, or of their legal personal representatives, to proof of the contents of the document should, if possible, be obtained and referred to in the affidavit.

The registrar may require an affidavit speaking as to due execution of the original document. Wherever possible such affidavit should be sworn to by one of the subscribing witnesses to the execution. Affidavit evidence from any person able to corroborate any of the facts sworn to in the affidavit of the applicant for the order may also be required and the registrar may direct that notice be given to persons who would be prejudiced by the application, if they have not consented. The order, if made, will direct that the grant be limited until the original testamentary document or a more authentic copy thereof be proved; but where it is known that the original document has been destroyed the order will direct a form of limitation appropriate to the circumstances.

PLIGHT AND CONDITION OF WILL OR CODICIL

2.148 A testamentary document should not be fastened in any way to other papers when lodging them in the registry.

2.149 If a testamentary document bears any sign which suggests that it has been interfered with in any way, or if there is any appearance of attempted revocation (*e.g.* by burning, tearing or otherwise) an affidavit as to the plight and condition of the document is required (Rule 15). Where possible, the affidavit evidence should be deposed to by the applicant for the grant, but an affidavit from any other person who has knowledge of the facts may be accepted. The registrar may also require an affidavit to be sworn by a subscribing witness to the will or codicil, speaking to the plight and condition of the document at the time of execution, and where such affidavit is called for the witness must also depose to the due execution of the document.

DEPOSIT OF WILL OF LIVING PERSONS

2.150 A testator may wish to deposit his will (or codicil) in the safe custody of the Record Keeper at the Principal Registry and a fee is payable. The will or codicil may be handed to the Record Keeper by the testator personally or by his authorised agent or may be handed in at any of the district probate registries or sub-registries for onward transmission to the Principal Registry. Alternatively, the will or codicil, contained in a sealed envelope appropriately endorsed, may be sent through the post to the Record Keeper by the testator (or his agent). Application for the withdrawal of a deposited will or codicil must be made in writing by the testator to the Principal Registry. Following the death of the testator, application may be made to the Principal Registry for the sealed envelope containing the deposited document to be opened and for the will or codicil to be handed over to the executor or other person entitled to possession of it.

2.151 The fee for depositing a will is £1 (Non-Contentious Probate Fees Order 1981 Sch. Fee 6). Printed forms and envelopes for use in connection with the deposit of wills may be obtained from the Record Keeper's Department of the Principal Registry or from any district probate registry.

PRECEDENTS

(1) *Affidavit as to execution of will (or codicil)*

[USUAL HEADING]

I. , *of*
make oath and say as follows:

1. That I am one of the subscribing witnesses to the (codicil to the) last will and testament of
of
formerly of
deceased, the said bearing date the
day of 19 being now produced to me and marked "A".

2. That the said deceased executed the said
on the day of
19 the date thereof by signing his name (*or* making his mark) at the foot or end thereof (*or* in the attestation clause) as the same now appears thereon, meaning and intending the same as h final signature to the said

in the presence of me and of
the other subscribed witness thereto, both of us being present at the same time, and we thereupon (to wit, after the deceased had so signed) attested and subscribed the said
in the presence of the said deceased.

3. That referring to the following alteration(s) in the said
namely

the said recited alteration(s) was/were (not) made as it/they now appear(s) previously to execution as aforesaid.

[4. That previous to execution as aforesaid the said
was read over to the said deceased by
and that the said deceased seemed perfectly to understand the same.]

5. That the only persons present at the time of execution of the said
were the said deceased, the said witnesses and [*insert names of other persons present* or *nobody else*].

Sworn by the said

at

on the day of 19

Before me

A Commissioner for Oaths (Solicitor)

(2) *Affidavit as to execution of will (or codicil)—Two signatures to will*

[USUAL HEADING]

I, of ,
make oath and say as follows:

1. That I am one of the subscribing witnesses to the last will and testament of
, of ,
deceased, the said will being now produced to me, and marked "A" bearing date the day of 19

2. That the said testat executed the said will on the day of the date thereof by signing h name [*on the second page of the said will opposite the printed words "signature of Testator" or as the case may be*] meaning and intending such signature in due and final execution of h said will as the same now appears thereon, in the presence of me and of the other subscribed witness thereto, both of us being present at the same time, and we thereupon attested and subscribed the said will in the presence of the said testat

3. *That prior to the said execution of the said will the said testat attempted to sign h name [opposite the first line of the attestation clause thereof or as the case may be] and being dissatisfied with such attempted signature abandoned same and executed the said will as before deposed to.]*

Sworn, etc.

(Note—The circumstances should be stated but it must be clearly shown by which signature the will was duly and finally executed.)

(3) *Affidavit of execution by person present at the execution of the will, both witnesses being dead or cannot be traced*

[USUAL HEADING]

I, of , make oath and say as follows:

1. That of , deceased, died on the day of 19 , having made and duly executed her last will and testament bearing date the day of 19 , which said will is now produced to me and marked "A".

2. That and , the two attesting and subscribing witnesses to the said will are both dead [*or I have caused enquiries to be made as to the whereabouts of and the attesting and subscribing witnesses to the said will but they have not been traced and it is not known whether they are alive or dead or as the case may be*].

3. That [*I am an executor named in the will of the deceased, or as the case may be, and*] I was present at the time of the execution of the said will, and that the said testatrix executed the said will on the said day of 19 by signing her name [*or making her mark*] at the foot or end thereof as the same now appears thereon in the presence of me and of the said two attesting witnesses thereto, all of us being present at the same time, and the said and thereupon attested and subscribed the said will in the presence of the said testatrix and in my presence.

(*The following clause to be added if execution by mark.*)

4. That previously to the execution of the said will by the said testatrix the same was read over to her by and she the said testatrix at such time seemed thoroughly to understand and approve of the contents of her said will.

Sworn, etc.

(4) *Affidavit in support of execution—Witnesses dead or cannot be traced—no other person present at execution*

[USUAL HEADING]

I, of ,
make oath and say as follows:

1. That I am the sole executor [*or as the case may be*] named in the last will and testament of , deceased, who died on the day of 19 , the said will bearing date the day of 19 , being now produced to me and marked "A". The deceased left no earlier will.

2. That *C.D.* and *E.F.*, the attesting and subscribing witnesses to the said will, are both now dead (*or* That I have caused enquiries to be made as to the whereabouts of *C.D.* and *E.F.*, the attesting and subscribing witnesses to the said will, but they have not been traced and it is not known whether they are alive or dead).

3. That I have been unable to ascertain whether any person other than the said *C.D.* and *E.F.* was present with the said testator at the time of execution of the said will.

4. That the said deceased died a bachelor without issue [*or as the case may be*] leaving *G.H.*, *P.H.*, and *S.H.*, his [*set out exact relationship, which must be lawful, and be described as such, where the deceased died before 4th April 1988*] together the only persons who would be entitled to share in his estate if he had died intestate, who are all *sui juris* and have consented to the said will being admitted to proof without further evidence as to the due execution thereof, as appears from the signed consents now produced to me and marked "B", "C" and "D" respectively.

Sworn, etc.

(*NOTE*—An affidavit identifying the signature to the will as being in the true and proper handwriting of the testator is also necessary (see form No. (12). Where affidavits identifying the handwriting of the witnesses can also be obtained, the consents of the persons prejudiced may often be dispensed with.)

(5) *Affidavit of plight and condition*

[USUAL HEADING]

I, of ,
make oath and say as follows:

1. That I am the executor (*or* one of the executors) named in the paper writing now produced to me and marked "A" purporting to be and contain the last will and testament (*or* a codicil to the last will and testament) of
late of

deceased, who died on the day of
19

the said will (*or* codicil) bearing date the day of 19 .

2. That having viewed and perused the said will (*or* codicil) and particularly observed [*Here describe the plight and condition of the will, and set forth finding it in its present state and if possible trace the will from the possession of the deceased in his lifetime up to the time of making the affidavit, giving (if known) explanation of present condition.*]

.
.
.
.
.
.

The said will (*or* codicil) is now in all respects in the same state, plight and condition as when found by me as aforesaid.

Sworn, etc.

(6)–*Affidavit of search*

[USUAL HEADING]

I, of , make oath and say as follows:

1. That I am the sole executor (*or* one of the executors) named in the paper writing now produced to me and marked "A" purporting to be and contain the last will and testament of late of deceased who died on the day of 19 , the said will bearing date (*or* bearing no date) the day of 19 .

2. That referring particularly to the fact that [*the blank spaces originally left in the said will for the insertion of the day and month of the date thereof have never been supplied, or that the said will is without date, or as the case may be*]. I have made enquiry of

the solicitor of the said deceased, and that I have also made diligent and careful search in all places where the said deceased usually kept h papers of moment and concern, and in h depositories, in order to ascertain whether he had left any other will or any codicil or list or memorandum of a testamentary character but that I have been unable to discover any such documents except the said will.

3. That I verily believe the said deceased died without having left any will, codicil, list or memorandum of a testamentary character whatever other than the said will hereinbefore deposed to by me.

Sworn, etc.

(7) *Affidavit as to alterations*

[USUAL HEADING]

I, , of , make oath and say as follows:

1. That I am one of the subscribing witnesses to the (*or* codicil to the) last will and testament of
of
.
.
deceased, the said will (*or* codicil) being now produced to me and marked "A" bearing date the day of 19 .

2. That I have carefully perused and inspected the said will (*or* codicil) and have particularly observed [*the words " " interlined between the and lines of the first side or page of the said will, the name " " interlined between the and lines of the said first side or page the words and figures " " struck through in ink in the line of the second side or page of the said will: and the word " " written upon an erasure in the line of the said second side or page (or, as the case may be, taking care to describe accurately the various interlineations, alterations, obliterations or erasures, in the order in which they appear in the document)*]
.
.
.
.
.
.
.

3. That the said testat executed the said will (*or* codicil) on the day of the date thereof, by signing h name [*"at the foot or end thereof" or, "in the testimonium clause thereof"*] [*or, "in the attestation clause thereof"*] *meaning and intending such recital and signature in final and due execution of* his *said will* as the same now appears thereon, in the presence of me and of

the other subscribed witness thereto, both of us being present at the same time, and we thereupon attested and subscribed the said in the presence of the said testat .

4. That all the said recited interlineations (*or* alterations *or* obliterations *or* erasures)
.
.
were written and made in the said will (*or* codicil) previously to the execution thereof [*or as the case may be*].

Sworn, etc.

(8) *Affidavit as to a draft will having been executed*

[USUAL HEADING]

I, of ,
make oath and say as follows:

1. That of ,
deceased, died on the day of 19 ,
having made his last will and testament bearing date the day
of 19 , now produced to me and marked "A".

2. That the said deceased gave me instruction to prepare his will on or about the day of 19 and a draft of such will was prepared by me and sent by me by post to the said deceased for his approval.

3. That the said deceased was very anxious to have his affairs settled at the earliest possible moment, and in order that there should be no delay in the execution of his said will he executed the said draft of the said will by signing his name at the foot or end thereof as the same now appears thereon.

4. That the said will was in due course of post sent by the said deceased to me, and that no engrossment of the said draft of the said will was made [*or if made that the same was not executed by the deceased*].

[*If deponent an attesting witness to the will add usual clauses as to due execution.*]

Sworn, etc.

(9) *Affidavit as to identity of executor—As to relationship*

[USUAL HEADING]

I, of ,
make oath and say as follows:

1. That of ,
deceased, died on the day of 19 ,
having made and duly executed his last will and testament bearing date the
day of 19 , and thereof appointed me, this deponent, sole executor.

2. That the said testator described me in his said will as his nephew, but I am not the nephew of the deceased. I am the lawful nephew of
the lawful wife of the said deceased.

3. That the said deceased in his lifetime always spoke of and referred to me as his nephew, and that he during his lifetime informed me that he had appointed me executor of is said will.

4. That I am well acquainted with the family and relatives of the said deceased, and that the said deceased had not at the date of his said will and never had a nephew of the name of

5. That I am the only person of the name of
residing at
as described in the said will, and was the only person of that name residing there at the date of the said will.

Sworn, etc.

(10) *Affidavit of identity of executor—As to name*

[USUAL HEADING]

I, of ,
make oath and say as follows:

1. That of ,
deceased died on the day of 19 ,
having made and duly executed his last will and testament bearing date the day of 19 .

2. That the said deceased in his said will appointed his friend (*name given in will*) to be one of the executors and trustees of his will meaning and intending the person so described to be me this deponent.

3. That the testator informed me that he had appointed me one of the executors of the said will and I thereupon agreed to act as such executor of such will [*or as the case may be to prove identity*].

4. That I am well acquainted with the friends of the said deceased having known him for over years and the said deceased had not at the date of his said will a friend of the name of (*name given in will*).

Sworn, etc.

(11) *Affidavit as to alias (will)*

[USUAL HEADING]

I, of ,
make oath and say as follows:

1. That John Winston, otherwise Wanstone, of ,
deceased, died on the day of 19 ,
having made and executed his last will and testament, bearing date the day of 19 , and thereof appointed me, this deponent, one of the executors.

2. That the said deceased in his said will is described as and subscribed his name thereto in execution thereof as John Winston, and was generally known by that name.

3. That the true name of the deceased was John Winston.

4. That at the time of the death of the said deceased, there was standing to his credit in Parrs Bank Ltd., a sum of money in the name of John Wanstone.

5. In the aforesaid circumstances it is desired that the grant of probate of the will of the said deceased should issue in the names of John Winston, otherwise John Wanstone.

Sworn, etc.

(12) *Affidavit of handwriting*

[USUAL HEADING]

I, *C.D.*, of , make oath and say as follows:

1. That I knew and was well acquainted with *A.B.*, of ,
deceased, who died on the day of 19 , for many years before and down to the time of his death, and that during such period I have frequently seen him write, and also subscribe his name

to writings, whereby I have become well acquainted with his manner and character of handwriting and subscription.

2. That having now with care and attention perused and inspected the paper writing now produced to me and marked "A" and purporting to be the last will and testament of the said deceased, bearing date the day of 19 , beginning thus " " ending thus " " and being thus subscribed "*A.B.*" [*or as the case may be*] I believe the whole of the said will, together with the names "*A.B.*" subscribed thereto as aforesaid [*or as the case may be*], to be of the true and proper handwriting and subscription of the said deceased.

Sworn, etc.

(13) *Affidavit of facts: Wills Act 1963*

[USUAL HEADING]

I, *A.B.*, of , make oath and say as follows:

1. That I am the sole executor [*or as the case may be*] named in the last will and testament [*or codicil to the last will and testament*] dated the day of 19 , of *C.D.* of , who died on the day of 19 , the said will (codicil) being now produced to me and marked "A".

2. That the said will (codicil) was executed at in

[*or*] 2. That at the time of execution of the said will (codicil) [*or* at the date of his death] the said *C.D.*, [was domiciled in] [*or* had his habitual residence at (address) in] [*or* was a national of (name of territory or state)]

[*Add, if necessary (see Section 6(2), Wills Act 1963)*].

3. That at the time of execution of the said will (codicil) [*or* at the time of his death] the said *C.D.* was connected with the and systems of internal law relating to the formal validity of wills as follows: (*give details of the connections with each so that it may be shown with which he was mostly closely connected*). The said *C.D.* was accordingly most closely connected with the system of internal law.

[*or* 3. That at the time of execution of the said will (codicil) [*or* That at the time of his death] the said *C.D.* was only connected with the system of internal law relating to the formal validity of wills (*give grounds on which this connection is claimed,* e.g. *place of birth, habitual residence, religion, caste etc.*)].

Sworn, etc.

CHAPTER 3

Probate

APPOINTMENT OF EXECUTOR

3.01 If a valid will of a testator, wherever domiciled at the date of death, is in the English or Welsh language and appoints an executor, he is accepted as having full rights and powers of executorship. No expression in a foreign tongue purporting to mean "executor" will be accepted as constituting an executor, but if the will sets out the duties of a person named therein in terms sufficient to constitute him executor according to the tenor thereof, he may obtain probate in that capacity.

3.02 Where the testator, by his will, has authorised a named person to nominate an executor and the named person has exercised his power, the appointment is effective. The instrument by which such an executor is appointed must be lodged with the papers to lead to the grant and the authorisation and appointment must be recited in the executor's oath to lead to the grant.

3.03 Where there is a gift of the residuary estate to a charity and the testator by his will gives power to the charity to nominate a person as executor of the will, on the nomination by the charity probate is granted to the nominee as executor. The facts must be recited in the oath. The nomination must be in writing under the hands of the duly appointed trustees of the charity and evidence of their right to act on behalf of the charity must be produced. The nomination must be filed with the papers.

3.04 The powers of the executor may be absolute or the terms of the appointment may impose restrictions as to time, place or subject-matter, or some other condition or limitation. Where the powers of an executor are in any way limited, the grant of probate will be similarly limited as to that executor. If a testator has appointed one executor for one special purpose, or in respect of one specific fund, together with another executor for all other purposes and effects, the executors can apply for probate together and one grant is issued, or separate grants can be applied for—one being limited to the specific fund, or purpose, and the other save and except such fund.

3.05 An appointment of one or two of three or more named persons as executors (e.g. "I appoint *A.B.* or *C.D.* or *E.F.* as executors") is void for uncertainty, but an appointment of "*A.B.* and/or *C.D.*" has been held to mean *A.B.* and *C.D.* together, or *A.B.* or failing him *C.D.* (*Re Lewis, Goronwy v. Richards* [1942] Ch. 424). An appointment of "*A.* or *B.*" is void for uncertainty. (But see para. 2.63 as to interpretation of will where the testator died on or after 1st January 1983.)

3.06 If a firm is appointed executor, probate is given to the partners, or to a person who was a member of the firm, or to the person trading under that firm's name. The appointment is of the individual members constituting the firm *at the date of the will*, unless a contrary intention appears in the will; the facts must be set out in the oath (*Re Fernie* (1849) 6 Notes of Cases 657; see also *Re Horgan decd.* [1971] P. 50).

3.07 When a person is appointed executor in his capacity as holder of an office and not by name, the appointment is of the person holding the office *at the date of death* of the testator, and not at the date of the will unless the context of the will indicates otherwise (*John Jones* (1927) 43 T.L.R. 324).

3.08 A valid testamentary document, whether containing an appointment of an executor or not, and disposing of the whole estate of a testator, revokes all previous testamentary dispositions, and an earlier testamentary document containing an appointment of an executor will not be admitted to probate on the ground that an executor has been appointed in that document (*Henfrey v. Henfrey* (1840) 4 Moore P.C.C. 29).

3.09 Where there is unnecessary delay on the part of the executor in making application for probate, or he refuses to do so and will not renounce his right, and a grant is sought by a person with a lower title, the executor should be cited to "accept or refuse a grant" (see para 15.23.)

Executor according to the tenor

3.10 When a testator does not expressly name any executor, but by direction to pay debts etc. or otherwise charges a person with the duties of an executor, such person may take a grant of probate as "executor according to the tenor of the will". In the following examples the person named has been held to be an executor according to the tenor of the will:

"I appoint *A.B.* to carry out these instructions".
" . . . to hold and administer in trust all my estate", (*Re Way* [1901] P. 345).

In another example, a testator appointed by his will *A.B.* as one of his executors and by a codicil substituted his son for *A.B.* as trustee; it was held that the son was executor according to the tenor (*Re Wright* (1908) 25 T.L.R. 15).

3.11 It is not essential that any estate should be given to the person directed by the will to pay debts, etc., in order to constitute him an executor according to the tenor (*In the Goods of Cook* [1902] P. 114). But a direction to a person to pay debts out of a particular fund will not constitute that person an executor according to the tenor (*Toomy* (1864) 3 Sw. & Tr. 562). There must be, however, some direction in the document that a person is to do some act of an executorial character, in order to constitute him an executor according to the tenor (*Re Brown* (1910) 54 S.J. 478). Where he is not given wider powers as above, a person appointed a trustee by the will is not an executor according to the tenor (*Re Punchard* (1872), 2 P. & D. 369).

3.12 A joint grant may be made to a person who is directly appointed as executor and to another who is an executor according to the tenor.

Executor a minor

3.13 Where the sole or sole surviving executor appointed is under the age of 18 years, a grant of administration with will annexed is made for his use and benefit until he attains the age of 18 years. (See Chapter 8.) Where one of the executors appointed is a minor, probate may be granted to the other executors with power reserved of making the like grant to the minor on his attaining the age of 18 years. A minor executor's right to probate on attaining the age of 18 years may not be renounced by any person in his behalf (Rule 34(1)).

Executor resides abroad

3.14 In this case the executor can, or course, prove the will himself, in which case the papers may be sworn abroad. Alternatively, if desired, a grant of administration with will annexed could be made to the attorney of such executor. (See paras. 8.44 ff.)

Passing over executor

3.15 An executor's title to probate is not defeasible by insolvency, commission of a crime (but see murder and manslaughter, para 12.18) or bankruptcy (*Smethurst v. Tomlin & Bankes* (1861), 2 Sw. & Tr. 143; *Drawmer* (1913) 108 L.T. 732). However, where good cause is shown the court may exercise its discretion to pass over the right of an executor by order under Section 116 of the Supreme Court Act 1981.

TRANSMISSION (CHAIN) OF EXECUTORSHIP

3.16 Where a sole executor, or last surviving executor, who has proved the will of his testator has died leaving part of the estate unadministered the grant of probate does not necessarily cease, and provided that there is an unbroken chain of executorship a further grant in the estate of the testator may not be required. Section 7 of the Administration of Estates Act, 1925, provides that:

> "(1) An executor of a sole or last surviving executor of a testator is the executor of that testator. This provision shall not apply to an executor who does not prove the will of his testator, and, in the case of an executor who on his death leaves surviving him some other executor of his testator who afterwards proves the will of that testator it shall cease to apply on such probate being granted.
> (2) So long as the chain of such representation is unbroken, the last executor in the chain is the executor of every preceding testator.
> (3) The chain of such representation is broken by:
> (*a*) an intestacy; or
> (*b*) the failure of a testator to appoint an executor; or
> (*c*) the failure to obtain probate of a will;
> but is not broken by a temporary grant of administration if probate is subsequently granted.
> (4) Every person in the chain of representation to a testator:
> (*a*) has the same rights in respect of the real and personal estate of that testator as the original executor would have had if living; and
> (*b*) is, to the extent to which the estate whether real or personal of that testator has come to his hands, answerable as if he were an original executor."

If the chain of executorship is broken, or remains in abeyance, and part of the estate of the deceased remains unadministered, a grant of letters of administration (with will) "*de bonis non*" may be applied for. (See para. 11.01.)

3.17 The chain of executorship is in abeyance where the sole executor, or surviving proving executor, has died testate appointing an executor, who for some reason does not prove his testator's will, or renounces probate of it. In these circumstances, a grant can be made (to a residuary legatee or residuary devisee or to the person otherwise entitled) of the unadministered estate of the original deceased, limited until the executor shall prove his testator's will, and the oath to lead to the grant must set out the reasons for the failure of the executor to prove his testator's will. A chain of executorship is not considered to exist through a grant to an attorney of an executor, nor through a grant to a special executor of settled land, and an executor for life or appointed for a special purpose only does not transmit his office to his own executor.

Colonial resealing

3.18 Where probate has been granted by a Court of Probate in a place to which the Colonial Probates Act 1892 applies, and the probate has been resealed in England, it is considered that a chain of executorship exists if the same Court has subsequently granted probate of the will of the executor (or the last surviving proving executor) to his executor (or executors), and this grant has also been resealed in England. For resealing Colonial grants, see paras. 13.06–16.

Northern Irish grants and Scottish confirmations

3.19 By virtue of the Administration of Estates Act 1971, a grant made in Northern Ireland in the estate of a testator domiciled there is treated as if it issued in England and Wales (see para. 13.03) and a chain of executorship can survive. No chain of executorship can survive through a Scottish confirmation.

OATH FOR EXECUTOR

3.20 The oath for executor is the document from which the information necessary for a grant of probate is obtained by the registrar. It is essential, therefore, that it should be accurately and carefully prepared. Except with the leave of a registrar, a grant of probate cannot be made within seven days of the death of the deceased (Rule 6(2).) A minority or life interest created by the will does not affect an executor's right to the grant as an executor is entitled as of right to probate. On obtaining probate of the will, the whole of the estate of the testator (whether disposed of by his will or not) which devolves on the personal representative devolves on and vests in the executor and, after payment of the debts and funeral and testamentary expenses, is to be administered by him; as to that part dealt with by the will, according to the terms of the will, and as to that part undisposed of by the will as under an intestacy.

3.21 In every oath to lead to a grant of probate, it must be stated whether or not there was land vested in the deceased immediately before his death, which was settled previously thereto and not by his will and which remained settled land. (The practice in cases where there is settled land is dealt with in Chapter 10.) A general executor may take a grant *save and except settled land* and in this case it is necessary only to show in the oath that there is settled land. If a grant has been taken in respect of settled land only, the oath for a grant in respect of the free estate must recite the grant already taken in respect of settled land. An office copy of the grant must be lodged with the papers.

3.22 There is no preference among the executors appointed by the will; any one may apply for the grant. A grant cannot be made to more than four persons. Where several executors are appointed any one or more of them not exceeding four in number may apply for probate and, provided that they have not renounced, power to obtain probate will be reserved to the other executors. If there are more than four executors who have not renounced and are competent to take probate, power will be reserved to the other executors exceeding four to apply for probate on vacancies occurring. On a vacancy any one of the others to whom power has been reserved may take a grant of double probate (see para. 3.28).

3.23 Where power is to be reserved a note should be inserted in the margin of the oath, "Power to be reserved to *A.B.* (and *C.D.*) the other executor (or executors)". Subject to the power of a registrar to dispense with giving notice where he is satisfied that the giving of notice is impracticable or would result in unreasonable delay or expense, notice of the application for probate must be given to each executor to whom power is to be reserved and a statement that it has must be included in the oath (Rule 27(1)). If notice has not been given to one or more of the executors, that should be made clear in the oath and the reasons why the registrar is being asked to dispense with the giving of the notice should be given in an accompanying letter. A preliminary enquiry may be made by similar letter, before the oath is prepared, to ascertain whether the registrar would be prepared to dispense with notice in the circumstances of the particular case. Where power is to be reserved to partners in a firm, notice may be given to them by sending it to the firm at its principal or last known place of business (Rule 27(2)).

3.24 If four executors are appointed by the will, and two only apply for the grant and one renounces and power is reserved to the other non-proving executor, the renunciation shoud be recited in the oath and filed with the application for the grant. An executor to whom power has been reserved may subsequently apply for a grant of double probate or may renounce probate. If one of the executors is a minor at the time of application for a grant of probate, power must be reserved to him to come in and prove (by taking out a grant of double probate) on attaining his majority and a marginal note should be made in the oath as follows: "Power to be reserved to *A.B.* the other executor named in the will on his attaining the age of 18 years".

Where one of two (or more) executors renounce

3.25 The oath should show that the applicant is one of the executors. Two or more executors may renounce on one form. The renunciation need not be recited in the oath, but the renunciation must be filed with the papers. An executor who renounces probate does not thereby lose any right which he may have to take representation to the same deceased in another character. A form of renunciation of probate by an executor who is also entitled in another character must also include a renunciation of his right to letters of administration (with will) if a grant to a person with a lower title is sought.

Affidavit of identity

3.26 The registrar may require evidence, in addition to any statement in the oath, as to the identity of the person applying for the grant (Rule 6(1)). Such evidence is given in the form of an "affidavit of identity" setting out the facts and disposing of the possibility of there being another person who can be identified with the description of the executor as appointed in the will (Forms of affidavit after para. 2.151 Nos. (9) and (10)).

Order of executors

3.27 Where two or more executors are appointed and apply for probate, the order in which they are appointed is usually followed in naming them in the grant. If it is required that the order be varied, the signed consents of all the executors to such variation should be furnished. (The request for variation, consents and signatures may be written on the back of the oath.)

Oath for executor

[USUAL HEADING]

I,[1]

of

make oath and say as follows:

1.[2]

of[3] deceased

formerly of

died on the [4] day of 19

aged years[5] domiciled in England and Wales[6]

2. I believe the paper writing now produced to and marked by me to contain the true and original last will and testament[7]
of the deceased.

3. To the best of my knowledge, information and belief there was (no)[8] land vested in the deceased which was settled previously to the death (and not by the will) of the deceased and which remained settled land notwithstanding such death.

[9]

4. [10]I am execut named in the said will [Notice of this application has been given to the executor(s) to whom power is to be reserved, (save)].

5. I will:
- (i) collect, get in and administer according to law the real and personal estate of the said deceased;
- (ii) when required to do so by the Court, exhibit in the Court a full inventory of the said estate and render an account thereof to the Court; and
- (iii) when required to do so by the High Court, deliver up to that Court the grant of probate.

6. To the best of my knowledge, information and belief the gross estate passing under the grant does not exceed/amounts to £[11] and the net

estate does not exceed/amounts to £(12)   (and that this is not a case in which an Inland Revenue Account is required to be delivered(13)).

Sworn, etc.

Notes

1 *Name and description, etc.* Insert full name, full postal address and occupation or description of each executor in the order that they appear in the will. An address at a club or hotel will not be accepted unless it is expressly stated in the oath that the executor permanently resides there and it is his only address. An address c/o Bankers or c/o Solicitors will be accepted if it is shown in the oath, or certified by the solicitor, that the deponent has no permanent or better address. The permanent address of a member of H.M. Forces must be given.

Any minor discrepancy in the executor's name should be dealt with in the oath. For instance—if the correct surname of an executor be "Phillips" and his name appears in the will as "Philips" he should be described in the oath as "Phillips (in the will spelt Philips)". If however, the difference between names is such to suggest the possibility that a person other than the applicant is intended by the testator, an affidavit of identity by the executor should be filed showing that the applicant is the person intended by the testator to act as executor of his will. The affidavit must show that the applicant is the person whose name and description most nearly satisfies the name and description in the will, and in such a case the oath must show that the executor's name is "Arthur Richard Jackson (in the will called Richard Jackson)", as the case may be. If the testator had informed the applicant that he had appointed him as executor that fact should be stated.

If the will appoints "my wife" as executor without naming her in any part of the will, the oath should include a paragraph (when she is an applicant for the grant) showing that the deponent was the lawful wife of the testator at the date of the will; this applies similarly to an appointment of "my husband".

If the executor has, since the date of the will, adopted a name other than that by which he is appointed in the will, either by deed poll, or by repute or constant use, the fact must be recited in the oath, and the deed, if any, in evidence of the change of name must be produced. Where a change of name has not been effected by deed, the oath should give details as to such change.

The occupation or description of every male deponent must be given immediately following his address in the oath. An executor who has no occupation should be described as "of no occupation"; if he is retired, his former occupation should be shown and he should be described as, "retired bank manager" or as the case may be. The description "of independent means", "esquire", "gentleman", and any other description of a similarly vague character cannot be accepted.

Officers in Her Majesty's Forces should be described as "Major, H.M. Army", "Captain, Royal Navy", "Squadron Leader, R.A.F." as appropriate; if retired, the description should be "Major (retired) H.M. Army", or as the case may be.

If the deponent is a female and has no occupation her status must be correctly shown in the oath, *e.g.* "spinster", "married woman (or the wife of ....)", "widow", or in the case of a divorcee "single woman". A married woman deponent who has married since the date of the will and is described therein by her former surname should be described in the oath as, "*A.B.*, wife of *B.B.*—formerly *A.C.*, spinster (widow, single woman)".

2 *Name of testator*. As a general rule the name with which the will is headed and signed is accepted as the true name of the testator. In practice the principle adopted is that the true name of the deceased must appear on the papers for the grant with the addition of any variation of that name in the will or in documents of title in which the testator held assets. In the case of a variance between the name of the testator in the heading of the will and the true name, the oath must state the true name of the testator followed by the word "otherwise" and the name in the heading of the will. Both names will be given in the grant, the true name coming first (Rule 9).

When the testator has changed his name as given in the will since the date of the will the fact must be stated, and if the change has been evidenced by a deed poll the date of the deed must be given and the deed produced. If the change has been made by assumption of another name and a deed has not been executed, the facts should be stated, in which case the oath must show the true name, with the reputed name as an alias.

3 *Address of testator*. The full address of the testator must be given and if his place of residence at the date of death does not correspond with that given in the will (or last codicil) both addresses should be inserted. In no case will more than four addresses be given in the grant.

If an address at a club or an hotel is given, it should be stated that is was the deceased's only and permanent address and that he resided at the place stated.

If the deceased was a member of Her Majesty's Forces and stationed abroad at the time of his death, his permanent address should be given, or it should be stated that he had no permanent address.

4 *Date of death*. If the exact date of death is known it must be given in the oath. Where the fact of death can be sworn to but the exact date thereof is uncertain, the oath should recite that the deceased "was last seen alive on the.............. day of.., and that his dead body was found on the ....day of................................' (*Long-Sutton* [1912] P. 97).

Presumed death: If there is no direct evidence of death and the applicant for the grant presumes the person to be dead, an order giving leave to swear to the death must be obtained prior to making application for the grant. (See paras. 12.10–17.)

Where an order giving leave to swear to death has been obtained the oath should state that the deceased died "on or since (the date mentioned in the order)".

Certificate of death—H.M. Forces: When a certificate from the Ministry of Defence has been received by the next of kin stating that death is presumed to have occurred on a specific date, no further evidence is required if such certificate is produced.

Where the deceased, or presumed deceased, was a member of a crew of a lost ship, certificates issued by the Registrar-General of Shipping and Seamen are accepted as evidence of death.

Place of death: The place of death need not be stated in the oath.

5 The age of the deceased should be shown.

6 *Domicile of deceased.* The domicile of the deceased must appear in the oath (e.g. "England and Wales").

7 Insert "with a codicil thereto" or as the case may be; the number of codicils, if more than one, should be given. It may be necessary to include a codicil which has been wholly revoked.

Where a revoked will or codicil is revived by a later will or codicil, the documents will be proved in chronological order as will and codicil, or as the case may be.

Where a will or codicil effects the incorporation of a non-duly executed testamentary document, such will or codicil should be referred to in the oath as "being contained in paper writings marked 'A' and 'B' ". The two documents should be so marked, and both must be marked by the applicants for the grant and the person who administers the oath with their signatures.

If the executor is sworn on a certified copy of the will (e.g. where an original will has been proved in a foreign court) the oath should read "to contain an official copy of the true and original last will, etc."

8 *Settled land.* It must be shown whether or not there was land vested in the deceased immediately before his death which was settled previously thereto and not by his will and which remained settled land. If there is such settled land, and the grant is to be taken in respect only of the free estate of the deceased it will be sufficient to state that there was such settled land, and the grant will be "save and except settled land".

9 This part of the form should be used to set out any special fact necessary to lead to the making of the grant.

Judge's or Registrar's Order. When a grant is to be issued pursuant to an order made by a judge or registrar, the order must be recited in the oath:

> Judge's Order: "That by an order made by Mr. Justice........................in this Division on the.................day of................................ 19......, it was ordered that ...."
> Registrar's order: "That by an order dated the..........................day of...............................19......, made by one of the Registrars (or, by a District Probate Registrar) of this Division, it was ordered that...........
> ...."

A copy of the order must be lodged with the papers to lead to the grant.

Omission from probate: If an order directs that part of a testamentary document be omitted from probate, a copy of the document, omitting such part, must be lodged at the registry for an endorsement to be made in the margin of the copy: "Let the will (and codicil) be registered in accordance with this copy in pursuance of Judge's (or Registrar's) Order dated............................... 19......," and signed by the Probate Officer or district probate registrar, before photography for probate purposes.

Relationship of executor to testator: It is only necessary to state the relationship if it is relevant to a question of identity or entitlement to the grant.

10 The style of the executors (of which the following are examples) is to be inserted.

One male executor	the sole executor
All males	the executors
One female	the sole executrix
All females	the executrixes
Male and female executors	the executors
One (or more) of the executors being dead the other (or others) proves	the surviving executor(s)
Power reserved to one (or more) and one proves	one of the executors
One or more of the executors renounces and one proves	one of the executors
Executor according to the tenor	the executor according to the tenor of the said will
Executrix for life or widowhood	the executrix for life or widowhood named in the said will
Two or more executors including a widow who is appointed during widowhood only	That we are the executors named in the said will, but as to the said *A.B.*, during widowhood only
Executrix appointed during spinsterhood only	the executrix during spinsterhood only named in the said will
Executor for life	the executor for life
Executor as to part of the estate	That I am the executor named in the said will in respect of the estate of the said deceased save and except (*state the terms of the will*).
	That I am the executor for England and Wales named in the said will.
	That we are the executors named in the said will, but as to the said *A.B.* only in respect of (*state terms of the will*).

11 *Gross amount of estate.* Insert in figures the gross amount of the "free" estate of the deceased which by law devolves on and vests in his legal personal representative, i.e. the amount shown in the corresponding paragraph relating to the estate in the Inland Revenue Account, if any. (For completion of the Inland Revenue Account, see paras. 6.58 ff). In those cases where an Inland Revenue Account is not required (see paras. 6.04–09) it will be sufficient to state that the gross estate does not exceed the upper figure of the brackets within which the estate falls.

The full value of the estate, or the appropriate bracket upper figure, should be sworn to, but in special circumstances an application for a grant will be entertained showing an amount, "so far as can at present be ascertained". Where the Inland Revenue Account shows that the applicant has not been able to ascertain the precise amount or value of the estate, or where it is desired to show the amount "so far as can at present be ascertained", the figure sworn to in the oath should so far as possible be an estimate of the final value of the whole estate, and not merely the total of those assets whose value is known.

Where the sole asset is a claim under the Law Reform (Miscellaneous Provisions) Act 1934, an estimated amount should, if possible, be given. If the practitioner satisfies the registrar of his inability to give an estimate he may if he wishes be allowed to proceed on a "NIL" figure. In these circumstances, the oath must contain a paragraph setting out the purpose for which the grant is required and should show the amount of the estate as "NIL, so far as can at present be ascertained".

Where the deceased died domiciled in England or Wales the gross value of the estate which must be sworn to in the oath is, for deaths on or after the 1st January 1972, the real and personal estate in the United Kingdom (i.e. England and Wales, Scotland and Northern Ireland).

If the deceased died domiciled out of England and Wales, the amount of the estate to be shown is the value of the real and personal property situate in England and Wales only and this should be so stated in the oath.

All the real and personal estate passing under the grant must be included in the gross figure notwithstanding that part thereof may be exempted from Inheritance Tax. The values of reversionary interests owned by the deceased and gratuities of Civil Servants, unless a nomination has been executed, and school teachers are to be included. Nominated property, property held on joint tenancy and gifts *inter vivos* should not be included. The gross value of freehold or leasehold property must be included in the amount without the deduction of mortgages. (For completion of the Inland Revenue Account, see paras. 6.58 ff.)

Community of property: Where, by the law of the domicile of the deceased, community of property exists between the spouses, the last paragraph of the oath should be amended to read "The whole of the estate in England and Wales in respect of which a grant is required amounts in value to the sum of £.........to the best of my knowledge, information and belief; and that £.........(half) of that sum has accrued to the surviving spouse by reason of the existence of community of property under the law of the place of the domicile of the said deceased at the date of the marriage".

Nil estate: The oath to lead to the grant must set out the reason why the grant is required, and a similar statement must be annexed to any Inland Revenue Account for the information of the Capital Taxes Office.

12 *Net amount of estate.* Insert here the net value of the "free estate", i.e. the value of the gross estate less any allowable debts, incumbrances etc. as shown in the corresponding paragraph relating to the same in the Inland Revenue Account, if any. In those cases where an Inland Revenue Account is not required it will be sufficient to state that it does not exceed the upper figure of the bracket within which the net estate falls for fee purposes (see Appendix 2, Schedule, fee no. 1).

13 *Excepted estate.* See paras. 6.04–09 for circumstances in which an Inland Revenue Account is not required.

DOUBLE PROBATE

3.28 A grant of double probate is made to executors to whom power was reserved in the original grant of probate. Double probate confers the same powers on an executor as an original grant and if any of the original grantees are living it runs concurrently with the original grant. The grant is in general terms, and is applicable to the whole estate of the testator. Application for double probate may be made at the Principal Registry or at any district probate registry. An executor who has proved the will may be called upon to furnish particulars of the estate to an executor to whom power was reserved (*Re Griffin* (1910) 54 S.J. 378). An applicant for a double grant is not entitled as of right to claim from the Commissioners a copy of the Inland Revenue account filed on the application for the original grant of probate. For the form of any necessary Inland Revenue account applicable, see para. 6.14.

3.29 The oath must recite the particulars of the former grant or grants, and where not more than four executors are appointed it must be shown that power was then reserved to the other executor or executors; if more than four executors are appointed it must be shown that power was reserved to the other executor or executors to apply on vacancies occurring, and that a vacancy has occurred by reason of the death of an executor who proved the will, stating the name and date of death of such deceased executor. If the applicant for double probate was under the age of 18 years at the date of the original grant, the oath must show that he has attained that age. Where power was reserved to an executor who was mentally incapacitated, medical evidence on affidavit showing that he has recovered his capacity is required in addition to the oath if such executor applies for double probate. Where application is made at the Principal Registry an office copy of the previous grant should be filed with the papers; and a copy should also be filed when application is made to a district probate registry other than that from which the original issued. The fee for a grant of double probate is £2.

Oath for double probate

[USUAL HEADING]

I, of ,
make oath and say as follows:
1.

of
formerly of

deceased died on the

day of 19 aged years domiciled in England and Wales.

2. I believe the paper writing now produced to and marked by me to contain the true and original (*or* an official copy of the true) last will and testament (and codicil *or* codicils) of the deceased.

3. To the best of my knowledge, information and belief there was no land vested in the deceased which was settled previously to the death (and not by the will) of the deceased and which remained settled land notwithstanding such death.

4. That on the day of 19 , probate of the said will was by authority of this Division at the Probate Registry thereof granted to of the executors named in the said will, power being reserved of making the like grant to the other executor named therein;

and that I am the other (*or* one of the other *or* the now surviving) executor named in the said will.

5. I will:

(i) collect, get in and administer according to law the real and personal estate of the said deceased;

(ii) when required to do so by the Court, exhibit in the Court a full inventory of the said estate and render an account thereof to the Court; and

(iii) when required to do so by the High Court, deliver up to that Court the grant of double probate.

6. To the best of my knowledge, information and belief the gross estate passing under the grant amounts to £ and the net estate to amounts to £ [and that this is not a case in which an Inland Revenue Account is required to be delivered].

Sworn, etc.

CHAPTER 4

Letters of Administration with Will Annexed

4.01 A grant of letters of administration with the will annexed is made where a will is proved by a person other than an executor appointed by the will or any codicil to it, as in the following circumstances:
(1) Where no executor is appointed.
(2) Where the executor appointed has died in the lifetime of the testator, or has survived the testator and died without proving the will.
(3) Where the executor has renounced probate, or has been cited to accept or refuse probate and has not appeared.
(4) Where the appointment of the executor is void by reason of uncertainty.
(5) Where the Court exercises its discretion under Section 116 of the Supreme Court Act 1981 to pass over the prior right of the executor.
(6) Where the executor appointed is incompetent by reason of his minority or his incapacity to manage his own affairs, or wishes to apply through an attorney. (In such cases a grant may be made for the use and benefit of the executor.)
(7) Where the executor appointed and the residuary legatees and residuary devisees named in the will all die in the life-time of the testator, even if there is no other gift in the will.
(8) Where the executor is appointed for the purpose only of dealing with the foreign estate of the testator; in such a case the grant will be made to the residuary legatee or devisee named in the will, or as the case may be.

4.02 A grant will not be made to more than four persons, and except with the leave of a registrar, a grant of letters of administration with will annexed cannot be issued within seven days of the death of the deceased (Rule 6(2)). The relevant parts of Rule 27 provide as follows:

> "(4) A grant of administration may be made to any person entitled thereto without notice to other persons entitled in the same degree.
> (5) Unless a registrar otherwise directs, administration shall be granted to a person of full age entitled thereto in preferenece to a guardian of a minor, and to a living person entitled thereto in preference to the personal representative of a deceased person.
> (6) A dispute between persons entitled to a grant in the same degree shall be brought by summons before a registrar.
> (7) The issue of a summons under this rule in a district probate registry

shall be notified forthwith to the registry in which the index of pending grant applications is maintained.
(8) If the issue of a summons under this rule is known to the registrar, he shall not allow any grant to be sealed until such summons is finally disposed of."

TO WHOM GRANTED

Interests, in order of preference, to be considered for the purpose of obtaining the grant

4.03 Each class must be dealt with in a specified order of preference and all prior interests must be cleared off in the oath to lead to the grant when application is made by a lower interest. Rule 20 provides:

> "Where the deceased died on or after 1 January 1926 the person or persons entitled to a grant in respect of a will shall be determined in accordance with the following order of priority, namely—
> (a) the executor (but subject to Rule 36(4)(d) below);
> (b) any residuary legatee or devisee holding in trust for any other person;"

The executor takes a grant of probate (see Chapter 3). Where there is a specific gift of residuary estate to named persons on certain trusts, such persons are preferred to persons entitled to the residuary estate.

4.04 The next class of persons entitled to a grant under Rule 20 is:

> "(c) any other residuary legatee or devisee (including one for life) or where the residue is not wholly disposed of by the will, any person entitled to share in the undisposed of residue (including the Treasury Solicitor when claiming bona vacantia on behalf of the Crown) provided that—
> (i) unless a registrar otherwise directs, a residuary legatee or devisee whose legacy or devise is vested in interest shall be preferred to one entitled on the happening of a contingency, and
> (ii) where the residue is not in terms wholly disposed of, the registrar may, if he is satisfied that the testator has nevertheless disposed of the whole or substantially the whole of the known estate, allow a grant to be made to any legatee or devisee entitled to, or to share in, the estate so disposed of, without regard to the persons entitled to share in any residue not disposed of by the will;"

"Other" residuary legatees and devisees (including one for life)

4.05 A person to whom residuary personal estate is bequeathed is termed a "residuary legatee" and a person to whom residuary real estate is devised is termed a "residuary devisee". Persons with a vested interest are preferred to those entitled on a contingency (Rule 20 (c)(i)). Persons given an immediate absolute interest in the residuary estate are entitled as "residuary legatees and/or devisees named in the will". Persons given a life interest in the residuary estate are entitled as "residuary legatees and/or devisees for life named in the will". Persons given an absolute interest in the residuary estate on the termination of a life interest are entitled as "residuary legatees and/or devisees substituted in the will". Where there is no qualification in the will as to a reversionary interest which follows a life interest, the reversionary interest vests in the reversioner notwithstanding that he may predecease the life tenant.

4.06 Where the interest of the reversioner is contingent upon his survival, or there is a gift over in the event of his pre-deceasing the life tenant, such interest is contingent during the lifetime of the life tenant and does not vest in the reversioner until it falls into possession: if applying for a grant before such interest has vested he should be described as "the contingent residuary legatee and/or devisee substituted by the will": if applying for a grant after the reversionary interest has vested he should be described as "the residuary legatee and/or devisee named in the will as therein mentioned". Unless there is anything to the contrary in the will, a gift to *A* "if he shall be living at the date of death of the survivor of myself and my wife and shall attain the age of twenty-one years or marry under that age" followed by a gift over, is a vested gift to *A* and not a contingent gift (*Re Heath, Public Trustee v. Heath* [1936] Ch. 259), but it is essential to the application of this principle that there be a gift over.

Residuary legatee on attaining the age of 18

4.07 If in connection with a gift to a minor there is a reference to the attaining of a specified age, the exact terms of the will must be considered in order to determine whether the gift is contingent or vested. Where there is a clear gift to the minor and a separate and distinct direction to pay when he attains 18 years, the vesting is not postponed until he attains that age (*Re Bartholomew* (1849), 1 Mac. & G. 354; *Shrimpton v. Shrimpton* (1862) 31 Beav. 425). A gift to a legatee at, or upon attaining, or as and when he shall attain, the age of 18 years, is, in the absence of any factor (such as a gift over, or a gift to the legatee of the intermediate income), a contingent gift (*Hanson v. Graham* (1801), 6 Vesey 239).

4.08 A gift to a minor on attaining the age of majority with a direction that the income is to be paid, after the death of a life tenant and during the child's infancy, to the child's parent for advancement, benefit and education is a contingent and not a vested gift (*Re Rogers* [1944] 1 All

E.R. 408). If there is an express direction that the whole of the income is to be paid for the benefit of the minor until he attains the specified age, such direction will vest what would otherwise have been a contingent gift (*Re Ussher; Foster v. Ussher* [1922] 2 Ch. 321).

Devisee on attaining a specified age

4.09 Under the rule of construction known as the rule in *Phipps v. Akers* (1842)9 Cl. & Fin. 583, where real estate is devised to *A* if or when he shall attain a specified age, with a gift over in the event of his dying under that age, the attainment of that age is held to be a condition subsequent and not precedent, and *A* takes an immediate vested estate, subject to being divested on death under that age; this applies equally to a gift of personal estate or a gift of mixed real and personal estate (*Re Heath, Public Trustee v. Heath* [1936] Ch. 259).

4.10 If a gift of residuary estate is made subject to a condition, the oath to lead to the grant must show that the condition has been complied with or fulfilled. Where a gift of residue is made to members of a class of persons not individually mentioned by name in the will, *e.g.* "to my children", and such persons apply for the grant, the oath must describe them as "lawful children of the testator and as such the residuary legatees and/or devisees named (or substituted) in the will". If there is no other devise or bequest in the will and the whole of the real and personal estate is given absolutely and finally to one person only, such person is "the universal legatee and devisee".

Persons entitled to share in undisposed of residuary estate

4.11 If there is no disposition of the residuary estate or any part of it, or if a gift of residue has lapsed, a partial intestacy arises in the estate of the testator and the persons entitled to share in such undisposed-of estate (as on an intestacy) are entitled to the grant. Where the residue is partially disposed of, the residuary legatees or devisees as to that part and the persons entitled to the undisposed-of estate are equally entitled to the grant.

4.12 If it is clear from the papers that there are kin entitled to share in any undisposed of estate, the Treasury Solicitor is not regarded as interested. Where this in not clear, the applicant will be required either to provide evidence that there are such kin or to give notice to the Treasury Solicitor under Rule 38 (even though the whole of the ascertained estate is disposed of). Where such notice is to be given, the registrar may direct that no grant shall issue within twenty-eight days after the notice has been given, in order to give the Treasury Solicitor opportunity to oppose the grant if he so wishes (Rule 38). A dispute between a residuary legatee (or devisee) and a person entitled to undisposed of estate shall be brought by summons before a registrar (Rule 27(6)).

Disposition of residuary estate not ascertainable

4.13 Although the residuary estate is wholly disposed of by the will, it may be that at the time of application for the grant the ultimate disposition of it cannot be ascertained. A grant may then be made to persons with a lower interest in order of priority under Rule 20.

No clear disposition of residuary estate

4.14 Where the will disposes of the whole of the residuary estate but its terms are ambiguous as to the ultimate disposition of it and no evidence can be produced to resolve the ambiguity (see para. 2.63), the oath to lead to the grant should state "that the deceased did not in his said will make any clear disposition of his residuary estate". In these circumstances, a grant may be made to the person who would have been entitled had the testator died intestate, but before preparing papers to lead to the grant, the matter should be referred to the registrar for his directions.

Grant to legatee or devisee, where the whole, or substantially the whole, of the known estate is disposed of (Rule 20(c)(ii))

4.15 Where the residue is not in terms wholly disposed of, the registrar may, if he is satisfied that the testator has nevertheless disposed of the whole or substantially the whole of the estate as ascertained at the time of the application for the grant, allow a grant to be made (subject, however, to Rule 38), to any legatee or devisee entitled to, or to share in, the estate so disposed of, without regard to the persons entitled to share in any residue not disposed of by the will. Although the registrar is given a discretion to make a grant to a legatee or devisee, it does not derogate from the right of a person entitled to undisposed of estate to take a grant if he wishes. A legatee or devisee applying for a grant must satisfy the registrar that the interest of persons entitled to the undisposed of estate is small enough to justify the exercise of the discretion.

4.16 Where the whole of the estate as ascertained at the time of making application for the grant has been left to one or more legatees or devisees, and a legatee or devisee having a substantial interest applies for the grant under Rule 20(c)(ii), the oath to lead to the grant should describe the applicant as "a legatee (or devisee) named in the will", and the words "all of which is disposed of by the said will" should be inserted.

4.17 Where a legatee or devisee applies on the basis that substantially the whole of the estate is disposed of, the words "of which £................. is disposed of by the said will" should be inserted in the oath. In this type of case it will be for the registrar, having regard to the size of the estate and the amount disposed of by the will, to decide whether the facts bring the case within Rule 20(c)(ii) and, if so, whether the grant should be made to the applicant. In cases of doubt the registrar may call for more detailed evidence and may direct that notice be given to the persons entitled to the undisposed of estate.

Lapse of gift

4.18 Unless a contrary intention is expressed by the will, a specific bequest or specific devise lapses if the beneficiary predeceases the testator, and it falls into the residuary estate. (See also paras. 2.81–82 as to devise or bequest to a former spouse lapsing on divorce etc. and paras. 4.19–23 below.)

Gift to a child or other issue of the testator saved

4.19 A gift of residuary estate to a person who predeceases the testator normally lapses, unless the will shows a contrary intention, and passes as on an intestacy under the provisions of Section 49 of the Administration of Estates Act 1925; but where a testator dies before 1st January 1983, Section 33 of the Wills Act 1837, as originally enacted, provides that where estate is bequeathed or devised to a person who is a lawful child or other lawful issue of the testator and such person dies in the lifetime of the testator leaving lawful issue living at the date of death of the testator, such devise or bequest does not lapse, but (unless a contrary intention appears in the will) takes effect as if the death of such person had happened immediately after the death of the testator. Consequently, the gift falls into the estate of the deceased child or other issue and passes under his will or intestacy and a grant may be made to his legal personal representative. Section 33 of the Wills Act 1837 is not applicable where the bequest or devise is to children (or other issue) of the testator as a class (*Re Harvey, Harvey v. Gillow* [1893] 1 Ch. 567).

4.20 Where, under Section 33 of the Wills Act 1837 a gift to issue of the testator is saved from lapse and such issue dies intestate, the person entitled to the interest under such intestacy must be ascertained in accordance with the law applicable at the date of death of such intestate legatee or devisee (*Re Basioli* [1953] Ch. 367; [1953] 1 All E.R. 301).

4.21 The terms "child" and "issue" in Section 33 of the Wills Act 1837 as originally enacted were extended:

(a) by Section 16 of the Family Law Reform Act 1969 to include illegitimate children in respect of testators dying on or after 1st January, 1970, and

(b) by paragraph 3(1) of Schedule 1 to the Children Act 1975 (now replaced by Section 39 of the Adoption Act 1976) to include adopted children in respect of testators dying on or after 1st January 1976.

4.22 Section 33 of the Wills Act 1837 *in respect of a testator who dies on or after 1st January 1983* has been substituted by a new section under Section 19 of the Administration of Justice Act 1982. Where a testator dies on or after 1st January 1983 and:

(a) his will contains a devise or bequest to a child or remoter issue of the testator; and

(b) the intended beneficiary dies before the testator, leaving issue; and

(c) issue of the intended beneficiary are living at the testator's death,

then, unless a contrary intention appears by the will, the devise or bequest shall take effect as a devise or bequest to the issue living at the testator's death. The substituted section also provides that, where the testator died on or after 1st January 1983, the illegitimacy of any person is to be disregarded for the purpose of the section (Section 33(4)(*a*)).

4.23 A child *en ventre sa mère* (subject to any special provision in the will) is not deemed to be "living" and does not save a gift to its deceased parent from lapse under Section 33 of the Wills Act 1837, where the testator dies before 1st Janaury 1983. However, where the testator dies on or after 1st January 1983 a person conceived before the testator's death and born living thereafter is deemed to have been living at the testator's death (Section 33(4)(b)).

Beneficiary a witness. Forfeiture of gift

4.24 Where a beneficiary, or the spouse of a beneficiary, is an attesting witness to the will, the beneficiary forfeits any gift under the will (Section 15, Wills Act 1837). But this does not apply where the testator has died on or since 30th May 1968 and the will (whatever the date of execution) is duly executed without the attestation of the beneficiary and without that of the spouse of the beneficiary (Wills Act 1968); see also *In the Estate of Bravada* [1968] 2 All E.R. 217. Nor does it apply where the beneficiary has become the spouse of the witness after the date of the will (*Thorpe and Others v. Bestwick* (1881) 6 Q.B.D. 311), or to a trustee of residuary estate (*Ryder* (1843), 2 N.C. 462), or to a beneficiary under a secret trust (*Re Young, Young v. Young* [1951] Ch. 344). The gift is not forfeited if the testator has effectively re-published the will by a codicil attested by other witnesses (*Anderson v. Anderson* (1872), L.R. 13 Eq. 381; *Trotter v. Trotter* [1889] 1 Ch. 764). Where a gift to any person is void as above, such person has no right to a grant as a beneficiary named in the will, but his right to a grant in any other capacity is not affected (Rule 21). As to gifts to attesting witnesses in privileged wills, see para. 2.97.

Grant to personal representative of residuary legatee and/or devisee or of any person entitled to share in any residue not disposed of by the will

4.25 The next class of persons entitled to a grant under Rule 20 is:

> "(d) the personal representative of any residuary legatee or devisee (but not one for life, or one holding in trust for any other person), or of any person entitled to share in any residue not disposed of by the will;"

If a beneficiary with an absolute interest in the residuary estate has survived the testator, the interest becomes vested by reason of his having survived. If he has since died, such vested interest devolves upon his legal personal representative and a grant may be made to such personal representative. Where a grant is sought by the legal personal representative of a deceased person, it must be shown in the oath how any living residuary legatee or devisee or person entitled to share in the undisposed of residue has been cleared off (*e.g.* by renunciation).

4.26 Where the testator has died leaving a surviving spouse, and the net value of the undisposed of residuary estate does not exceed the statutory sum to which the spouse is entitled as on intestacy, the whole of the undisposed of estate devolves on such spouse. The legal personal representative of such spouse who has since died is entitled to the grant. If the net value of the undisposed of estate does not exceed the statutory sum to which a spouse is entitled, and the surviving spouse has since died, no grant having been taken in his or her estate, any person having the right to such grant also has a potential right to the grant in the estate of the testator, and if these persons are cleared off (e.g. by renunciation) legatees, devisees or creditors have equal right to a grant of administration with the will annexed.

4.27 Where the net value of the undisposed of estate exceeds the statutory sum to which a spouse is entitled, all living persons entitled to share in the undisposed of estate must be cleared off before the legal personal representative of a spouse who has since died can apply, unless the testator left no kin entitled to share with the spouse.

4.28 If the testator left a spouse and other persons entitled to share in the undisposed of estate and they are all now dead, the legal personal representative of the spouse has a prior right to the grant. If there are no legal personal representatives of the spouse, or if such representatives renounce the right to a grant in the estate of the testator, the grant will be made to the representatives of any of the other persons entitled to share with the spouse; the oath to lead to such grant must recite that there are no representatives of the spouse, or that they have renounced, as the case may be.

4.29 Rule 20 provides the next in order of priority as:

> (e) "any other legatee or devisee (including one for life or one holding in trust for any other person) or any creditor of the deceased, provided that, unless a registrar directs otherwise a legatee or devisee whose legacy or devisee is vested in interest shall be preferred to one entitled on the happening of a contingency;"

On clearing off all prior classes, a grant may be made to any other legatee or devisee named in the will or to any creditor of the deceased. As in Rule 20(c) a vested interest is preferred to a contingent one.

4.30 Rule 20 provides the next in order of priority as:

> "(f) the personal representative of any other legatee or devisee (but not one for life or one holding in trust for any other person) or of any creditor of the deceased."

When all other classes have been cleared off in order of priority, a grant may be made to the personal representative of a member of the previous class (other than of a legatee or devisee for life or one holding in trust for another person). All members of the previous class must be cleared off. A grant will be made without preference to any member of these classes.

Life or minority interests

4.31 Section 114(2) of the Supreme Court Act 1981 requires that in all cases where a life or minority interest arises under the will, or in respect of estate undisposed of by the will, administration with will annexed shall be granted either to a trust corporation, with or without an individual, or to normally not less that two individuals. The oath to lead to the grant must in every case show whether there is or is not any life or minority interest. In any case where a life or minority interest may arise (although such interest does not actually exist at the time of making application for the grant), the oath should be worded accordingly, and normally at least two individuals (or a trust corporation) must apply.

4.32 Where two administrators are required the second administrator should, where possible, be a person equally entitled with the first administrator. For example, on clearing off executors, administration (with will) may be granted to two of the residuary legatees and devisees in trust, or if none, to two members of a lower class entitled under Rule 20. If there is no person equally entitled with the first administrator, a person next entitled in order of priority may be joined. In the latter case the oath to lead to the grant must show by clearings off that such person is next entitled. For further information and procedure see paras. 5.07–09.

4.33 If application is to be made for a grant to issue to one individual notwithstanding that a life or minority interest arises (e.g. because the minor is very close to attaining his majority), the facts should be placed before the Principal of the Probate Department at the Principal Registry or the district probate registrar before swearing the papers to lead to the grant and his directions obtained. If a grant has been made to one individual only and it is afterwards discovered that there is a subsisting life or minority interest, the court may appoint one or more additional personal representatives. (See para. 5.10.)

Persons interested in the residuary estate

4.34 Where there is no executor named, or the executors are dead, or have renounced probate, or are otherwise cleared off, persons interested in the residuary estate of the testator are first entitled to a grant of letters of administration with will annexed.

Residue

4.35 The question often arises as to whether a testamentary document contains a gift of the residuary estate, or as to the extent of the gift, or as to the persons entitled to the gift. In such cases the words of the document must be construed in their natural and grammatical sense unless there is something in the context of the document which places a different meaning on them. Whenever doubt arises it is advisable to obtain the decision of the registrar before preparing the papers to lead to the grant. To constitute a gift of the residuary estate there must be a disposition of the whole of the residue; even though the testator has by specific bequest or devise disposed of all the estate which he possessed at the time of his death there must be an expression that includes anything of whatever character, which may fall into his estate.

4.36 It is often necessary to decide whether a testator has used the word "money" or "moneys" in the popular or strict legal sense, and whether the word was meant as "possessions" or the equivalent. In deciding whether the expression may be construed as a gift of residue, the sense in which it is used and the testator's intention must be ascertained from the context and general tenor of the testamentary document, the circumstances of the case and of the testator, his relationship to the beneficiary and the provision made for the other beneficiaries (*Perrin v. Morgan* [1943] A.C. 399 and *Re Barnes' Will Trusts, Prior v. Barnes* [1972] 2 All E.R. 639).

4.37 Ambiguous wording in a testamentary document often gives rise to difficulty in deciding whether a gift is an absolute gift or a gift of a life interest only, *e.g.* a gift of what would appear to be an absolute interest in the residuary estate followed by a gift over of what remains. In such cases the wording of the document as a whole must be fully considered to discover the construction which would most effectively express the intentions of the testator (*Re Last* [1958] P. 137).

4.38 In respect of a testator who dies on or after 1st January 1983, Section 22 of the Administration of Justice Act 1982 states that:

> "Except where a contrary intention is shown it shall be presumed that if a testator devises or bequeaths property to his spouse in terms which in themselves would give an absolute interest to the spouse, but by the same instrument purports to give his issue an interest in the same property, the gift to the spouse is absolute notwithstanding the purported gift to the issue."

Where the deceased has died on or after 1st January 1983, recourse to Section 21 of the Administration of Justice Act 1982 as regards interpretation of a testator's will may also be appropriate (see para. 2.63).

4.39 Where there is only a partial disposition of the residuary estate, the persons entitled on an intestacy are equally entitled to a grant with the residuary legatees and devisees under such disposition. Where there is no disposition of residuary estate, the persons entitled to a grant are those who would have been entitled to it had the testator died intestate.

Assignment of interest in estate

4.40 Where all the persons entitled to the estate of the deceased (whether under a will or on intestacy) have assigned their whole interest in the estate to one or more persons, the assignee or assignees shall replace, in the order of priority for the grant of administration, the assignor or, if there are two or more assignors, the assignor with the highest priority. Where there are two or more assignees, administration may be granted with the consent of the others to any one or more (not exceeding four) of them. Where an assignee applies for administration, the original instrument of assignment must be produced and a copy of it must be lodged in the registry (Rule 24).

Grant to trust corporation

4.41 Where there is no executor named in the will, or the executors are dead or have been cleared off by renunciation or citation, a trust corporation named in the will as residuary legatee and devisee in trust is entitled to letters of administration with will annexed in its own right. On the consent of all persons interested in the residuary estate, a grant may be made to a trust corporation alone, or jointly with an individual having an interest in the residuary estate. A grant of administration with will may be made to a trust corporation where an executor appointed is a minor, or where a person interested in the residuary estate is a minor. (See paras. 10.08ff.)

Corporation (not a trust corporation)

4.42 Where a corporate body (not being a trust corporation) would, if an individual, be entitled to a grant, letters of administration with will annexed for its use and benefit, limited until further representation be granted, may be granted to its nominee or to its lawfully constituted attorney (Rule 36(4)). If there is any minority or life interest in the estate, a grant cannot normally be made to a single individual as nominee or attorney: two individuals, or a trust corporation with or without an individual, should be appointed. (See paras. 10.08ff.)

Trustee in bankruptcy

4.43 A trustee in bankruptcy of a beneficiary under a will or an intestacy has no title under the Rules to a grant as such. He cannot be regarded as a trust corporation for the purposes of administering the estate of the deceased. He may, however, in proper cases obtain an order under Section 116 of the Supreme Court Act 1981 for a grant to himself as an individual; such order and grant will be limited to such period as he shall remain trustee of the property of the beneficiary. (See paras. 11.20–24.)

Trustee under deed of arrangement

4.44 A trustee under a deed of arrangement, may, if the terms of the deed and the circumstances of the case permit, be able to establish title to a grant under Rule 24. Failing this, he may apply for an order for a grant under Section 116 of the Supreme Court Act 1981. In either event the grant will describe him as trustee under the deed and be limited to such period as he shall remain trustee. (See paras. 11.20–24.)

THE OATH

4.45 An oath to lead to a grant of administration shall state whether, and if so, in what manner, all persons having a prior right to a grant have been cleared off, and whether any life or minority interest arises in the estate of the deceased (Rule 8(4)). Where the deceased died on or after 1st January 1926, the oath shall state whether, to the best of the applicant's knowledge, information and belief, there was land vested in the deceased which was settled previously to his death and not by his will and which remained settled land notwithstanding his death (Rule 8(3)).

Oath for administrator—Will

[USUAL HEADING]

I,[1]

of

make oath and say as follows:

1. That believe the paper writing now produced to and marked by to contain the true and original last will and testament[2] of[3]

of[4]

formerly of

deceased, who died on the[5] day of 19

aged years[6]

domiciled in England and Wales.[7]

2. That[8] minority interest arises in the estate, that[8] life interest arises in the estate, that to the best of knowledge, information and belief, there was[9] (no) land vested in the said deceased which was settled previously to death and not by h will and which remained settled land notwithstanding death.

3. That the sole executor named in the said will died in the lifetime of the said deceased (*or as the case may be*).[10]

4. That I am the residuary legatee and devisee in trust named in the said will (*or as the case may be*).[11]

5. That will:

(i) collect, get in and administer according to the law the real and personal estate of the said deceased[12]

(ii) when required to do so by the Court, exhibit in the court a full inventory of the said estate and render an account thereof to the Court; and

(iii) when required to do so by the High Court, deliver up to that Court the letters of administration (with will).

6. That to the best of knowledge, information and belief the gross estate passing under the grant does not exceed/amounts to £ (13) and the net estate does not exceed/amounts to £ (14) [and that this is not a case in which an Inland Revenue Account is required to be delivered(15)].

Sworn, etc.

Notes

1 Name and description, etc. Insert full name, full postal address and occupation or description of deponent (for further information see after para. 3.27—oath for executor). If there is more than one deponent with equal interests and they are named in the will, their names, etc. should be inserted in the oath in the order in which they are mentioned in the will. Deponents not of equal interests or not named in the will should appear in the oath in the order of priority of entitlement to the grant.

2, 3, 4, 5, 6, and 7 For the particulars to be inserted in these sections of the oath see respectively explanatory notes 7, 2, 3, 4, 5 and 6 relating to the oath for executors, after para. 3.27.

8 It must be shown whether or not any minority or life interest arises in the estate. If there is such an interest the grant must normally be made to at least two individuals or to a trust corporation with or without an individual (Section 114(2), Supreme Court Act 1981). Where a life interest appears in the terms of the will but has ceased to exist at the date of application for the grant, the oath should show that no life interest *now* arises in the estate; the cessation of such an interest under the will should be explained by an additional paragraph in the oath reciting the name and fact of death of the person concerned.

9 See explanatory note 8 to oath after para. 3.27.

10 It must here be clearly shown how the executors (if any) named in the will and all other interests prior to that of the applicant for the grant are cleared off.

11 The precise capacity in which the grant is claimed should be set out but the relationship (if any) of the applicant to the testator need only be stated if it is needed to establish title or identification. For example, if the will is incorrect as to the actual relationship of the applicant the discrepancy must be dealt with and the identity of the applicant established by a paragraph in the oath or by a separate affidavit.

If application for a grant is made by a person in a representative capacity, the date and nature of the grant by which he was constituted legal personal representative and the registry from which such grant issued must be correctly recited in the oath; the grant, or an official copy of it, must be produced.

12 Here insert any limitation as to the extent of the grant or the estate to be administered.

13, 14 and 15 For the particulars to be inserted in these sections of the oath see respectively explanatory notes 11, 12 and 13 relating to the oath for executors, after para. 3.27.

CLEARING OFF EXECUTORS

4.46 The following examples show how executors may be cleared off:

"That the said deceased did not in his said will name any executor."
"That *A.B.* the sole executor named in the said will died in the lifetime of the said deceased."
"That *A.B.* the sole executor named in the said will survived the said deceased and has since died without having proved the said will."
"That *A.B.* the sole (or surviving) executor named in the said will has renounced probate thereof."
"That *A.B.* one of the executors named in the said will died in the lifetime of the said deceased, that *C.D.* the other executor named in the said will survived the said deceased and has since died without having proved the said will."
"That the appointment of executor in the said will is void for uncertainty."

PRECEDENTS

4.47 The following examples cover a wide variety of cases and should assist in the completion of oaths; they are appropriate where there is no settled land or where a grant "save and except settled land" is required.

[Note: The "statutory sum" referred to in some of the examples is the amount payable to a surviving spouse (as on an intestacy) where the whole or part of the estate is undisposed of by the will. See para. 5.13 and tables in Appendix 3.]

(1) *Grant to the residuary legatee and devisee in trust (Clear off executor)*: That I am the residuary legatee and devisee in trust named in the said will.

(2) *Wife and children (minors) not specifically named in the will appointed residuary legatees and devisees—Grant to widow and nominee (Clear off executor)*: That the said deceased in his said will appointed his wife and his children as residuary legatees and devisees; that I the said *A.B.* am the lawful widow of the said deceased and was his lawful wife at the date of the said will; that the only children of the said deceased are *C.B.* now a minor of the age of years only and *D.B.* now a minor of the age of years only; that there is no testamentary or other lawfully appointed guardian of the said minors and that I the said *A.B.* am the lawful mother and the statutory guardian of the said minors and one of

the residuary legatees and devisees named in the said will; and I the said *E.F.* am the person nominated by the said *A.B.* to apply with her for letters of administration with the will annexed of the estate of the said deceased.

(3) *Residuary legatee and devisee in trust renounces or is dead—Grant to residuary legatee and devisee (Clear off executor)*: That *A.B.* the residuary legatee and devisee in trust named in the said will died in the lifetime of the said deceased (*or* survived the said deceased and has since died without having taken upon h self letters of administration (with the said will annexed) of the estate of the said deceased *or* has duly renounced letters of administration (with the said will annexed) of the estate of the said deceased); that I am the residuary legatee and devisee named in the said will.

(4) *Grant to widow of testator the residuary legatee and devisee for life, and child, a residuary legatee and devisee substituted, on renunciation or death of residuary legatee and devisee in trust (Clear off executor and residuary legatee and devisee in trust)*: That I the said *A.B.* am the lawful widow of the said deceased the residuary legatee and devisee for life named in the said will; that I the said *C.B.* am the child of the deceased and as such (having attained the age of 18 years) one of the residuary legatees and devisees substituted in the said will.

(5) *Grant to residuary legatee and devisee, or residuary legatee or residuary devisee (Clear off executor)*: That I am the residuary legatee and devisee (*or* residuary legatee *or* residuary devisee) named in the said will.

(6) *Grant to husband (or widow) the residuary legatee and devisee for life and son (or daughter) residuary legatee and devisee substituted (Clear off executor)*: That I the said *A.B.* am the lawful husband (or widow) of the said deceased and the residuary legatee and devisee for life named in the said will; that I the said *C.B.* am the son (*or* daughter) of the deceased and (having attained the age of 18 years) the residuary legatee and devisee substituted in the said will.

(7) *Grant to residuary legatee and devisee and a legatee or devisee (Clear off executor)*: That I the said *A.B.* am the residuary legatee and devisee named in the said will; that I the said *C.D.* am a legatee (devisee) named in the said will.

(8) *Grant to residuary legatee and devisee for life and attorney of residuary legatee and devisee substituted (Clear off executor)*: That I the said *A.B.* am the residuary legatee and devisee for life named in the said will; that I the said *E.F.* am the lawful attorney of *C.D.* the residuary legatee and devisee substituted in the said will.

(*Note*: The residuary legatee and devisee for life should consent to a limited grant being made and the limitation will be: "until further representation be granted". If the residuary legatee and devisee for life does not consent to the limitation, the attorney must be joined by Registrar's Order under Rule 25.)

(9) *Grant to residuary legatee and devisee in trust and a residuary legatee and devisee (Clear off executor)*: That I the said *A.B.* am the residuary legatee and devisee in trust named in the said will; that I the said *C.D.* am the residuary legatee and devisee (for life) named in the said will.

(10) *No residuary legatee or residuary devisee named in the will which disposes of the whole (or substantially the whole) of the known estate—Grant under Rule 20(c)(ii) to legatee or devisee named in the will (Clear off executor)*: That I am a legatee (*or* devisee) named in the said will.....................The gross value of the said estate amounts to £.....................and no more, *all of which is disposed of by the said will (or, of which £.....................is disposed of by the said will*) to the best of my knowledge, information and belief.

(11) *No residuary legatee or devisee—Grant to husband (or widow)—Net value of undisposed of estate less than amount of statutory sum (Clear off executor)*: That the said deceased did not in her (his) said will name any residuary legatee or devisee; that I am the lawful husband (widow) and the only person now entitled to the undisposed of estate of the said deceased.

(12) *No residuary legatee or devisee—Grant to representative of husband (or widow)—Net value of undisposed of estate less than amount of statutory sum (Clear off executor)*: That the said deceased did not in her (his) said will name any residuary legatee or devisee; that *A.B.* her lawful husband (his lawful widow) and only person entitled to the estate undisposed of by the said will has since died without having taken upon himself (herself) letters of administration with will of the estate of the said deceased; That I am the sole executor of the will of the said *A.B.* deceased, probate of his (her) will having been granted to me at the .... Probate Registry on the .... day of........................ 19...... (*or* That I am the administrator of the estate of the said *A.B.*, letters of administration thereof having been granted to me at the .... Probate Registry on the...........day of..........................19.........).

(13) *No residuary legatee or devisee—Spouse entitled to undisposed of estate—Grant to spouse and a legatee (or devisee)—Net value of undisposed of estate less than the amount of statutory sum (Clear off executor)*: That the said deceased did not in h said will name any residuary legatee or devisee; that I the said *A.B.* am the lawful widow (lawful husband) and only person now entitled to the undisposed of estate of the said deceased; that I the said *C.D.* am a legatee (or devisee) named in the said will.

(14) *No residuary legatee or devisee—Grant to husband or widow and child—Net value of undisposed of estate exceeds amount of statutory sum (Clear off executor)*: That the said deceased did not in his (her) said will name any residuary legatee or devisee; that I the said *A.B.* am the lawful husband (*or* the lawful widow of the said deceased; that I the said *C.B.* am the lawful* child of the said deceased: that we are two of the persons (*or* the only persons) entitled to share in the estate of the said deceased undisposed of by his (her) said will.

(*Where the deceased died on or after 4th April 1988 "lawful" is not relevant and may be omitted).

(15) *No residuary legatee or devisee—Grant to husband (or widow) and only surviving parent of deceased (no issue)—Net value of undisposed of estate exceeds amount of statutory sum (Clear off executor)*: That the said deceased did not in his (her) said will name any residuary legatee or devisee; that the said deceased died without issue; that I the said *A.B.* am the lawful husband (lawful widow) of

the said deceased and that I the said *C.D.* am the lawful * father (mother) of the said deceased; that we are the only persons entitled to share in the estate of the said deceased undisposed of by his (her) said will.

(*Where the deceased died on or after 4th April 1988 "lawful" is not relevant and may be omitted.)

(16) *Grant to widow residuary legatee and devisee for life (or during widowhood) and her nominee—Residuary legatees and devisees substituted being minor children of the deceased (Clear off executor)*: That the I said *C.D.* am the lawful widow of the said deceased and the residuary legatee and devisee for life (*or* during widowhood) named in the said will; that *E.D.* and *F.D.*, the lawful children of the said deceased and the residuary legatees and devisees substituted in the said will are now minors, the said *E.D.* being of the age of years only and the said *F.D.* being of the age of years only; that there is no testamentary or other lawfully appointed guardian of the said minors; that I the said *C.D.* am the lawful mother and only surviving parent and the statutory guardian of the said minors; that I the said *H.D.* am the person nominated by the said *C.D.* to apply with her for administration with the will annexed of the estate of the said deceased.

(17) *Son of testator residuary legatee and devisee for life and his daughter (a minor) residuary legatee and devisee substituted—Grant to son and nominee (Clear off executor)*: That the said deceased in his said will named me the said *A.B.* his son residuary legatee and devisee for life and his grand-daughter *C.B.* (daughter of me the said *A.B.*) residuary legatee and devisee substituted; that the said *C.B.* is now a minor aged..............years; that there is no testamentary or other lawfully appointed guardian of the said minor and that I the said *A.B.* am the lawful father and only surviving parent and statutory guardian of the said minor; that I, the said *D.B.* am the person nominated by the said *A.B.* to join with him in the administration of the estate of the said deceased.

(18) *Widow of testator the residuary legatee and devisee named is an attesting witness to will—Grant to widow—Net value of undisposed of estate less than amount of statutory sum (Clear off executor)*: That the said deceased in his said will named me his wife *A.B.* as his residuary legatee and devisee; that I the said *A.B.* was an attesting witness to the execution of the said will whereby the said gift to me is void; that I am the lawful widow and the only person now entitled to the undisposed of estate of the said deceased.

(19) *No residuary legatee or devisee—Grant to husband (or widow) (as one of the persons entitled to share in undisposed of estate and as guardian of minors entitled to share) and a nominee—Net value of undisposed of estate exceeds amount of statutory sum (Clear off executor)*: That the said deceased did not in his (her) said will name any residuary legatee or devisee; that I the said *C.D.* the lawful husband (lawful widow) and *D.D.* and *E.D.* the lawful children of the said deceased are the only persons entitled to share in the estate of the said deceased undisposed of by his (her) said will; that the said *D.D.* is a minor of the age of..............years only; that the said *E.D.* is a minor of the age of..............years only; that there is no testamentary or other lawfully appointed guardian of the said minors; that I the said *C.D.* am the lawful father (mother) and only surviving parent and statutory guardian of the said minors;

and that I the said *E.F.* am the person nominated by the said *C.D.* to join with him (her) in the administration of the estate of the said deceased.

(20) *Grant to widow residuary legatee and devisee for life (or during widowhood) and child residuary legatee and devisee substituted (Clear off executor)*: That I the said *A.B.* am the lawful widow of the said deceased and the residuary legatee and devisee for life (*or* during widowhood) named in his said will; that I the said *C.B.* am the child of the deceased and (having attained the age of 18 years) one of the residuary legatees and devisees substituted in the said will.

(21) *No residuary legatee or devisee (deceased died a widower or widow)—Grant to person entitled to estate undisposed of by the will (Clear off executor)*: That the said deceased did not in his (her) said will name any residuary legatee or devisee, that the said deceased died a widower (*or* widow); that I am the (lawful) (child) of the deceased and the only person entitled to the estate (or one of the persons entitled to share in the estate) undisposed of by the said will.

(NOTE: The grant is given to any person entitled to undisposed of estate by clearing off prior rights as under an intestacy. In respect of deaths on or after 4th April 1988, with the exception of a husband or wife, the relationships need not be lawful.)

(22) *Residuary legatee and devisee the wife (or husband) of attesting witness—Grant to person entitled to the undisposed of estate (Clear off executor)*: That the said deceased in his said will named *A.B.* residuary legatee and devisee; that *C.B.* the lawful husband (*or* lawful wife) of the said *A.B.* at the date of the said will was a subscribing witness to the execution thereof whereby the gift of the residuary estate to the said *A.B.* is void; that the said deceased died a widow (widower) (*or* bachelor *or* spinster) without issue or parent or any other person entitled in priority to share in the estate by virtue of any enactment; that I am the (lawful) (sister) of the whole blood and only person entitled to the undisposed of estate (*or* one of the persons entitled to share in the undisposed of estate) of the said deceased. (See note to form (21) above).

(23) *Sole executor and residuary legatee and devisee survives testator and dies without proving—Grant to representative of residuary legatee and devisee*: That *A.B.* the sole executor and residuary legatee and devisee named in the said will, survived the said deceased and has since died without having proved the said will; that I am the sole executor of the will of the said *A.B.* deceased, probate thereof having been granted to me at the .... Probate Registry on the .... day of .... 19........., (*or* that I am the administrator of the estate of the said *A.B.* deceased, letters of administration of his estate having been granted to me at the .... Probate Registry on the .... day of .... 19.........).

(*Note*: The grant, or an office copy of it, in the estate of *A.B.* must be produced. If a life or minority interest arises in the estate there must normally be two applicatns for the grant; and if there is only one representative of the residuary legatee and devisee, the next person entitled (*e.g.* a legatee or devisee) should be joined as co-administrator).

(24) *Residuary legatee and devisee for life renounces—Grant to the residuary legatees and devisees substituted (Clear off executor)*: That *C.D.* the residuary legatee and devisee for life named in the said will has duly renounced letters of

administration (with the said will annexed) of the estate of the said deceased; that we are the residuary legatees and devisees substituted in the said will.

(25) *Sole executrix and residuary legatee and devisee for life survives and dies without proving—Grant to residuary legatees and devisees substituted*: That *A.B.* the widow, the relict of the deceased and the sole executrix and residuary legatee and devisee for life named in his said will, survived him and has since died without having proved the said will; that we are the lawful children of the said deceased, and (as such) the residuary legatees and devisees substituted in the said will.

(26) *Residuary legatee and devisee dies in testator's lifetime—Grant to the persons entitled to the estate undisposed of by the will (Clear off executor)*: That *A.B.* the wife of the said deceased and the residuary legatee and devisee named in his said will died in his lifetime; that the said deceased died a widower; that we are the (lawful) children and the only persons entitled to (or two of the persons entitled to) share in the said estate of the deceased undisposed of by his said will.
(*Note*: See note to form 21 above.)

(27) *Residuary legatee and devisee lawful issue of testator dies in the lifetime of the testator but leaves lawful issue—Testator dies before 1st January 1983—Grant to representative of dead residuary legatee and devisee (Wills Act 1837, Section 33 as originally enacted) (Clear off executor)*: That *C.D.* the lawful son (daughter) of the said testator and the residuary legatee and devisee named in the said will died in the lifetime of the said testator leaving lawful issue living at the death of the said testator; that I am the sole executor of the will (*or* the administrator of the estate) of the said *C.D.* deceased, probate of his said will (*or* letters of administration of his estate) having been granted to me at the .... Probate Registry on the .... day of ....19.........
(The grant, or an office copy, in the estate of *C.D.* must be produced.)

(28) *Residuary legatee and devisee issue of testator dies in the lifetime of the testator but leaves issue—Testator dies on or after 1st January 1983—Grant to issue of dead residuary legatee and devisee (Wills Act 1837, Section 33 as substituted by Section 19, Administration of Justice Act 1982) (Clear off executor)*: That *C.D.* the son (daughter) of the said testator and the residuary legatee and devisee named in the said will died in the lifetime of the said testator leaving issue living at the death of the said testator; that I am the son (daughter) of the said *C.D.* and (one of) his (her) said issue living at the death of the said testator.

(29) *Grant to residuary legatee and devisee for life and residuary legatee and devisee for life substituted (Clear off executor)*: That I the said *A.B.* am a (sister) of the deceased and the residuary legatee and devisee for life named in the said will; that I the said *B.B.* am a (niece) of the said deceased and the residuary legatee and devisee for life substituted in the said will.

(30) *Residuary legatee and devisee survives and dies without taking a grant—Grant to representative of residuary legatee and devisee (Clear off executor)*: That *E.F.* the residuary legatee and devisee named in the said will, survived the said testator, and has since died without having taken upon himself

letters of administration (with the said will annexed) of the estate of the said testator; that I am the sole executor of the will (*or* administrator of the estate) of the said *E.F.* deceased, probate of his will (*or* letters of administration of his estate) having been granted to me at the..................Probate Registry on the.................day of........................19.........

(*Note*: The grant, or an office copy, in the estate of *E.F.* must be produced.)

(31) *Residuary estate bequeathed to children as a class, and not by name—Grant to (lawful) children as residuary legatees and devisees (Clear off executor)*: That we are the (lawful) children of the said deceased, and as such (having attained the age of 18 years) the residuary legatees and devisees named in his said will.

(*Note*: If there is a life or minority interest more than one administrator is normally required. If the will was executed on or after 4th April 1988 the relationships need not be lawful, unless a contrary intention appears in the will.)

(32) *Residuary legatee and devisee renounces—Grant to legatee or devisee (Clear off executor)*: That *A.B.* the residuary legatee and devisee named in the said will has duly renounced letters of administration (with the will annexed) of the estate of the said deceased; that I am a legatee (*or* devisee) named in the said will.

(33) *No residuary legatee or devisee—Person entitled to estate undisposed of by the will renounces—Grant to legatee or devisee (Clear off executor)*: That the said deceased did not in his said will name any residuary legatee or devisee; that the said deceased died a bachelor (*or* spinster *or* widow *or* widower) without issue or any other person entitled in priority to share in his/her estate by virtue of any enactment; that *A.B.*, widow the lawful mother and the only person entitled to the estate of the said deceased undisposed of by his said will has duly renounced letters of administration with will annexed of the estate of the said deceased; that I am a legatee (*or* devisee) named in the said will.

(34) *Sole executor cited to accept or renounce probate does not appear—Grant to one of the residuary legatees and devisees*: That *A.B.* the sole executor named in the said will, has been cited to accept or refuse probate of the said will, but has in no wise appeared, and that by a Registrar's Order dated the .... day of.................19........., it was ordered that letters of administration, with the said will annexed of the estate of the said deceased be granted to me; that I am one of the residuary legatees and devisees named in the said will.

(*Note:* If there is a life or minority interest, normally more than one person must apply).

(35) *Sole executor and residuary legatee and devisee renounces—Grant to creditor of deceased*: That *A.B.* the sole executor named in the said will has duly renounced probate thereof and as the residuary legatee and devisee named therein has also renounced letters of administration with will annexed of the estate of the deceased; that I am a creditor of the deceased.

CHAPTER 5

Letters of Administration

5.01 A grant of letters of administration is appropriate when the deceased died wholly intestate, including cases where the deceased left no estate but a grant is required:

(a) in respect of settled land, or
(b) for the purpose of making title, or
(c) for the purpose of being a party to legal proceedings.

Letters of administration are also appropriate in the majority of cases where the deceased left a will appointing no executor and disposing only of personal estate abroad, but died leaving estate in England and Wales.

5.02 It may happen that, although no will is forthcoming on the death of the deceased, the person entitled on intestacy cannot in conscience make oath that the deceased actually died intestate, for he may know, or have reason to believe, that there was a will in existence after the death. But if the executor and all persons interested under the document have been cited to propound it and have not appeared, or having appeared have failed to proceed with reasonable diligence, the person entitled on an intestacy can then apply for letters of administration.

5.03 Letters of administration will be granted where there is a paper writing duly executed in the same manner as a will but merely revoking all testamentary dispositions and therefore effective to create an intestacy. The document must be lodged with the application for the grant. The grant of administration will bear a note that it was so made in consequence of the execution of the revoking document. When a grant of letters of administration is applied for following a decree pronouncing against the validity of a purported last will of the deceased, the oath leading to the grant must recite the decree and an office copy of the same must be produced. Except with the leave of a registrar, no grant of administration may issue within fourteen days of the death of the deceased (Rule 6(2)).

5.04 In any case in which it appears that the Crown has, or may have, a beneficial interest in an estate, notice of the intended application for a grant must be given to the Treasury Solicitor (or to the Solicitor to the Duchy of Lancaster, or Duchy of Cornwall, as the case may be), and the registrar may direct that no grant shall issue within twenty-eight days after such notice has been given (Rule 38).

5.05 When the deceased died on or after the 1st January 1926, every application for a grant of administration must show whether or not there was land vested in the deceased which was settled previously to his death and which remained settled land notwithstanding his death (Rule 8(3)).

5.06 In granting administration, living interests are generally preferred to the representatives of dead interests, and where there are conflicting interests the nearer interest is preferred to the more remote. However, in special circumstances the registrar does have power to allow a grant to be made to the legal personal representative of a dead interest without living interests in the same degree as the dead interest being cleared off by renunciation or otherwise (Rule 27(5)).

Number of administrators—Minority or life interest in estate

5.07 Under Section 114 of the Supreme Court Act 1981, a grant of administration cannot be made to more than four persons and if a minority or life interest arises in the estate, administration must be granted either to a trust corporation, with or without an individual, or to normally not less than two individuals. This applies to all cases irrespective of the date of death. If an application is to be made for a grant to issue to one individual notwithstanding that a minority or life interest arises, the relevant facts should be placed before the Principal of the Probate Department at the Principal Registry or the district probate registrar for his directions, before the papers to lead to the grant are sworn.

Second administrator

5.08 Where a life or minority interest arises in the estate (and a trust corporation is not the sole applicant for the grant), the second administrator should, where possible, be a person equally entitled with the first administrator. If there is no person equally entitled, a person next entitled in the order of priority should, if possible, be joined; in these circumstances it must be shown by clearings off in the oath leading to the grant that such person is next entitled.

5.09 Rule 25 provides:

"(1) A person entitled in priority to a grant of administration may, without leave, apply for a grant with a person entitled in a lower degree, provided that there is no other person entitled in a higher degree to the person to be joined, unless every other such person has renounced.

(2) Subject to paragraph (3) below, an application for leave to join with a person entitled in priority to a grant of administration a person having no right or no immediate right thereto shall be made to a registrar, and shall be supported by an affidavit by the person entitled in priority, the consent of the person proposed to be joined as administrator and such other evidence as the registrar may direct.

(3) Unless a registrar otherwise directs, there may without any such application be joined with a person entitled in priority to administration—
(a) any person who is nominated under paragraph (3) of rule 32 or paragraph (3) of rule 35;
(b) a trust corporation."

Where a joint grant is required and the proposed second administrator is a person who is not equally or next entitled with the first administrator, an application to the registrar is necessary. The guardian of a minor can be joined as co-administrator with a person who is of full age having an equal interest with the minor. No order is required and the grant will not be limited.

Appointment of additional administrator

5.10 If a grant has been made to one individual only and it is subsequently discovered that there is a subsisting life or minority interest, the court may, on application by any person interested in the estate or the guardian or receiver of any such person, appoint one or more personal representatives in addition to the original grantee (Section 114(4), Supreme Court Act 1981). Such application is made *ex parte* to a registrar and must be supported by an affidavit by the applicant setting out the facts, together with the signed consent of the proposed additional administrator and such other evidence as the registrar may require (Rule 26(1).) The registrar may direct that the original grant be noted as to the appointment of the additional representative, or he may revoke or impound the grant or make such other order as the circumstances may require (Rule 26(2)). If the grant issued at the Principal Registry, the application is made by lodging the requisite documents with the Record Keeper at that registry. If the grant issued at a district registry, the application is made by lodging the requisite documents at that registry.

TO WHOM GRANTED

5.11 In order to determine who are the persons entitled to a grant of letters of administration, regard must be had to the law of distribution at the date of death of the deceased, also to the principles and rules, subject to any statutory modification, governing the making of grants at the date of the death.

Death on or after 1st January 1926

5.12 Rule 22 provides:

> "(1) Where the deceased died on or after 1 January 1926, wholly intestate, the person or persons having a beneficial interest in the estate shall be entitled to a grant of administration in the following classes in order of priority, namely—
>
> (a) the surviving husband or wife;
> (b) the children of the deceased and the issue of any deceased child who died before the deceased;
> (c) the father and mother of the deceased;
> (d) brothers and sisters of the whole blood and the issue of any deceased brother or sister of the whole blood who died before the deceased;
> (e) brothers and sisters of the half blood and the issue of any deceased brother or sister of the half blood who died before the deceased;
> (f) grandparents;
> (g) uncles and aunts of the whole blood and the issue of any deceased uncle or aunt of the whole blood who died before the deceased;
> (h) uncles and aunts of the half blood and the issue of any deceased uncle or aunt of the half blood who died before the deceased.
>
> (2) In default of any person having a beneficial interest in the estate, the Treasury Solicitor shall be entitled to a grant if he claims bona vacantia on behalf of the Crown.
>
> (3) If all persons entitled to a grant under the foregoing provisions of this rule have been cleared off, a grant may be made to a creditor of the deceased or to any person who, notwithstanding that he has no immediate beneficial interest in the estate, may have a beneficial interest in the event of an accretion thereto.
>
> (4) Subject to paragraph (5) of rule 27, the personal representative of a person in any of the classes mentioned in paragraph (1) of this rule or the personal representative of a creditor of the deceased shall have the same right to a grant as the person whom he represents provided that the persons mentioned in sub-paragraphs (b) to (h) of paragraph (1) above shall be preferred to the personal representative of a spouse who has died without taking a beneficial interest in the whole estate of the deceased as ascertained at the time of the application for the grant.

Beneficial interests in the estate

5.13 *Where the intestate died on or after the 1st January 1953 leaving a husband or wife surviving,* Section 46(1) of the Administration of Estates Act 1925, as amended by Section 1 of the Intestates' Estates Act 1952, provides that:

(1) If the intestate leaves no issue, no parent, or brother or sister of the whole blood, or issue of a brother or sister of the whole blood, the surviving husband or wife is entitled to the residuary estate absolutely.

(2) If the intestate leaves issue, the surviving husband or wife shall take the personal chattels absolutely and a net sum of £75,000 in the case of deaths on or after 1st June 1987 (£5,000 where death occurred before 1st January 1967; £8,750 where death occurred after 31st December 1966 but before 1st July 1972; £15,000 where death occurred after 30th June 1972 but before 15th March 1977; £25,000 where death occurred after 14th March 1977 but before 1st March 1981; £40,000 where death occurred after 28th February 1981 but before 1st June 1987), free of tax and costs, with interest thereon from the date of death at the appropriate rate (currently 6 per cent per annum) until paid or appropriated and shall have a life interest in half the residuary estate.

(3) If the intestate leaves a parent, or a brother or sister of the whole blood, or issue of a brother or sister of the whole blood, but leaves no issue, the surviving husband or wife shall take the personal chattels absolutely and a net sum of £125,000 in the case of deaths on or after 1st June 1987 (£20,000 where death occurred before 1st January 1967; £30,000 where death occurred after 31st December 1966 but before 1st July 1972; £40,000 where death occurred after 30th June 1972 but before 15th March 1977; £55,000 where death occurred after 14th March 1977 but before 1st March 1981; £85,000 where death occurred after 28th February 1981 but before 1st June 1987), free of tax and costs, with interest thereon from the date of death at the appropriate rate (currently 6 per cent per annum) until paid or appropriated, and one half of the residuary estate absolutely.

5.14 Where the net value of the estate does not exceed the amount of the statutory sum to which a surviving spouse is entitled, and where there is no life or minority interest in the estate, a surviving spouse may apply for a grant alone. If the gross value of the estate exceeds the amount of the statutory sum to which the surviving spouse is entitled, the following deductions may be made in order to ascertain whether the net value exceeds that sum:

(a) the value of the personal chattels as provided by Section 55(1)(x) of the Administration of Estates Act 1925,
(b) inheritance tax,
(c) costs incurred or to be incurred in the obtaining of the grant and administering the estate,
(d) probate fees payable on appliction for the grant,
(e) debts and funeral expenses.

Where any of such deductions are made in order to bring the net value of the estate below the statutory sum, the oath leading to the grant must set them out in detail.

General information: death on or after 1st January 1926

5.15 A grant of administration may be made to any person entitled thereto without notice to other persons entitled in the same degree (Rule 27(4)). A person entitled or two or more persons equally entitled to the grant may apply but the number of applicants must not exceed four. A dispute between persons entitled to a grant in the same degree must be brought by summons before a registrar (Rule 27(6)). If the issue of a summons under this Rule is known to a registrar, he shall not allow any grant to be sealed until such summons is finally disposed of (Rule 27(8)).

Surviving spouse

5.16 A surviving spouse has first right to a grant (Administration of Estates Act 1925, and as amended by the Intestates' Estates Act 1952 in the case of death on or after 1st January 1953) and subject to this there is no preference as to the right to a grant among the persons entitled to the estate of the deceased. For example, the lawful issue of pre-deceasing lawful children of the deceased are equally entitled to a grant with the lawful children of the deceased living at his death; similarly, the lawful issue of pre-deceasing lawful brothers or sisters of the deceased are equally entitled with the lawful brothers or sisters of the deceased living at his death, and so on with regard to the lawful issue of other lawful relatives who pre-decease the deceased. *Where the intestate dies on or after 4th April 1988 the relationships (other than that of husband and wife) need not be lawful ones*—see Parts I and III of the Family Law Reform Act 1987. Where, in a case of intestacy or partial intestacy, a spouse survives, the question as to whether a life interest arises must be determined by reference to the value of all the estate from whatever source that will eventually come into the hands of the administrators. A surviving spouse is entitled to take a grant alone where the deceased left no relatives entitled to share in the estate, where the net value of the estate does not exceed the amount of the statutory sum to which he or she is entitled, or where other persons are entitled to share in the estate but no life or minority interest arises.

5.17 If the net value of the estate does not exceed the amount of the statutory sum, and the surviving spouse does not wish to apply for the grant, he or she may renounce the right thereto and a grant can then be made to the next person entitled in order of priority as "a person who may have a beneficial interest in the estate of the intestate in the event of an accretion thereto". Alternatively the spouse may appoint an attorney to take a grant for his or her use and benefit (see paras. 8.44 ff).

5.18 If there is a life or minority interest the surviving spouse and a person entitled to share in the estate may jointly apply for the grant. Alternatively, a trust corporation may be joined as co-administrator with the spouse, or on filing the required consents and, if necessary, renunciations, a grant may be made to a trust corporation alone.

5.19 If a surviving spouse has a life interest and renounces the right to a grant, the grant may be made to normally not less than two other of the persons entitled to share in the estate, or, with the necessary consents, to a trust corporation alone or with one of such persons. Where a spouse entitled to a life interest has died without having applied for a grant, a grant may be made to any other person with a beneficial interest in the estate. If there is a minority interest, a grant will normally be made to not less than two individuals or to a trust corporation with or without an individual. A grant will not be made to the legal personal representative of the spouse unless all other persons entitled to share in the estate are cleared off (Rule 22(4)).

5.20 Where the surviving spouse and all other persons entitled to share in the estate have died, the legal personal representative of the spouse has the prior right to the grant (Rule 22(4)). If there is no such representative, the persons entitled to be constituted representatives of the spouse are usually required to renounce the potential right to a grant in the estate of the deceased (*i.e.* the spouse who died first) before a grant is made to the personal representative of another person who was entitled to share in the estate.

5.21 If a surviving spouse who was entitled to all the estate of the deceased (as ascertained at the time of making application for the grant) has since died, his (or her) legal personal representative has the same right to a grant as was possessed by the spouse he represents. If such representative does not wish to apply for the grant in the estate of the deceased he should renounce the right thereto, and in this event the grant can then be made to, "a person who may have a beneficial interest in the estate of the intestate in the event of an accretion thereto". If there is no duly constituted representative of the spouse, and the persons entitled to be so constituted renounce the rights they would have if they were so constituted, the grant in the estate of the deceased can be made to "a person who may have a beneficial interest, etc.," as above.

Divorce or annulment of marriage

5.22 For the obvious reason that the relationship of husband and wife no longer existed at the time of death, a party to a marriage which has been dissolved or annulled has no title to a grant on the intestacy of his or her former spouse, except as the statutory guardian of a minor child. The oath to lead to a grant in the estate of one of such parties must refer to the final decree of divorce or nullity and recite the date thereof and state the court which made it. The oath should show that the intestate died a "single man" or "single woman" and state that he or she did not re-marry.

5.23 The recognition of foreign divorces, annulments and legal separations is now governed by Part II of the Family Law Act 1986, the relevant parts of which are as follows:

"PART II

RECOGNITION OF DIVORCES, ANNULMENTS AND LEGAL SEPARATIONS

Divorces, annulments and judicial separations granted in the British Islands

44.—(1) Subject to section 52(4) and (5)(*a*) of this Act, no divorce or annulment obtained in any part of the British Islands shall be regarded as effective in any part of the United Kingdom unless granted by a court of civil jurisdiction.

(2) Subject to section 51 of this Act, the validity of any divorce, annulment or judicial separation granted by a court of civil jurisdiction in any part of the British Islands shall be recognised throughout the United Kingdom.

Overseas divorces, annulments and legal separations

45.—Subject to sections 51 and 52 of this Act, the validity of a divorce, annulment or legal separation obtained in a country outside the British Islands (in this Part referred to as an overseas divorce, annulment or legal separation) shall be recognised in the United Kingdom if, and only if, it is entitled to recognition–

(*a*) by virtue of sections 46 to 49 of this Act, or
(*b*) by virtue of any enactment other than this Part.

46.—(1) The validity of an overseas divorce, annulment or legal separation obtained by means of proceedings shall be recognised if—

(*a*) the divorce, annulment or legal separation is effective under the law of the country in which it was obtained; and
(*b*) at the relevant date either party to the marriage—
  (i) was habitually resident in the country in which the divorce, annulment or legal separation was obtained; or
  (ii) was domiciled in that country; or
  (iii) was a national of that country.

(2) The validity of an overseas divorce, annulment or legal separation obtained otherwise than by means of proceedings shall be recognised if—

(*a*) the divorce, annulment or legal separation is effective under the law of the country in which it was obtained;

(*b*) at the relevant date—

(i) each party to the marriage was domiciled in that country; or

(ii) either party to the marriage was domiciled in that country and the other party was domiciled in a country under whose law the divorce, annulment or legal separation is recognised as valid; and

(*c*) neither party to the marriage was habitually resident in the United Kingdom throughout the period of one year immediately preceding that date.

(3) In this section "the relevant date" means—

(*a*) in the case of an overseas divorce, annulment or legal separation obtained by means of proceedings, the date of the commencement of the proceedings;

(*b*) in the case of an overseas divorce, annulment or legal separation obtained otherwise than by means of proceedings, the date on which it was obtained.

(4) Where in the case of an overseas annulment, the relevant date fell after the death of either party to the marriage, any reference in subsection (1) or (2) above to that date shall be construed in relation to that party as a reference to the date of death.

(5) For the purpose of this section, a party to a marriage shall be treated as domiciled in a country if he was domiciled in that country either according to the law of that country in family matters or according to the law of the part of the United Kingdom in which the question of recognition arises.

47.—(1) Where there have been cross-proceedings, the validity of an overseas divorce, annulment or legal separation obtained either in the original proceedings or in the cross-proceedings shall be recognised if—

(*a*) the requirements of section 46(1)(*b*)(i), (ii) or (iii) of this Act are satisfied in relation to the date of the commencement either of the original proceedings or of the cross-proceedings, and

(*b*) the validity of the divorce, annulment or legal separation is otherwise entitled to recognition by virtue of the provisions of this Part.

(2) Where a legal separation, the validity of which is entitled to recognition by virtue of the provisions of section 46 of this Act or of subsection (1) above is converted, in the country in which it was obtained, into a divorce which is effective under the law of that country, the validity of the divorce shall be recognised whether or not it would itself be entitled to recognition by virtue of those provisions.

48.—(1) For the purpose of deciding whether an overseas divorce, annulment or legal separation obtained by means of proceedings is entitled to recognition by virtue of section 46 and 47 of this Act, any finding of fact made (whether expressly or by implication) in the proceedings and on the basis of which jurisdiction was assumed in the proceedings shall—

(*a*) if both parties to the marriage took part in the proceedings, be conclusive evidence of the fact found; and (*b*) in any other case, be sufficient proof of that fact unless the contrary is shown.

(2) In this section "finding of fact" includes a finding that either party to the marriage—

(*a*) was habitually resident in the country in which the divorce, annulment or legal separation was obtained; or

(*b*) was under the law of that country domiciled there; or

(*c*) was a national of that country.

(3) For the purposes of subsection (1)(*a*) above, a party to the marriage who has appeared in judicial proceedings shall be treated as having taken part in them.

Supplemental

49.—(1) In relation to a country comprising territories in which different systems of law are in force in matters of divorce, annulment or legal separation, the provisions of this Part mentioned in subsections (2) to (5) below shall have effect subject to the modifications there specified.

(2) In the case of a divorce, annulment or legal separation the recognition of the validity of which depends on whether the requirements of subsection (1)(*b*)(i) or (ii) of section 46 of this Act are satisfied, that section and, in the case of a legal separation, section 47(2) of this Act shall have effect as if each territory were a separate country.

(3) In the case of a divorce, annulment or legal separation the recognition of the validity of which depends on whether the requirements of subsection (1)(*b*)(iii) of section 46 of this Act are satisfied—

(*a*) that section shall have effect as if for paragraph (*a*) of subsection (1) there were substituted the following paragraph—

"(*a*) the divorce, annulment or legal separation is effective throughout the country in which it was obtained;"; and

(*b*) in the case of a legal separation, section 47(2) of this Act shall have effect as if for the words "is effective under the law of that country" there were substituted the words "is effective throughout that country".

(4) In the case of a divorce, annulment or legal separation the recognition of the validity of which depends on whether the requirements of subsection (2)(*b*) of section 46 of this Act are satisfied, that section and section 52(3) and (4) of this Act and, in the case of a legal separation, section 47(2) of this Act shall have effect as if each territory were a separate country.

(5) Paragraphs (*a*) and (*b*) of section 48(2) of this Act shall each have effect as if each territory were a separate country.

50.—Where, in any part of the United Kingdom—

(*a*) a divorce or annulment has been granted by a court of civil jurisdiction, or

(*b*) the validity of a divorce or annulment is recognised by virtue of this Part,

the fact that the divorce or annulment would not be recognised elsewhere shall not preclude either party to the marriage from re-marrying in that part of the United Kingdom or cause the re-marriage of either party (wherever the re-marriage takes place) to be treated as invalid in that part.

51.—(1) Subject to section 52 of this Act, recognition of the validity of—

(*a*) a divorce, annulment or judicial separation granted by a court of civil jurisdiction in any part of the British Islands, or

(*b*) an overseas divorce, annulment or legal separation,

may be refused in any part of the United Kingdom if the divorce, annulment or separation was granted or obtained at a time when it was irreconcilable with a decision determining the question of the subsistence or validity of the marriage of the parties previously given (whether before or after the commencement of this Part) by a court of civil jurisdiction in that part of the United Kingdom or by a court elsewhere and recognised or entitled to be recognised in that part of the United Kingdom.

(2) Subject to section 52 of this Act, recognition of the validity of—

(*a*) a divorce or judicial separation granted by a court of civil jurisdiction in any part of the British Islands, or

(*b*) an overseas divorce or legal separation,

may be refused in any part of the United Kingdom if the divorce or separation was granted or obtained at a time when, according to the law of that part of the United Kingdom (including its rules of private international law and the provisions of this Part), there was no subsisting marriage between the parties.

(3) Subject to section 52 of this Act, recognition by virtue of section 45 of this Act of the validity of an overseas divorce, annulment or legal separation may be refused if—

(*a*) in the case of a divorce, annulment or legal separation obtained by means of proceedings, it was obtained—

(i) without such steps having been taken for giving notice of the proceedings to a party to the marriage as, having regard to the nature of the proceedings and all the circumstances, should reasonably have been taken; or

(ii) without a party to the marriage having been given (for any reason other than lack of notice) such opportunity to take part in the proceedings as, having regard to those matters, he should reasonably have been given; or

(*b*) in the case of a divorce, annulment or legal separation obtained otherwise than by means of proceedings—

(i) there is no official document certifying that the divorce, annulment or legal separation is effective under the law of the country in which it was obtained; or

(ii) where either party to the marriage was domiciled in another country at the relevant date, there is no official document certifying that the divorce, annulment or legal separation is recognised as valid under the law of that other country; or

(*c*) in either case, recognition of the divorce, annulment or legal separation would be manifestly contrary to public policy.

(4) In this section—

"official", in relation to a document certifying that a divorce, annulment or legal separation is effective, or is recognised as valid, under the law of any country, means issued by a person or body appointed or recognised for the purpose under that law;

"the relevant date" has the same meaning as in section 46 of this Act;

and subsection (5) of that section shall apply for the purpose of this section as it applies for the purposes of that section.

(5) . . .

52.—(1) The provisions of this Part shall apply—

(*a*) to a divorce, annulment or judicial separation granted by a court of civil jurisdiction in the British Islands before the date of the commencement of this Part, and

(*b*) to an overseas divorce, annulment or legal separation obtained before that date,

as well as to one granted or obtained on or after that date.

(2) In the case of such a divorce, annulment or separation as is mentioned in subsection (1)(*a*) or (*b*) above, the provisions of this Part shall require or, as the case may be, preclude the recognition of its validity in relation to any time before that date as well as in relation to any subsequent time, but those provisions shall not—

(*a*) affect any property to which any person became entitled before that date, or

(*b*) affect the recognition of the validity of the divorce, annulment or separation if that matter has been decided by any competent court in the British Islands before that date.

(3) Subsections (1) and (2) above shall apply in relation to any divorce or judicial separation granted by a court of civil jurisdiction in the British Islands before the date of the commencement of this Part whether granted before or after the commencement of section 1 of the Recognition of Divorces and Legal Separations Act 1971.

(4) The validity of any divorce, annulment or legal separation mentioned in subsection (5) below shall be recognised in the United Kingdom whether or not it is entitled to recognition by virtue of any of the foregoing provisions of this Part.

(5) The divorces, annulments and legal separations referred to in subsection (4) above are—

(*a*) a divorce which was obtained in the British Islands before 1st January 1974 and was recognised as valid under rules of law applicable before that date;

(*b*) an overseas divorce which was recognised as valid under the Recognition of Divorces and Legal Separations Act 1971 and was not affected by section 16(2) of the Domicile and Matrimonial Proceedings Act 1973 (proceedings otherwise than in a court of law where both parties resident in United Kingdom);

(*c*) a divorce of which the decree was registered under section 1 of the Indian and Colonial Divorce Jurisdiction Act 1926;

(*d*) a divorce or annulment which was recognised as valid under section 4 of the Matrimonial Causes (War Marriages) Act 1944; and

(*e*) an overseas legal separation which was recognised as valid under the Recognition of Divorces and Legal Separations Act 1971.

53.. . .

54.—(1) In this Part—

"annulment" includes any decree or declarator of nullity of marriage, however expressed;

"part of the United Kingdom" means England and Wales, Scotland or Northern Ireland;

"proceedings" means judicial or other proceedings.

(2) In this Part "country" includes a colony or other dependent territory of the United Kingdom but for the purposes of this Part a person shall be treated as a national of such a territory only if it has a law of citizenship or nationality separate from that of the United Kingdom and he is a citizen or national of that territory under that law."

5.24 Where the decree was made outside the British Islands an official copy of the decree (and a notarial translation of the decree if not in English) should be lodged with the application for the grant. Where the divorce or annulment was not obtained by proceedings and there is no official document certifying the effect under the law of the relevant country (see Section 51(3)(*b*) in para. 5.23) the directions of a registrar should be sought as to what evidence will be required. Evidence of the law in question may be required, in addition to the official copy of the decree, in any case, and the oath should always confirm all the relevant matters as to habitual residence, domicile or nationality at the relevant date etc., as appropriate to the particular application, *e.g.* that at the date upon which the proceedings leading to the decree were commenced either party to the marriage (naming the party), was habitually resident in the country in which the divorce was obtained (or, at that date, was domiciled in that country or, at that date, was a national of that country). For other possible grounds for recognition, see para. 5.23.

5.25 Where the decree was made in any part of the British Islands the oath should contain the same details as for an English divorce. An official copy of the decree should be lodged with the application for the grant.

Separation

5.26 Following a decree of judicial separation, and where the separation is subsisting at the date of death, where one of the spouses dies on or after 1st August 1970 wholly or partially intestate, his or her estate passing on or as on an intestacy devolves as if the other spouse were dead. This applies equally to husbands and wives and to all property whether acquired before or after the date of the decree. A separation order made by a magistrates' court, where death occurs on or after 1st August 1970, does not now deprive the surviving spouse of his rights on an intestacy or partial intestacy.

Children or other issue

5.27 If the intestate has left no spouse surviving, the lawful children, or other issue, of the intestate living at the date of death are entitled to a grant; such other issue must be lawful issue (but see para. 5.28 where the intestate died on or after 4th April 1988) of a lawful child of the intestate who pre-deceased the intestate, and they are entitled *per stirpes* to their deceased parent's share of the estate. Issue of an intestate must attain the age of 18 years, or marry under that age, to have a vested interest in the estate. Where issue die without having attained a vested interest, the estate is divided as though they had not survived the intestate. A child *en ventre sa mère* has the same rights as issue living at the date of death (Section 55(2), Administration of Estates Act 1925), and in such a case it must be sworn in the oath leading to the grant that the deceased died leaving an unborn child and that a minority interest may arise in the estate.

Illegitimate children

5.28 Section 14(1) of the Family Law Reform Act 1969 provided in respect of deaths on or after 1st January 1970 (but before 4th April 1988):

> "Where either parent of an illegitimate child dies intestate as respects all or any of his or her real or personal property, the illegitimate child, or, if he is dead, his issue, shall be entitled to take any interest therein to which he or such issue would have been entitled if he had been born legitimate."

Illegitimate children were therefore placed in the same category as legitimate children regarding their right of succession to the estate of either parent dying intestate. Section 14(2) of the Family Law Reform Act 1969 gave parents the same rights on an intestacy of an illegitimate child as they would have had if that child had been born legitimate. This sub-section related only to deaths occurring on or after 1st January 1970. Section 14 of the Family Law Reform Act 1969 was repealed on 4th April 1988 by Sch. 4 of the Family Law Reform Act 1987. The repeal does not affect any rights arising under the intestacy of a person dying before the coming into force of the repeal (Sch. 3 para. 8, Family Law Reform Act 1987). In respect of a person dying intestate *on or after 4th April 1988* illegitimacy is not to be taken into consideration in determining the rights of succession of an illegitimate person, the rights of succession to the estate of an illegitimate person and the rights of succession through an illegitimate relationship (Section 18, Family Law Reform Act 1987).

Legitimated persons

5.29 The Legitimacy Act 1976 consolidated the law relating to legitimacy and legitimation. If the intestate died before 4th April 1988 and if a declaration of legitimacy has been obtained from a court of competent jurisdiction, or if the birth has been re-registered under the

Legitimacy Act 1976, the applicant for a grant should produce a copy of the declaration or the amended birth certificate. If a declaration has not been made nor a re-registration effected, and it appears that it is open to the applicant to obtain such a declaration or re-registration, the court may require him to do so.

5.30 If re-registration is impossible, and either it is not open to the applicant to obtain a declaration, or to insist on his doing so would impose undue hardship, evidence in support of his contention of legitimation should be submitted to a registrar at the Principal Registry, or to the district probate registrar. The affidavit evidence should, with regard to the person who, it is claimed, became legitimated, speak to the following: whether the name of his father was entered in the certificate of birth; particulars of the marriage of his parents, and whether at the time of that marriage his father was domiciled in England and Wales; whether the father in any way acknowledged the child as being his own, and whether he contributed to its maintenance; whether there was an affiliation order; whether the child resided with the parents and whether it was brought up as a member of the family. Any other relevant fact supporting the contention of legitimation should be set out and, if possible, corroborative evidence should be obtained from any other person having knowledge of the facts. If, on the evidence, the registrar is not satisfied, he may direct that an application be made to a judge on summons in chambers or open court, in either case with notice to the Attorney-General. If the intestate died on or after 4th April 1988 the question of legitimacy is not relevant to succession.

5.31 Where the applicant does produce a declaration or certificate of re-registration, the oath leading to the grant must state that the person who it is claimed has been legitimated is the person referred to in the declaration or re-registration. In any case in which the Crown is or could be beneficially concerned, notice to the Treasury Solicitor must be given under Rule 38.

Children of void marriages

5.32 Section 1 of the Legitimacy Act 1976 provides that a child of a void marriage, whenever born, is to be treated as the legitimate child of his parents if at the time of the act of intercourse resulting in his birth (or at the time of the celebration of the marriage, if later) both or either of his parents believed that the marriage was valid. However, this section applies only where the father of the child was domiciled in England or

Wales, at the time of the birth, or, if he died before the birth, was so domiciled at the time of his death. Subsection (1) of Section 1 of the Legitimacy Act 1976 was amended, as from 4th April 1988, by Section 28 of the Family Law Reform Act 1987 by substituting for the words "the act of intercourse resulting in his birth" the words "the insemination resulting in the birth or, where there was no such insemination, the child's conception".

Children of voidable marriages

5.33 A voidable marriage annulled by a final decree (after 31st July 1971) is treated as if it had existed up to that time and therefore a child born during the marriage is legitimate.

Adopted children

5.34 Until the Adoption Act 1958 came into force on the 1st April 1959, rights of succession on an intestacy were not afforded to adopted persons. The present law affecting the rights of succession of adopted persons in respect of deaths occurring on or after 1st January 1976 is contained in the Adoption Act 1976, the relevant sections of which replaced those contained in the Children Act 1975 as from 1st January 1988. Adopted persons are treated as children of the adopter or adopters for the purposes of determining rights of priority to a grant of administration of the estate of an adopted person, the adopter or any other person whenever the adoption order was made. The definition of "adoption" in the Adoption Act 1976 includes adoption orders made in Scotland, Northern Ireland, the Isle of Man or any of the Channel Islands and therefore for the purposes of determining rights of succession they are to be treated as having been made in England or Wales.

5.35 It must be shown in the oath leading to the grant that an adoption order has been made under the appropriate Act, the effect of the order and that it is still subsisting. It is not necessary for the applicant for a grant specifically to clear off adopted persons and persons claiming through such adopted persons unless it is disclosed in the oath that an adoption order has been made.

Overseas adoptions

5.36 The Adoption Act 1968 provided in the case of deaths on or after 1st February 1973, that adoptions made in the designated overseas countries listed below shall have effect as if made in the British Isles:

Commonwealth countries and United Kingdom dependent territories

Australia
Bahamas
Barbados
Bermuda
Botswana
British Honduras (now Belize)
British Virgin Islands (now Tortola)
Canada
Cayman Islands
Republic of Cyprus
Dominica
Fiji
Ghana
Gibraltar
Guyana
Hong Kong
Jamaica
Kenya
Lesotho
Malawi
Malaysia
Malta
Mauritius
Montserrat
New Zealand
Nigera
Pitcairn
St. Christopher (or St. Kitts), Nevis & Anguilla
St. Vincent
Seychelles
Singapore
Southern Rhodesia (now Zimbabwe)
Sri Lanka
Swaziland
Tanzania
Tonga
Trinidad & Tobago
Uganda
Zambia

Other countries and territories:

Austria
Belgium
Denmark (including Greenland and the Faroes)
Finland
France (including Réunion, Martinique, Guadeloupe and French Guyana)
The Federal Republic of Germany and Land Berlin (West Berlin)
Greece
Iceland
The Republic of Ireland
Israel
Italy
Luxembourg
The Netherlands (including Surinam and the Antilles)
Norway
Portugal (including the Azores and Madeira)
South Africa and South West Africa (now Namibia)
Spain (including the Balearics and the Canary Islands)

Sweden
Switzerland
Turkey
The United States of America
Yugoslavia

The Adoption Act 1968 was repealed, and replaced by, the Adoption Act 1976, on 1st January 1988, but the above list is still applicable.

Evidence of an overseas adoption order may be a certified copy of the entry in a public register of the country concerned, or a certificate as to the adoption signed by a person authorised so to do by the law of the country concerned or a certified copy of such a certificate.

Parents

5.37 If the intestate died a bachelor or spinster, or a widow or widower, or a single man or a single woman without issue or any other person entitled in priority to share in the estate by virtue of any enactment, leaving both parents surviving, they are equally entitled to the grant and one or both may apply. If only one parent survived, he or she is solely entitled. Adoptive parents are in the same position as lawful parents in the case of an adopted child who has died intestate on or after 1st January 1950. Where the deceased died on or after 1st January 1970 (but before 4th April 1988) the natural parent or parents are entitled (subject, in the case of a natural father, to sufficient evidence of paternity being produced). Where the deceased died on or after 4th April 1988 it is not necessary to show whether the relationship is lawful or not, or to produce evidence of paternity.

Brothers and sisters or their issue

5.38 Where the intestate died a widow or widower, a bachelor or spinster, or a single man or woman without issue and without parent or any other person entitled in priority to share in the estate by virtue of any enactment, the persons entitled to a grant in order of priority are:

(1) Brothers and sisters of the whole blood and issue of any deceased brother or sister of the whole blood who died before the deceased.

If no person as mentioned above, then:

(2) Brothers and sisters of the half blood and issue of any deceased brother or sister of the half blood who died before the deceased.

The issue of predeceasing brothers and sisters take *per stirpes* the share in the estate which their parent would have taken had he or she survived the intestate. Where the deceased died on or after 4th April 1988 it does not matter whether the relationship is lawful or not.

Grandparents

5.39 If the intestate leaves no surviving spouse, issue, parent, brother or sister of the whole or half blood or their issue or any other person entitled in priority to share in the estate by virtue of any enactment, any or all of his grandparents who survive may take a grant. Where the deceased died on or after 4th April 1988 it does not matter whether the relationship is lawful or not.

Uncles and aunts or their issue

5.40 Where the intestate leaves no surviving spouse and dies without issue and without parent, brother or sister of the whole blood or half blood or their issue, or grandparent or any other person entitled in priority to share in the estate by virtue of any enactment, the persons entitled to a grant in order of priority are:

(1) Uncles and aunts of the whole blood and issue of any deceased uncle or aunt of the whole blood who died before the deceased.

If no person as mentioned above, then:

(2) Uncles and aunts of the half blood and issue of any deceased uncle or aunt of the half blood who died before the deceased.

The issue of predeceasing uncles and aunts take *per stirpes* the share in the estate which their parent would have taken had he or she survived the intestate. Where the deceased died on or after 4th April 1988 it does not matter whether the relationship is lawful or not.

The Crown, Duchy of Lancaster, Duchy of Cornwall

5.41 Where an intestate dies leaving no spouse and no relative entitled to the estate (including illegitimate children or their issue in respect of deaths on or after 1st January 1970 and any relative, including illegitimate relatives or those related through an illegitimate person in respect of deaths on or after 4th April 1988), a grant may be made to the Treasury Solicitor.

Creditors

5.42 Where all persons entitled to share in the estate, and the personal representatives of such persons who are now dead, are cleared off by renunciation or citation proceedings, a grant may be made to a creditor of the intestate. Such grant may also be made in a case of intestacy upon the renunciation of a surviving spouse who is entitled to the whole of the net estate as ascertained at the time of application for the grant, or upon the renunciation of the personal representative of a spouse who was so entitled. There is no preference of right to a grant among creditors.

5.43 If it is clear that the intestate left no person entitled to the estate, the Crown (or Duchy of Lancaster or Duchy of Cornwall, as the case may be) has an interest and the renunciation of the Treasury Solicitor (or for the Duchy) must be obtained before a grant can be made to a creditor, unless *bona vacantia* is not claimed on behalf of the Crown.

5.44 Where a creditor who seeks to obtain a grant is able only to swear that the intestate died without any "known" kin, a citation must normally be issued calling upon the kin who may be living to accept or refuse a grant. Notice of the intended application for a grant must be given to the Treasury Solicitor or Solicitor for the Duchy as the case may be (Rule 38).

5.45 If a life or minority interest arises under the intestacy and there is more than one creditor, normally at least two of them must apply. If there is only one creditor, a trust corporation may be joined as co-administrator, or the creditor may apply to a registrar for an order that a joint grant be made to him and some suitable person.

5.46 Where a firm is a creditor application for a grant may be made by one or more (but not exceeding four) of the partners. The oath leading to the grant must show that the applicants are members of the firm, and that the other partners have been consulted and that they each consent to the application being made.

5.47 An undertaker wishing to recover the funeral expenses is not *prima facie* a creditor of the deceased, but in special circumstances (*e.g.* where the persons entitled to a grant are unable or unwilling to apply) he may obtain an order for a "discretionary" grant to be made to him pursuant to Section 116 of the Supreme Court Act 1981 (see paras. 11.20 ff). The registrar should be consulted as to the affidavit evidence required to lead to such order.

Assignment of interest in estate

5.48 Rule 24 provides:

> "(1) Where all the persons entitled to the estate of the deceased (whether under a will or on intestacy) have assigned their whole interest in the estate to one or more persons, the assignee or assignees shall replace, in the order of priority for a grant of administration, the assignor or, if there are two or more assignors, the assignor with the highest priority.
> (2) Where there are two or more assignees, administration may be granted with the consent of the others to any one or more (not exceeding four) of them.

(3) In any case where administration is applied for by an assignee the original instrument of assignment shall be produced and a copy of the same lodged in the registry."

A grant will be made to a surviving spouse (or other life tenant who is the first person entitled) as sole administrator where persons entitled to a reversionary interest have assigned all their rights and interests in the estate to the applicant for the grant. (The reversioners are not required to renounce in this case.) In the case of a life tenant who is the first person entitled to the grant assigning his interest to a person having a lower title, the renunciation of the life tenant is required before a grant can be made to the assignee. A deed of assignment (and renunciation where applicable) must be referred to in the oath leading to such a grant.

Grant to legal personal representatives

5.49 Rule 22(4) provides that the legal personal representative of any next of kin entitled to a grant, or the personal representative of a creditor, shall have the same right to a grant as the person whom he represents; but, unless a registrar otherwise directs, administration will be granted to a living person in preference to the personal representative of a deceased person who would, if living, be entitled in the same degree (Rule 27(5)). A representative grant may be made to one or more of the proving executors of the will of a deceased person without reference to the others, but where a grant of administration has been made in the estate of a deceased person all his surviving administrators should join in taking the representative grant. It is, however, the practice to permit a grant to be made to some of the administrators provided that the others renounce or consent.

Oath for administrator

[USUAL HEADING]

I,(1)

of

make oath and say as follows:

1. That(2)

of(3)

deceased died on the (4) day of 19

aged years(5)

domiciled in[(6)]

and intestate[(7)]

[(8)]or any other person entitled in priority to share in h estate by virtue of any enactment.

2. That [(9)] minority interest arises under the intestacy.

3. That [(9)] life interest arises under the intestacy.

4. That to the best of knowledge, information and belief, there was[(10)] land vested in the said deceased which was settled previously to h death and which remained settled land notwithstanding h death.

5. That I am the[(11)]

of the said deceased.

6. That will:

(i) collect, get in and administer according to the law the real and personal estate of the said deceased;[(12)]

(ii) when required to do so by the court, exhibit in the Court a full inventory of the said estate and render an account thereof to the Court; and

(iii) when required to do so by the High Court, deliver up to that Court the letters of administration.

7. That to the best of knowledge, information and belief the gross estate passing under the grant does not exceed/amounts to £ [(13)] and the net estate does not exceed/amounts to £ [(14)] [and that this is not a case in which an Inland Revenue Account is required to be delivered].[(15)]

Sworn, etc.

Notes

1. Name and description, etc. Insert full name, full postal address and occupation or status of deponent (for further information see after para. 3.27, oath for executor). Not more than four persons may apply for a grant. If there is more than one deponent and they are not of equal interests their names, etc. should be inserted in the oath in the order of priority of entitlement to the grant.

2, 3, 4, 5 and 6. For the particulars to be inserted in these sections of the oath, see explanatory notes 2, 3, 4, 5 and 6 relating to the oaths for executors, after para. 3.27.

7. It must be shown whether the deceased died a bachelor, spinster, widow, widower, single man or single woman as the case may be, and in what manner all classes of persons who would have a right prior to that of the applicant or applicants are cleared off. If the deceased died a single man or single woman, particulars of the decree of dissolution or annulment of marriage must be recited. Where persons in a class prior to that of the applicant or applicants did not survive the deceased that fact must be stated (e.g. by showing that the deceased died, "a widow without issue or parent" or as the case may be), clearing off all degrees of relationship down to the applicant or applicants. (See Rule 22, as to order of priority.)

8. The words following down to "enactment" should be struck out if the applicants are the spouse and/or a child.

9. It must be shown whether or not any minority or life interest arises in the estate. If there is such an interest the grant must normally be made to at least two individuals or to a trust corporation with or without an individual (Section 114(2), Supreme Court Act 1981). Where a life interest has ceased to exist at the date of application for the grant, the oath should show that no life interest *now* arises in the estate; the cessation of such an interest should be explained by an additional paragraph in the oath reciting the name and fact of death of the person concerned.

10. See explanatory note 8 after para. 3.27.

11. The precise capacity in which the grant is claimed should be set out together with the relationship (if any) of the applicant to the deceased.

If application for a grant is made by a person in a representative capacity, the date and nature of the grant by which he was constituted legal personal representative and the registry from which such grant issued must be correctly recited in the oath, and the grant, or an official copy of it, must be produced.

12. Here insert any limitation as to the extent of the grant or the estate to be administered.

13, 14 and 15. See explanatory notes 11, 12 and 13 after para. 3.27.

PRECEDENTS

5.50 The relationship to the intestate and interest of the applicant for the grant should be shown as in the following examples:

A Husband	"The lawful husband."*
A wife	"The lawful widow."*

*If the net value of the estate does not exceed the amount of the statutory sum payable to a surviving spouse, the husband or widow should also be described in the oath as "*The only person now entitled to the estate of the intestate*."

Child or issue of deceased child ...	"The lawful** son (*or* daughter *or* grandson *or* granddaughter) and only person entitled to (*or* one of the persons entitled to share in) the estate of the said intestate."
Adopted child ...	"The lawful adopted son (*or* daughter) and only person entitled to (*or* one of the persons entitled to share in) the estate of the said intestate."
Father or mother ...	"The lawful** father (*or* mother) and only person entitled to (*or* one of the persons entitled to share in) the estate of the said intestate."

Father or mother by adoption ...	"The lawful adoptive father (or mother) and only person entitled to (*or* one of the persons entitled to share in) the estate of the said intestate."
Brother or sister, or issue of deceased brother or sister (whole blood) ...	"The lawful** brother (*or* sister *or* nephew *or* niece) of the whole blood and only person entitled to (*or* one of the persons entitled to share in) the estate of the said intestate."
Brother or sister by adoption, or issue of deceased brother or sister by adoption (whole blood) ...	"The lawful brother (*or* sister *or* nephew *or* niece) of the whole blood by adoption and only person entitled to (*or* one of the persons entitled to share in) the estate of the said intestate."
Brother or sister, or issue of deceased brother or sister (half blood)	"The lawful** brother (*or* sister, *or* nephew *or* niece) of the half-blood and only person entitled to (*or* one of the persons entitled to share in) the estate of the said intestate."
Brother or sister by adoption, or issue of deceased brother or sister by adoption (half-blood)	"The lawful brother (*or* sister *or* nephew *or* niece) of the half-blood by adoption and only person entitled to (*or* one of the persons entitled to share in) the estate of the said intestate."
Grandparent ...	"The lawful** grandfather (*or* grandmother) and only person entitled to (*or* one of the persons entitled to share in) the estate of the said intestate."
Uncle or aunt or issue of deceased uncle or aunt (whole blood)	"The lawful** uncle (*or* aunt *or* cousin-german) of the whole blood and only person entitled to (*or* one of the persons entitled to share in) the estate of the said intestate."
Uncle or aunt or issue of deceased uncle or aunt (half-blood) ...	"The lawful** uncle (*or* aunt *or* cousin-german) of the half-blood and only person entitled to (*or* one of the persons entitled to share in) the estate of the said intestate."

** If the intestate died on or after 4th April 1988 it does not matter whether the relationship is lawful and the word "lawful" may be omitted.

5.51 ***The following precedents are designed to assist in the completion of oaths; they are applicable where there is no settled land or where a grant "save and except settled land" is required. Note:*** **The "statutory sum" referred to in some of the precedents is the amount payable to a surviving spouse where the deceased has died intestate. (See paras. 5.13–14.)**

(1) *Husband (or wife) survives—Grant to husband (or wife) alone:* That I am the lawful husband (widow) and only person now entitled to the estate of the said intestate (add when the gross estate exceeds the amount of the statutory sum and it is not apparent from the value of the net estate shown for probate purposes, in the Inland Revenue account and/or the oath, that the surviving spouse is entitled to the net estate as his or her statutory sum "that the gross value of the said estate is £.................. and after deducting (see paras. 5.13–14) the net value of the estate does not exceed £..................").

(*Note:* If the net value of the estate exceeds the amount of the statutory sum and there are no relatives of the deceased, the husband (or wife) is the only person entitled to the whole estate, and the oath must clear off all other rights and show that the husband (or wife) is "the only person entitled to the estate".)

(2) *Husband (or wife) survives and dies without taking grant—Net value of estate exceeds the statutory sum—No issue or parent—Grant to brother of whole blood—No life interest now arises:* That the said deceased died intestate leaving *C.D.* her lawful husband (widow) who has since died without having taken upon himself letters of administration of her estate; that the said intestate died without issue or parent or any other person entitled in priority to share in the estate by virtue of any enactment; that a (*or* no) minority interest arises, that no life interest now arises under the intestacy; that I am the lawful** brother of the whole blood and one of the persons entitled to share in the estate of the said intestate.

(3) *Husband (or wife) survives—Net value of estate exceeds the statutory sum—Life interest—Grant to husband (or widow) and child of age:* That a life interest arises under the intestacy; that no (*or* a) minority interest arises under the intestacy; and that I *C.B.* am the lawful husband (widow) and that I *D.B.* am the lawful** child and that we are two of the persons entitled to share in the estate of the said intestate.

(*Note:* If the deceased died without issue any other person entitled to share in the estate can be joined with the husband on the facts being recited in the oath.)

(4) *Husband (or wife) survives and dies without taking grant—Net value of estate does not exceed the statutory sum—Grant to representative of husband (or wife):* That *A.B.* the lawful husband (widow) and only person entitled to the estate of the said intestate has since died without having taken upon himself letters of administration of her estate (add where appropriate (see para. 5.14) "that the gross value of the estate of the said deceased is £......... and after deducting.................. the net value of the said estate does not exceed the sum of £.................."); that I am the executor of the will (*or* the administrator of the estate) of the said *A.B.* deceased, probate of his will (*or* letters of administration of his estate) having been granted to me at the........................ Probate Registry on the.................... day of.................... 19...

(*Note:* The grant, or an office copy thereof, in the estate of *A.B.* must be produced.)

(5) *Husband (or wife) survives and renounces—Net value of estate does not exceed the statutory sum—Grant to child of deceased:* That *A.B.* the lawful husband (widow) and only person now entitled to the estate of the said intestate has duly renounced letters of administration of her estate (add where appropriate (see para. 5.14) "that the gross value of the estate of the said deceased is £............. and after deducting .... the net value of the said estate does not exceed the sum of £..............."); that I am the lawful** child and a person who may have a beneficial interest in the estate of the said intestate in the event of an accretion thereto.

(6) *Husband (or wife) survives—Net estate exceeds the statutory sum—Children under age—Minority and life interest—Grant to husband (or widow) (statutory guardian of minors) and his (her) nominee:* That the said deceased died intestate leaving *A.B.* her lawful husband (widow) and *C.B.* and *E.B.*, her lawful** children, who are both minors, the said *C.B.* being of the age of .... years and the said *E.B.* being of the age of .... years; that the said *A.B.*, *C.B.* and *E.B.* are the only persons entitled to share in the estate of the said intestate, and there is no testamentary or other lawfully appointed guardian of the said minors; that I the said *A.B.* am the lawful father (mother) and only surviving parent and the statutory guardian of the said minors; that I the said *F.D.* am the person nominated by the said *A.B.* to apply with him (her) for a grant in the estate of the said intestate; that a minority and life interest arises under the intestacy.

(*Note:* The nomination may be of one, two or three persons.)

(7) *Grant to husband or widow (statutory guardian of minors entitled to share in the estate) and a trust corporation nominated—Minority and life interest:* That the said deceased died intestate leaving *A.B.* her lawful husband (*or* his lawful widow) and *B.B.* and *D.B.* h lawful** children the only persons entitled to share in h estate; that the said *B.B.* is a minor of the age of .... years, and the said *D.B.* is a minor of the age of .... years; that there is no testamentary or other lawfully appointed guardian of the said minors; that I the said *A.B.* am the lawful father (mother) and only surviving parent and the statutory guardian of the said minors and have nominated the said .... Bank PLC to apply with me for administration of the estate of the said intestate; that a minority and life interest arises under the intestacy; that the said .... Bank PLC is a trust corporation as defined by Rule 2(1) of the Non-Contentious Probate Rules 1987, and has by a resolution dated the .... day of .... 19........ (a certified copy of which is hereunto annexed) appointed me the said *E.F.* for the purpose of applying on its behalf with the said *A.B.* for letters of administration of the estate of the said intestate; that I the said *A.B.* and the said .... Bank PLC will collect, get in and administer, etc.

(8) *Spouses judicially separated—No life interest:* That the said *A.B.* died intestate leaving *B.B.* her lawful husband surviving; that on the .... day of .... 19........ by decree of the High Court of Justice (*or* of the................................ County Court) it was decreed that the said *A.B.* be judicially separated from the said *B.B.*; that the separation under the said decree

continued from the making thereof to the time of the death of the said intestate; that the said intestate died (without issue or parent, or any other person entitled in priority to share in her estate by virtue of any enactment); that I am the (lawful** brother of the whole blood) and one of the persons entitled to share in the estate of the said intestate.

(9) *Deceased a divorced person who did not re-marry—Grant to daughter (or son):* That the said deceased died intestate a single man (*or* single woman); that the marriage of the said intestate with.......................... was dissolved by final decree of the High Court of Justice (*or* of the.......................... County Court) on the.......................... day of .... 19........, and that the said intestate did not re-marry; that I am the lawful** daughter (son) and only person (or one of the persons) entitled to (share in) the estate of the said intestate.

(10) *Husband (or wife) survives and renounces—Net value of estate exceeds amount of statutory sum—Grant to children—Life interest:* That the said deceased died intestate leaving *A.B.* her lawful husband (his lawful widow) who has duly renounced letters of administration of h estate; that a life interest (but no) (*or* and a) minority interest arise under the intestacy; that we are the lawful** children and two of the persons entitled to share in the estate of the said intestate.

(11) *Husband (or wife) survives and dies without taking a grant—Net value of estate exceeds amount of statutory sum—Grant to child or children:* That the said deceased died intestate leaving *A.B.* her lawful husband (his lawful widow) who has since died without having taken upon himself letters of administration of her estate; that I am the lawful** child (*or* that we are the lawful** children) and one (*or* two) of the persons entitled to share in the estate of the said intestate; that no life interest now arises under the intestacy.

(12) *Husband (or wife) survives—Net estate exceeds amount of statutory sum—No issue—Grant to husband (or wife) and parent:* That the said deceased died intestate without issue or any other person entitled in priority to share in the estate by virtue of any enactment; that the said *A.B.* is the lawful husband (widow) and the said *C.D.* is the lawful** father (mother) and only persons entitled to share in the estate (*or* two of the persons entitled to share in the estate) of the said intestate.

(*Note:* A similar grant is given to the husband (or widow) and any other person entitled to share in the estate on clearing off prior rights.)

(13) *Grant to husband (widow) and attorney of child—Net value of estate exceeds statutory sum—Life interest:* That the said deceased died intestate; that no (*or* a) minority interest arises under the intestacy; that a life interest arises under the intestacy; that the said *A.B.* is the lawful husband (widow) of the said intestate and the said *E.F.* is the lawful attorney of *B.B.* the lawful** child of the said intestate, and that the said *A.B.* and the said *B.B.* are the only (*or* two of the) persons entitled to share in the estate of the said intestate. And that we will collect, get in and administer according to law, *etc.* for the use and benefit of the said *B.B.* and until further representation be granted, *etc.*

(*Note:* The husband (or widow) must consent to the grant being limited for the use and benefit of the child and until further representation be granted. If the widower (or widow) does not consent to the limitation, the attorney must be joined by a registrar's order under Rule 25.)

(14) *Husband (or widow) renounces—Net value of estate exceeds statutory sum—Grant to nieces or nephews of the whole blood:* That the said deceased died intestate leaving *C.D.* her lawful husband (his lawful widow) who has duly renounced letters of administration of her estate; that the said intestate died without issue, or parent, and without brother of sister of the whole blood or any other person entitled in priority to share in the estate by virtue of any enactment and that we are the lawful** nieces of the whole blood (*or* nephew and niece of the whole blood), and two of the persons entitled to share in the estate of the said intestate.

(15) *Deceased died a widow (or widower)—Grant to child:* That the said deceased died intestate a widow (*or* widower) and that I am the lawful** child and the only person entitled to (*or* one of the persons entitled to share in) the estate of the said intestate.

(16) *Deceased died a widower (widow)—Child only person entitled to estate survives but dies without taking grant—Grant to legal personal representative of child:* That the said deceased died intestate a widow (widower) leaving *A.B.* her (his) lawful** child and only person entitled to her (his) estate who has since died without having taken upon herself (himself) letters of administration thereof; that I am the administrator of the estate (*or* executor of the will) of the said *A.B.* deceased, letters of administration of h... estate (*or* probate of h... will) having been granted to me at the.................... Probate Registry on the .... day of .... 19......

(*Note:* The grant, or an office copy thereof, in the estate of *A.B.* must be produced.)

(17) *Deceased died a widower (widow)—Minority interest—Grant to child and statutory guardian of grandchild a minor:* That the said deceased died intestate a widower (widow); that a minority interest but no life interest arises under the intestacy; that I the said *A.B.* am the lawful** son and one of the persons entitled to share in the estate of the said intestate; that *C.B.* (spinster), the lawful** grandchild (being the lawful** child of *D.B.* deceased a lawful** son (daughter) of the said intestate who died in h ... lifetime) the only other person entitled to share in the estate of the said intestate is now a minor of the age of .... years only; that there is no testamentary or other lawfully appointed guardian of the said minor; that I the said *E.B.* am the lawful father (mother) and only surviving parent and statutory guardian of the said minor.

(18) *Deceased died a widower (widow)—Minority interest—Grant to child and guardian assigned of grandchild a minor—Statutory guardian of minor renounces administration:* That the said deceased died intestate a widower (widow) leaving me the said *A.B.* his lawful** child and *C.D.* his lawful** grandchild (being the lawful** child of *H.D.* deceased the lawful** child of the said intestate who died in his lifetime) the only persons entitled to share in his estate; that the said *C.D.* is now a minor of the age of........... years only; that *E.D.* the lawful father (mother) and only surviving parent and statutory guardian of the said minor has renounced letters of administration of the estate of the said intestate; that there is no testamentary or other lawfully appointed guardian of the said minor; that I the said *F.G.* am the guardian of the said minor duly assigned by Registrar's order dated .... for the purpose of taking letters of administration

of the estate of the said intestate; that a minority interest but no life interest arises under the intestacy.

(19) *Deceased died a widow (widower)—Only issue died without attaining a vested interest in the estate—Grant to parent(s) of the intestate:* That the said deceased died intestate a widow (*or* widower) without issue other than *A.B.* h ... lawful** child a minor of the age of .... years only and without any other person entitled in priority to share in the estate by virtue of any enactment; that the said *A.B.* did not attain the age of 18 years and died on the .... day of .... 19 .... a bachelor (spinster) without having attained a vested interest in the estate of the said intestate; that I am the lawful** father (mother) (*or* the lawful** father and mother) the only person (persons) entitled to the estate (*or* one of the persons entitled to share in the estate) of the said intestate.

(20) *Deceased died a widow (widower)—Grant to child and a grandchid:* That the said deceased died intestate a widower (widow); that I the said *A.B.* am the lawful** daughter of the said intestate; that I the said *C.D.* am the lawful** grandchild of the said intestate (being the lawful** child of *E.D.* deceased the lawful** child of the intestate who died in h ... lifetime); that we are two of the (*or* the only) persons entitled to share in the estate of the said intestate.

(21) *Grant to adopted child—Deceased died a widow or widower, or bachelor or spinster:* That the said deceased died intestate a widow (*or* widower, *or* spinster, *or* bachelor); that by an order dated the .... day of .... 19........., made by the .... Court at .... under the Adoption Act 1976 (or as the case may be) I was duly adopted by the said intestate (and *X.Y.*, his deceased wife, *or* her deceased husband) and that the said order is still subsisting; that I am the lawful adopted son (*or* daughter) and the only person entitled to the estate (*or* one of the persons entitled to share in the estate) of the said intestate.

(22) *Grant to adopter or adopters—Deceased died a bachelor (or spinster, widow or widower) without issue:* That the said deceased died intestate a bachelor (*or* spinster, widow *or* widower) without issue or any other person entitled in priority to share in the estate by virtue of any enactment; that by an order dated the .... day of .... 19........., made by the .... Court at .... under the Adoption Act 1976 (or as the case may be) the said intestate was duly adopted by me (us) and that the said order is still subsisting; that I am (we are) (one of) the lawful adopter(s) and one of the persons (*or* the only person(s)) entitled to (share in) the estate of the said intestate.

(23) *Deceased died a widower (widow) without child—Grant to grandchild:* That the said deceased died intestate a widower (widow) without child; that I am the lawful** grandchild of the said intestate (being the lawful** child of *A.B.* deceased the lawful** child of the intestate who died in h ... lifetime) and the only person entitled to (*or* one of the persons entitled to share in) the estate of the said intestate.

(24) *Grant to child beneficially interested in estate under Family Law Reform Act 1969; date of death between 1st January 1970 and 3rd April 1988 inclusive:* That the said deceased died intestate a spinster (*or* widow); that I am the natural child

and only person entitled to (*or* one of the persons entitled to share in) the estate of the said intestate.

(25) *Deceased died a bachelor (or spinster, widower or widow) without issue—Grant to father and mother:* That the said deceased died intestate a bachelor (spinster, widower *or* widow) without issue or any other person entitled in priority to share in the estate by virtue of any enactment; that we are the lawful** father and mother and only persons entitled to share in the estate of the said intestate.

(26) *Deceased died a bachelor (spinster, widow or widower) without issue—Father (mother) only person entitled to estate has since died—Grant to representative of father (mother):* That the said deceased died intestate a bachelor (spinster, widow *or* widower) without issue or any other person entitled in priority to share in the estate by virtue of any enactment; that *A.B.* the lawful** father (mother) and only person entitled to the estate of the said intestate has since died without having taken upon h ... self letters of administration thereof; that I am the executor of the will (*or* administrator of the estate) of the said *A.B.*, probate of his (her) will (*or* letters of administration of h ... estate) having been granted to me at the .... Probate Registry on the .... day of .... 19........

(*Note:* The grant, or an office copy thereof, in the estate of *A.B.* must be produced. If both parents survive and die without taking a grant the legal personal representative of either of them may apply.)

(27) *Deceased died a bachelor (spinster, widow or widower) without issue without parent—Grant to brother or sister of whole blood:* That the said deceased died intestate a bachelor (spinster, widow *or* widower) without issue or parent or any other person entitled in priority to share in the estate by virtue of any enactment; that I am the lawful** brother of the whole blood (*or* sister of the whole blood) and the only person entitled to (*or* one of the persons entitled to share in) the estate of the said intestate.

(28) *Deceased died a bachelor (spinster, widow or widower) without issue without parent—Grant to brother (sister) and nephew (niece) of whole blood:* That the said deceased died intestate a bachelor (spinster, widow *or* widower) without issue or parent or any other person entitled in priority to share in the estate by virtue of any enactment; that I the said *A.B.* am the lawful** brother (sister) of the whole blood and that I the said *C.B.* am a lawful** nephew (niece) of the whole blood (being the lawful** child of *E.B.* the lawful** brother (sister) of the whole blood of the said intestate who died in the lifetime of the said intestate) and that we are two of the persons entitled to share in the estate of the said intestate.

(29) *Deceased died a bachelor (spinster, widow or widower) without issue without parent (brother or sister survives)—Grant to nephew or niece of whole blood:* That the said deceased died intestate a bachelor (spinster, widow *or* widower) without issue or parent or any other person entitled in priority to share in the estate by virtue of any enactment; that I the said *A.B.* am the lawful** nephew (niece) of the whole blood (being the lawful** child of *C.B.* deceased the lawful** brother (sister) of the whole blood of the said intestate who died in the lifetime of the said intestate) and one of the persons entitled to share in the estate of the said intestate.

(30) *Grant to brother (or sister) and the statutory guardian of minor nephews (or nieces) also entitled to share in the estate:* That the said deceased died intestate a bachelor (spinster, widow *or* widower) without issue or parent or any other person entitled in priority to share in the estate by virtue of any enactment leaving me *A.B.* h ... lawful** brother (sister) of the whole blood and *B.B.* and *C.B.* h ... lawful** nephews (nieces) of the whole blood being the lawful** children of *E.B.* the lawful** brother (sister) of the whole blood of the said intestate who died in h ... lifetime; that I the said *A.B.* and the said *B.B.* and *C.B.* are the only persons entitled to share in the estate of the said intestate; that the said *B.B.* and *C.B.* are now minors the said *B.B.* being of the age of .... years only and the said *C.B.* being of the age of .... years only; that there is no testamentary or other lawfully appointed guardian of the said minors; that I the said *D.B.* am the lawful mother (father) and only surviving parent and the statutory guardian of the said minors; that a minority interest but no life interest arises under the intestacy.

(31) *Deceased died a bachelor (spinster, widow or widower) without issue without parent, brother or sister of whole blood—Grant to nephew (or niece) of whole blood:* That the said deceased died intestate a bachelor (spinster, widow *or* widower) without issue or parent and without brother or sister of the whole blood or any other person entitled in priority to share in the estate by virtue of any enactment and that I am the lawful** nephew (niece) of the whole blood and the only person entitled to (*or* one of the persons entitled to share in) the estate of the said intestate.

(32) *Deceased died a bachelor (spinster, widow or widower) without issue and without parent, or brother or sister of whole blood (nephew and niece survives)—Grant to great-nephew or great-niece of whole blood:* That the said deceased died intestate a bachelor (spinster, widow *or* widower) without issue or parent and without brother or sister of the whole blood or any other person entitled in priority to share in the estate by virtue of any enactment; that I am the lawful** great-nephew (great-niece) of the whole blood (being the lawful** child of *C.D.* deceased, the lawful** niece (nephew) of the whole blood of the said intestate who died in h ... lifetime and that the said *C.D.* was a lawful** child of *F.D.* a lawful** brother (sister) of the whole blood of the said intestate who died in h ... lifetime) and one of the persons entitled to share in the estate of the said intestate.

(33) *Deceased died a bachelor (spinster, widow or widower) without issue without parent, brother or sister, or nephew or niece of whole blood—Grant to great-nephew (or great-niece) of whole blood:* That the said deceased died intestate a bachelor (spinster, widow *or* widower) without issue or parent and without brother or sister of the whole blood or nephew of niece of the whole blood or any other person entitled in priority to share in the estate by virtue of any enactment, and that I am the lawful** great-nephew (great-niece) of the whole blood and one of the persons entitled to share in (*or* the only person entitled to) the estate of the said intestate.

(34) *Grant to great-niece and statutory guardian of another great-niece, a minor:* That the said deceased died intestate a bachelor (spinster, widow *or* widower) without issue or parent and without brother or sister of the whole blood or nephew or niece of the whole blood or any other person entitled in priority to

share in the estate by virtue of any enactment; that I the said *A.B.* am the lawful** great-niece of the whole blood and one of the persons entitled to share in the estate of the said intestate; that *C.D.* spinster the lawful** great-niece of the whole blood and only other person entitled to share in the estate of the said intestate is now a minor of the age of .... years only; that there is no testamentary or other lawfully appointed guardian of the said minor; that I the said *E.D.* am the lawful mother (father) and only surviving parent and statutory guardian of the said minor; that a minority but no life interest arises under the intestacy.

(35) *Grant to brother or sister of the half blood:* That the said deceased died intestate a bachelor (spinster, widow *or* widower) without issue or parent or brother or sister of the whole blood or their issue or any other person entitled in priority to share in the estate by virtue of any enactment; that I am the lawful** brother (or sister) of the half blood and one of the persons entitled to share in the estate of the said intestate (or the only person entitled to the estate of the said intestate).

(36) *Grant to nephew or niece of the half blood—Brother or sister of the half blood survived:* That the said deceased died intestate a bachelor (spinster, widow *or* widower) without issue or parent or brother or sister of the whole blood or their issue or any other person entitled in priority to share in the estate by virtue of any enactment; that I am the lawful** nephew (niece) of the half blood (being the lawful** child of .... deceased the lawful** brother (or sister) of the half blood of the said intestate who died in his/her lifetime) and one of the persons entitled to share in the estate of the said intestate.

(37) *Grant to nephew or niece of the half blood (no surviving brother or sister of the half blood):* That the said deceased died intestate a bachelor (spinster, widow *or* widower) without issue or parent or brother or sister of the whole blood or their issue and without brother or sister of the half blood or any other person entitled in priority to share in the estate by virtue of any enactment; that I am the lawful** nephew (or niece) of the half blood and one of the persons entitled to share in the estate (or the only person entitled to the estate) of the said intestate.

(38) *Deceased died a bachelor (spinster, widow or widower) without issue without parent or brother or sister or their issue (whole or half blood)—Grant to grandfather or grandmother or both:* That the said deceased died a bachelor (spinster, widow *or* widower) without issue or parent or brother or sister of the whole or half blood or their issue or any other person entitled in priority to share in the estate by virtue of any enactment; that I am (we are) the lawful** grandfather (and/or grandmother) and (one of) the persons entitled to share in the estate (*or* the only person entitled to the estate) of the said intestate.

(39) *Deceased died a bachelor (spinster, widow or widower) without issue without parent, or brother or sister or their issue, or grandparent—Grant to uncle or aunt of whole blood:* That the said deceased died intestate a bachelor (spinster, widow *or* widower) without issue or parent, without brother or sister of the whole or half blood or their issue, and without grandparent or any other person entitled in priority to share in the estate by virtue of any enactment; that I am the lawful**

uncle (aunt) of the whole blood and one of the persons entitled to share in (*or* the only person entitled to) the estate of the said intestate.

(40) *Grant to uncle (aunt) and cousin german of whole blood:* That the said deceased died intestate a bachelor (spinster, widow *or* widower) without issue or parent or brother or sister of the whole or half blood or their issue or grandparent or any other person entitled in priority to share in the estate by virtue of any enactment; that I the said *A.B.* am the lawful** uncle (aunt) of the whole blood and that I the said *C.B.* am the lawful** cousin german of the whole blood of the said intestate (being a lawful** child of *E.B.* a lawful** uncle (aunt) of the whole blood of the said intestate who died in h ... lifetime); that we are two of the persons entitled to share in the estate of the said intestate.

(41) *Grant to cousin german once removed of the whole blood:* That the said deceased died intestate a bachelor (spinster, widow *or* widower) without issue or parent or brother or sister of the whole or half blood or their issue or grandparent, or uncle or aunt of the whole blood or cousin german of the whole blood or any other person entitled in priority to share in the estate by virtue of any enactment; that I am a lawful** cousin german once removed of the whole blood and one of the persons entitled to share in (*or* the only person entitled to) the estate of the said intestate.

(42) *Deceased died a bachelor (spinster, widow or widower) without issue without parent, or brother or sister, or issue of brother or sister, or grandparent—Grant to uncle or aunt of half blood:* That the said deceased died intestate a bachelor (spinster, widow *or* widower) without issue or parent or brother or sister of the whole or half blood or their issue or grandparent or uncle or aunt of the whole blood or their issue or any other person entitled in priority to share in the estate by virtue of any enactment; that I am the lawful** uncle (aunt) of the half blood and one of the persons entitled to share in (*or* the only person entitled to) the estate of the said intestate.

(43) *Deceased died a bachelor (spinster, widow or widower) without issue without parent—On renunciation of only person entitled to estate—Grant to creditor:* That the said deceased died intestate a bachelor (spinster, widow *or* widower) without issue or parent or any other person entitled in priority to share in the estate by virtue of any enactment leaving (*A.B.* h ... lawful** sister of the whole blood) and only person entitled to h ... estate, who has duly renounced letters of administration thereof; that I am a creditor of the said intestate.

(44) *Deceased died without known relation—Grant to creditor by order:* That the said deceased died intestate a bachelor (spinster, widow *or* widower) and without any known relation; that the kin (if any) entitled to share and all other persons having or claiming any interest in the estate of the said intestate have been duly cited but no one has appeared; that by Registrar's order dated the .... day of .... 19........ it was ordered that letters of administration of the estate of the said intestate be granted to me a creditor of the said intestate.

(*Note:* Notice must be given to the Treasury Solicitor prior to the application for the order. (See Rule 38.))

(45) *Deceased died without spouse or blood relatives—Treasury Solicitor renounces—Grant to creditor:* That the said deceased died intestate a bachelor (spinster, widow *or* widower) without issue or parent or brother or sister of the whole or half blood or their issue and without grandparent or uncle or aunt of the whole or half blood or their issue or any other person entitled in priority to share in the estate by virtue of any enactment: that the Solicitor for the affairs of Her Majesty's Treasury has renounced letters of administration of the estate of the said intestate: that I am a creditor of the said intestate.

(46) *Oath for discretionary grant by order:* That the said deceased died intestate; that by a Registrar's order made on the .... day of .... 19 .... it was ordered that letters of administration of the estate of the said intestate be granted to me by virtue of Section 116 of the Supreme Court Act 1981.

**If the intestate died on or after 4th April 1988 it does not matter whether the relationship is lawful and the word "lawful" may be omitted.

CHAPTER 6

Inland Revenue Account

6.01 In addition to the other requirements of the probate registries mentioned elsewhere in this volume, an appropriate form of Inland Revenue Account may have to be completed and lodged before a grant of representation can be obtained. Where Inheritance Tax (or its predecessor Capital Transfer Tax when the death was before 18.3.86) is payable on delivery of the Inland Revenue Account, the form must be receipted to show payment of the tax and any interest thereon before the application for the grant may proceed. (For general information concerning applications for a grant, see paras. 1.06–19.)

6.02 To comply with this additional requirement it is necessary to know:

(a) when an Inland Revenue Account is required;
(b) which is the appropriate form;
(c) how payment should be arranged.

After dealing with these questions a general outline of both Inheritance Tax and Capital Transfer Tax will be given followed by a guide to how the forms should be completed.

6.03 First, a few words about Estate Duty are necessary. The Finance Act 1975 abolished Estate Duty (and introduced Capital Transfer Tax) in connection with deaths on or after 13.3.75. If it is necessary to obtain a grant (be it original or second or subsequent) in connection with a death during the Estate Duty regime, the 21st edition of this work should be consulted, but it is important to mention that instead of an Inland Revenue Account, an Inland Revenue Affidavit (*i.e.* a form which has been sworn or affirmed by the executors or intending administrators) is required. Further, the current prints of the Inland Revenue Account should not be used. There is no objection to the use of the earliest prints of the Capital Transfer Tax forms (described as for use where the deceased died on or after 13.3.75) if they are suitably modified and sworn, or alternatively the appropriate Estate Duty Inland Revenue Affidavits (A-12, A-13 or A-14) can be completed. Prints of all these forms are obtainable from the Capital Taxes Office, Minford House, Rockley Road, London W14 0DF.

WHEN AN INLAND REVENUE ACCOUNT IS REQUIRED

6.04 Whereas in the case of deaths before 1.4.81 probate or letters of administration were refused except on production of an Inland Revenue Account (showing either that tax had been paid or that no tax was payable) now, in certain circumstances, the requirement is waived.

6.05 Section 256, Inheritance Tax Act 1984 (see 6.28) empowers the Board of Inland Revenue to make regulations dispensing with the delivery of accounts required under Section 216 of that Act. These regulations dispense with the need to deliver an Inland Revenue Account in relation to certain smaller estates called "excepted estates".

6.06 An "excepted estate" for deaths on or after 1.4.87 means the estate of a person immediately before his death where:

(a) the estate consists only of property passing under that person's will or intestacy or under a nomination of an asset taking effect on the death or by survivorship;
(b) the total gross value of the property does not exceed £70,000;
(c) no more than £10,000 represents the value of property situated outside the United Kingdom; and
(d) that person died domiciled in the United Kingdom and without having made any transfers chargeable to either Inheritance Tax or Capital Transfer Tax.

6.07 The original regulations (deaths between 1.4.81 and 31.3.83) were contained in the Capital Transfer Tax (Delivery of Accounts) Regulations 1981 S.I. No. 880 and an "excepted estate" was where the total gross value of the property did not exceed £25,000 with no more than 10% or £1,000 situated outside the United Kingdom. These regulations were amended in relation to deaths between 1.4.83 and 31.3.87 by 1983 S.I. No. 1039 with the upper limits being increased from £25,000 to £40,000 and £1,000 to £2,000. The current regulations were introduced in relation to deaths on or after 1.4.87 by S.I. No. 1127.

It is most important to note that an estate where the deceased had a beneficial interest in settled property cannot be an "excepted estate". In the case of an "excepted estate" applicants will be able to obtain a grant of representation without delivering an account and without needing to swear to the exact value of the estate. They will merely be required to swear that the value is under £70,000 and that the other conditions are satisfied.

6.08 If, after the grant, the applicant discovers that the estate was not an "excepted estate", he must deliver to the Board an account of all the property comprised in the estate within 6 months of the discovery. The Board retains the right to call for a completed account of an "excepted estate" after the grant but a notice in writing must be issued to the personal representatives within the "prescribed period" (*i.e.* 35 days after the making of the first full grant of representation to the deceased in England and Wales). The Capital Taxes Office will send a notice (Cap 214) with an account (Cap 204) to the first named personal representative and an informative notice to any other personal representatives.

6.09 Unless an estate qualifies as an "excepted estate", an Inland Revenue Account must be completed and delivered.

WHICH IS THE APPROPRIATE FORM?

6.10 There are four Inland Revenue Accounts which require consideration:

Cap 202

6.11 This is a shortened version of the Inland Revenue Account and is for use in respect of an application for an original full grant where:

(a) the deceased died on or after 27.3.81 domiciled (by general law) in the United Kingdom;
(b) the estate comprises only property which passes under the deceased's will or intestacy, or by nomination or beneficially by survivorship and all that property was situated in the United Kingdom;
(c) the total net value of the estate, after deducting any exemptions and reliefs claimed does not exceed the threshold above which tax is payable at the date of death;
(d) the deceased made no transfers of value chargeable with tax (*i.e.* no transfers of value that were not covered by the tax exemptions) after 26.3.74 and within the cumulation period (see 6.33 below).

An earlier print of the form is available for use where the deceased died before 27.3.81 and full details of the circumstances when it should be used are to be found in the 21st edition of this Manual.

Cap 200

6.12 This is the full version of the Inland Revenue Account and is for use in respect of an application for an original grant (whether full or limited to settled land) where:

(a) the deceased died on or after 27.3.81 domiciled (by general law) in the United Kingdom;
(b) the Cap 202 is not appropriate because for example:
  (i) the estate exceeds the tax threshold; or
  (ii) the estate includes settled property or foreign property; or
  (iii) the deceased made chargeable lifetime transfers.

An earlier print of the form is available for use where the deceased died before 27.3.81.

Cap 201

6.13 This is the only Inland Revenue Account which may be used to obtain an original grant where the deceased died on or after 27.3.81 domiciled (by general law) outside the United Kingdom. It is emphasised that the Cap 201 form should be used even though the deceased is treated as domiciled in the United Kingdom by virtue of Section 267, I.H.T.A. 1984—see para 6.45. There is no shorter version of the Cap 201 and the "excepted estates" procedure does not apply to persons who die domiciled outside the United Kingdom. An earlier print of the form is available for use where the deceased died before 27.3.81.

Cap A—5C

6.14 This form of Inland Revenue Affidavit/Account is for use whenever it is desired to obtain a second or subsequent grant of representation in respect of property which came within the operation of the original grant; this will be:

(i) a grant of double probate (see para. 3.28);
(ii) a grant de bonis non (see para. 11.01);
(iii) a cessate grant (see para. 11.13);

Cap A—5C is not appropriate where application is being made for:

(i) a full grant following a grant pending suit (para. 11.29) or *ad colligenda bona* (paras. 11.25–28),
(ii) a grant *caeterorum*, or
(iii) a new grant following the revocation of a previous grant (paras. 14.17–23).

In all these cases, the form of affidavit or account appropriate for an original grant should be used.

6.15 The Cap A—5C (which has a simplified Inland Revenue Certificate on the back) has superseded the earlier forms A—5A (which was appropriate in Estate Duty cases only) and A—5B. Where stocks are held, the old forms may still be used, but as many applications for grants of letters of administration *de bonis non* are in respect of deaths which occurred prior to 13.3.75, it should be borne in mind that, whichever form is used in such a case, it MUST be sworn or affirmed by the intended administrators.

6.16 Prints of Cap 200 and 202 can be obtained from the Capital Taxes Office, Inland Revenue, Minford House, Rockley Road, London W14 0DF, or on personal application only at the Stamp Office, Room 2, South West Wing, Bush House, Strand WC2B 4QN; the London Chief Post Office, King Edward Street EC1A 1AA; the Branch Post Offices at Fleet Street EC4Y 1BT, Chancery Lane WC2A 1EA, East Strand WC2R 1EL, High Holborn WC1V 6RN, 11 Regent Street SW1 and The Stock Exchange EC2M 5TP: and at Main Post Offices outside the Metropolitan Postal District. Prints of Cap 201 and A—5C are obtainable only from the Capital Taxes Office, Minford House, or on personal application at the Stamp Office (addresses above).

6.17 Instructions for the completion of Cap 200 and 201 issued by the Board of Inland Revenue (Cap 213) can be obtained from the Capital Taxes Office, Minford House, or on personal application only at the Stamp Office, or at any of the Post Offices mentioned in the preceding paragraph.

HOW PAYMENT SHOULD BE ARRANGED

6.18 The personal representatives are required to pay all the tax for which they are liable on delivery of their account (Section 226(2), I.H.T.A. 1984). It is accordingly necessary for any tax to be calculated and paid before the application for the grant can proceed. Except in the cases mentioned below the tax is calculated by the applicant without reference to the Capital Taxes Office.

Cap 200

6.19 In the following instances, the Cap 200 MUST be submitted to the Capital Taxes Office for assessment:

(i) where conditional exemption from tax is claimed in respect of articles considered to be of national, scientific, historic or artistic interest, or in respect of land or buildings (together with associated land or objects) considered to be of outstanding interest (Sections 30 & 31 I.H.T.A. 1984; see para. 6.49(xi)).

(ii) where payment of tax is to be made out of deposits in the National Savings Bank or out of the proceeds of National Savings Certificates or Premium Bonds which formed part of the deceased's estate at the date of his death, or

(iii) where the application is for a grant of representation limited to settled land (see para. 10.25).

In any other case where the assessment of the Cap 200 appears to give rise to special difficulty, it may be submitted to the Capital Taxes Office with an indication of the nature of the problem.

Cap 201

6.20 This form (for use only where the deceased died domiciled outside the United Kingdom) MUST always be submitted to the Capital Taxes Office for consideration of the domicile and assessment of the tax payable before the grant is issued. This is so even where it appears that under the provisions of Section 267 I.H.T.A. 1984 the deceased had a deemed domicile in the United Kingdom at the date of his death (see para 6.45). In some cases, it may be necessary for the Capital Taxes Office to call for further evidence of the domicile of the deceased, but in many cases consideration of the matter will be deferred until after the grant has been issued.

Cap 202

6.21 As this form is only appropriate when the estate is below the tax threshold, no assessment of tax will be necessary. As indicated above, if any of the conditions set out at the head of the form are not satisfied it should not be used.

Form A—5C

6.22 This form leading to a second or subsequent grant of representation in the circumstances explained at para. 6.14 must be examined and certified by the Capital Taxes Office before the grant can be issued. Where application for the grant is made to the Principal Registry, the applicant should first submit the form to the Capital Taxes Office. If the grant is to be obtained at a district registry, the form will be directed to the Capital Taxes Office for control.

6.23 After assessment of the tax and interest (if any) payable thereon, the Inland Revenue Account accompanied by the remittance should be sent to Finance Division, Inland Revenue (A), Barrington Road, Worthing, West Sussex BN12 5BR. A cheque should be made payable to "Inland Revenue" and crossed. It should not relate to more than one estate and should not include Court fees. Alternatively, but not where the application is to be made to the Principal Registry, the Inland Revenue Account and remittance may be forwarded direct to the probate registry to which the application for the grant of representation is being made.

PROCEDURE WHERE MORE THAN ONE GRANT OF REPRESENTATION IN THE UNITED KINGDOM IS REQUIRED

6.24 Where more than one grant of representation in the United Kingdom is required, *e.g.* because the deceased died domiciled abroad owning assets in more than one part of the United Kingdom, the applicants for the grant should make their *first* application in that part of the United Kingdom in which they wish to have the overall tax liability of the deceased's free estate dealt with. When the first Inland Revenue Account (or Inventory in Scotland) is delivered, it should contain particulars of *all* assets liable to Inheritance Tax in the United Kingdom and the personal representatives must pay all the tax for which they are liable on delivery of that Account (or Inventory).

6.25 After the first grant has issued (and whether or not the estate was below the taxable limit at the date of the deceased's death), the personal representatives should send to the Capital Taxes Office *in the part of the United Kingdom where the original grant was obtained* the further Inland Revenue Account (or Inventory) to lead to the second grant to the deceased. That office will have the Account (or Inventory) endorsed to show either (a) that no tax is payable on the assets shown therein, or (b) the amount of the tax and interest (if any) paid in respect of the assets included therein. When the Inland Revenue Account (or Inventory) is returned, it should then be submitted to the Principal Registry or district probate registry as appropriate (or, in Scotland, the Commissary Court in Edinburgh) in that part of the United Kingdom in which the further grant of representation is required. (For the acceptance of English, Scottish and Northern Irish grants within the United Kingdom, see paras. 13.02–05.)

6.26 The addresses of the Capital Taxes Office in Scotland and Northern Ireland are as follows:

Scotland: 16 Picardy Place,
Edinburgh.
EH1 3NB.

Northern Ireland: Law Court Buildings
Chichester Street,
Belfast,
BT1 3NU.

AN OUTLINE OF CAPITAL TRANSFER TAX AND INHERITANCE TAX

6.27 It is impossible in this work to deal with all aspects of what has become a complex area of taxation but it is hoped that the brief description that follows will assist the practitioner. It is proposed to consider various topics under the following main headings:

(a) Capital Transfer Tax—lifetime transfers;
(b) Inheritance Tax—lifetime gifts;
(c) The effect of death on the above;
(d) The death estate;
(e) Exemptions and reliefs;
(f) Payment of tax.

It is not intended to provide any details of the operation of Capital Transfer Tax or Inheritance Tax in the field of discretionary and similar trusts (Sections 58–85).

6.28 Although Capital Transfer Tax only commenced with the 1975 Finance Act, the legislation was altered to such an extent and with such frequency prior to its abolition that a consolidation Act was necessary. The Capital Transfer Tax Act 1984, a pure consolidation measure which did not make any changes to the then existing legislation, came into force on 1.1.85. With the introduction of Inheritance Tax the Act was renamed the Inheritance Tax Act 1984 for deaths and transfers on or after 18.3.86. Any reference to a statutory section in the remainder of this part is a reference to the 1984 Act, as amended by subsequent Finance Acts, unless otherwise shown.

(A) Capital Transfer Tax—Lifetime transfers

6.29 Capital Transfer Tax (a tax on transfers of capital) was introduced by the Finance Act 1975 with effect from 27.3.74 in the case of lifetime transfers and from 13.3.75 for transfers on death. The Finance Act 1986 abolished Capital Transfer Tax and introduced Inheritance Tax in respect of lifetime transfers and transfers on death on or after 18.3.86.

6.30 The basic concept of Capital Transfer Tax was that any transfer of capital (subject to certain exceptions) by an individual was valued at the time it was made, added to the total of the transfers made by that individual (after 26.3.74) in the preceding ten years (see para. 6.33) and taxed (if the threshold was exceeded) at the rate appropriate to the revised cumulative total. Rates increased as the total progressed. The transfer of a person's estate on his death was treated as his final gift and added to his lifetime cumulative total to form the top slice for tax purposes. The cumulative total was the total of his chargeable lifetime transfers (made after 26.3.74) in the ten years preceding his death. There were different rates of tax for lifetime transfers and on death—after 13.3.84 all lifetime rates were half the death rates. However additional tax could be payable in respect of lifetime transfers made within three years of the death (see para. 6.38). The table of rates at the end of this chapter shows the rates at the various dates.

6.31 Capital Transfer Tax was charged on the value transferred by a chargeable transfer and a chargeable transfer was any transfer of value made by an individual after 26.3.74, unless an exemption applied. A transfer of value was any disposition as a result of which the value of a person's estate immediately after the disposition was less than it would have been but for the disposition. The amount by which it was less was the value transferred by the transfer.

Valuation

6.32 Normally, *e.g.* with a gift of quoted shares, the value of a gift is identical to the consequential reduction in the value of the transferor's estate but this is not always the case. For example, a transferor owning a pair of valuable ornaments gives one away. Individually each is worth

£10,000 but as a pair they are worth substantially more than £20,000. Supposing the pair were worth £25,000, the loss to the transferor's estate would be the difference between £25,000 (the value of the pair before the transfer) and £10,000 (the value of the ornament left in the estate after the transfer). This concept is particularly relevant in connection with transfers of shares in unquoted companies, in that the transfer of value is not the value of the gifted holding but rather the difference between the value of the transferor's interest in the company immediately before and immediately after the disposition. The statutory provisions regulating the valuation of any assets provide for an open market basis of valuation (see Section 160 and para 6.73). See also Section 161 regarding related property.

Cumulation

6.33 The original legislation provided for cumulation throughout the transferor's lifetime but this principle was amended by Section 93, F.A. 1981, so that when a transfer was made, it was now only added to the total of the transfers made by the transferor in the preceding 10 years. Examples as to how the cumulation principle operates and how the tax is calculated may assist (ignoring all exemptions).

T makes his first gift of £100,000 on 1.1.81.	
According to the rates in table 3B:	
Tax on first £90,000	= £7,250
Tax on balance of £10,000 at 22.5%	= £2,250
	£9,500
T makes a further gift of £50,000 on 1.1.83	
His cumulative total is now £150,000	
and tax on this must first be calculated	
According to the rates in table 5B:	
Tax on £130,000	=£13,375
Tax on balance of £20,000 at 22.5%	= £4,500
	£17,875
Less Tax on previous cumulative Total of £100,000	= £7,375
Tax now due	£10,500

Grossing up

6.34 The amount of tax payable on a transfer depended on who was paying the tax. If it was paid by the transferor, the value transferred by the transfer (the amount by which the transferor's estate was reduced) included his liability for the tax. Accordingly if T made a first gift of

£100,000 on 1.1.81 and paid the tax, the gift of £100,000 had to be "grossed up" in accordance with Table 3D:

$$£110{,}000 + \left(\frac{40}{29} \times £1{,}750\right) = £112{,}413$$

This was the chargeable transfer and the tax thereon (Table 3B) amounted to £12,413.

(B) Inheritance tax—Lifetime gifts

6.35 The Finance Act 1986 abolished Capital Transfer Tax and introduced Inheritance Tax in respect of lifetime transfers and transfers on death on or after 18.3.86. The fundamental change was that the immediate charge for tax in connection with lifetime transfers between individuals was removed. Such transfers (and those into accumulation and maintenance trusts and trusts for the disabled) were now to be described as potentially exempt transfers (PETs) with the exemption becoming absolute if the transferor survived for seven years. If he does not so survive a PET becomes a chargeable transfer and Inheritance Tax may then be payable. Originally transfers into settlements where an interest in possession existed and terminations of such interests retained the immediate tax charge but since 17.3.87 these transfers are also regarded as PETs. Basically after 17.3.87 the main transfers by an individual which attract an immediate charge to Inheritance Tax are those into a discretionary settlement.

6.36 With all chargeable transfers (whether subject to an immediate tax charge or to a charge following the transferor's death within seven years) the value transferred is calculated as for Capital Transfer Tax as at the date of the transfer (see paras. 6.31 and 6.32). The cumulation principle also applies (see para. 6.33) but the period for cumulation is reduced from 10 to seven years. If the transferor is paying the tax in connection with a transfer that attracts an immediate tax charge, "grossing up" will apply (see para. 6.34).

6.37 Where there is an immediate charge to tax on a lifetime transfer made on or after 18.3.86, tax is charged at half the death rates then in operation. To return to the example in para. 6.33:

> If T made a further gift to a discretionary settlement on 1.6.88 resulting in a chargeable transfer of £100,000, the amount of tax immediately payable is calculated as follows:

Cumulative total of transfers within 7 years	= £50,000
Present chargeable transfer	= £100,000
New cumulative total	£150,000
Tax on £150,000 at half death rates on 1.6.88 (Table 11A)	= £8,000
Tax on £50,000 at half death rates on 1.6.88 (Table 11A)	= NIL
Tax payable	£8,000

As is apparent from Table 11A, the progressive rate bands were abandoned for transfers on or after 15.3.88, with a flat rate of tax for the balance of the value transferred once the tax threshold is exceeded.

(C) The effect of death

6.38 For Capital Transfer Tax purposes, the amount of tax payable in respect of a lifetime transfer could increase if the transferor died within the following three years, as the death rather than the lifetime rates of tax might apply. Tax was first assessed at the lifetime rates operative *at the date of transfer* and this assessment was usually concluded in the lifetime. The amount so assessed was compared with the tax on the transfer at the death rates operative *at the date of death*. If the latter exceeded the former, the extra tax was payable by the transferee(s).

6.39 In the case of deaths on or after 18.3.86, where lifetime transfers have been made before that date there are transitional provisions which preserve the treatment described above for such transfers, e.g. suppose T dies on 10.6.86 having made a single transfer of £110,000 on 1.1.84. Ignoring any exemptions, the tax on £110,000 using the lifetime rates appropriate at the date of transfer (Table 6B) is £8,250. On the death on 10.6.86 the tax thereon, calculated using the rates in force at that date (Table 9A), is £12,450 and the additional sum payable is thus £4,200.

6.40 As regards lifetime transfers after 18.3.86, the position is more complicated. Tax will only have been paid in the lifetime if the transfers were chargeable rather than potentially exempt (see para. 6.35). On the death it may be necessary not only to recalculate and pay additional tax in respect of the chargeable transfers, but also to pay tax on any PETs which have become chargeable transfers by reason of the death occurring within seven years. Suppose the following series of events have occurred before the transferor's death on 1.2.89:

1.1.88—chargeable transfer of £20,000
1.2.87—PET of £10,000
1.1.85—chargeable transfer of £50,000
1.2.81—chargeable transfer of £100,000

During the lifetime, tax will have been assessed as described in para. 6.33 in respect of the transfers within the Capital Transfer Tax regime on 1.2.81 and 1.1.85, and as follows for the Inheritance Tax transfer on 1.1.88:

Cumulative total of chargeable transfers within 7 years of 1.1.88	= £150,000
transfer on 1.1.88	= £20,000
	£170,000
Tax on £170,000 (Table 10B)	= £13,500
Less tax on £150,000 (Table 10B)	= £9,500
Payable	£4,000

On death:

(i) the PET becomes chargeable and the tax thereon is calculated using the death rates in force at the date of the transferor's death as follows:

Cumulative total of transfers within 7 years of the gift on 1.2.87	= £150,000
Transfer on 1.2.87	= £10,000
	£160,000
Tax on £160,000 using rates appropriate at the date of death (Table 11A)	= £20,000
less tax on £150,000 using rates appropriate at the date of death (Table 11A)	= £16,000
Tax due (none paid in lifetime)	£4,000

(ii) the death also results in additional tax being paid in respect of the chargeable transfer made on 1.1.88. The tax is to be recalculated at the death rates and the transfer made on 1.2.87 (the PET that becomes chargeable by reason of the death) is to be taken into account. This gives a cumulative total of £180,000.

Tax on £180,000 using rates appropriate at the date of death (Table 11A)	= £28,000
Tax on £160,000 using rates appropriate at the date of death (Table 11A)	= £20,000
	£8,000
Tax already assessed in the lifetime	= £4,000
Additional tax due	= £4,000

6.41 It has already been stated that transfers on or after 18.3.86 but within seven years of death will be taxed on their value at the date of the gift but the death rate scale (*i.e.* that in force at the date of death) applies. However there is taper relief which reduces the amount of this charge where the transfer is made more than three years before the death. The relief takes the form of a percentage reduction in the tax payable in respect of any relevant transfers. The value of the transfers are not reduced.

Years between gift and death	*% of full charge at death rates*
0–3	100
3–4	80
4–5	60
5–6	40
6–7	20

Gifts with reservation

6.42 There are special rules for the taxation of property taken under a gift subject to a reservation. This is property where either (i) possession and enjoyment is not *bona fide* assumed by the donee, or (ii) not enjoyed to the entire (or virtually the entire) exclusion of the donor and of any benefit to him by contract or otherwise. A simple example is the gift of a house in which the donor continues to reside rent free. If he remains in residence to the time of the donor's death, the property is treated as property to which the donor was beneficially entitled immediately before his death, and is treated as forming part of his estate on death. When the residence ceases before the donor's death, he is treated as having made a PET at that time. As with all PETs, tax is charged if the donor then dies within seven years.

(D) The death estate

6.43 For Capital Transfer Tax purposes on the death of any person tax was charged as if, immediately before his death, he had made a transfer of value and the value transferred had been equal to the value of his estate immediately before his death. The position remains the same for Inheritance Tax. A person's estate is defined in Section 4(1) as the aggregate of all the property to which he is benefically entitled, except that the estate of a person immediately before his death does not include excluded property—Section 5(1) and see para. 6.44 below. In addition to the free estate the death estate includes:

(i) settled property in which he had a beneficial interest in possession—Section 49(1);
(ii) his severable share of joint property passing by survivorship on his death;
(iii) property nominated by the deceased in his lifetime;
(iv) *donationes mortis causa.*

For Inheritance Tax purposes only a further category is added, viz:

(v) gifts with a reservation retained to the date of death—see para. 6.42.

In determining the value of a person's estate at any time, his liabilities at that time shall be taken into account—Section 5(3). The statutory provisions regarding valuation of assets on death are the same as those for lifetime transfers, viz. Section 160, and again the "related property" provisions of Section 161 may be relevant.

Excluded property

6.44 Excluded property is defined in Section 6 and Section 48 as being:

(i) certain reversionary interests (see para 6.85);
(ii) settled property situated abroad at the date of the deceased's death where the settlor was domiciled outside the United Kingdom at the date the settlement was made;
(iii) property (not being settled property) situated outside the United Kingdom when the deceased was himself domiciled outside the United Kingdom at his death;
(iv) certain Government securities issued by the Treasury with a condition that they should be exempt from taxation so long as they are in the beneficial ownership of a person neither domiciled nor ordinarily resident in the United Kingdom;
(v) certain National Savings owned by persons domiciled in the Channel Islands or the Isle of Man.

The only circumstances in which the "deemed domicile" provisions of Section 267 can be relevant is when determining a person's domicile in connection with categories (ii) and (iii) above.

6.45 Even though a person may have acquired or retained a domicile outside the United Kingdom under general law, he is treated, in certain circumstances, as domiciled in the United Kingdom *for Capital Transfer Tax and Inheritance Tax purposes.* Broadly speaking, by virtue of the provisions of Section 267 persons:

(i) who had a domicile in the United Kingdom do not acquire a foreign domicile for three years; and

(ii) who have been resident in the United Kingdom for seventeen out of the last twenty years are regarded as having acquired a United Kingdom domicile.

Until 15.3.83, persons who had a United Kingdom domicile but then acquired a domicile in the Channel Islands or the Isle of Man under general law were treated for Capital Transfer Tax purposes as remaining domiciled in the United Kingdom.

6.46 In arriving at the value of the deceased's estate, deduction is allowable for liabilities and incumbrances on the property. Unless the liability was imposed by law (*e.g.* income tax) it must have been "incurred for a consideration in money or money's worth"—Section 5(5). Where the liability falls to be discharged after the death (*e.g.* dilapidations under a lease etc), the liability has to be valued as at the death. Where the liability is one in respect of which there is a right to reimbursement (*e.g.* a liability under a guarantee), deduction is allowable only to the extent that such reimbursement cannot reasonably be expected to be obtained. Liabilities to persons resident outside the United Kingdom (unless contracted to be paid here or charged on property situated in the United Kingdom) must, *so far as possible*, be taken to reduce the value of the property outside the United Kingdom. Hence, if a person dies domiciled outside the United Kingdom leaving a substantial estate and liabilities in the country of his domicile, such liabilities will only reduce the value of the chargeable property in the United Kingdom to the extent that they exceed the value of the "excluded property" abroad—see Section 162. Deduction is also allowed for the deceased's funeral expenses which includes the cost of a tombstone—see Section 172.

Cumulation

6.47 As stated at para. 6.43 the transfer of a person's estate on his death is treated as his final gift and added to his lifetime cumulative total for determining the tax payable in connection with the death. By way of example:

T, having a lifetime cumulative total of	£150,000
dies, on 16.4.88 leaving a chargeable death estate of	£200,000
	£350,000

1. Tax on £350,000 (using table 11A) is 40% of £240,000	= £96,000
2. Tax on lifetime cumulative total of £150,000 (using table 11A) is 40% of £40,000	= £16,000
3. Tax on death estate of £200,000 is £96,000 less £16,000	= £80,000

(E) Exemptions and reliefs

6.48 There were a whole range of exemptions and reliefs which had the effect of mitigating the burden of the charge to Capital Transfer Tax. They are shown below with, as necessary, the manner in which they continue to apply for Inheritance Tax. Many of them apply both to lifetime transfers and to the transfer on death. Some apply only on death and others only to lifetime transfers. These last are still important to the practitioner concerned with the position on death for two reasons:

(a) they have a bearing on the way in which page 3 of the Inland Revenue Account should be completed (see para 6.69);
(b) they may affect the deceased's cumulative total for the purpose of arriving at the value of the aggregate chargeable transfers on death.

6.49

(i) Transfers of value made by a transferor in any one year (i.e. from 6 April to the following 5 April inclusive) by outright gift to any one person are exempt if the values transferred by them do not exceed (since 6.4.81) £250—Section 20.

(ii) Transfers of value made by a transferor in any one year (*i.e.* year ended 5 April as above) are exempt to the extent that the values transferred by them do not exceed (since 6.4.81) £3,000. Where the values in any one year exceed £3,000, only the excess is taxable. Any unused exemption in any one year may be carried forward to the following year but only after the exemptions for that year have been exhausted—Section 19. For Inheritance Tax purposes the annual exemptions remain but the application is less straightforward. They reduce the value of transfers attracting an immediate tax charge, and unused amounts from the previous year can be carried forward in a calculation of the lifetime tax. On death adjustment for any exemptions carried forward may be necessary if a PET made in the earlier year becomes a chargeable transfer. This is most easily illustrated by an example.

1.1.87—T makes a PET of £100,000
1.6.87—T makes a further PET of £200,000
1.1.88—T makes a lifetime transfer of £300,000 which attracts an immediate charge to tax

The £3,000 annual exemption for 1987/88 and that carried forward from 1986/87 are available to reduce the chargeable transfer to £294,000. On 12.3.88 T dies and the PETs on 1.1.87 and 1.6.87 become chargeable. In calculating the tax liabilities in connection with the death, the 1986/87 annual exemption will now be taken against the 1.1.87 transfer (reducing the value to £97,000) and so cannot be used against the transfer in 1987/88. However the applicaton of the annual exemption for 1987/88 is not changed, even though the PET of £200,000 was made earlier in that year. The 1.6.87 transfer is taken at £200,000 and, in calculating the additional tax payable, the transfer on 1.1.88 is taken at £297,000.

(iii) Transfers of value if or to the extent it is shown that they form a part of the transferor's normal expenditure out of his income and do not affect his usual standard of living are exempt—Section 21.

(iv) Transfers of value made by gifts "in consideration of marriage" are exempt to the extent that the value transferred by a transferor on a marriage does not exceed:

(a) £5,000 in the case of a transfer by a parent to the bride or groom.
(b) £2,500 in the case of a transfer by the bride or groom to the other party.
(c) £2,500 in the case of a transfer by a grandparent (or great-grandparent) to the bride or groom.
(d) £1,000 in the case of a transfer by any other person to the bride or groom—Section 22.

(v) Exemption in respect of contributions made by a transferor to an approved retirement benefits scheme for employees—Section 12.

N.B. All the above exemptions apply to lifetime transfers only and are not applicable to the deemed transfers on death which arise under the provisions of Section 4.

(vi) Exemption in respect of transfers of value to the extent that the value transferred is attributable to property which becomes comprised in the estate of the transferor's spouse—Section 18.

The above exemption applies to *both* lifetime transfers and transfers made on death, and extends not only to property passing to the deceased's surviving spouse under his will or intestacy, but also to settled property, joint property, nominated property and policies of insurance effected or kept up for the benefit of a spouse.

In the unusual case where the transferor is domiciled in the United Kingdom and his spouse has acquired or retained an independent domicile outside the United Kingdom, the relief is limited to a maximum of £55,000. (Prior to 27.10.77 the maximum relief was £15,000; between 27.10.77 and 25.3.80 it was £25,000 and between 26.3.80 and 8.3.82 it was £50,000.)

(vii) Transfers of value made to recognised charities established within the United Kingdom, are exempt—Section 23. The original Capital Transfer Tax provisions limited the exemption for transfers on (or within one year of) the transferor's death to £100,000. The limit was increased to £200,000 for transfers on or after 26.3.80 and to £250,000 for transfers on or after 4.3.82. The limit was removed in the case of deaths on or after 15.3.83.

(viii) Exemption in respect of transfers of value made to any political party which at the last general election prior thereto had:

(a) two members elected to the House of Commons or
(b) one member elected to the House of Commons and not less than one hundred and fifty thousand votes given to candidates who were members of that party—Section 24.

For transfers made more than 12 months prior to the transferor's death, the exemption has always been unlimited. As regards transfers made on or within one year of the transferor's death, the exemption was limited to a maximum of £100,000 but since 15.3.88 the limit has been removed.

(ix) Under Section 25 exemption in respect of transfers of value made for National purposes without limit as to amount to:

(a) The National Gallery.
(b) The British Museum.
(c) The National Museum of Scotland.
(d) The National Museum of Wales.
(e) The Ulster Museum
(f) Any other similar national institution which exists wholly or mainly for the purpose of preserving for the public benefit a collection of scientific, historic or artistic interest and which is approved for the purposes of the exemption by the Treasury.

(g) Any museum or art gallery in the United Kingdom which exists wholly or mainly for that purpose and is maintained by a local authority or university in the United Kingdom.
(h) Any library the main function of which is to serve the needs of teaching and research at a university in the United Kingdom.
(i) The Historic Buildings and Monuments Commission for England.
(j) The National Trust for Places of Historic Interest or Natural Beauty.
(k) The National Trust for Scotland for Places of Historic Interest or Natural Beauty.
(l) The National Art Collections Fund.
(m) The Trustees of the National Heritage Memorial Fund.
(n) The Friends of the National Libraries.
(o) The Historic Churches Preservation Trust.
(p) The Nature Conservancy Council.
(q) Any local authority.
(r) Any Government department (including the National Debt Commissioners).
(s) Any university or university college in the United Kingdom.

(x) Under Section 26 exemption without limit in respect of transfers of value made to a body not established or conducted for profit (where the Treasury so directs) of any of the following types of property:
(a) Land which in the opinion of the Treasury is of outstanding scenic or historic or scientific interest.
(b) A building for the preservation of which special steps should in the opinion of the Treasury be taken by reason of its outstanding historic or architectural or aesthetic interest and the cost of preserving it.
(c) Land used as the grounds of such a building.
(d) An object which at the time of the transfer is ordinarily kept in and which is given with a building within paragraph (b) above.
(e) Property given as a source of income for the upkeep of property within (a) to (d) above.
(f) A picture, print, book, manuscript, work of art or scientific collection which in the opinion of the Treasury is of national, scientific, historic or artistic interest.

All the exemptions at (vi) to (x) above are subject to certain conditions. Briefly these are as follows:

(1) The gift effected by the transfer must vest *immediately* in the transferee. (But the exemption in respect of a transfer to a surviving spouse is not lost because the property is given to him or her only if he or she survives the deceased for a specified period. In such event, the spouse will normally be entitled to the *income* of the property during the period in question.)

(2) The gift must not be dependent on a condition which is not satisfied within 12 months after the deceased's death.

(3) The gift to a charity, political party or public body, etc. must not be defeasible.

(4) The property transferred by the gift to a charity, etc. must not be less than the deceased's whole interest in the property or given for a limited period only.

(5) The property or any part of it must not become applicable for purposes other than those of the charity, political party or public body to which it is given.

(6) Where the property transferred to a charity, etc. is land or a building, the gift must not be subject to any interest reserved or created by the deceased entitling his spouse or any person connected with him to occupy the property at less than a full rack-rent.

(7) Where the property transferred to a charity, etc. is other than land or a building, the gift must not be subject to any interest created by the deceased which substantially affects the enjoyment of the property by the body to which it is given.

(xi) Conditional exemption under Section 30 in respect of certain types of property designated by the Treasury under Section 31 of the Act. Under Section 31 the Treasury may designate:

(a) any pictures, prints, books, manuscripts, works of art, scientific collections or other things not yielding income which appear to the Treasury to be of national, scientific, historic or artistic interest;

(b) any land which in the opinion of the Treasury is of outstanding scenic or historic or scientific interest;

(c) any building for the preservation of which special steps should in the opinion of the Treasury be taken by reason of its outstanding historic or architectural interest;

(d) any land which adjoins such a building as is mentioned in paragraph (c) above and which in the opinion of the Treasury is essential for the protection of the character and amenities of the building;

(e) any object which in the opinion of the Treasury is historically associated with such a building as is mentioned in paragraph (c) above.

The exemption must be claimed and certain undertakings must be given before exemption will be granted (*e.g.* to preserve the property and allow reasonable public access). The exemption is conditional only, and tax will become payable on the first occurrence after the death of a "chargeable event", *e.g.* a breach of the undertaking or a disposal of the property by sale (other than a sale by private treaty to one of the bodies listed at (ix) above).

(xii) Exemption under Section 154 in respect of the death of a person in whose case it is certified by the Defence Council or Secretary of State that the deceased died from a wound inflicted, accident occurring or disease contracted at a time when he or she was:

(a) a member of the armed forces of the Crown, or

(b) subject to the law governing any of those forces by reason of association with or accompanying any body of those forces,

and was on active service against an enemy or on other service of a warlike nature or which, in the opinion of the Treasury, involved the same risks as service of a warlike nature; *or* that the deceased died from a disease contracted at some earlier time, death being due to or hastened by aggravation of the disease during a period when the above conditions were satisfied.

(xiii) Exemption under Section 152 in respect of cash options under approved annuity schemes.

(xiv) The "surviving spouse exemption"—para 2 Sch. 6—is a continuation of an Estate Duty exemption. If, when the first spouse died, Estate Duty was paid on property that he (or she) settled on trust for the surviving spouse, no claim for Estate Duty arose on the cesser of that spouse's life interest (or annuity) unless the spouse had been competent to dispose of the settled property. If, after 13.3.75, the surviving spouse's interest ceases (on death or otherwise) "there shall be left out of account the value of any property" that would have qualified for the Estate Duty exemption.

(xv) The "revertor to settlor" exemption appears in Section 54(1). If on the termination (by death or otherwise) of an interest in possession in settled property the property reverts to the settlor, the value of the settled property is "left out of account" in determining the value of the deceased's estate. The settlor must be living and he must not have acquired his reversionary interest (absolute or otherwise) by purchase.

If the settled property reverts to the settlor's living spouse a comparable provision applies—Section 54(2).

(xvi) If the deceased's estate includes land upon which timber (*i.e.* trees and underwood) is growing, the value of the timber can be left out of account in determining the value of the estate and will not then be taxed until it is sold or otherwise disposed of. The exemption only applies if the taxpayer so elects, if the land is non-agricultural and if it has been owned by the deceased for the previous five years—Sections 125–130.

(xvii) The present relief for agricultural land found in Sections 115 to 124 was first contained in Sch.14, F.A. 1981 and applies in the case of transfers on or after 10.3.81. (For transfers before that date, the provisions of Sch. 8, F.A. 1975 as amended by Section 74, F.A. 1976 operate.)

The relief, which applies to the agricultural value of agricultural land (including settled land) situated in the United Kingdom, the Channel Islands and the Isle of Man, takes the form of a percentage reduction from the value transferred. Relief at 50% is available where:

(i) immediately before the transfer the land carries the right to vacant possession or the right to obtain it within the next twelve months; or

(ii) the transitional provisions operate (see below).

In all other cases, the relief is 30% (20% until 15.3.83).

In order to qualify for the relief, the land must either have been occupied by the transferor for the purposes of agriculture throughout the period of two years ending with the date of transfer or it must have been owned by him for seven years and occupied throughout that period by him (or others) for the purposes of agriculture. Where the occupation is by a company which was controlled by the transferor, it is treated as occupied by the transferor. Where agricultural property owned by the transferor on the date of transfer has replaced other agricultural land, the provisions of Section 118 may operate to enable the occupation or ownership conditions to be satisfied. The relief is not available where the land was under a contract for sale at the date of transfer.

Prior to 10.3.81, the relief was generally only available for "working farmers" (although a retired farmer could qualify) and he usually had to occupy the land for the two years prior to the transfer. The relief reduced the agricultural value of the land by 50% but only to the extent that the value did not exceed

£250,000 or the area of land did not exceed 1,000 acres (whichever was the more favourable).

The original relief could operate to reduce the value of tenanted agricultual land by 50%. This "double relief" can still apply even after 10.3.81 by virtue of the "transitional provisions". If the transferor owned tenanted land which would have qualified for relief on a transfer before 10.3.81 and if he could not have obtained vacant possession between that date and the date of transfer, the 50% relief will apply on that transfer after 10.3.81.

The above describes the position for lifetime transfers and transfers on death for Capital Transfer Tax purposes. It remains wholly relevant as regards property comprised in the death estate for Inheritance Tax purposes and in the calculation of the lifetime tax in respect of a chargeable transfer. Additional conditions apply, however, in connection with chargeable transfers that involve a charge for tax or for additional tax on the transferor's death within seven years. The gifted property must have been retained by the transferee throughout the period between the gift and the death of the transferor (although there is relief for replacement property in certain circumstances) and the gifted property must have qualified for relief at the time of the death in accordance with the original conditions and have remained agricultural property to the time of the transferor's death.

(xviii) The business relief provisions are contained in Sections 103–114. Relief is available in respect of "relevant business property" which has been owned by the transferor throughout the period of two years ending with the transfer.

"Relevant business property" means:

(a) property consisting of a business or interest in a business;
(b) shares in or securities of a company which (either by themselves or together with other such shares or securities owned by the transferor) gave him control of the company immediately before the transfer;
(c) shares in the company which do not fall within (b) above and are not quoted on a recognised stock exchange;
(d) any land or building, machinery or plant which, immediately before the transfer, was used wholly or mainly for the purposes of a business carried on by a company of which the transferor then had control or by a partnership of which he then was a partner; and
(e) any land or building, machinery or plant which, immediately before the transfer, was used wholly or mainly for the

purposes of a business carried on by the transferor and was settled property in which he was then beneficially entitled to an interest in possession.

The relief is not available where the property is subject to a binding contract for sale or if the shares are in a company that is being liquidated. Further, a business, or interest in a business or shares in a company are not "relevant business property" if the business carried on consists wholly or mainly of one or more of: dealing in securities, stocks and shares, land or buildings or making or holding investments. Assets which are not needed in the business may be excluded from the relief ("excepted assets").

As regards category (c) above, it should be noted that from 17.3.87 shares dealt with on the Unlisted Securities Market (USM) are treated for all Inheritance Tax purposes as if they were quoted shares.

The relief (in common with agricultural relief) is given by allowing a percentage reduction against the value transferred by a transfer of value. The percentage reductions have been amended by successive Finance Acts as follows:

7.4.76–26.10.77 (incl.)	30% for (a) (b) & (d) above nil for (c) & (e)
27.10.77–9.3.81 (incl.)	50% for (a) & (b) 30% for (d) 20% for (c) nil for (e)
10.3.81–14.3.83 (incl.)	50% for (a) & (b) 30% for (d) & (e) 20% for (c)
15.3.83 onwards	50% for (a) & (b) 30% for (c) (d) & (e).

The F.A. 1987 (relevant as regards transfers after 17.3.87) increased business relief from 30% to 50% on transfers out of a minority holding of more than 25% in unquoted companies.

As described for agricultural relief at para. (xvii) above, additional conditions apply for business relief to operate in connection with chargeable transfers that involve a charge for tax or for additional tax on the transferor's death within seven years.

(xix) *Fall in value relief*—Section 131. For Capital Transfer Tax, when additional tax became payable by reason of the transferor's death within three years of the transfer, relief was available to take account of reductions in the value of the gifted property (on sale or otherwise) between the transfer and the death. For Inheritance Tax purposes the relief has been extended to include falls in value in the seven years between the gift and the death when additional tax is payable in respect of a chargeable transfer by reason of the death. The relief has to be claimed by the transferee.

(xx) Relief is available in respect of certain securities which are sold (within twelve months of the deceased's death) at a loss compared with their market value on death—Sections 178–189. The relief, which has to be claimed, can only be obtained in respect of "qualifying investments", principally shares quoted on a recognised stock exchange and units in an authorised Unit Trust (as defined in Section 358 of the Taxes Act). In order to quantify the loss (which operates as a reduction in the value of the estate), all sales, within twelve months of the death, and all purchases between the date of death and two months after the date of the final qualifying sale must be taken into account.

(xxi) Relief under the provisions of Sections 190–199 in respect of sales of land within three years of the deceased's death (or land compulsorily acquired more than three years after the death where the notice to treat was served before or within three years of the death). Under this provision, the "sale value" of *all* land sold by the executors or administrators within the relevant period may be substituted for the "value on death" of the land, unless the sale value would differ from the value on death by less than the lower of (a) £1,000, or (b) 5 per cent of the value on death.

(xxii) Section 158 enables arrangements with foreign governments to be made that avoid or reduce the effects of double taxation. The arrangements can provide relief by means of a credit for one tax against another and/or by an alteration to the taxing rights of the respective territories. To date only five arrangements have been made—with the Republic of Ireland, South Africa, the United States of America, Sweden and the Netherlands—but by virtue of Section 158(6) existing arrangements made for Estate Duty remain in force (unless and until specifically repealed) in relation to Inheritance Tax on death. Five agreements can still operate—with India, Pakistan, France, Switzerland and Italy.

(xxiii) Relief under Section 159 is available in respect of tax paid in any territory outside the United Kingdom on property taxable on the deceased's death. Where the property is situated in the overseas territory and *not* in the United Kingdom, a credit for the foreign tax (not exceeding the amount of U.K. tax in respect of the property) may be claimed. In any other case, reference should be made to the provisions in sub-sections (3) to (5) of Section 159.

(xxiv) Relief under Section 141 is available where the estate of the deceased is increased by a chargeable transfer made not more than five years before his death. The tax chargeable on the deceased's death is reduced by a percentage of the tax attributable to the increase to the deceased's estate charged on the previous occasion.

The relevant reductions for the various periods are:

(a) 1 year or less	100%
(b) more than 1 year but not more than 2	80%
(c) more than 2 years but not more than 3	60%
(d) more than 3 years but not more than 4	40%
(e) more than 4 years but not more than 5	20%

It is important to note that the relief is given by reducing the tax on the whole of the deceased's estate on his death. If, say, the taxable estate comprises free estate and settled property the reduction will be apportioned between them even if the property which was the subject of the earlier transfer became comprised in only one of the two constituent parts of the estate.

This relief applies in connection with deaths on or after 10.3.81. Prior to that date, the relief to successive charges to tax was in two forms depending on whether the charge on the deceased's death was in respect of settled or non-settled property. Relief for the former was contained in para. 5 Sch. 5, F.A. 1975 (taking the form of a percentage reduction in the value of the settled property) and for the latter in Section 30, F.A. 1975 (taking a similar form to the current relief). In both cases the maximum period between the charges was four years.

(xxv) *Commorientes*—the provisions of Section 4(2) will prevent any double charge for tax that might arise by virtue of the presumption in Section 184, Law of Property Act 1925 that the younger is deemed to have survived the elder when they die in circumstances where it cannot be known which of them actually survived the other. For tax purposes the deaths are treated as simultaneous—even though the younger may inherit the elder's estate, the inheritance will not be taxed as part of the younger's estate (see para.12.01).

Instruments of variation

6.50 In any consideration of the exemptions and reliefs available practitioners should bear in mind the provisions of Section 142. The dispositions (whether effected by will, under the rules of intestacy or otherwise) of the property comprised in the deceased's estate can be varied by an instrument in writing made by the persons who benefit or who would benefit under the dispositions. The variation must be effected within two years of the death and if the provisions of Section 142(1) are to apply, the parties to the instrument must give written notice to the Board of Inland Revenue within the six months following the date of the instrument—Section 142(2). The devolution of property settled at the date of the death cannot be varied within the provision.

(F) Payment of tax

Lifetime transfers

6.51 What follows in this section is no more than an outline of the detailed liability provisions contained in Sections 199–210.

For Capital Transfer Tax purposes (*i.e.* transfers made before 18.3.86) both the transferor and the transferee (including trustees in the case of a transfer into settlement) had a liability to pay the tax. If additional tax became payable by reason of the transferor's death within three years, only the transferee was liable for this additional amount.

With transfers made on or after 18.3.86 which give rise to an immediate charge for tax, the liability remains with both the transferor and the transferee (or trustees). On death within seven years additional tax may be payable and the transferee (or trustees) are primarily liable. The transferor's personal representatives can, however, be required in certain circumstances to pay all or part of this additional amount. As regards PETs (and gifts with a reservation) the charge for tax arises on the death with the transferee primarily liable, although again the transferor's personal representatives can be required to pay any tax not paid by the transferee.

Death Estate

6.52 Under Section 200(1) the deceased's personal representatives are liable for the tax attributable to the value of property which either:

(i) was not immediately before the death comprised in a settlement, or

(ii) was so comprised and consists of land in the United Kingdom which devolves upon or vests in them.

Under Section 226(2) the personal representatives are required to pay all the tax for which they are liable on delivery of the Inland Revenue Account of the deceased's estate.

Instalment-option property

6.53 Sections 227–228 enable the persons liable for tax to give notice to the Board of Inland Revenue that they wish to pay the tax in respect of certain types of property by 10 yearly instalments (until 15.3.83 it was 8 yearly or 16 half-yearly instalments). This relief is available in connection with tax payable on the death whether for the death estate or for lifetime transfers. It is also available in relation to lifetime tax but only if the tax is being borne by the person benefiting from the transfer. If a PET becomes chargeable by reason of the death, the tax attributable may qualify for payment by instalments providing the property is still owned by the beneficiary. The types of property on which tax may be paid by instalments are as follows:

(a) Land of any description, wherever situated.

(b) Shares or securities of a company which gave the deceased control of the company immediately before his death.

(c) Other unquoted shares or securities of a company transferred on the death if not less than 20 per cent of the tax for which the personal representatives (as such) are liable consists of the tax on the said shares and any other instalment-option property.

(d) Unquoted shares or securities of a company (other than at (b) above) if the Board of Inland Revenue are satisfied that the tax attributable to their value cannot be paid in one sum without undue hardship.

(e) Unquoted shares of a company (other than at (b) above) if the value transferred attributable to them exceeds £20,000 (until 15.3.83 it was £5,000), and the shares transferred comprise at least 10 per cent of the nominal value of all the shares of the company at the date of the deceased's death (or, if they are ordinary shares, at least 10 per cent of the nominal value of all the ordinary shares of the company at the date of the deceased's death).

(f) Unincorporated businesses and interests (*e.g.* partnership interests) in such businesses. The word "business" includes a business carried on in the exercise of a profession or vocation but does not include a business carried on otherwise than for gain.

6.54 Where the instalment-option property (or part of it) is sold, or a payment (under a partnership agreement or otherwise) of any sum in satisfaction of the whole or any part of an interest in a business is made, the tax unpaid (or the proportionate part thereof) becomes immediately payable, unless such sale (or payment) takes place before the first instalment is due. In the latter case, the full tax in respect of the sold property is payable six months after the end of the month in which the death occurred.

Interest

6.55 Capital Transfer Tax was normally due and payable 6 months after the end of the month in which the chargeable transfer (including a transfer on death) was made but the tax on lifetime transfers made after 5th April and before 1st October was not due until the end of April in the next year. With Inheritance Tax the rules for transfers which attract an immediate lifetime tax charge remain as for Capital Transfer Tax. The tax in respect of lifetime transfers that become chargeable only by reason of the transferor's death within seven years (and in respect of gifts with reservation) is due and payable, as with the tax due in respect of the death estate, six months after the end of the month in which the death occurs.

As can be seen from the table below, until 15.12.86 interest on tax in respect of lifetime transfers was at a separate (higher) rate than on tax in respect of the transfer of the death estate, but since that date the rate has been the same for all transfers.

	Lifetime tax	*Death tax*
Until 31.12.79	9%	6%
1.1.80 to 30.11.82	12%	9%
1.12.82 to 30.4..85	8%	6%
1.5.85 to 15.12.86	11%	9%
16.12.86 to 5.6.87	8%	8%
6.6.87 to 5.8.88	6%	6%
6.8.88 to 5.10.88	8%	8%
After 6.10.88	9%	9%

6.56 Where tax is being paid by instalments interest continues to accrue on the *whole tax* from time to time unpaid unless the provisions of Section 234 apply to afford relief from interest. The relief extends to tax attributable to:

(i) the value of any shares or securities except as mentioned at Section 234(2);
(ii) a business or interest in a business;
(iii) property which qualifies for the current agricultural relief introduced on 10.3.81.

With these types of property each instalment of tax carries interest only from the date that it is due to be paid, so that interest is only payable in respect of and to the extent that any instalment is in arrear. (In relation to chargeable transfers made before 10.3.81 only £250,000 of property could enjoy this relief from interest.)

6.57 If the personal representatives wish to pay part of the Inheritance Tax in connection with the deceased's death out of Savings Certificates, Premium Bonds or a Savings Bank Account which formed part of the death estate, a letter to this effect should be sent to The Controller, Capital Taxes Office, Affidavits Division, Minford House, Rockley Road, London W14 0DF with the Inland Revenue Account. A letter from the appropriate Director of Savings, showing the value of the relevant Certificates, Bonds or Savings Account at the date of the deceased's death should also be enclosed. (It should, however, be noted that the necessary formalities in connection with the transfer of the monies to the Finance Division of the Inland Revenue will inevitably mean some delay in the issue of the grant of representation.)

COMPLETION OF THE INLAND REVENUE ACCOUNT

Cap 200 and 201

6.58 As stated at the beginning of this chapter (paras. 6.10 ff) the principal forms of Inland Revenue Account to lead to a grant of representation are Cap 200 and Cap 201. The forms are similar in design, the chief difference being that the Cap 200 is appropriate only where the deceased died domiciled in some part of the United Kingdom, and the Cap 201 *must* be used where the deceased died domiciled outside the United Kingdom. It will be convenient to consider the various parts of each form of Account together, pointing out the differences between them where these are material. A guide for completing forms Cap 200 and Cap 201 is to be found in Inland Revenue form Cap 213.

Pages 1 and 2

6.59 These pages require full particulars of the deceased, and on page 2 is a declaration which must be signed by the applicant(s) for the grant that the facts stated are true to the best of his/their knowledge and belief. Immediately beneath the space for the applicants' signatures, there appears the following warning:

> Warning
>
> An executor or intending administator who fails to make the fullest enquiries that are reasonably practicable in the circumstances may be liable to penalties. If he fails to disclose in sections 1A, 1B, 2A, 2B and 3 (as appropriate) and in his answers to the questions on page 3 all the property to the best of his knowledge and belief in respect of which tax may be payable on the death of the deceased (whether or not he is liable for the tax and whether or not the property is under his control) he may be liable to penalties or prosecution.

6.60 The name and address of the solicitors acting on behalf of the applicant(s) should be shown at the top of page 1 of the form and their reference and telephone number should also be inserted in the appropriate spaces to facilitate any enquiries which may prove to be necessary.

6.61 The name of the probate registry (*e.g.* "Principal Registry", "Bristol District Probate Registry") should be shown in the space immediately beneath the heading "In The High Court of Justice, Family Division (Probate)", and then, in the relevant spaces *and in block capitals*, the deceased's surname and forenames (in full), the dates of his birth and death, his last usual address, particulars of his marital status, surviving relatives and occupation and his domicile at the date of his death. The dates of birth and death should be shown numerically using two digits for each of the day, month and year (*e.g.* 07–07–88 for 7 July 1988). It is particularly important where relief under the provisions of Section 18 is being claimed to indicate that the deceased left a surviving husband or wife. Where the deceased had no occupation at the date of his death, his last occupation followed by the word "Retired" should be inserted, or, where this is not appropriate, his or her personal description (*e.g.* "Gentleman", "Spinster" or "Widow") will suffice.

6.62 Where the application is being made on Cap 200 in respect of a person who died domiciled in the United Kingdom, it is necessary to indicate the relevant part of the United Kingdom but no further information concerning the domicile will be required. Where, however, the application is being made on a CAP 201 in respect of a person who died domiciled outside the United Kingdom under the general law, the name of the country of domicile (and, where appropriate, the state or province of that country) must be inserted in the relevant space on page 1 of the form. If, in such a case, the deceased had a "deemed domicile" in the United Kingdom under the provisions of Section 267 a statement to this effect should be added.

6.63 As stated at para 6.20, if a domicile outside the United Kingdom under the general law is claimed, the Cap 201 *must* be submitted to the Controller, Capital Taxes Office, Affidavits Division, Minford House, Rockley Road, London W14 0DF, *before* the application for the grant can proceed. In such cases, a statement of domicile explaining the circumstances relied upon to establish the domicile and containing a short history of the deceased's life commencing with his domicile of origin must be filed with the Inland Revenue Account. It is not sufficient for this purpose simply to lodge an Account showing that the deceased died domiciled in............... without any supporting evidence. Where this is done or the evidence does not appear to support the domicile claimed, the Inland Revenue Account will be returned by the Capital Taxes Office with "observations" calling for the evidence or clarification of the position, thus delaying the issue of the grant. Paragraph 5 on page 2 of the form must also be completed.

6.64 The last section on page 1 showing the names and addresses of the executors or intended administrators should be completed.

6.65 Page 2 sets out the declaration to be completed and signed by the applicants. Paragraphs 1–4 are identical for both forms, but there is an additional fifth paragraph for the Cap 201. Paragraph 1 of the declaration should be completed to show the kind of grant (*e.g.* "Probate of the Will", "Letters of Administration with the Will annexed") for which application is being made. If the grant is required only for settled land (*i.e.* land which was settled *prior* to the death of the deceased and which remained settled land notwithstanding his or her death) the phrase "limited to the Settled Land of which true particulars and values are given in Section 3 hereof" should be inserted immediately after "of the afore named deceased" at the end of the paragraph.

6.66 Paragraph 3 must be either completed or deleted in all cases. It is essential that, where the account includes property, the precise amount or value of which has not been ascertained by the executors or intended administrators paragraph 3 should be completed. An Exhibit setting out the circumstances should be annexed to the Account, and the best estimate of value included in the appropriate section. If there is *no* such property, the paragraph must be deleted by the applicants. Failure to do so may delay the issue of the grant.

6.67 Paragraph 4 must be completed where the estate includes instalment option property [*i.e.* property on which the person paying the tax thereon may, by notice in writing to the Board, elect to pay it by instalments—see para 6.53 above].

Page 3

6.68 This contains a series of questions with alternative YES and NO boxes printed alongside. The object of the questions is to ascertain whether there is any other property, apart from the deceased's free estate, which must be taken into account in determining the total value on which tax is chargeable in connection with the death. It is essential that the fullest enquiries that are reasonably practicable are made and that all questions are answered. Even if it is considered that no claim for tax arises, the material facts should nevertheless still be supplied where the affirmative answer is appropriate.

6.69 Question 1 relates to gifts etc made by the deceased during his lifetime. As explained at paras. 6.30–37 the extent to which the deceased made transfers during his lifetime (whether before or after 18.3.86) may affect the amount of tax payable on the death estate. Certain lifetime transfers which are exempt from tax need not be reported: the footnote on page 3 contains full details of these.

6.70 Question 2 falls into two parts:

(a) whether the deceased had an interest in possession in settled property *at the time of his death*, *e.g.* as life tenant or annuitant; and
(b) whether the deceased *ceased to be entitled* to any such interest after 26.3.74 or within ten years of his death (whichever is the shorter period).

A person beneficially entitled to an interest in possession in settled property is treated as beneficially entitled to the property in which that interest subsists and that property will be subject to tax as part of his taxable estate unless:

(i) an exemption applies; or
(ii) it is to be left out of account (see Section 54(1) and (2) and para 2 Sch. 6).

Whether or not any of these exceptions apply, the applicant should give the required details of the title under which the property is held and if it is considered that the property is not subject to tax, give the reasons. If the interest ceased (by a release or otherwise) in the deceased's lifetime, the property in which that interest subsisted may form the subject-matter of a lifetime transfer by the deceased—Section 52.

6.71 Question 3 relates to assets which the deceased may have nominated in favour of another person prior to his death. If any such nomination was made, full particulars should be given.

6.72 Question 4 deals with property held in the joint names of the deceased and any other person(s) at his death. Tax repercussions may arise when property is put into the joint names, on any dealings that follow and also on death. If the deceased's involvement with the property arises only in his capacity as trustee, details are not required.

Pages 4 and 5

6.73 Details of property to which the deceased was beneficially entitled (excluding property over which he had a general power of appointment) are included in this section of the form. There is a difference between the requirements of the Cap 200 and the Cap 201. Both require details of property which does not qualify for the instalment option, but in the case of the Cap 200 all such property within the United Kingdom should be listed, whereas in the case of Cap 201 only such property in England and Wales is required here. The provisions regulating the way in which property is to be valued are contained in Section 160 and specify that:

> "the value of any property shall for the purposes of this Act be the price which the property might reasonably be expected to fetch if sold on the open market at that time."

Under Section 4(1) the relevant time for valuing property is immediately before the death. Any provisions in the deceased's will which seek to restrict the executors' right of disposal of the property should be disregarded in a valuation for tax purposes.

Stocks and shares

6.74 The total value of the deceased's portfolio of stocks, shares, debentures and other securities should be included under two separate headings:

(i) those which are quoted in the Stock Exchange Daily Official List; and
(ii) others.

Securities which are eligible for the instalment option (see para. 6.53) should not be included here but rather on page 7 of the Account.

6.75 Full details of the deceased's holdings should be given on the form Cap 40 annexed to the Inland Revenue Account. Where space is insufficient, a further copy of the form or a separate schedule should be attached. If obtained, a professional valuation may be enclosed. Securities quoted on the Stock Exchange should be listed first in the order in which they appear in the Stock Exchange Daily Official List, followed by those quoted on any other recognised Stock Exchange. The full title of the holding (as shown in the share certificate or scrip) together with the nominal amount of the deceased's holding at the date of his death should be shown on the Cap 40. Regard should be had to the unit of quotation shown in the list as, owing to capital reorganisation, this may differ from that shown on the certificates.

6.76 The principal value for tax is normally taken as the "quarter-up" price on the day of the deceased's death, *i.e.* one quarter of the way from the lower (bid) to the higher (offer) limit of quotation on the day. For example where the range is (70–90) the quarter-up price will be 75p. As an alternative a price half way between the highest and lowest bargains recorded for the day may be taken but any bargains struck at special prices must be ignored. Where the deceased died at a weekend or any other day when the Stock Exchange was closed for business, the executors or intending administrators may select prices from either the last list prior to the date of death or the first list available after the death. The actual date chosen should be indicated on the Cap 40.

6.77 Certain symbols on the Stock Exchange Daily Official List may affect the value of a shareholding, *e.g.*:

- XD— As a dividend has been declared prior to the death, the net sum payable should be accounted for.
- IK— This applies to certain short-dated stocks and to arrive at their market value the gross accrued interest to the date of death should be added to the quarter-up price.
- IK.XD—As a dividend has been declared on a short-dated stock, to arrive at market price the gross interest accruing from the date of death to the date of payment of the dividend should be deducted from the quarter-up price. The net amount of the dividend due should be included separately.
- X Cap— As a bonus issue of shares has been declared the new shares to which the deceased was entitled at his death should be included in his estate.
- X Rts— A rights issue has been declared and the method for dealing with this situation depends upon the way in which the deceased dealt with the rights before he died. If he took up the new shares, they should be included on the Cap 40. If he sold the rights, the proceeds should be reflected in the estate. If he did nothing, the market value of the rights should be accounted for.

When either of the last two markings appear beside a holding, it is helpful to add a note to the Cap 40 making the position regarding the new shares clear.

6.78 Units of unit trusts should be valued at the manager's published bid price and the management group should be stated. If no price was published on the day of the deceased's death, the price last published prior to that date should be shown.

6.79 Unquoted securities which are not "instalment-option property" under Section 228 (see para. 6.53) should be included at the best available estimate of value. Where possible, a letter from the company giving a reasoned estimate of the market value of the shares at the date of the deceased's death and particulars of any recent dealings should be attached. The value of any National Savings Certificates owned by the deceased at the date of his death should be evidenced by a letter from the Director of Savings, Savings Certificates & S.A.Y.E. Office, Durham DH99 1NS.

Debts due to the deceased

6.80 Debts due to the deceased at the date of his death (other than business debts which are instalment-option property and reflected on page 7) must be included at their full nominal value together with interest thereon up to the date of death. If the market value of the loan at the deceased's death is considered to be less than the nominal value, a statement showing the precise terms of the loan and the circumstances in which the value for tax is considered to be lower than the nominal value should be annexed.

Proceeds of sale of real/leasehold property

6.81 Where real or leasehold property has been contracted to be sold by the deceased prior to his death, the option to pay tax thereon by instalments does not apply to the property. The amount to be included is the proceeds of sale of the property after deducting any deposit received in the lifetime.

Policies

6.82 As regards all policies, only those where the proceeds are (or will be) payable to the estate should be included on page 4 (see also question 1(c) on page 3 of the account). The total amount payable under policies of insurance on the deceased's life (including accident policies) must be included. With regard to policies not payable on the death of the deceased (*e.g.* policies payable on the death of some other person, sinking fund policies etc.), the amount to be included is the saleable value of the policy at the date of the deceased's death. This is not necessarily the surrender value, although this will normally be acceptable in the first instance.

Household goods and personal effects

6.83 The deceased's household and personal effects should be included at their estimated open-market value at the date of the deceased's death. If any actual sales have taken place, the gross amount realised should be shown separately and where a formal valuation has been made a copy should be annexed to the papers. If nil or a very small value is included, a brief explanation of the circumstances will assist.

6.84 If conditional exemption under the provisions of Section 30 is claimed in respect of any articles considered to be of national, scientific, historic or artistic interest (see para. 6.49(xi)) the *full* value of the items should be included on page 5 and an appropriate deduction taken in the summary on page 10. In such a case, the Cap 200 (or 201) *must* be forwarded to the Controller, Capital Taxes Office, Affidavits Division, Minford House, Rockley Road, London W14 0DF, for consideration of the claim and for assessment of the Inland Revenue Account—see para. 6.19. A schedule giving particulars of the items in respect of which exemption is claimed should be annexed to the papers. If exemption in respect of any of the articles has been granted in connection with a previous death, the full name and date of death of the person concerned should be stated.

Reversionary interests

6.85 Where the deceased was the owner of a reversionary interest (whether vested or contingent), full particulars including the estimated value at the date of death should be shown on page 5. Unless the reversionary interest:

(i) had at any time been acquired (whether by the deceased or by a previous owner) for a consideration in money or money's worth; or

(ii) was under a settlement made on or after 16.4.76 by the deceased or his or her spouse; or

(iii) is an interest expectant on the determination of a lease treated as a settlement;

it is "excluded property" and exempt from tax in connection with the death, and the value should be deducted in the summary on page 10 of the Account.

Repayments of income tax

6.86 Any repayment of income tax to which the deceased may have been entitled at the date of his death forms a part of his estate and should accordingly be included. Where the amount of the repayment has not been quantified, the best possible estimate should be shown.

Other property

6.87 Any other property which formed a part of the deceased's estate at the date of his death (other than property with the instalment option) not shown elsewhere in Section 1A should be included in the space provided on page 5. Examples of such property are:

(a) benefits payable on the deceased's death under a superannuation scheme (where the personal representatives are entitled as of right to such benefits);
(b) sums payable under the Law Reform (Miscellaneous Provisions) Act 1934;
(c) arrears of salary or holiday pay to which the deceased was entitled at his death;
(d) refunds of season tickets, air-line reservations and similar payments made by the deceased prior to his death.

The total of the deceased's assets included in section 1A of the Account should now be calculated and the figure carried forward to page 6 and to the Probate Summary on page 12.

Page 6

6.88 Page 6 should contain particulars of the deceased's liabilities at the date of his death in respect of which deduction is claimed (other than debts charged on the instalment-option property or liabilities of a business) and his funeral expenses. The liabilities must have been due and owing by the deceased at the date of his death to persons resident in the United Kingdom, or if due to persons resident abroad must have been contracted to be paid or charged on property situated in the United Kingdom.

6.89 In order to be admissible as deductions against the deceased's estate, the liabilities must be either imposed by law (*e.g.* income tax, rates etc.) or incurred by the deceased for a consideration in money or money's worth—Section 5(5). This provision covers all the ordinary simple contract debts, *e.g.* for food, clothing, gas, electricity etc, owing by the deceased at the date of his death, but not voluntary payments *e.g.* under a covenant made by the deceased in consideration of his "natural love and affection" for the covenantee. The name and address of the creditor and a brief description of the liability, together with the amount (or where this has not been ascertained, the best possible estimate thereof) should be shown. It should be noted that no deduction for administration expenses is allowable for tax purposes and such items should not be included.

6.90 A liability in respect of which there is a right to reimbursement (*e.g.* a guarantee debt) is deductible only to the extent (if any) that reimbursement cannot reasonably be expected to be obtained—Section

162(1). If deduction for such a debt is claimed, a statement setting out the circumstances and (where possible) giving details of the principal debtor's financial position should be annexed to the Inland Revenue Account. If a liability does not become due for payment until some future date, the full amount may not be deductable and in view of Section 162(2) a valuation of the debt at the date of death will be necessary.

6.91 Deduction may be taken for "reasonable funeral expenses"—Section 172. This will not cover the cost of a memorial service to the deceased, but will include items such as the tombstone, obituary notices, and by concession a reasonable amount for the mourning expenses of the family.

6.92 Where the total amount of the debts and funeral expenses in Section 1A is greater than the total of the assets therein, a deduction for the excess may be taken in the Schedule to section 1B on page 7 of the Inland Revenue Account. Deduction is allowable only against the value of property which is available to meet the debts.

6.93 The summary at the foot of page 6 must be completed in every case. This should show the total of the assets from page 5, the total of the debts and funeral expenses (as above) and the resulting net value should be carried to page 11 part A 1a. The total of the liabilities in section 1A should be carried forward to the Probate Summary on page 12.

Page 7

6.94 This section of the Inland Revenue Account should contain particulars of the deceased's property with the instalment option. Here again the two forms differ—the Cap 200 should be completed to show details of property in the United Kingdom, whereas the Cap 201 relates to property in England and Wales. At the top of the page, two questions concerning the payment of tax should be answered by ticking the appropriate box. The person paying the tax in respect of the property included in this section can elect to pay it be ten yearly instalments. If the election is made, only the instalments that are already due and payable need be assessed on the Inland Revenue Account. If the taxpayer wishes to discharge the tax in one sum, the whole tax must be assessed on the account if the due date has passed, but otherwise, payment can be deferred until after the Grant. The Capital Taxes Office will issue an assessment of the tax payable when payment is due.

6.95 It should be noted:

(a) that the option to pay the tax by instalments does not relate to property which is under contract to be sold, and,
(b) payment by ten yearly instalments is possible only in connection with deaths on or after 15.3.83. Prior to that date the tax could be paid by either 8 yearly or 16 half-yearly instalments.

Land

6.96 The total value of appropriately situated freehold and leasehold land (not being settled land) should be included here. A sufficient description of each property (to enable it to be identified by the Valuation Office) should be given on the form Cap 37 together with details of tenure and of any leases or other lettings relating to the property. A form Cap 37 should always be completed for any land owned and the detailed instructions on that form followed. If a professional valuation of any of the land is available, a copy may be annexed. The amount to be shown in the value at the date of death column in section 1**B** is the gross value, that is the value before deduction of any liabilities, reliefs or exemptions.

Business interests

6.97 The net value of any business interests, and, separately, interests in partnerships owned by the deceased at his death, should be included. An explanation of the way in which the value has been arrived at with full supporting evidence in the form of balance sheets and articles of partnership (where appropriate) should be supplied. The value to be shown on page 7 is the value before any reliefs and exemptions.

Stocks, shares etc.

6.98 The circumstances in which shares etc. qualify for the instalment option are shown at para. 6.53 (b) to (e) inclusive and the value of the deceased's holdings that do qualify should be entered here. The value of the holdings in companies that he controlled at his death should be separated from the value of the other qualifying holdings but in each case the holdings should be detailed on the form Cap 40. The values inserted on page 7 of the Account should be gross, ignoring all claims for exemption and reliefs. The total gross value of all the property in the free estate that qualifies for the instalment option can now be calculated with the figure carried forward to the Probate Summary on page 12 of the Account.

6.99 The last section on page 7 of the Account is for liabilities charged on property that qualifies for the instalment option. The most common liabilities will be mortgage debts or bank advances charged on the land. Individual business debts should not be listed here, as they will have been taken into account in calculating the net value of the business interest above. The nature of each liability should be stated with details of the property charged, to whom the liability is payable and the amount due at the date of death. The total of these liabilities should be:

(i) carried forward to the Probate Summary on page 12 of the Account.
(ii) deducted from the gross value of the property with the instalment option.

The net value resulting at (ii) should be carried to page 11 of the Account at part A 1c.

Page 8

6.100 Section 2 on page 8 is for the remainder of the deceased's property in respect of which the personal representatives are liable to pay the tax. This liability is dealt with by Section 200(1) of the Act.

6.101 The requirements of the Cap 200 and the Cap 201 are different in some respects (as explained below) but both must be completed to include property nominated by the deceased during his lifetime and the deceased's interest in jointly-owned property passing by survivorship to the other joint owner(s) on the death. Particulars of the property, using forms Cap 40 and Cap 37 as appropriate, and of the disposition under which it devolved on the death, together with its gross value at the date of death, should be shown. The main difference between the Cap 200 and the Cap 201 is in connection with property situated abroad. The Cap 200 (used where the deceased dies domiciled in some part of the U.K.) requires that all property situated outside the U.K. should be included in section 2. The Cap 201, however, is for use where the deceased died domiciled outside the U.K. so that property situated abroad is "excluded property" under Section 6(1) and accordingly exempt on the death. With the Cap 201 property situated outside the U.K. need only be shown in section 2:

(i) if the deceased is "deemed" to have had a U.K. domicile at his death by virtue of section 267; or
(ii) to the extent that assets are "deemed" to be situated in the U.K. by virtue of a double taxation agreement or convention.

A further difference between the forms is in connection with property situated in Scotland or Northern Ireland. With the Cap 200 such property will have been included in section 1 of the account but with the Cap 201 it will have to be shown now in section 2.

6.102 Particulars of the property with its local situation should be given. Where the property consists of stocks and shares quoted on an overseas stock exchange, the name of exchange should be shown when completing the Cap 40. The gross value at the date of death has to be included in sterling terms and where the valuation of foreign property is made in terms of an overseas currency, a conversion into sterling will be necessary. Rates of exchange can be obtained from the *Financial Times*. The London buying rate should be used for major world currencies and the world value of the pound rate for any others.

6.103 Deduction can be taken for the deceased's liabilities charged upon, incurred in connection with or otherwise affecting the property included in section 2. Liabilities due to persons resident outside the United Kingdom (unless already taken into account in section 1) will normally be deducted from the value of the property outside the United Kingdom. Only if the property is included in the section should deduction be taken here—see Section 162(5). The name and address of each creditor and a brief description of each liability should be shown together with the amount owed (and its sterling equivalent where appropriate) at the date of death. Under Section 173 deduction may be claimed for any additional expense incurred in administering or realising property situated outside the United Kingdom. The expense must be shown to be attributable to the situation of the property and the deduction cannot exceed 5% of the value of the property.

6.104 As with section 1 of the Inland Revenue Account, section 2 is divided into parts A and B, relating respectively to property without and to property with the instalment option (see above regarding completion of section 1B, in connection with instalment option property). The net values calculated for both parts A and B of the section should be carried to page 11 and included at part A 1a and 1c respectively. These net values are before all claims for reliefs and exemptions.

Page 9

6.105 The requirements of the Cap 200 and Cap 201 are identical in connection with section 3 of the Account. If the applicant has answered "yes" in reply to question 2a on page 3 (see para 6.70) the net value of the settled property as at the date of death should normally be entered here. Details of the assets comprised in the fund(s) and of any liabilities are required. In addition the title under which the property is held (see question 2 on page 3 of the account) and the names and addresses of the trustees and their solicitors should always be provided. As space is limited, it is often more convenient to provide these details in schedules annexed to the account. Even though it is considered that some exemption applies in connection with the death, the property should be detailed and included in the section—the exemption can be claimed on page 10 of the Account—but if the circumstances enable the property to be left out of account (Section 54(1) and (2) and para 2 Sch. 6) the property need not be included. This property, will, of course, have been disclosed in the applicant's reply to question 2 on page 3 of the Account.

6.106 The section requires details of property wherever situated and this is the case whether it is the Cap 200 or Cap 201 that is being used. It should be remembered that with settled property, assets situated outside the United Kingdom are not excluded property unless the settlor was domiciled for tax purposes otherwise than in the United Kingdom when the settlement was made. The domicile of the deceased as the person entitled to the beneficial interest in possession is not the relevant aspect.

6.107 The applicant is required to separate the property upon which he intends to pay the tax on delivery of the Account from property on which he does not. The former should be listed under a heading "Part 1" and the latter under a heading "Part 2". Applicants are required to insert these headings as necessary in the column provided. If any of the "Part 1" property qualifies for the instalment option, the applicant should indicate by ticking the relevant box whether the option is to be exercised. Separate net totals are required for instalment and non-instalment-option property, the former being carried to page 11 part A 1b and the latter to page 11 part A 1a. With "Part 2" property, the net value has to be carried forward to page 11 part A 1d and separate totals for the property with and the property without the instalment option are not required there.

Page 10

6.108 It is on this page that any exemptions and reliefs (see para 6.49) due against the death estate should be claimed. The page divides into three parts so that each exemption and relief can be deducted against the appropriate property and separate totals for each section of the Inland Revenue Account carried forward to page 11. The requirements are identical for both the Cap 200 and the Cap 201 and the manner in which it should be completed may best perhaps be explained by the following illustration in which the columns are numbered instead of their heading being set out in full.

1.	2.	3.	4.
Legacy to the RSPCA	Charity exemption	£15,000	£15,000
Homeside Farm	Agricultural relief (50%)	£100,000	£50,000
Residuary estate	Spouse exemption	£123,333	£123,333

Grossing up

6.109 Calculation of the residuary estate (in the final example above) can be complicated where:

(a) part of an estate is taxable and part is exempt *and*
(b) the tax is in fact payable out of the exempt part.

Example

By the deceased's will, his son is given a pecuniary legacy of £150,000 with his wife taking the remainder of his £300,000 estate. Tax is payable in respect of the legacy only but as a pecuniary legacy is taken free of tax (unless the will indicates otherwise), the tax will be paid out of the residuary estate. The exempt part of the estate is therefore not worth £150,000—rather £150,000 less the tax on the legacy.

The legacy must be grossed up according to the rates in Table 11C (assuming a death on 6.4.88) *viz:* £150,000 − £110,000 = £40,000. £110,000 + (5/3 × £40,000) = £176,666. The taxable estate (the grossed up legacy) is £176,666 and the tax payable is £26,666 (Table 11C).

The exempt residuary estate is £300,000 less £176,666 = £123,334 and it is this last figure that is exempt and shown in the third and fourth columns.

The grossing calculations can be more complex:

(a) if the death follows chargeable lifetime transfers or
(b) if the taxable death estate consists not only of specific gifts not bearing their own tax but also specific gifts that do bear their own tax and/or shares of residue.

Page 11

6.110 It is *essential* that the relevant parts of page 11 of the Account are completed except in those cases where it *must* be submitted to the Capital Taxes Office prior to the issue of the grant. If there is any difficulty in completing the assessment of tax on page 11, the papers may be forwarded to the Controller, Capital Taxes Office, Affidavits Division, Minford House, Rockley Road, London W14 0DF, with a brief explanation of the difficulty. If the papers are submitted direct to the probate registry or the Finance Division at Worthing without pages 11 and 12 having been completed, delay in the issue of the grant will be inevitable.

6.111 Part A on page 11 is a summary for determining chargeable rates. Item 1 headed "Capital value now transferred" includes the individual net totals from sections 1A, 1B, 2A, 2B and 3. and the total reliefs (from page10) due for each section. These will have been brought forward to this page as each section was completed. Now all that remains is to insert the totals at b and e. The latter is the total death estate chargeable to tax.

6.112 Item 2 is the total of all chargeable lifetime transfers made by the deceased within 7 years of death or for deaths before 18.3.86, made on or after 27.3.74 and within 10 years of his death. Item 3 is the aggregate of 1e and 2. This figure is the total chargeable estate and determines the tax calculations at 4 to 6 below.

Examples

Deceased died in May 1988 leaving a taxable free estate of £200,000 comprising non-instalment-option property of £144,000 and instalment-option property of £56,000.

(a) Having made no chargeable lifetime transfers (see Table 11A for rates)

e. Total after all reliefs			200,000	
2. **Cumulative total of chargeable transfers made prior to the deceased's death**			NIL	
3. **Aggregate Chargeable Transfers**			200,000	
4. Tax thereon				
On first	£110,000		NIL	—
On balance of	£90,000 at 40%		36,000	—
5. **Total**			36,000	—
less tax (at death rate) on 2 above				
On first	£	= £	NIL	
On balance of	£	= £		
Less relief for successive charges			NIL	
6. **Tax payable**			36,000	—

Where chargeable lifetime transfers have been made, their addition to the death estate affects the rate at which tax is payable thereon.

(b) Having made chargeable lifetime transfers of £150,000 (see Table 11A for rates)

e. Total after all reliefs		200,000	
2. **Cumulative total of chargeable transfers made prior to the deceased's death**		150,000	
3. **Aggregate Chargeable Transfers**		350,000	
4. Tax thereon			
On first	£110,000	NIL	—
On balance of	£ 240,000 at 40%	96,000	—
5. **Total**		96,000	—
less tax (at death rate) on 2 above			
On first	£110,000 = NIL		
On balance of	£ 40,000 = £16,000 (at 40%)	16,000	—
Less relief for successive charges		NIL	—
6. **Tax payable**		80,000	—

Value on which tax is now being paid	Value of Property	
	Non-instalment £	Instalment Option £
7. Total Value at 1b	144,000	—
8. That part of 1c on which tax now to be paid	—	56,000

It will be seen that where relief for successive charges is due (see para. 6.49(xxiv)) it is reflected in these calculations. The figure at 7 is always the total shown at 1b above and by its nature will always have to be included under the non-instalment heading. The figure at 8 will, of course, always be included under the instalment-option heading and will represent that part of the property at 1c above on which tax is being paid on delivery of the account. Although the executors will be responsible for the tax on all the property at 1c they may defer payment if the tax is not yet due (*i.e.* where the application for the grant is made within 6 months of the death).

Part B

6.113 The amount of tax and interest payable on the delivery of the Account on the property shown at 7 and 8 is calculated in this section. The tax on the non-instalment property is calculated using the formula:

$$\frac{(7)}{(3)-(2)} \times (6).$$

and using the figures in example (b) above produces:

$$\frac{144{,}000}{350{,}000 - 150{,}000} \times 80{,}000 = £57{,}600$$

Tax on the instalment option property is calculated using:

$$\frac{(8)}{(3)-(2)} \times (6).$$

Again adopting the figures in example (b) produces:

$$\frac{56{,}000}{350{,}000 - 150{,}000} \times 80{,}000 = £22{,}400.$$

6.114 If a claim for double taxation relief (see para. 6.49(xxiii)) is appropriate, deduction should be taken here. Where the tax has actually been paid, the receipts (or copies thereof) should be annexed to the Inland Revenue Account. Otherwise a reasoned estimate of the amount of duty or tax payable in the other country should be made. The amount of the relief (which must not exceed the tax payable in this country on the relevant property) is the cost in sterling to the deceased's estate. For the purpose of a provisional deduction, the London selling rate of exchange for major world currencies or the world value of the pound rate for lesser known currencies, should be used (both may be obtained from the *Financial Times*).

6.115 As regards the instalment-option property, if the applicant has exercised the option to pay the tax by instalments, only those instalments which are already due and payable need to be paid on delivery of the Account. If, for example, only one instalment has fallen due then (in the case of deaths on or after 15.3.83) one tenth of the total net tax will have to be paid.

6.116 Para. 6.55 contains details regarding interest on tax. Whether and to what extent interest is payable on delivery of the Inland Revenue Account is shown in the following table.

Non-instalment-option property and instalment-option property (where the whole tax is paid on delivery of the Account).	—	Interest is due on the whole of the unpaid tax from the due date to the date of payment of the tax.

Instalment-option property where tax is being paid by instalments that do not qualify for interest relief.	—	Interest is due on the whole tax up to the date when the last instalment being paid became due. (Nil where only the first instalment is due.) To this is added interest on the instalments now being paid from the last mentioned date to the date of payment of the tax.
Instalment-option property where tax is being paid by instalments that do qualify for interest relief.	—	Interest is chargeable on each instalment only from the date on which the instalment is due.

6.117 At the foot of part B, there is a space to include the amount of any additional tax and interest due under Section 7(2) which the applicant wishes to pay on delivery of the Account. The relevant provisions are explained at para 6.38 and as there stated this additional tax is the liability of the transferee(s). It becomes due and payable, like the tax on the death estate, 6 months after the end of the month in which the death occurred. A schedule showing how any amount inserted in schedule B has been calculated should be annexed.

Example
If the deceased died on 6.4.88 having made only one lifetime transfer of £156,000 on 8.9.85, the Schedule might contain the following details. (The transfer will, of course, have been reported to the Capital Taxes Office and the lifetime tax paid.)

Lifetime transfer on 8.9.85	£156,000
less annual exemptions:	
1985/86 £3,000	
1984/85 £3,000	£ 6,000
Cumulative total	£150,000
Tax on £150,000 at death rates [Table 11A]:	
on first £110,000 = NIL	
on balance of £40,000 at 40% = £16,000	£16,000
Less tax paid in the lifetime [Table 8B]:	
£9,075 + 20% × £28,000 =	£14,675
Additional tax now due	£ 1,325

Similarly where the deceased has made transfers in his lifetime that have become chargeable by reason of his death within 7 years of the transfer, the tax will be calculated in the manner described at para. 6.40. If this tax is to be paid on delivery of the Inland Revenue Account, a schedule showing how it has been calculated should be annexed.

Page 12

6.118 This page provides the probate summary—this is the aggregate gross value of the property which devolves on and vests in the personal representatives of the deceased for and in respect of which the grant is to be made. The figures to be carried forward are indicated in sections 1A and 1B and as regards section 3 only the property in which the deceased had a beneficial interest in possession and over which he had and exercised a general power of appointment should be included. The total of the liabilities in section 1A and 1B are then deducted to provide the net value for probate purposes. The totals for tax and interest paid have to be carried from page 11 and the total tax and interest payable on the Account should be shown. Where no tax is payable on the Account, the word "nil" should be stated.

Cap form 202

6.119 The circumstances in which this pink, four-page form may be used are set out at para. 6.11. In any other case, the full twelve-page version of the Inland Revenue Account must be used.

Page 1

6.120 The layout of this page is almost the same as that of the Cap 200 and reference should be made to para. 6.59 for completion details.

Page 2

6.121 This page contains the declaration which has to be signed by all applicants. Paragraph 1 should be completed to show the kind of grant that is required. No alteration is permitted to paragraphs 2 to 7 and if any of the statements are incorrect, then a full Inland Revenue Account (Cap 200) must be used. Account A should on page 2 contain details of all property without the instalment option in respect of which the grant is to be made. The value included for each item should be its gross value without any deduction for exemptions or reliefs and the total carried forward to page 4. The more detailed discussion relating to the completion of the Cap 200 at paras. 6.73–92 may be of assistance.

Page 3

6.122 The top portion of this page is for the deceased's debts and funeral expenses. The lower portion is for property with the instalment option and debts due in respect of such property. The total in each case should be carried forward separately to page 4.

Page 4

6.123 This page begins with enquiries regarding jointly owned property and then space is available (Account B) for details of both joint and nominated property and debts and incumbrances thereon. The summaries should then be completed resulting in the net estate for tax purposes. Again reference may usefully be made to the relevant instructions for the Cap 200 in connection with exemptions and reliefs.

After the grant

6.124 After the papers have been lodged at the probate registry and the grant issued, the Inland Revenue Account will be sent to the Capital Taxes Office for examination and for the collection of any further tax payable. The Office may raise enquiries regarding the figures shown for assets or liabilities or seek clarification of the reliefs and exemptions claimed. If, of course, any amendments to the values returned or to any statements made in the Inland Revenue Account come to the notice of the personal representatives, they should be notified to the Capital Taxes Office—Section 217.

APPENDIX I: CAPITAL TRANSFER TAX RATES

TABLE 1A

Scale of rates in respect of transfers made on (or within three years of) death from 13th March 1975 to 26th October 1977 (inclusive)

Range of cumulation				*Cumulative tax to bottom of range*	*Rate of tax on value within range*
	£		£	£	%
Exceeds	15,000	but not	20,000	NIL	10
Exceeds	20,000	but not	25,000	500	15
Exceeds	25,000	but not	30,000	1,250	20
Exceeds	30,000	but not	40,000	2,250	25
Exceeds	40,000	but not	50,000	4,750	30
Exceeds	50,000	but not	60,000	7,750	35
Exceeds	60,000	but not	80,000	11,250	40
Exceeds	80,000	but not	100,000	19,250	45
Exceeds	100,000	but not	120,000	28,250	50
Exceeds	120,000	but not	150,000	38,250	55
Exceeds	150,000	but not	500,000	54,750	60
Exceeds	500,000	but not	1,000,000	264,750	65
Exceeds	1,000,000	but not	2,000,000	589,750	70
Exceeds	2,000,000			1,289,750	75

TABLE 1B

Scale of rates in respect of lifetime transfers made from 27th March 1974 to 26th October 1977 (inclusive)

Range of cumulation			*Cumulative tax to bottom of range*	*Rate of tax on value within range*
	£	£	£	%
Exceeds	15,000 but not	20,000	NIL	5
Exceeds	20,000 but not	25,000	250	7.5
Exceeds	25,000 but not	30,000	625	10
Exceeds	30,000 but not	40,000	1,125	12.5
Exceeds	40,000 but not	50,000	2,375	15
Exceeds	50,000 but not	60,000	3,875	17.5
Exceeds	60,000 but not	80,000	5,625	20
Exceeds	80,000 but not	100,000	9,625	22.5
Exceeds	100,000 but not	120,000	14,125	27.5
Exceeds	120,000 but not	150,000	19,625	35
Exceeds	150,000 but not	200,000	30,125	42.5
Exceeds	200,000 but not	250,000	51,375	50
Exceeds	250,000 but not	300,000	76,375	55
Exceeds	300,000 but not	500,000	103,875	60
Exceeds	500,000 but not	1,000,000	223,875	65
Exceeds	1,000,000 but not	2,000,000	548,875	70
Exceeds	2,000,000		1,248,875	75

TABLE 1C

Grossing table for use on deaths from 13th March 1975 to 26th October 1977 (inclusive)

Range of net value		*Gross equivalent*		
£	£	£		£
15,000 to	19,500	15,000 plus £10/9	for each £1 over	15,000
19,500 to	23,750	20,000 plus £20/17	for each £1 over	19,500
23,750 to	27,750	25,000 plus £5/4	for each £1 over	23,750
27,750 to	35,250	30,000 plus £4/3	for each £1 over	27,750
35,250 to	42,250	40,000 plus £10/7	for each £1 over	35,250
42,250 to	48,750	50,000 plus £20/13	for each £1 over	42,250
48,750 to	60,750	60,000 plus £5/3	for each £1 over	48,750
60,750 to	71,750	80,000 plus £20/11	for each £1 over	60,750
71,750 to	81,750	100,000 plus £2	for each £1 over	71,750
81,750 to	95,250	120,000 plus £20/9	for each £1 over	81,750
95,250 to	235,250	150,000 plus £5/2	for each £1 over	95,250
235,250 to	410,250	500,000 plus £20/7	for each £1 over	235,250
410,250 to	710,250	1,000,000 plus £10/3	for each £1 over	410,250
Over £710,250		2,000,000 plus £4	for each £1 over	710,250

TABLE 1D

Grossing table for lifetime transfers made from 27th March 1974 to 26th October 1977 (inclusive)

Range of net value £	£	*Gross Equivalent* £		£
15,000 to	19,750	15,000 plus £20/19	for each £1 over	15,000
19,750 to	24,375	20,000 plus £40/37	for each £1 over	19,750
24,375 to	28,875	25,000 plus £10/9	for each £1 over	24,375
28,875 to	37,625	30,000 plus £8/7	for each £1 over	28,875
37,625 to	46,125	40,000 plus £20/17	for each £1 over	37,625
46,125 to	54,375	50,000 plus £40/33	for each £1 over	46,125
54,375 to	70,375	60,000 plus £5/4	for each £1 over	54,375
70,375 to	85,875	80,000 plus £40/31	for each £1 over	70,375
85,875 to	100,375	100,000 plus £40/29	for each £1 over	85,875
100,375 to	119,875	120,000 plus £20/13	for each £1 over	100,375
119,875 to	148,625	150,000 plus £40/23	for each £1 over	119,875
148,625 to	173,625	200,000 plus £2	for each £1 over	148,625
173,625 to	196,125	250,000 plus £20/9	for each £1 over	173,625
196,125 to	276,125	300,000 plus £5/2	for each £1 over	196,125
276,125 to	451,125	500,000 plus £20/7	for each £1 over	276,125
451,125 to	751,125	1,000,000 plus £10/3	for each £1 over	451,125
Over £751,125		2,000,000 plus £4	for each £1 over	751,125

TABLE 2A

Scale of rates in respect of transfers made on (or within three years of) death from 27th October 1977 to 25th March 1980 (inclusive)

Range of cumulation	£		£	*Cumulative tax to bottom of range* £	*Rate of tax on value within range* %
Exceeds	25,000	but not	30,000	NIL	10
Exceeds	30,000	but not	35,000	500	15
Exceeds	35,000	but not	40,000	1,250	20
Exceeds	40,000	but not	50,000	2,250	25
Exceeds	50,000	but not	60,000	4,750	30
Exceeds	60,000	but not	70,000	7,750	35
Exceeds	70,000	but not	90,000	11,250	40
Exceeds	90,000	but not	110,000	19,250	45
Exceeds	110,000	but not	130,000	28,250	50
Exceeds	130,000	but not	160,000	38,250	55
Exceeds	160,000	but not	510,000	54,750	60
Exceeds	510,000	but not	1,010,000	264,750	65
Exceeds	1,010,000	but not	2,010,000	589,750	70
Over 2,010,000				1,289,750	75

TABLE 2B

Scale for rates in respect of lifetime transfers made from 27th October 1977 to 25th March 1980 (inclusive)

Range of cumulation			*Cumulative tax to bottom of range*	*Rate of tax on value within range*
	£	£	£	%
Exceeds	25,000 but not	30,000	NIL	5
Exceeds	30,000 but not	35,000	250	7.5
Exceeds	35,000 but not	40,000	625	10
Exceeds	40,000 but not	50,000	1,125	12.5
Exceeds	50,000 but not	60,000	2,375	15
Exceeds	60,000 but not	70,000	3,875	17.5
Exceeds	70,000 but not	90,000	5,625	20
Exceeds	90,000 but not	110,000	9,625	22.5
Exceeds	110,000 but not	130,000	14,125	27.5
Exceeds	130,000 but not	160,000	19,625	35
Exceeds	160,000 but not	210,000	30,125	42.5
Exceeds	210,000 but not	260,000	51,375	50
Exceeds	260,000 but not	310,000	76,375	55
Exceeds	310,000 but not	510,000	103,875	60
Exceeds	510,000 but not	1,010,000	223,875	65
Exceeds	1,010,000 but not	2,010,000	548,875	70
Over 2,010,000			1,248,875	75

TABLE 2C

Grossing table for use on deaths from 27th October 1977 to 25th March 1980 (inclusive)

Range of net value		*Gross equivalent*			
£	£	£			£
25,000 to	29,500	25,000	plus £10/9	for each £1 over	25,000
29,500 to	33,750	30,000	plus £20/17	for each £1 over	29,500
33,750 to	37,750	35,000	plus £5/4	for each £1 over	33,750
37,750 to	45,250	40,000	plus £4/3	for each £1 over	37,750
45,250 to	52,250	50,000	plus £10/7	for each £1 over	45,250
52,250 to	58,750	60,000	plus £20/13	for each £1 over	52,250
58,750 to	70,750	70,000	plus £5/3	for each £1 over	58,750
70,750 to	81,750	90,000	plus £20/11	for each £1 over	70,750
81,750 to	91,750	110,000	plus £2	for each £1 over	81,750
91,750 to	105,250	130,000	plus £20/9	for each £1 over	91,750
105,250 to	245,250	160,000	plus £5/2	for each £1 over	105,250
245,250 to	420,250	510,000	plus £20/7	for each £1 over	245,250
420,250 to	720,250	1,010,000	plus £10/3	for each £1 over	420,250
Over £720,250		2,010,000	plus £4	for each £1 over	720,250

TABLE 2D

Grossing table for lifetime transfers made from 27th October 1977 to 25th March 1980 (inclusive)

Range of net value		*Gross equivalent*			
£	£	£			£
25,000 -	29,750	25,000 plus	£20/19	for each £1 over	25,000
29,750 -	34,375	30,000 plus	£40/37	for each £1 over	29,750
34,375 -	38,875	35,000 plus	£10/9	for each £1 over	34,375
38,875 -	47,625	40,000 plus	£8/7	for each £1 over	38,875
47,625 -	56,125	50,000 plus	£20/17	for each £1 over	47,625
56,125 -	64,375	60,000 plus	£40/33	for each £1 over	56,125
64,375 -	80,375	70,000 plus	£5/4	for each £1 over	64,375
80,375 -	95,875	90,000 plus	£40/31	for each £1 over	80,375
95,875 -	110,375	110,000 plus	£40/29	for each £1 over	95,875
110,375 -	129,875	130,000 plus	£20/13	for each £1 over	110,375
129,875 -	158,625	160,000 plus	£40/23	for each £1 over	129,875
158,625 -	183,625	210,000 plus	£2	for each £1 over	158,625
183,625 -	206,125	260,000 plus	£20/9	for each £1 over	183,625
206,125 -	286,125	310,000 plus	£5/2	for each £1 over	206,125
286,125 -	461,125	510,000 plus	£20/7	for each £1 over	286,125
461,125 -	761,125	1,010,000 plus	£10/3	for each £1 over	461,125
Over 761,125		2,010,000 plus	£4	for each £1 over	761,125

TABLE 3A

Scale of rates in respect of transfers made on (or within 3 years of) deaths from 26th March 1980 to 8th March 1982 (inclusive)

Range of cumulation		*Cumulative tax to bottom of range*	*Rate of tax on value within range*
£	£	£	%
Exceeds 50,000 but not	60,000	NIL	30
Exceeds 60,000 but not	70,000	3,000	35
Exceeds 70,000 but not	90,000	6,500	40
Exceeds 90,000 but not	110,000	14,500	45
Exceeds 110,000 but not	130,000	23,500	50
Exceeds 130,000 but not	160,000	33,500	55
Exceeds 160,000 but not	510,000	50,000	60
Exceeds 510,000 but not	1,010,000	260,000	65
Exceeds 1,010,000 but not	2,010,000	585,000	70
Over 2,010,000		1,285,000	75

TABLE 3B

Scale of rates in respect of lifetime transfers made from 26th March 1980 to 9th March 1981 (inclusive)

Range of cumulation		*Cumulative tax to bottom of range*	*Rate of tax on value within range*
£	£	£	%
Exceeds 50,000 but not	60,000	NIL	15
Exceeds 60,000 but not	70,000	1,500	17.5
Exceeds 70,000 but not	90,000	3,250	20
Exceeds 90,000 but not	110,000	7,250	22.5
Exceeds 110,000 but not	130,000	11,750	27.5
Exceeds 130,000 but not	160,000	17,250	35
Exceeds 160,000 but not	210,000	27,750	42.5
Exceeds 210,000 but not	260,000	49,000	50
Exceeds 260,000 but not	310,000	74,000	55
Exceeds 310,000 but not	510,000	101,500	60
Exceeds 510,000 but not	1,010,000	221,500	65
Exceeds 1,010,000 but not	2,010,000	546,500	70
Over 2,010,000		1,246,500	75

TABLE 3C

Grossing table for use on deaths from 26th March 1980 to 8th March 1982 (inclusive)

Range of net value		*Gross equivalent*		
£	£	£		£
50,000 to	57,000	50,000 plus £10/7	for each £1 over	50,000
57,000 to	63,500	60,000 plus £20/13	for each £1 over	57,000
63,500 to	75,500	70,000 plus £5/3	for each £1 over	63,500
75,500 to	86,500	90,000 plus £20/11	for each £1 over	75,500
86,500 to	96,500	110,000 plus £2	for each £1 over	86,500
96,500 to	110,000	130,000 plus £20/9	for each £1 over	96,500
110,000 to	250,000	160,000 plus £5/2	for each £1 over	110,000
250,000 to	425,000	510,000 plus £20/7	for each £1 over	250,000
425,000 to	725,000	1,010,000 plus £10/3	for each £1 over	425,000
Over 725,000		2,010,000 plus £4	for each £1 over	725,000

TABLE 3D

Grossing table for lifetime transfers made from 26th March 1980 to 9th March 1981 (inclusive)

Range of net value		*Gross equivalent*			
£	£	£			£
50,000 -	58,500	50,000	plus £20/17	for each £1 over	50,000
58,500 -	66,750	60,000	plus £40/33	for each £1 over	58,500
66,750 -	82,750	70,000	plus £5/4	for each £1 over	66,750
82,750 -	98,250	90,000	plus £40/31	for each £1 over	82,750
98,250 -	112,750	110,000	plus £40/29	for each £1 over	98,250
112,750 -	132,250	130,000	plus £20/13	for each £1 over	112,750
132,250 -	161,000	160,000	plus £40/23	for each £1 over	132,250
161,000 -	186,000	210,000	plus £2	for each £1 over	161,000
186,000 -	208,500	260,000	plus £20/9	for each £1 over	186,000
208,500 -	288,500	310,000	plus £5/2	for each £1 over	208,500
288,500 -	463,500	510,000	plus £20/7	for each £1 over	288,500
463,500 -	763,500	1,010,000	plus £10/3	for each £1 over	463,500
Over 763,500		2,010,000	plus £4	for each £1 over	763,500

TABLE 4B

Scale of rates in respect of lifetime transfers made from 10th March 1981 to 8th March 1982 (inclusive)

Range of cumulation			*Cumulative tax to bottom of range*	*Rate within range*
	£	£	£	%
Exceeds	50,000 but not	60,000	NIL	15
Exceeds	60,000 but not	70,000	1,500	17.5
Exceeds	70,000 but not	90,000	3,250	20
Exceeds	90,000 but not	110,000	7,250	22.5
Exceeds	110,000 but not	130,000	11,750	25
Exceeds	130,000 but not	160,000	16,750	30
Exceeds	160,000 but not	510,000	25,750	35
Exceeds	510,000 but not	1,010,000	148,250	40
Exceeds	1,010,000 but not	2,010,000	348,250	45
Over 2,010,000			798,250	50

TABLE 4D

Grossing table for lifetime transfers made from 10th March 1981 to 8th March 1982 (inclusive)

Range of net value £	£	*Gross equivalent* £		£		£
50,000 -	58,500	50,000	plus 20/17	for each £1 over		50,000
58,500 -	66,750	60,000	plus 40/33	for each £1 over		58,500
66,750 -	82,750	70,000	plus 5/4	for each £1 over		66,750
82,750 -	98,250	90,000	plus 40/31	for each £1 over		82,750
98,250 -	113,250	110,000	plus 4/3	for each £1 over		98,250
113,250 -	134,250	130,000	plus 10/7	for each £1 over		113,250
134,250 -	361,750	160,000	plus 20/13	for each £1 over		134,250
361,750 -	661,750	510,000	plus 5/3	for each £1 over		361,750
661,750 -	1,211,750	1,010,000	plus 20/11	for each £1 over		661,750
Over 1,211,750		2,010,000	plus 2	for each £1 over		1,211,750

For death rates during this period see tables 3A & 3C

TABLE 5A

Scale of rates in respect of transfers made on (or within 3 years of) deaths from 9th March 1982 to 14th March 1983 (inclusive)

Range of cumulation £		£	*Cumulative tax at bottom of range* £	*Rate of tax on value within range* %
Exceeds	55,000 but not	75,000	NIL	30
Exceeds	75,000 but not	100,000	6,000	35
Exceeds	100,000 but not	130,000	14,750	40
Exceeds	130,000 but not	165,000	26,750	45
Exceeds	165,000 but not	200,000	42,500	50
Exceeds	200,000 but not	250,000	60,000	55
Exceeds	250,000 but not	650,000	87,500	60
Exceeds	650,000 but not	1,250,000	327,500	65
Exceeds	1,250,000 but not	2,500,000	717,500	70
Over 2,500,000			1,592,500	75

TABLE 5B

Scale of rates in respect of lifetime transfers made from 9th March 1982 to 14th March 1983 (inclusive)

Range of cumulation			*Cumulative tax at bottom of range*	*Rate of tax on value within range*
	£	£	£	%
Exceeds	55,000 but not	75,000	NIL	15
Exceeds	75,000 but not	100,000	3,000	17.5
Exceeds	100,000 but not	130,000	7,375	20
Exceeds	130,000 but not	165,000	13,375	22.5
Exceeds	165,000 but not	200,000	21,250	25
Exceeds	200,000 but not	250,000	30,000	30
Exceeds	250,000 but not	650,000	45,000	35
Exceeds	650,000 but not	1,250,000	185,000	40
Exceeds	1,250,000 but not	2,500,000	425,000	45
Over 2,500,000			987,500	50

TABLE 5C

Grossing table for use on deaths from 9th March 1982 to 14th March 1983 (inclusive)

Range of net value		*Gross equivalent*				
£	£	£		£		£
55,000 -	69,000	55,000	plus	10/7	for each £ over	55,000
69,000 -	85,250	75,000	plus	20/13	for each £ over	69,000
85,250 -	103,250	100,000	plus	5/3	for each £ over	85,250
103,250 -	122,500	130,000	plus	20/11	for each £ over	103,250
122,500 -	140,000	165,000	plus	2	for each £ over	122,500
140,000 -	162,500	200,000	plus	20/9	for each £ over	140,000
162,500 -	322,500	250,000	plus	5/2	for each £ over	162,500
322,500 -	532,500	650,000	plus	20/7	for each £ over	322,500
532,500 -	907,500	1,250,000	plus	10/3	for each £ over	532,500
Over 907,500		2,500,000	plus	4	for each £ over	907,500

TABLE 5D

Grossing table for lifetime transfers made from 9th March 1982 to 14th March 1983 (inclusive)

Range of net value		*Gross equivalent*			
£	£	£			£
55,000 -	72,000	55,000	plus £20/17	for each £1 over	55,000
72,000 -	92,625	75,000	plus £40/33	for each £1 over	72,000
92,625 -	116,625	100,000	plus £5/4	for each £1 over	92,625
116,625 -	143,750	130,000	plus £40/31	for each £1 over	116,625
143,750 -	170,000	165,000	plus £4/3	for each £1 over	143,750
170,000 -	205,000	200,000	plus £10/7	for each £1 over	170,000
205,000 -	465,000	250,000	plus £20/13	for each £1 over	205,000
465,000 -	825,000	650,000	plus £5/3	for each £1 over	465,000
825,000 -	1,512,500	1,250,000	plus £20/11	for each £1 over	825,000
Over 1,512,500		2,500,000	plus £2	for each £1 over	1,512,500

TABLE 6A

Scale of rates in respect of lifetime transfers made from 15th March 1983 to 12th March 1984 (inclusive)

Range of cumulation			*Cumulative tax at bottom of range*	*Rate of tax on value within range*
	£	£	£	%
Exceeds	60,000 but not	80,000	NIL	30
Exceeds	80,000 but not	110,000	6,000	35
Exceeds	110,000 but not	140,000	16,500	40
Exceeds	140,000 but not	175,000	28,500	45
Exceeds	175,000 but not	220,000	44,250	50
Exceeds	220,000 but not	270,000	66,750	55
Exceeds	270,000 but not	700,000	94,250	60
Exceeds	700,000 but not	1,325,000	352,250	65
Exceeds	1,325,000 but not	2,650,000	758,500	70
Over 2,650,000			1,686,000	75

TABLE 6B

Scale of rates in respect of lifetime transfers made from 15th March 1983 to 12th March 1984 (inclusive)

Range of cumulation			*Cumulative tax at bottom of range*	*Rate of tax on value within range*
	£	£	£	%
Exceeds	60,000 but not	80,000	NIL	15
Exceeds	80,000 but not	110,000	3,000	17.5
Exceeds	110,000 but not	140,000	8,250	20
Exceeds	140,000 but not	175,000	14,250	22.5
Exceeds	175,000 but not	220,000	22,125	25
Exceeds	220,000 but not	270,000	33,375	30
Exceeds	270,000 but not	700,000	48,375	35
Exceeds	700,000 but not	1,325,000	198,875	40
Exceeds	1,325,000 but not	2,650,000	448,875	45
Over 2,650,000			1,045,125	50

TABLE 6C

Grossing table for use on deaths from 15th March 1983 to 12th March 1984 (inclusive)

Range of net value		*Gross equivalent*				
£	£	£		£		£
60,000 -	74,000	60,000	plus	10/7	of each £ over	60,000
74,000 -	93,500	80,000	plus	20/13	of each £ over	74,000
93,500 -	111,500	110,000	plus	5/3	of each £ over	93,500
111,500 -	130,750	140,000	plus	20/11	of each £ over	111,500
130,750 -	153,250	175,000	plus	2	of each £ over	130,750
153,250 -	175,750	220,000	plus	20/9	of each £ over	153,250
175,750 -	347,750	270,000	plus	5/2	of each £ over	175,750
347,750 -	566,500	700,000	plus	20/7	of each £ over	347,750
566,500 -	964,000	1,325,000	plus	10/3	of each £ over	566,500
Over 964,000		2,650,000	plus	4	of each £ over	964,000

TABLE 6D

Grossing table for lifetime transfers made from 15th March 1983 to 12th March 1984 (inclusive)

Range of net value		*Gross equivalent*		
£	£	£	£	£
60,000 -	77,000	60,000 plus 20/17	for each £ over	60,000
77,000 -	101,750	80,000 plus 40/33	for each £ over	77,000
101,750 -	125,750	110,000 plus 5/4	for each £ over	101,750
125,750 -	152,875	140,000 plus 40/31	for each £ over	125,750
152,875 -	186,625	175,000 plus 4/3	for each £ over	152,875
186,625 -	221,625	220,000 plus 10/7	for each £ over	186,625
221,625 -	501,125	270,000 plus 20/13	for each £ over	221,625
501,125 -	876,125	700,000 plus 5/3	for each £ over	501,125
876,125 -	1,604,875	1,325,000 plus 20/11	for each £ over	876,125
Over 1,604,875		2,650,000 plus 2	for each £ over	1,604,875

TABLE 7A

Scale of rates in respect of transfers made on (or within 3 years of) deaths from 13th March 1984 to 5th April 1985 (inclusive)

Range of cumulation		*Cumulative tax to bottom of range*	*Rate of tax on value within range*
£	£	£	%
Exceeds 64,000	but not 85,000	NIL	30
Exceeds 85,000	but not 116,000	6,300	35
Exceeds 116,000	but not 148,000	17,150	40
Exceeds 148,000	but not 185,000	29,950	45
Exceeds 185,000	but not 232,000	46,600	50
Exceeds 232,000	but not 285,000	70,100	55
Exceeds 285,000		99,250	60

TABLE 7B

Scale of rates in respect of lifetime transfers made from 13th March 1984 to 5th April 1985 (inclusive)

Range of cumulation		*Cumulative tax to bottom of range*	*Rate of tax on value within range*
£	£	£	%
Exceeds 64,000	but not 85,000	NIL	15
Exceeds 85,000	but not 116,000	3,150	17.5
Exceeds 116,000	but not 148,000	8,575	20
Exceeds 148,000	but not 185,000	14,975	22.5
Exceeds 185,000	but not 232,000	23,300	25
Exceeds 232,000	but not 285,000	35,050	27.5
Exceeds 285,000		49,625	30

TABLE 7C

Grossing table for use on deaths from 13th March 1984 to 5th April 1985 (inclusive)

Range of net value £	£	*Gross equivalent* £		£
64,000 to	78,700	64,000 plus 10/7	for each £ over	64,000
78,700 to	98,850	85,000 plus 20/13	for each £ over	78,700
98,850 to	118,050	116,000 plus 5/3	for each £ over	98,850
118,050 to	138,400	148,000 plus 20/11	for each £ over	118,050
138,400 to	161,900	185,000 plus 2	for each £ over	138,400
161,900 to	185,750	232,000 plus 20/9	for each £ over	161,900
Over 185,750		285,000 plus 5/2	for each £ over	185,750

TABLE 7D

Grossing table for lifetime transfers made from 13th March 1984 to 5th April 1985 (inclusive)

Range of net value £	£	*Gross equivalent* £		£
64,000 to	81,850	64,000 plus 20/17	for each £ over	64,000
81,850 to	107,425	85,000 plus 40/33	for each £ over	81,850
107,425 to	133,025	116,000 plus 5/4	for each £ over	107,425
133,025 to	161,700	148,000 plus 40/31	for each £ over	133,025
161,700 to	196,950	185,000 plus 4/3	for each £ over	161,700
196,950 to	235,375	232,000 plus 40/29	for each £ over	196,950
Over 235,375		285,000 plus 10/7	for each £ over	235,375

TABLE 8A

Scale of rates in respect of transfers made on (or within 3 years of) deaths from 6th April 1985 to 17 March 1986 (inclusive)

Range of cumulation £	£	*Cumulative tax to bottom of range* £	*Rate of tax on value within range* %
Exceeds 67,000 but not	89,000	NIL	30
Exceeds 89,000 but not	122,000	6,600	35
Exceeds 122,000 but not	155,000	18,150	40
Exceeds 155,000 but not	194,000	31,350	45
Exceeds 194,000 but not	243,000	48,900	50
Exceeds 243,000 but not	299,000	73,400	55
Exceeds 299,000		104,200	60

TABLE 8B

Scale of rates in respect of lifetime transfers made from 6th April 1985 to 17th March 1986 (inclusive)

Range of cumulation		*Cumulative tax to bottom of range*	*Rate of tax on value within range*
£	£	£	%
Exceeds 67,000	but not 89,000	NIL	15
Exceeds 89,000	but not 122,000	3,300	17.5
Exceeds 122,000	but not 155,000	9,075	20
Exceeds 155,000	but not 194,000	15,675	22.5
Exceeds 194,000	but not 243,000	24,450	25
Exceeds 243,000	but not 299,000	36,700	27.5
Exceeds 299,000		52,100	30

TABLE 8C

Grossing table for use on deaths from 6th April 1985 to 17th March 1986 (inclusive)

Range of net value		*Gross equivalent*			
£	£	£			£
67,000 to	82,400	67,000	plus 10/7	for each £ over	67,000
82,400 to	103,850	89,000	plus 20/13	for each £ over	82,400
103,850 to	123,650	122,000	plus 5/3	for each £ over	103,850
123,650 to	145,100	155,000	plus 20/11	for each £ over	123,650
145,100 to	169,600	194,000	plus 2	for each £ over	145,100
169,600 to	194,800	243,000	plus 20/9	for each £ over	169,600
Over 194,800		299,000	plus 5/2	for each £ over	194,800

TABLE 8D

Grossing table for lifetime transfers made from 6th April 1985 to 17th March 1986 (inclusive)

Range of net value		*Gross equivalent*			
£	£	£			£
67,000 to	85,700	67,000	plus 20/17	for each £ over	67,000
85,700 to	112,925	89,000	plus 40/33	for each £ over	85,700
112,925 to	139,325	122,000	plus 5/4	for each £ over	112,925
139,325 to	169,550	155,000	plus 40/31	for each £ over	139,325
169,550 to	206,300	194,000	plus 4/3	for each £ over	169,550
206,300 to	246,900	243,000	plus 40/29	for each £ over	206,300
Over 246,900		299,000	plus 10/7	for each £ over	246,900

APPENDIX II: INHERITANCE TAX RATES

TABLE 9A

Scale of rates in respect of transfers made on or within seven years of death from 18th March 1986 to 16th March 1987 (inclusive)

Range of cumulation	*Cumulative tax to bottom of range*	*Rate of tax on value within range*
£ £	£	%
Exceeds 71,000 but not 95,000	NIL	30
Exceeds 95,000 but not 129,000	7,200	35
Exceeds 129,000 but not 164,000	19,100	40
Exceeds 164,000 but not 206,000	33,100	45
Exceeds 206,000 but not 257,000	52,000	50
Exceeds 257,000 but not 317,000	77,500	55
Exceeds 317,000	110,500	60

TABLE 9B

Scale of rates of tax for transfers taxed at half of death rates from 18th March 1986 to 16th March 1987 (inclusive)

Range of cumulation	*Cumulative tax to bottom of range*	*Rate of tax on value within range*
£ £	£	%
Exceeds 71,000 but not 95,000	NIL	15
Exceeds 95,000 but not 129,000	3,600	17.5
Exceeds 129,000 but not 164,000	9,550	20
Exceeds 164,000 but not 206,000	16,550	22.5
Exceeds 206,000 but not 257,000	26,000	25
Exceeds 257,000 but not 317,000	38,750	27.5
Exceeds 317,000	55,250	30

TABLE 9C

Grossing table for transfers on deaths from 18th March 1986 to 16th March 1987 (inclusive)

Range of net value	*Gross equivalent*	
£ £	£	£
71,000 to 87,800	71,000 plus £10/7	for each £1 over 71,000
87,800 to 109,900	95,000 plus £20/13	for each £1 over 87,800
109,900 to 130,900	129,000 plus £5/3	for each £1 over 109,900
130,900 to 154,000	164,000 plus £20/11	for each £1 over 130,900
154,000 to 179,500	206,000 plus £2	for each £1 over 154,000
179,500 to 206,500	257,000 plus £20/9	for each £1 over 179,500
Over 206,500	317,000 plus £5/2	for each £1 over 206,500

TABLE 9D

Grossing table for transfers taxed at half of death rates from 18th March 1986 to 16th March 1987 (inclusive)

Range of net value		*Gross equivalent*	
£	£	£	£
71,000 to	91,400	71,000 plus £20/17 for each £1 over	71,000
91,400 to	119,450	95,000 plus £40/33 for each £1 over	91,400
119,450 to	147,450	129,000 plus £5/4 for each £1 over	119,450
147,450 to	180,000	164,000 plus £40/31 for each £1 over	147,450
180,000 to	218,250	206,000 plus £4/3 for each £1 over	180,000
218,250 to	261,750	257,000 plus £40/29 for each £1 over	218,250
Over 261,750		317,000 plus £10/7 for each £1 over	261,750

TABLE 10A

Scale of rates in respect of transfers made on or within seven years of death from 17th March 1987 to 14th March 1988 (inclusive)

Range of cumulation		*Cumulative tax to bottom of range*	*Rate of tax on value within range*
£	£	£	%
Exceeds 90,000	but not 140,000	NIL	30
Exceeds 140,000	but not 220,000	15,000	40
Exceeds 220,000	but not 330,000	47,000	50
Exceeds 330,000		102,000	60

TABLE 10B

Scale of rates of tax for transfers taxed at half of death rates from 17th March 1987 to 14th March 1988 (inclusive)

Range of cumulation		*Cumulative tax to bottom of range*	*Rate of tax on value within range*
£	£	£	%
Exceeds 90,000	but not 140,000	NIL	15
Exceeds 140,000	but not 220,000	7,500	20
Exceeds 220,000	but not 330,000	23,500	25
Exceeds 330,000		51,000	30

TABLE 10C

Grossing table for transfers on deaths between 17th March 1987 to 14th March 1988 (inclusive)

Range of net value		*Gross equivalent*	
£	£	£	£
90,000 to 125,000		90,000 plus £10/7 for each £1 over	90,000
125,000 to 173,000		140,000 plus £5/3 for each £1 over	125,400
173,000 to 228,000		220,000 plus £2 for each £1 over	173,450
Over 228,000		330,000 plus £5/2 for each £1 over	228,450

TABLE 10D

Grossing table for transfers taxed at half of death rates from 17th March 1987 to 14th March 1988 (inclusive)

Range of net value		*Gross equivalent*	
£	£	£	£
90,000 to 132,500		90,000 plus £20/17 for each £1 over	90,000
132,500 to 196,500		140,000 plus £5/4 for each £1 over	132,500
196,500 to 279,000		220,000 plus £4/3 for each £1 over	196,500
Over 279,000		330,000 plus £10/7 for each £1 over	279,000

TABLE 11A

Scale of rates in respect of transfers made on or within seven years before death from 15th March 1988

Range of cumulation	*Cumulative tax*	*Rate of tax %*
Exceeds £110,000	£NIL	40

TABLE 11B

Scale of rates of tax for transfers taxed at half of death rates from 15th March 1988

Range of cumulation	*Cumulative tax*	*Rate of tax %*
Exceeds £110,000	£NIL	20

TABLE 11C

Grossing table for transfers on deaths on or after 15th March 1988

Range of net value	*Gross equivalent*
Over £110,000	£110,000 plus £5/3 for each £1 over £110,000

TABLE 11D

Grossing table for transfers taxed at half of death rates from 15th March 1988

Range of net value	*Gross equivalent*
Over £110,000	£110,000 plus £5/4 for each £1 over £110,000

CHAPTER 7

Foreign Domicile

7.01 When a person dies domiciled outside England and Wales, the practice in making a grant of representation is governed by Rule 30. The normal rules as to priority of entitlement to a grant are not applicable except in certain cases (Rule 28(2)). Where the deceased died domiciled in any of the countries to which the Colonial Probates Acts 1892 and 1927 have been applied (see para. 13.08), it may not be necessary to obtain a separate English grant, and consideration should be given to obtaining representation in England by the simpler and less costly method of applying for the resealing of the foreign grant (see paras. 13.06ff). A grant cannot be made to a person disqualified by English law, such as a minor.

Evidence of foreign law

7.02 In making application for a grant in England and Wales, it may be necessary to refer to a foreign system of law for the purpose of:

(a) establishing the validity of any testamentary document left by the deceased;

(b) showing that the applicant is entitled to the grant,

and affidavit evidence or notarial evidence as to such law may be required in respect of either or both of these matters. Rule 19 provides:

> "Where evidence as to the law of any country or territory outside England and Wales is required on any application for a grant, the registrar may accept—
>
> (a) an affidavit from any person whom, having regard to the particulars of his knowledge or experience given in the affidavit, he regards as suitably qualified to give expert evidence of the law in question; or
>
> (b) a certificate by, or an act before, a notary practising in the country or territory concerned."

ADMISSIBILITY TO PROOF OF WILLS OF PERSONS DYING DOMICILED OUT OF ENGLAND AND WALES

(1) Deaths before 1st January 1964

7.03 Subject to the four exceptions referred to in the following paragraphs, the general rule is that the will of a testator dying domiciled out of England and Wales is admissible to proof in the English court if it has been accepted as a valid testamentary document by the court having jurisdiction at the place of his domicile at the time of his death (*Deshais* (1865) 4 Sw. Tr. 13; 34 L.J. 58 and *Re Yahuda* [1956] P.388), or at the time when it was executed. (In cases of death on or after 1st January 1964, this general rule is modified by the provisions of the Wills Act 1963—see paras. 2.101ff.)

Exception (1)—Will disposing of immovable estate in England or Wales

7.04 Whatever the domicile of the testator, a will is not valid to pass immovable estate in England or Wales unless it has been executed in the manner prescribed by the Wills Act 1837. (In cases of deaths on or after 1st January 1964, this rule is also modified by the Wills Act 1963.) A will executed in accordance with English law which disposes of immovables in England or Wales, may be admitted to proof and a grant made limited to the immovables, notwithstanding that the will may be invalid by the law of the domicile of the testator.

Exception (2)—Wills of British subjects

7.05 Sections 1 and 2 of the Wills Act 1861 (Lord Kingdown's Act) provide that a will made before 1st Janaury 1964 by a British subject whatever his domicile, shall as regards to personal estate be held to be well executed for the purpose of being admitted to proof in England and Wales:

(a) if, having been made out of the United Kingdom, it is formally valid by the law of the place where it was made, or by the law of the place where the testator was domiciled when he made the will, or by the law then in force in that part of Her Majesty's dominions where the testator had his domicile of origin; or
(b) if, having been made within the United Kingdom, it is formally valid by the law then in force in that part of the United Kingdom where it was made.

The grant will be limited to the personal estate of the deceased unless the will is executed in English form. The Wills Act 1861 was repealed as from 1st January 1964, but without prejudice to the validity of wills made before that date, and was replaced by the Wills Act 1963.

Exception (3)—Wills which exercise a power of appointment

7.06 In the case of a testator dying domiciled outside England and Wales, that part of his will as exercises a power of appointment under an English settlement is admissible to proof in England and Wales provided that the will is executed as prescribed by the Wills Act 1837.

Exception (4)—Change of domicile

7.07 Section 3 of the Wills Act 1861 provides:

> "No will..............shall be held to be revoked or to have become invalid, nor shall the construction thereof be altered, by reason of any subsequent change of domicil of the person making the same."

Will proved in the court of the domicile

7.08 A will which has been accepted as a valid testamentary instrument by the court of the country in which the testator died domiciled is admissible to proof in England and Wales. It is normally necessary that the will should dispose of estate situated in England and Wales or contain a valid appointment of an executor (but see *Re Wayland* [1951] 2 All E.R. 1041). Where the documents produced include a sealed copy of the grant made in that court, this is usually accepted as sufficient evidence as to the validity of the will. If the documents produced do not clearly indicate that the will has been accepted as valid by the court of the domicile of the testator, an affidavit of law, or a certificate of law by a notary practising in the country or territory concerned, is required. For the procedure where the original will is not available, see paras 2.144 ff.

Wills in English or Welsh language and made in English form: domicile in certain countries

7.09 A will in the English or Welsh language and made in English form will normally be accepted as valid without further enquiry if the testator died domiciled in Northern Ireland, the Republic of Ireland, Australia, Canada or New Zealand. If, however, the testator died domiciled in any other British Commonwealth country, colony or protectorate, the validity of any will (if not already proved in the court of the domicile) must be established by other evidence. Where the testator died on or after 1st January 1964, see also Wills Act 1963, paras. 2.101 ff.

Will valid by the law of the domicile of the testator

7.10 A will executed in the manner required by the law of the place where the testator was domiciled at the date of his death or executed according to the law of the place of his domicile at the time of making the will is admissible to proof in England and Wales. It is normally necessary that the will should dispose of estate situate in England or Wales or contain a valid appointment of an executor. Affidavit or foreign notarial certificate evidence is required to establish the validity of the will and, if necessary, the authenticity of the copy will produced. Where the testator died on or after 1st January 1964, see also Wills Act 1963, paras. 2.101 ff.

(2) Death on or after 1st January 1964

7.11 In the case of persons dying on or after 1st January 1964, the rules as to recognising the validity of wills and codicils (whether made before or on or after that date) are contained in the Wills Act 1963 (see paras. 2.101 ff). A will (or other testamentary instrument or act) of a person, whatever his domicile, is to be treated as properly executed if its execution was in accordance with any of the alternatives contained in that Act.

PROCEDURE FOR PROVING WILLS OF PERSONS DYING DOMICILED OUT OF ENGLAND AND WALES

Testamentary documents in a foreign language

7.12 Wills and other documents in a foreign language must be accompanied by translations which should, if possible, be verified by the certificate of an English notary public or a British consular official. Where such English notarial or consular translation cannot be obtained, the matter should be referred to a registrar who may accept a translation made by some other sufficiently qualified person, together with an affidavit by the translator as to his qualifications and in verification of the translation.

7.13 Where the testator's will, written in English, has been lodged with a notary abroad, the notarially certified document lodged may contain a copy of the original will or it may merely contain a translation into a foreign language and a re-translation into English. In the latter case a photographic copy or a duly verified copy of the original will will be called for. In view of the decision in *In the Goods of Rule* (1878) 4 P.D. 76, however, if the applicant for the grant objects the registry cannot insist on the production of such photographic or other copy of the original will. If, however, it appears on the face of the document that the re-translation is or may be inaccurate, the registry will require that the re-translation be checked with the original. The copy of the will to be annexed to the grant is made in the registry by the photographic process. However, foreign wills are frequently accompanied by or attached to extraneous matter, and in such cases the Principal at the Principal Registry, or the district probate registrar, should be consulted as to whether an engrossment of the will only is required.

7.14 The original will, or official copy thereof, and not the translation into English, must be marked by the applicant for the grant and the person before whom the oath is sworn with their signatures.

Original will not available

7.15 If the original will is not available because it is in the custody of a foreign court or notary, a copy of it (under seal where possible) duly authenticated by the court or official having custody of the original is accepted (Rule 54(2)).

7.16 Where the original will has been proved in a foreign court its non-availability is normally accepted, but if an affidavit or certificate of law is required as to the validity of the will it should confirm that the original will is in the custody of the foreign court (or foreign notary, as the case may be), and also state that the copy will produced is acceptable in the foreign court as sufficient evidence of the contents of the original. (For form of affidavit of law, see after para. 7.29.) If neither the original will nor an official copy can be produced, an order is necessary for the admission to proof of a less formal copy (Rule 54). For the practice, see paras. 2.144–147.

ENTITLEMENT TO AN ENGLISH GRANT WHERE DECEASED DIED DOMICILED OUTSIDE ENGLAND AND WALES

(1) Executor

7.17 If a formally valid will of a testator, wherever domiciled, is in the English or Welsh language and appoints an executor, he will be accepted as having full rights of executorship and may obtain probate or appoint an attorney in that capacity, without any order being required. However, no expression in a foreign tongue purporting to mean "executor" is accepted as constituting an executor, but if such a will sets out the duties of a person named in it in terms sufficient to constitute him executor according to the tenor, he may obtain probate or appoint an attorney in that capacity without any order being required.

Renunciation by executor in the court of domicile

7.18 If an executor has renounced probate in the court of the country of domicile of the testator, his right to probate in England and Wales is not thereby extinguished. An English grant of probate may be made to him notwithstanding his renunciation elsewhere. If probate is granted to other executors, then unless he renounces probate in England and Wales also, power to obtain probate is reserved to him.

Executors and persons entrusted with administration by the court of domicile

7.19 There is no order of priority of right to a grant as between an executor and a person who has been entrusted by the court of domicile of the testator with the administration of the estate. A person entrusted who applies for a grant (whether direct or through an attorney) does not have to clear off executors. An executor may obtain probate or appoint an attorney to apply for a grant for his use and benefit notwithstanding that some other person has been entrusted with the administration of the estate by the court of the domicile (Rule 30(3)(a)).

(2) Person entrusted with administration by the court of domicile of the deceased

7.20 A grant may be made by order under Rule 30(1)(a) to the person entrusted with the administration of the estate of the deceased by the court having jurisdiction at the place where the deceased died domiciled, or to his attorney or attorneys. The grant, decree or order made by the foreign court must show that the person entrusted has been given powers of administration generally corresponding to those conferred upon a personal representative in England and Wales. The original grant, decree or order issued by the foreign court, or an officially certified copy (under seal, where possible) including an official copy of the will, if any, must be lodged. If a document is in a foreign language, a translation is required (see para. 7.12). If the copies of the grant and will are contained in separate documents they are acceptable only where it is clear that the documents relate to the same deceased person, and to each other. No other evidence of law is required to lead to the order, nor to set up validity of the will where it is clear from the documents that the court of the domicile has accepted the will as valid. The applicant for the order and the grant must depose to the facts of the case usually in the oath leading to the grant. The grant will be one of letters of administration, with or without the will, as the case may be.

(3) Person beneficially entitled to the estate by the law of domicile of the deceased

7.21 Where there is no person entrusted with the administration of the estate by the court having jurisdiction at the place where the deceased died domiciled, application may be made for an order that a grant be made under Rule 30(1)(b) to the person beneficially entitled to the estate by the law of the place where the deceased died domiciled. Where there is more than one person beneficially entitled, the registrar may order that the grant issue to such of them as he directs. Unless there is an order or certificate from the court of domicile establishing the beneficial interest(s) in the estate, the application for an order must be supported by affidavit, or notarially verified, evidence (see after para. 7.29) of the law of the country of domicile which must refer to the facts, state the law applicable and show who, according to such law, is beneficially entitled to the estate. The applicant for the grant must depose to the facts of the case, either in a separate affidavit or in the oath leading to the grant. The person or persons beneficially entitled may appoint an attorney, or attorneys, to apply for the order and the grant.

(4) Grant by order under Rule 30(1)(c)

7.22 If there is no person entrusted with the administration of the estate of the deceased by the court having jurisdiction at the place where he died domiciled, and if no person who is beneficially entitled to the estate by the law of the place where the deceased died domiciled wishes to apply for a grant, or in special circumstances, the registrar may make an order under Rule 30(1)(c) for a grant to be made to such person as he may direct. This type of order and grant may be appropriate where the law of the country in which the deceased died domiciled entitles a person who is not beneficially entitled to the estate to administer it, without having to obtain a grant or order from the court of domicile.

7.23 An applicant for an order and grant must furnish an affidavit setting out the facts of the case. If the law of the country of domicile entitles the applicant to administer the estate without first obtaining the authority of the court of domicile, evidence as to such law of the country of domicile is required (see after para 7.29). The affidavit, or certificate, should refer to the facts of the case and state who, according to the law of that country, is beneficially entitled to the estate and who is entitled to administer the estate. If the deceased left a will, the affidavit or certificate should also speak to the validity of it, unless the will has already been admitted to proof in the court of the country of domicile.

The whole, or substantially the whole, of the estate in England and Wales immovable

7.24 Where the whole, or substantially the whole, of the estate in England and Wales of a person who died domiciled outside England and Wales consists of immovable property, a grant in respect of the whole estate in England and Wales may be made to the person who would have been entitled to a grant if the deceased had died domiciled in England and Wales without any order being required (Rule 30(3)(b)). This is applicable whether the deceased died testate or intestate. The oath leading to the grant must include a statement of the domicile of the deceased, and state that the whole, or substantially the whole (as the case may be), of the estate in England and Wales consists of immovable property. Where it is asserted that substantially the whole of the estate in England and Wales consists of immovable property, brief details of the estate and the respective values of the immovable estate and the movable estate should be included in the oath.

APPLICATION FOR ORDER FOR GRANT UNDER RULE 30

7.25 An order for a grant under Rule 30 is obtained by way of *ex parte* application to a registrar of the Principal Registry or, if the grant is to be obtained at a district registry, to the appropriate district probate registrar. Where the application for the order is made prior to making application for the grant, the affidavits and documents (including the will, if any) necessary to lead to the order may be posted to or left with the Probate Department of the Principal Registry or the district probate registrar. When an application under Rule 30(1)(a) or (b) is straightforward, it may be made simultaneously with the application for the grant and all the papers necessary to lead to the making of the order and grant may be posted to or lodged with the appropriate registry, as above. Provided that the papers contain all the necessary information and are not defective, the order and grant will be made and the grant will be despatched in the usual way. Notice of any defect in the papers will be given by post or telephone.

Oath

7.26 In all cases where the deceased died domiciled outside England and Wales, the oath must state specifically the place of domicile (Rule 8(2)). Where (as in Canada, Australia or the United States of America) there are separate jurisdictions, the particular Province of State must be specified. The grant will only cover estate situated in England and Wales and the value of estate in any other country must be excluded in arriving at the figures to be inserted in the oath. Where an order has already been obtained for a grant to be made to the person entrusted with administration by the court of the domicile or beneficially entitled to the estate by the law of the domicile, the oath will normally be accepted if it merely describes the applicant as the person so entrusted or entitled, as the case may be, without actually reciting the order. However, in practice, it is always wise to recite the order in the oath.

Community of property

7.27 Where, by the law of the place of domicile of the deceased, community of property exists between the spouses, the following concluding paragraph to the oath leading to the grant should be used:

> "The whole of the estate in England and Wales in respect of which a grant is required amounts in value to the sum of £.................to the best of my knowledge, information and belief; and that £.............................(half) ....of that sum has accrued to the surviving spouse by reason of the existence of community of property under the law of the place of domicile of the said deceased at the date of the marriage."

The grant will be in respect of the whole estate, but a court fee will be payable in respect of half of it only.

Minority or life interests

7.28 Where a minority or life interest arises in any estate, except in the case of a grant of probate to an executor, the grant must normally be made to not less than two individuals or to a trust corporation, with or without an individual (Section 114(2), Supreme Court Act 1981). This applies even where the law of the domicile of the deceased allows a single individual to take a grant or to administer the estate. The statement in the oath as to minority and life interests must be based on the law appropriate to the circumstances of the case, including that of the domicile.

Inland Revenue Account

7.29 In all cases where the deceased died domiciled outside the United Kingdom, the Inland Revenue Account must be submitted to, and must be assessed by, the Capital Taxes Office before application is made for the grant (see para. 6.20). The Account must be accompanied by a statement of domicile (see para. 6.63). For the appropriate form of Inland Revenue Account, see para. 6.20.

FORM OF AFFIDAVIT AS TO FOREIGN LAW

[USUAL HEADING]

I, , of ,
make oath and say as follows:

1. I am conversant with the laws and constitution of..............and practise (*or* have practised for.........years) as an advocate in the courts of that country.
2. A single system of law as to the formal validity of testamentary documents is in force in...........

3. I have referred to the (official (*or* notarial) copy of the) last will and testament of C.D., of.............., deceased, bearing date the........... day of................. 19......, and now produced to me and marked "A"; and I say that the said will was made in conformity with and is valid by the aforesaid laws and constitution. (*Add where necessary*: Under the aforesaid laws and constitution the original will is deposited permanently at the (Wills Registry at..............) (office of E.F., a notary at...............) and cannot be removed from such custody. The aforesaid copy of the will is acceptable in the courts of.......................as evidence of the contents of the original will).
4. I am informed and verily believe (*set out facts leading to the deponent's conclusions*)*.
5. In the aforesaid circumstances I say that *G.H* and *I.J.* are according to the aforesaid laws and constitution the persons beneficially entitled to the estate of the said deceased [*and (if neither G.H. nor I.J. are to apply for the grant, but instead the person or persons entitled to administer the estate are to apply*) *K.L.* and *M.N.* are the persons jointly and severally (or jointly) entitled to administer the estate of the said deceased]).
6. That no life or minority interest arises in the said estate under the said laws and constitution.

Sworn, etc.

*(The relevant facts upon which the expert relies must be verified; if not by an order of the court of domicile, then usually by the applicant(s) for the order and the grant deposing to the same in an affidavit of facts or, in straightforward cases, in the oath.)

(*Note*: In a case of intestacy the above form may be adapted to fit the circumstances.)

Example forms of oath

(1) *Oath for grant of letters of administration, with or without will annexed, to* person entrusted *with administration by the court of the domicile of the deceased*

[USUAL HEADING]

I, A.B. of.................(occupation) make oath and say as follows:

1. That C.D. of..............deceased, died on the...........day of................. 19......, aged...........years, domiciled in .... intestate (*or* having made and duly executed his last will and testament).

2. [That I believe the paper writing now produced to and marked by me to contain a true and official copy of the last will and testament (with a codicil thereto) of the said deceased.]

3. That I am the person entrusted with the administration of the estate of the said deceased by the Court having jurisdiction at the place where the said deceased died domiciled.

4. That no life or minority interest arises in the said estate; that there was (no) land vested in the said deceased immediately before his death which was settled previously thereto [and not by his will (and codicil)] and which remained settled land notwithstanding his death.

5. That I will:
   (i) collect, get in and administer according to the law the real and personal estate of the said deceased;
   (ii) when required to do so by the Court, exhibit in the Court a full inventory of the said estate and render an account thereof to the Court; and
   (iii) when required to do so by the High Court, deliver up to that Court the grant of letters of administration.

6. That to the best of my knowledge, information and belief the gross estate in England and Wales passing under the grant amounts to £ and the net estate amounts to £ .

Sworn, etc.

(2) *Oath for grant of letters of administration, with or without will annexed, to* person beneficially entitled *to the estate by the law of the place where the deceased died domiciled*

[USUAL HEADING]

I, A.B. of..............(occupation) make oath and say as follows:

1. That C.D. of.................deceased, died on the...........day of.............. 19......, aged years, domiciled in.................intestate (*or* having made and duly executed his last will and testament).

2. [That I believe the paper writing now produced to and marked by me to contain a true and official copy of the last will and testament (with a codicil thereto) of the said deceased.]

3. That no one has been entrusted with the administration of the estate of the deceased by the court having jurisdiction at the place where he died domiciled.

4. That I am the person beneficially entitled to the estate of the said deceased by the law of the place where the said deceased died domiciled.

5. That no minority or life interest arises in the said estate: that there was (no) land vested in the said deceased immediately before his death which was settled previously thereto [and not by his will (and codicil)] and which remained settled land notwithstanding his death.

6.That I will:
   (i) collect, get in and administer according to law the real and personal estate of the said deceased;
   (ii) when required to do so by the Court, exhibit in the Court a full inventory of the said estate and render an account thereof to the Court; and
   (iii) when required to do so by the High Court, deliver up to that Court the grant of letters of administration.

7. That to the best of my knowledge, information and belief the gross estate in England and Wales passing under the grant amounts to £ and the net estate amounts to £

Sworn, etc.

(3) *Oath for grant of letters of administration, or letters of administration with will*, under Rule 30(1)(c) of the Non-Contentious Probate Rules 1987

[USUAL HEADING]

I, A.B., of.............., (occupation) make oath and say as follows:

1. That C.D., of.........................., deceased, died on the...........day of .... 19........., aged years, domiciled in................. intestate (*or* having made and duly executed his last will and testament).

2. [That I believe the paper writing now produced to and marked by me to contain the true and original (*or an official copy of the true and original*) last will and testament of the said deceased.]

3. (*Insert statements as to minority and life interests and settled land.)*

4. That on the..............day of.................19......, it was ordered by a Registrar of this Division that letters of administration (*with will annexed*) of the estate of the said deceased be granted to me under and by virtue of Rule 30(1)(c) of the Non-Contentious Probate Rules 1987.

5. That I will:

(i) collect, get in and administer according to the law the real and personal estate of the said deceased;

(ii) when required to do so by the Court, exhibit in the Court a full inventory of the said estate and render an account thereof to the Court; and

(iii) when required to do so by the High Court, deliver up to that Court the grant of letters of administation.

6. That to the best of my knowledge, information and belief the gross estate in England and Wales passing under the grant amounts to £ and the net estate amounts to £

Sworn, etc.

CHAPTER 8

Grants for use of Minors and Persons Mentally Incapable and to Attorneys

GRANTS FOR USE OF MINORS

8.01 The practice in the making of grants for the use and benefit of minors is governed by Rule 32. A grant may not issue to a person under the age of 18 years and a grant limited for the use and benefit of a minor remains in force until he attains the age of 18 years. A grant made to guardians of a minor ceases upon the death of such guardians. If all the minor beneficiaries are still under the age of 18 years another grant may be made to newly assigned guardians (see paras. 11.13 ff). If all the minor beneficiaries die without having attained the age of 18 years, a grant made for their use and benefit is dead, and the form of the subsequent grant is *de bonis non* (see para. 11.01 ff).

Guardians entitled in priority

8.02 Under Rule 32(1) priority of right to a grant for the use and benefit of a minor is given equally to both parents of the minor *jointly*, the statutory guardian, testamentary guardian and any guardian appointed by a court of competent jurisdiction.

Number of grantees

8.03 It is provided by Section 114(2) of the Supreme Court Act 1981, that whenever a minority or life interest arises under a will or intestacy, administration shall be granted either to a trust corporation with or without an individual, or to not less than two individuals unless it appears to the court to be expedient in all the circumstances to appoint an individual as sole administrator. Section 114(1) provides that a grant shall not be made to more than four persons in respect of the same part of the estate of a deceased person.

8.04 Where several minors are entitled, and they belong to different branches of a family, it is desirable, when practicable, that the applicants for the grant represent the several branches.

Minors and persons of full age equally entitled

8.05 Unless a registrar otherwise directs, a person of full age entitled to a grant is preferred as grantee to a guardian of a minor (Rule 27(5)). If it is desired that a grant be made to the guardians of a minor notwithstanding that there are persons of full age, the facts of the case must be referred to a registrar.

Limitation in grant

8.06 A grant made on behalf of one minor is usually limited "for his use and benefit and until he shall attain the age of 18 years". If there is more than one minor, the grant is usually limited "for their use and benefit until one of them shall attain the age of 18 years". The grant ceases when the minor, or one of them, attains his majority. A grant made on behalf of more than one minor does not cease if one of them dies under the age of 18 years.

Renunciation on behalf of minor

8.07 A minor executor's right to probate on attaining the age of 18 years may *not* be renounced by any person on his behalf (Rule 34(1)). A minor's right to administration (with or without will) may be renounced only by a person assigned as guardian under Rule 32(2) and authorised to renounce by a registrar (Rule 34(2)).

Sole, or sole surviving, executor a minor

8.08 It should be noted that in the case of a minor sole, or sole surviving, executor who has no interest in the residuary estate of the deceased, administration for his use and benefit until he attains the age of 18 years shall, unless a registrar otherwise directs, be granted to the person entitled to the residuary estate (Rule 32(1)). (Forms of oath after para. 8.24, nos. (1) and (2)).

One of the executors a minor

8.09 Where a minor is one of a number of executors, probate may be granted to the other or others not under disability, with power reserved of making a like grant to the minor on his attaining the age of 18 years (Rule 33(1)). If the other executor or executors who are not under disability renounce probate, or, on being cited to accept or refuse a grant, fail to make an effective application for a grant, administration (with will) for the use and benefit of the minor limited until he attains the age of 18 years may be granted under Rule 32 as allowed by Rule 33(2). A minor executor, on attaining full age, may then take a grant or renounce probate as he may wish.

Testamentary guardians

8.10 By section 4 of the Guardianship of Minors Act 1971, the father and mother of a (minor) child may, by deed or will, appoint any person to be guardian of the child after their death. A guardian so appointed must act jointly with the surviving parent. Where guardians are appointed by both parents they shall, after the death of the surviving parent, act jointly. The mother of an illegitimate child has the right to appoint a testamentary guardian (*Re A: S. v. A.* (1940) 164 L.T. 230), so may the natural father of such a child who is entitled to its custody under the Guardianship of Minors Act 1971, but, in this latter instance, the appointment is effective only if the father is entitled to the custody of the child immediately before his death. (Form of oath after paras. 8.24, nos. (2) and (4).)

Statutory guardian

8.11 Where a minor has only one lawful parent living, that parent is the statutory guardian and has a right to the grant without being assigned as guardian by the court. If such a parent is willing to take the grant he or she should, where the circumstances of the case require it, nominate a suitable person, preferably of kin to the minor, to act as co-administrator. (Forms of oath after para. 8.24, nos. (3) and (5).)

Guardians appointed by the court

8.12 Section 5(1) of the Guardianship of Minors Act 1971 provides:

> "Where a child has no parent, no guardian of the person, and no other person having parental rights with respect to him, the court, on the application of any person, may, if it thinks fit, appoint the applicant to be the guardian of the child."

Illegitimate child

8.13 The mother of an illegitimate child is not the statutory guardian of such child and if she wishes to apply for a grant on its behalf she must be assigned as guardian. Where the natural father of the minor is entitled to its custody by virtue of an order in force under Section 9 of the Guardianship of Minors Act 1971, he is, on the death of the mother, regarded as if he were the lawful father and statutory guardian of the minor (Section 14, Guardianship of Minors Act 1971).

Adoptive parents and "kin" by adoption

8.14 By virtue of the Children Act 1975 adoptive parents acquired all the rights of lawful parents. The relevant part of that Act was repealed, and replaced by, the Adoption Act 1976 on 1st January 1988. If a child has been adopted by one person only, the adoptive parent is not the statutory guardian, but the survivor of two adoptive parents is the statutory guardian of the child. Relationship by adoption did not previously constitute persons other than adoptive parents as next of kin of a child. However, the Children Act 1975 provided that an adopted child is to be treated in law as if it were the child of the adopter or adopters. Section 39 of the Adoption Act 1976 contains similar provisions. Particulars of the adoption order should be recited in the oath leading to the grant and it should also be confirmed in the oath that the order still subsists. A copy of the order or of the entry in the Adopted Children Register may be called for by the Court.

Assigned guardians

8.15 An order assigning a guardian or guardians to a minor is necessary in the following circumstances:

(1) Where the parents of the minor are unable or unwilling to act jointly in taking a grant on his behalf and there is no statutory or testamentary guardian or guardian appointed by a competent court, or if there is no such guardian able and willing to act.

(2) Where good cause is shown why the parents of the minor, or a statutory or testamentary guardian, or guardian appointed by a competent court, should be passed over.

Application for order assigning guardians

8.16 An order may be obtained by lodging an affidavit at the Probate Department at the Principal Registry, or at a district probate registry if it is proposed to apply for the grant at that registry. The affidavit should be sworn by the proposed guardian or guardians, and must set out the facts of the case, stating in particular whether both parents of the minor are living, and whether or not there is any statutory, testamentary or other lawfully appointed guardian, and the reason must be given if it is sought to pass over both parents or such a guardian. Renunciations and consents must be referred to. The affidavit should also state with whom each minor is residing, the age of each minor and relationship, if any, to the proposed guardians. (Forms of oath and affidavits after para. 8.24, nos. (6), (7) and (8).) Any supporting affidavits and other relevant documents should be lodged with the affidavit of facts.

8.17 If one guardian only is to be assigned for the purpose of taking a grant jointly with a person who is entitled to administration, such other person should furnish a signed consent as to his willingness to act with the proposed guardian.

Grants for use and benefit of minors in care under Child Care Act 1980

8.18 Section 3 of the Child Care Act 1980 provides that a local authority may resolve that all parental rights and duties shall vest in the authority with respect to any child in its care, in whose case it appears that his parents are dead, and that he has no guardian or custodian, or that his parent has abandoned him, or suffers from some disability rendering him incapable of caring for that child, or suffers from a mental disorder within the meaning of the Mental Health Act 1983 which renders him unfit to have care of the child, or is of such habits or mode of life as to be unfit to have care of the child, or has so consistently failed without reasonable cause to discharge the obligations of a parent as to be unfit to have the care of the child. For further details reference should be made to the text of Section 3 of the Act.

8.19 Section 5 of the Act provides that the resolution shall continue in force until the child attains the age of 18, unless the child is adopted or an order is made freeing the child for adoption, or a guardian is appointed under Section 5 of the Guardianship of Minors Act 1971, or an event mentioned in para. (*a*) or (*b*) of Section 25(1) of the Child Abduction and Custody Act 1985 occurs with respect to the child (see the Act for further details), or the resolution is rescinded by the local authority, or determined by order of a juvenile court.

8.20 Under the Public Trustee Rules 1912, as substitued by the Public Trustee (Custodian Trustee) Rules 1971 and amended by the Public Trustee (Custodian Trustee) Rules 1975, 1976, 1981, 1984 and 1987, certain local authorities are enabled to act as trust corporations. In all child "care" applications, whether made by the authority as a trust corporation or through its nominees, the local authority should apply for a registrar's order under Rule 32(2) assigning the authority itself as guardian of the child.

8.21 Where the local authority applies as a trust corporation, the oath to lead to the grant should, in addition to the usual recitals, state that the local authority is entitled to act as custodian trustee under the Public Trustee Act 1906 and thereby as a trust corporation as defined by Rule 2(1) of the Non-Contentious Probate Rules 1987, and that it has power to accept a grant. Copies of the resolution of the local authority assigning parental rights and of the resolution authorising the officer of the authority to apply on its behalf should be authenticated by the certificate of the Town Clerk, Chief Executive, Director of Administration or other appropriate officer and lodged with the application.

Minors domiciled out of England and Wales—Deceased died domiciled in England and Wales

8.22 If the deceased died domiciled in England and Wales, and all persons entitled to a grant are minors and are domiciled out of England and Wales, a grant will be made to the guardians lawfully constituted according to the law of the place of the domicile of the minors, or to the attorneys of such guardians. The right to guardianship must be proved by producing a copy of the document by which the guardians have been constituted, under the seal of the Court having jurisdiction at the place of the domicile of the minors. If guardians have not been so constituted, the right to guardianship must be proved by an affidavit, or by a certificate by a notary practising in the country or territory concerned, as to the law of the place of the domicile of the minors. An affidavit must be sworn to by someone suitably qualified (*e.g.* a barrister or advocate who is practising, or who has practised, in the Court of the domicile), and must give particulars of the deponent's knowledge or experience regarding the law in question and show that the deponent is conversant with such law. If the document, or affidavit or certificate does not make it clear that the guardianship provides for the custody of the property of the minors, an order assigning guardians to the minors will be necessary. The domicile of the minors must be sworn to in the oath leading to the grant.

Minors domiciled in England and Wales—Deceased died domiciled out of England and Wales

8.23 If the persons entitled to the grant are all minors and are domiciled in England and Wales, the guardianship is governed by English law, whatever the domicile of the deceased; but the entitlement to a grant will depend upon the law of the place of the domicile of the deceased (see Chapter 7). For the appropriate form of and assessment of Inland Revenue Account and statement of domicile, see paras. 6.13, 6.20, 6.62 and 6.63.

Wardship

8.24 After the making of a wardship order, and during the subsistence of such order, material decisions relating to the child or his property should not be taken without the concurrence of the judge or registrar dealing with the wardship. Accordingly, the directions of such judge or registrar should be taken when application is made for the assignment of guardians to a ward or for the making of a grant to any person for the use and benefit of a minor who is a ward of court.

EXAMPLE FORMS OF OATH FOR GUARDIANS

(1) *Sole executor and residuary legatee and devisee a minor—Oath for administration (with will) to both parents of minor*

[USUAL HEADING]

We, *A.B.* and *B.B.* both of ,
make oath and say as follows:

1. That we believe the paper writing now produced to and marked by us to contain the last will and testament of *C.B.* of deceased, who died on the day of 19 , aged years, domiciled in England and Wales.

2. That *D.B.* (grandson of the deceased) the sole executor and residuary legatee and devisee named in the said will is now a minor aged years.

3. That there is no testamentary or other lawfully appointed guardian of the said minor.

4. That a minority but no (*or* a) life interest arises in the estate.

5. That there was (no) land vested in the said deceased which was settled previously to his death (and not by his will) and which remained settled land notwithstanding his death.

6. That we are the lawful parents of the said minor.

7. That we will

(i) collect, get in and administer according to the law the real and personal estate of the said deceased for the use and benefit of the said minor and until he shall attain the age of 18 years;

(ii) when required to do so by the Court, exhibit in the Court a full inventory of the said estate and render an account thereof to the Court; and

(iii) when required to do so by the High Court, deliver up to that Court the letters of administration.

8. That to the best of our knowledge, information and belief the gross estate passing under the grant does not exceed/amounts to £ and that the net estate does not exceed/amounts to £ [and that this is not a case in which an Inland Revenue Account is required to be delivered]. (*See notes at paras. 6.04–09.*)

Sworn, etc.

(2) *Sole executor and residuary legatee and devisee a minor—Oath for administration (with will) to testamentary guardian appointed by same will and to his nominee.*

[USUAL HEADING]

We, *A.B*of ,
and *C.D*of ,
make oath and say as follows:

1. That we believe (*continue as in preceding form*).

2. That *E.F.* son of the deceased the sole executor and residuary legatee and devisee named in the said will is now a minor aged 15 years.

3. That the said deceased by his said will appointed me the said *A.B.* to be the guardian of the said minor.

4. That there is no statutory or other lawfully appointed guardian of the said minor.

5. (*Insert statements as to minority and life interests*).

6. (*Insert statement as to settled land*).

7. That I the said *A.B.* am the testamentary guardian of the said minor.

8. That I the said *C.D.* am the person nominated by an instrument in writing under the hand of the said *A.B.* dated the day of 19 , to be co-administrator with will of the estate of the said deceased.

9. That we will (*complete as in preceding form, including paragraph as to the value of estate etc*).

(3) *No executor named, or executors cleared off—Minor residuary legatee and devisee—Oath for administration (with will) to statutory guardian and nominee*

[USUAL HEADING]

We, *A.B.* of
and *G.R.* of
make oath and say as follows:

1. That we believe—(*continue as in form (1) above*).

2. *Clear off executor.*

3. That *C.B.*, spinster, niece of the said deceased the residuary legatee and devisee named in the said will is now a minor aged 17 years.

4. That there is no testamentary or other lawfully appointed guardian of the said minor.

5. (*Insert statements as to minority and life interests*).

6. (*Insert statement as to settled land*).

7. That I the said *A.B.* am the lawful mother and only surviving parent and the statutory guardian of the said minor.

8. That I the said *G.R.* am the person nominated by an instrument in writing under the hand of the said *A.B.* dated the day of 19 , to be co-administrator with will of the estate of the said deceased.

9. That we will (*Complete as in form (1) above, including paragraph as to value of estate etc*).

(4) *Minor only person entitled—Oath for administration to testamentary guardians of minor*

[USUAL HEADING]

We, *E.D.* of ,
and *H.D.* of ,
make oath and say as follows:

1. That *A.B.* of , deceased, died on the day of 19 , aged years domiciled in England and Wales, intestate, a widower (widow) leaving *B.B.* his (her) lawful child and only person entitled to his (her) estate who is now a minor aged years.

2. That there is no statutory or other lawfully appointed guardian of the said minor.

3. (*Insert statements as to minority and life interests*).

4. (*Insert statement as to settled land*).

5. That we are the testamentary guardians of the said minor duly appointed by the will of *C.B.* deceased, the lawful mother (father) of the said minor, probate of the said will having been granted at the Probate Registry on the day of 19 .

6. That we will (*complete as in form (1) above, including paragraph as to value of estate etc*).

(*Note*: The grant, or office copy thereof, in the estate of *C.B.* must be produced)

(5) *Minor only person entitled—Oath for administration to statutory guardian and his nominee*

[USUAL HEADING

We, *B.B.* of ,
and *F.D.* of ,
make oath and say as follows:

1. That *A.B.* of , deceased, died on the day of 19 , aged years domiciled in England and Wales, intestate, a widower (widow) without child leaving *C.B.* his (her) lawful grandchild and only person entitled to his (her) estate who is now a minor aged years.

2. That there is no testamentary or other lawfully appointed guardian of the said minor.

3. (*Insert statements as to minority and life interests*).

4. (*Insert statement as to settled land*).

5. That I the said *B.B.* am the lawful father (mother) and only surviving parent and the statutory guardian of the said minor.

6. That I the said *F.D.* am the person nominated in an instrument in writing under the hand of the said *B.B.* dated the day of 19 , to be co-administrator of the estate of the said intestate.

7. That we will (*complete as in form (1) above, including paragraph as to the value of estate etc.*).

(6) *Minor only person entitled—Oath for administration to assigned guardians*

[USUAL HEADING]

We, *E.D.* of ,
and *F.D.* of ,
make oath and say as follows:

1. That *A.B.* of , deceased died on the day of 19 , aged years domiciled in England and Wales, intestate, a bachelor (spinster) without issue or parent or any other person entitled in priority to share in the estate by virtue of any enactment leaving *B.B.* his (her) lawful** brother (sister) of the whole blood and only person entitled to his (her) estate who is now a minor aged years.

2. That there is no statutory, testamentary or other lawfully appointed guardian of the said minor.

3. (*Insert statements as to minority and life interests*).

4. (*Insert statement as to settled land*).

5. That we are the guardians duly assigned of the said minor by a Registrar's order dated the day of 19 , for the purpose of taking out letters of administration of the estate of the said intestate for the use and benefit of the said minor until he shall attain the age of 18 years.

6. That we will (*complete as in form (1) above, including paragraph as to the value of estate etc*).

(7) *Affidavit to lead registrar's order assigning guardians of minor*

[USUAL HEADING]

We, *A.B.* of ,
and *C.D.* of ,
make oath and say as follows:

1. That of , deceased, died on the day of 19 , domiciled in England and Wales intestate, a widow(er), leaving bachelor (spinster) his lawful and only child, and only person entitled to his estate, who is now a minor of the age of years.

2. That there is no statutory, testamentary or other lawfully appointed guardian of the said minor.

3. That we are the lawful [uncles] and two of the next of kin of the said minor, and [*if the deponents are not next of kin of the minor, recite the fact that the next of kin has renounced guardianship*] are ready and willing to undertake the guardianship of the said minor for the purpose of taking letters of administration of the estate of the said deceased, for the use and benefit of the said minor until he/she shall attain the age of 18 years.

4, That the said minor lives with and is in the care of at .

5. That the said minor is not a ward of court and no proceedings are pending for his/her adoption.

6. That the gross value of the estate of the deceased is £ and the net value of the said estate is £

7. That (*set out any other relevant facts relied on in support of the application*).

8. That we hereby apply for an order assigning us as guardians of the said minor for the purpose of taking letters of administration of the estate of the said deceased for the use and benefit of the said minor until he/she attains the age of 18 years.

Sworn. etc.

(8) *Affidavit to lead to registrar's order assigning guardians of a minor who has no living blood relative*

[USUAL HEADING]

We, *A.B.* of ,
and *C.D.* of ,
make oath and say as follows:

1. That *E.F.* of deceased, died on the day of 19 , domiciled in England and Wales, intestate, a widower, leaving *G.F.*, his lawful** son and only person entitled to his estate who is now a minor aged years.

2. That the said minor has no living blood relatives, and is now residing with and in the care of at

3. That there is no statutory, testamentary or other lawfully appointed guardian of the said minor.

4. That we are ready and willing to undertake the guardianship of the said minor for the purpose of taking out letters of administration of the estate of the said intestate for the use and benefit of the said minor and until he shall attain the age of 18 years.

(*For paragraphs 5, 6, 7 and 8 see form (7) above.*)

Sworn, etc.

**Where the intestate died on or after 4th April 1988 the relationship need not be lawful and the word "lawful" may be omitted.

GRANTS FOR USE OF PERSONS MENTALLY INCAPABLE

8.25 Where the person entitled to a grant is mentally incapable of managing his affairs, administration may be granted for his use and benefit during his incapacity. Rule 35 governs the making of such grants and provides:

"(1) Unless a registrar otherwise directs, no grant shall be made under this rule unless all persons entitled in the same degree as the incapable person referred to in paragraph (2) below have been cleared off.

(2) Where a registrar is satisfied that a person entitled to a grant is by reason of mental incapacity incapable of managing his affairs, administration for his use and benefit, limited until further representation be granted or in such other way as the registrar may direct, may be granted in the following order of priority—

(a) to the person authorised by the Court of Protection to apply for a grant;

(b) where there is no person so authorised, to the lawful attorney of the incapable person acting under a registered enduring power of attorney;

(c) where there is no such attorney entitled to act, or if the attorney shall renounce administration for the use and benefit of the incapable person, to the person entitled to the residuary estate of the deceased.

(3) Where a grant is required to be made to not less than two administrators, and there is only one person competent and willing to take a grant under the foregoing provisions of this rule, administration may, unless a registrar otherwise directs, be granted to such person jointly with any other person nominated by him.

(4) Notwithstanding the foregoing provisions of this rule, administration for the use and benefit of the incapable person may be granted to such two or more other persons as the registrar may by order direct.

(5) Notice of an intended application under this rule shall be given to the Court of Protection."

Other persons equally entitled with incapable person

8.26 Unless a registrar otherwise directs, a grant for the use of a person incapable of managing his affairs will not be made unless all other persons equally entitled with him are cleared off. If one of several executors is incapable, the other executors may obtain probate, and power will be reserved to the incapable executor to prove the will when he regains his capacity.

8.27 Where one of two executors is incapable administration (with will) may be granted to the attorney of the other limited until further representation be granted.

Number of grantees

8.28 Under Section 114(1) of the Supreme Court Act 1981, a grant of administration cannot be made to more than four persons in respect of the same part of the estate of a deceased person, and under Section 114(2) of the Act if a minority or life interest arises under the will or intestacy, administration shall be granted either to a trust corporation, with or without an individual, or to not less than two individuals unless it appears to the Court to be expedient in all the circumstances to appoint an individual as administrator.

8.29 Where a minority or life interest arises in the estate, and there is only one person authorised or entitled because of a registered enduring power of attorney to apply for a grant for the use and benefit of an incapable person, or only one such person willing to apply for a grant, that person may nominate his co-administrator.

Person authorised by order of the Court of Protection

8.30 Where the person entitled to a grant is mentally incapable of managing his affairs, the person authorised by order of the Court of Protection has priority of right to the grant. An official copy of the order must be lodged with the oath on the grant application. Such order is made under the provisions of the Mental Health Act 1983, and usually takes into account that some other person will be required under the Non-Contentious Probate Rules, as co-administrator, to apply for the grant with the person authorised, in the event of there being a minority or life interest in the estate. Where two grantees are necessary the person authorised now has power to nominate a co-administrator.

Attorney acting under a registered enduring power of attorney

8.31 Where no one has been authorised by the Court of Protection to apply for a grant (and this should be confirmed in the oath), the person next entitled to apply is a lawful attorney of the incapable person acting under an enduring power of attorney given under the Enduring Powers of Attorney Act 1985 and registered with the Court of Protection. The power of attorney sealed by the Court of Protection showing that it has been registered, or an office copy issued by the Court of Protection, must be produced on the application for the grant. Where two administrators are necessary, the attorney may nominate his co-administrator under Rule 35(3) if any other attorney is not competent or willing to take a grant.

Person entitled to the residuary estate of the deceased

8.32 Where no one has been authorised by the Court of Protection and there is no attorney acting under a registered enduring power of attorney or if such attorney has renounced administration for the use and benefit of the incapable person, a grant may be issued to the person entitled to the residuary estate of the deceased. The oath should confirm that no one has been authorised by the Court of Protection to apply for a grant and that there is no lawful attorney of the incapable person acting under a registered enduring power of attorney.

Grant to persons appointed by registrar's order

8.33 Under Rule 35(4) the registrar may by order direct that a grant of administration for the use and benefit of the incapable person be issued to such two or more persons as he may direct, whether or not anyone is entitled to apply for a grant under the preceding parts of Rule 35. Such an order will usually direct that the grant be limited until further representation be granted. An application for an order under Rule 35(4) should be made by affidavit of the proposed grantees, setting out the relevant facts. The affidavit and evidence of mental incapacity (see para. 8.35) should be left at the Probate Department at the Principal Registry, or with the district probate registrar of the appropriate district probate registry if the grant is to be applied for there.

Notice to Court of Protection

8.34 In cases of mental incapacity, where no person is authorised by the Court of Protection to apply for the grant, notice of the intended application must be given to the Court of Protection. Receipt of such notice will be acknowledged by the Court of Protection, and must be filed with the papers leading to the grant. The notice must be given by the solicitor acting for the proposed grantee, and must show the name, address and date of death of the deceased, the name and address of the proposed grantee with his relationship (if any) to the incapable person and the name and address of the latter. The notice should be addressed to "The Court of Protection, 25 Store Street, Bedford Square, London WC1E 7BP".

Evidence of mental incapacity

8.35 Where the person entitled is mentally incapable of managing his own affairs, and the applicant for the grant is not a person authorised by the Court of Protection to apply or a lawful attorney acting under a registered enduring power of attorney, evidence of incapacity must be furnished. If the incapable person is a patient who is resident in an institution, the registrar will normally accept a certificate from the responsible medical officer in the following terms:

(Name of Institution)

(Name of patient)

I certify that:

1. The above-named patient, who is now resident in this institution, is in my opinion by reason of mental disorder incapable of managing and administering his property and affairs.
2. In my opinion the above-named patient is unlikely to be fit to manage and administer his property and affairs within a period of three months.

Date............................ Signed.....................................

Responsible Medical Officer

If the responsible medical officer is unable to give such a certificate, the matter should be referred to the registrar for directions. Evidence of the incapacity of a person not a resident patient should be in the form of a certificate, in similar terms to that above, by the patient's doctor.

Passing over an incapable person

8.36 If it is sought to pass over an incapable person, as distinct from obtaining a grant for his use and benefit, application must be made for a "discretionary" grant under Section 116 of the Supreme Court Act 1981 (see paras. 11.20–24).

Oath

8.37 The oath leading to the grant must state that the person entitled to the grant "is now by reason of mental incapacity incapable of managing his own affairs". A Court of Protection order, or any other relevant order or registered enduring power of attorney must be referred to in the oath, and the order or power of attorney (or an official copy of it), must be lodged with the papers for the grant. The appropriate limitation (*e.g.* "for the use and benefit of *A.B.*, (the incapable person) and until further representation be granted") must also be included.

Recovery of incapable person

8.38 A grant made for the use and benefit of an incapable person and limited "during his incapacity" ceases upon his recovery, and he may then apply for a cessate grant (see paras. 11.13–16.) A grant limited "until further representation be granted" continues until another grant issues and takes its place (or the grantee or incapable person dies).

Physical incapacity

8.39 The Rules make no special provision where a person entitled to a grant is physically incapable. In such cases he may appoint an attorney—see paras 8.48 ff.

EXAMPLE FORMS OF OATH FOR INCAPACITY

(1) *Sole executor mentally incapable—Grant of administration (with will) to person authorised by Court of Protection*

[USUAL HEADING]

I, *A.B.* of ,
make oath and say as follows:

1. That *C.D.* of , deceased, died on the day of 19 , aged years, domiciled in England and Wales having made and duly executed his last will and testament wherein he appointed *D.D.* sole executor.

2. That the said *D.D.*, is now by reason of mental incapacity incapable of managing his affairs.

3. That by an order made by the Court of Protection on the day of 19 , I was duly authorised to apply for letters of administration (with will) of the estate of the said deceased, for the use and benefit of the said *D.D.*

4. (*Insert statement as to any minority or life interest**)

5. (*Insert statement as to settled land*).

6. That I believe the paper writing now produced to and marked by me to contain the true and original last will and testament of the said deceased.

7. That I will:

(i) collect, get in and administer according to the law the real and personal estate of the said deceased for the use and benefit of the said *D.D.* and until further representation be granted;

(ii) when required to do so by the Court, exhibit in the Court a full inventory of the said estate and render an account thereof to the Court; and

(iii) when required to do so by the High Court, deliver up to that Court the letters of administration (with will).

8. That to the best of my knowledge, information and belief the gross estate passing under the grant does not exceed/amounts to £ and that the net estate does not exceed/amounts to £ [and that this is not a case in which an Inland Revenue Account is required to be delivered].

Sworn, etc.

*(*Note:* If a minority or life interest does arise, the person authorised to apply by the Court of Protection may nominate his co-administrator who must join in deposing to the oath in that capacity.)

(2) *Sole executor mentally incapable—Grant of administration (with will) to lawful attorney acting under a registered enduring power of attorney*

[USUAL HEADING]

I, *A.B.* of ,
make oath and say as follows:

1. That *C.D.* of ,
deceased, died on the day of
19 , aged years, domiciled in England and Wales having made and executed his last will and testament wherein he appointed *D.D.* sole executor.

2. That the said *D.D.* is now by reason of mental incapacity incapable of managing his affairs.

3. That no one has been authorised by the Court of Protection to apply for letters of administration (with will) of the estate of the said deceased.

4. That I am the lawful attorney of the said *D.D.* acting under an enduring power of attorney registered with the Court of Protection.

5. (*Insert statement as to any minority or life interest*)*

6. (*Insert statement as to settled land*).

7. That I believe the paper writing now produced to and marked by me to contain the true and original last will and testament of the said deceased.

8. That I will (*Continue as in para. 7 of form (1) above*).

9. That to the best (*Continue as in para 8. of form (1) above*).

Sworn, etc.

*(*Note*: If a minority or life interest does arise and there is no other lawful attorney acting under a registered enduring power of attorney who is competent and willing to take a grant, the applying attorney may nominate his co-administrator who must join in deposing to the oath in that capacity.)

(3) *Sole executor mentally incapable—Grant of administration (with will) to residuary legatee and devisee*

[USUAL HEADING]

I, *A.D.* of ,
make oath and say as follows:

1. That *C.D.* of , deceased, died on the
day of 19 , aged years, domiciled in England and Wales, having made and duly executed his last will and testament wherein he appointed *D.D.* sole executor.

2. That the said *D.D.* is now by reason of mental incapacity incapable of managing his affairs.

3. (*Insert statement as to any minority or life interest.*)*

4. (*Insert statement as to settled land*).

5. That I believe the paper writing now produced to and marked by me to contain the true and original last will and testament of the said deceased.

6. That no person has been authorised by the Court of Protection to apply for letters of administration (with will) of the estate of the said deceased.

7. That there is no lawful attorney of the said *D.D.* acting under a registered enduring power of attorney. (*or* That *E.F.* the lawful attorney of the said *D.D.* acting under a registered enduring power of attorney has renounced administration for the use and benefit of the said *D.D.*).

8. That I am (*relationship to deceased, if any*), the residuary legatee and devisee named in the said will.

9. That I will:

(i) collect, get in and administer according to law the real and personal estate, etc. (*continue as in para. (7) of form (1)*).

10. That to the best (*continue as in para. (8) of form (1) above*).

Sworn, etc.

*(*Note*: If a minority or life interest arises and there is only one person entitled to, or entitled to share in, the residue, who is competent and willing to take a grant, the applying residuary legatee and devisee may nominate his co-administrator, who must join in deposing to the oath in that capacity.)

(4)*Intestacy—Only person entitled to estate mentally incapable—Grant of administration to person authorised by Court of Protection*

[USUAL HEADING]

I, *A.B.* of ,
make oath and say as follows:

1. That *C.D.* of , deceased, died on the day of 19 , aged years, domiciled in England and Wales, intestate a (*widower*) leaving *D.D.*, his lawful* (*son*) and only person entitled to his estate who by reason of mental incapacity is now incapable of managing his affairs.

2. (*Insert statement as to any minority or life interest*).

3. (*Insert statement as to settled land*).

4. That I am the person authorised by the Court of Protection under an order dated the day of 19 , to apply for letters of administration of the estate of the said intestate for the use and benefit of the said *D.D.*

5. That I will:

(i) collect, get in and administer according to the law the real and personal estate of the said deceased for the use and benefit of the said *D.D.* and until further representation be granted;

(ii) when required to do so by the Court, exhibit in the Court a full inventory of the said estate and render an account thereof to the Court; and

(iii) when required to do so by the High Court, deliver up to that Court the letters of administration.

6. That to the best of my knowledge, information and belief the gross estate passing under the grant does not exceed/amounts to £ and that the net

estate does not exceed/amounts to £ [and that this is not a case in which an Inland Revenue Account is required to be delivered].

Sworn, etc.

*If the intestate died on or after 4th April 1988 "lawful" is not relevant and may be omitted.

(5) *Intestacy—Only person entitled to estate incapable—Grant of administration to lawful attorney acting under a registered enduring power of attorney*

[USUAL HEADING]

I, *A.B.* of ,
make oath and say as follows:

1. That *C.D.* of , deceased, died on the day of 19 , aged years, domiciled in England and Wales, intestate leaving *D.D.* his lawful widow the only person entitled to his estate who by reason of mental incapacity is now incapable of managing her affairs.
2. (*Insert statement as to any life or minority interest*).
3. (*Insert statement as to settled land*).
4. That no one has been authorised by the Court of Protection to apply for letters of administration of the estate of the said deceased.
5. That I am the lawful attorney of the said *D.D.* acting under an enduring power of attorney registered with the Court of Protection.
6. That I will (*Continue as in para. 5 of form (4) above*).
7. That to the best (*Continue as in para. 6 of form (4) above*).

Sworn, etc

GRANTS WHERE SOLE GRANTEE BECOMES INCAPABLE

Sole, or sole surviving, proving executor becomes incapable

8.40 Where a sole, or sole surviving, proving executor has become incapable, a grant of administration (with will annexed) in respect of the unadministered estate (*de bonis non*) may be made "for his use and benefit and during his incapacity" to the person authorised by the Court of Protection or, failing such person, to the person who is otherwise entitled to a grant for the use and benefit of the incapable executor (see para. 8.25). Where the incapable proving executor is one of a number of executors and power has been reserved to the other executors, the latter may apply for a grant of double probate. The former practice whereby the original grant was impounded has been discontinued.

Sole, or sole surviving, administrator becomes incapable

8.41 Where a sole, or sole surviving, administrator becomes incapable of managing his affairs, subject to the preferred right to a grant of a person entitled in the same degree as the person incapable (Rule 35(1)), a grant in respect of the unadministered estate (*de bonis non*) may be made "for his use and benefit and during his incapacity" to the person authorised by the Court of Protection or, failing such person, to the person who would otherwise be entitled to a grant for the use and benefit of the incapable person (see para. 8.25). The former practice whereby the original grant was impounded has been discontinued.

Recovery of incapable grantee

8.42 If the incapable grantee regains his capacity, the temporary grant, and the original grant when it has not been impounded under the former practice, must be brought into, or sent by post to, the Record Keeper's Department of the Principal Registry, or the appropriate district probate registry, and upon evidence as to the grantee's recovery (*i.e.* a doctor's affidavit or where the temporary grant was made to a person authorised by the Court of Protection, the order of that court determining the proceedings) and the consent of the temporary grantee, the registrar will order that the temporary grant be noted as to its cessation, and that where the original grant had been impounded it be re-delivered to the original grantee. The temporary grant is also given out.

Death of executor grantee before recovery

8.43 If a sole, or sole surviving executor grantee dies without having recovered his capacity, having made a will appointing executors who duly prove it, the grant, where impounded under the former practice, may be delivered to them, by order of a registrar, for the purpose of establishing a chain of executorship.

GRANT TO ATTORNEY

8.44 Rule 31 provides that—

> "(1) Subject to paragraphs (2) and (3) below, the lawfully constituted attorney of a person entitled to a grant may apply for administration for the use and benefit of the donor, and such grant shall be limited until further representation be granted, or in such other way as the registrar may direct.
>
> (2) Where the donor referred to in paragraph (1) above is an executor, notice of the application shall be given to any other executor unless such notice is dispensed with by the registrar.
>
> (3) Where the donor referred to in paragraph (1) above is mentally incapable and the attorney is acting under an enduring power of attorney, the application shall be made in accordance with rule 35."

It is not essential that a person residing out of the jurisdiction of the court should appoint an attorney; he may, if he so wishes, make application for a direct grant to himself.

8.45 The person entitled may appoint a trust corporation as attorney, or individuals as attorneys, and may execute the power of attorney in this country.

Donor resident in England or Wales

8.46 It should be noted that under the new Rules a grant may be made to the attorney of a person *resident in England or Wales* without any leave of a registrar being necessary. As the new Rules contain no specific provisions for where a person is *physically incapable* of managing his affairs or for where a person may renounce his right to a grant and consent to administration being granted to the person or persons who would be entitled to his estate if he had died intestate (*spes successionis*), the appointment of an attorney or attorneys to take a grant offers a convenient alternative.

Minority of life interest

8.47 Section 114(2) of the Supreme Court Act 1981 provides that where a minority or life interest arises in the estate of the deceased, administration shall be granted either to a trust corporation, with or without an individual, or to not less than two individuals, unless it appears to the court to be expedient in all the circumstances to appoint an individual as sole administrator. Therefore, where no minority or life interest arises in the estate one attorney is sufficient, but where such an interest arises at least two attorneys, or a trust corporation, must normally be appointed.

Power of attorney

8.48 Powers of attorney are governed by the Powers of Attorney Act 1971 (and the Enduring Powers of Attorney Act 1985—see para. 8.49). A power of attorney given for the purpose of obtaining a grant remains operative indefinitely unless the document states otherwise. Where the power is not of recent date, evidence may be required to show that the circumstances and conditions under which it was given have not changed. The power of attorney should be under seal and witnessed by a disinterested person, but the registrar has a discretion to accept less formal documents. The power should specifically refer to the deceased by name and clearly show that it is given for the purpose of obtaining representation to the estate of the deceased, unless it is a general power of attorney under Section 10 of the Powers of Attorney Act 1971. The attorney or attorneys must be appointed in an identifiable form, and it is best if the attorney or attorneys are directly appointed by name.

Enduring power of attorney

8.49 The Enduring Powers of Attorney Act 1985 came into force on 10th March 1986. The Act provides that an enduring power of attorney, within the meaning of the Act, is not revoked by the subsequent mental incapacity of the donor, but once the donor has become incapable the rights of the attorney are limited (see the Act for further information) until the power has been registered with the Court of Protection. See para. 8.31 as to a grant, for the use and benefit of a mentally incapable person, to an attorney acting under a registered enduring power of attorney, and see the Enduring Powers of Attorney (Prescribed Form) Regulations 1987, which replaced the Enduring Powers of Attorney (Prescribed Form) Regulations 1986 on 1st November 1987, and see also the Court of Protection (Enduring Powers of Attorney) Rules 1986 for further information.

8.50 It is not necessary that the attorney reside within the jurisdiction of the court; if resident abroad he may obtain a grant under his power. Where two or more attorneys are appointed jointly and severally, one of them may apply for the grant but if there is a minority or life interest arising in the estate, normally at least two must apply. However, if they are appointed *jointly* both (or all) must apply and if one of them is dead a new power is necessary.

8.51 A power of attorney limited to a specific portion of an estate should be referred to a registrar before making application for a grant. Where appropriate a limited grant will be made, but if the donor of the power is entitled to a general grant the attorney should be authorised to take a grant in respect of all the estate.

Power of attorney given in a non-English speaking country

8.52 If the power of attorney is in the English language and is executed in an English-speaking country the usual attestation clause only is necessary. Where the power of attorney is executed in a non-English speaking country the following practice must be observed:

(a) If the power is in the language of such country, a translation certified by a competent authority is necessary.

(b) If in English the power will be accepted if witnessed by a notary or British Consul.

(c) A power in English and not witnessed as in "(b)" above will be rejected unless there is evidence (such as a certificate by the extracting solicitor) or other sufficient indication that the donor understood English.

The Republic of South Africa and the Republic of Ireland are regarded as English-speaking countries. Where the donor of the power appears to be a native of India, Pakistan, Sri Lanka or Malaysia the requirements stated in "(c)" above must be observed.

Power of attorney to be filed in the registry

8.53 The original power of attorney or, if appropriate a sufficiently athenticated copy, must be filed in all cases. A power given for purposes additional to the obtaining of a grant will be given out after issue of the grant provided that a copy is filed in the registry. The contents of an instrument creating a power of attorney may be proved by means of a copy which:

(a) is a reproduction of the original made with a photographic or other device for reproducing documents in facsimile; and
(b) contains the following certificate or certificates signed by the donor of the power or by a solicitor or stockbroker, that is to say:
   (i) a certificate at the *end* to the effect that the copy is a *true and complete copy* of the original; and
   (ii) if the original consists of two or more pages, a certificate at the *end of each page* of the copy to the effect that it is a *true and complete* copy of the *corresponding* page of the original.

(Section 3(1), Powers of Attorney Act 1971).

8.54 Where a copy of an instrument creating a power of attorney has been made which complies with the requirements indicated above, the contents of the instrument may also be proved by means of a copy of that copy if the copy itself complies with the requirements indicated above, taking references in it to the original as references to the copy from which the further copy is made (Section 3(2) of the Act).

8.55 Where, in accordance with the law of the domicile of the deceased, a power of attorney has been deposited in a court of law or with a notary, a notarial copy of it will be accepted provided that it is shown by evidence of the law of the country concerned that such copy, having been prepared by and issued under the hand of the notary, is as valid as the original and would be accepted in lieu of the original by the court of the domicile. A certificate to that effect by a notary practising in the country concerned is sufficient.

8.56 If, prior to 1st October 1971, the original power of attorney had been deposited at the Central Office of the Supreme Court an office copy of it is acceptable. An office copy of a power deposited in the Supreme

Court of Northern Ireland or registered in the books of Council and Session in Scotland is accepted without further evidence as to the contents of the power or of the fact that it has been deposited and registered.

Status of an attorney

8.57 An attorney acting under a power has the same status as the donor of the power (see *Re Rendell, Wood v Rendell* [1901] 1 Ch. 230), but a chain of executorship is not constituted through a grant to an attorney, although it is not finally broken. For "chain of executorship" see paras. 3.16–19.

Attorney of executor

8.58 The grant made to the attorney of an executor is one of letters of administration with will annexed. A grant to the attorney of a sole, or sole surviving, executor, or to the attorney of more than one executor, is made for the use and benefit of the executor(s) and limited until further representation be granted.

8.59 Where the application for a grant is by an attorney appointed by some of a number of executors, the oath leading to the grant must show that notice of the application has been given to the other executors, unless the registrar has dispensed with such notice (Rule 31(2)).

8.60 A joint grant may be made to the attorneys of two executors where each executor has appointed his own attorney separately. The grant would normally be made for the use and benefit of the executors during their joint lives, and would cease upon the death of either of the executors or either of the attorneys or upon further representation being granted.

Attorneys of persons entitled to administration (with or without will)

8.61 All or any of the persons entitled to administration (with or without will) may appoint an attorney for the purpose of taking a grant. The attorney of one of several persons so entitled may take a grant without notice to the others. A grant made to the attorney of several persons entitled to administration is limited until further representation be granted. If made to the attorney of one of several persons entitled, the grant is limited in the same way. A joint grant may be made to attorneys appointed separately by two persons entitled to administration, for their use and benefit during their joint lives, and the grant would cease upon the death of either of the attorneys or of either donor or upon further representation being granted.

Attorneys of guardian

8.62 Where the guardian of a minor appoints attorneys for the purpose of taking a grant, the grant is made for the use and benefit of the minor and until he shall attain the age of 18 years, or until further representation be granted. If there is more than one minor, the grant is made for their use and beneift and until one of them attains the age of 18 years, or until further representation be granted.

Death of donor of power of attorney

8.63 If the donor of the power of attorney dies before the estate has been fully administered, the power of attorney and the grant made under it cease to be operative. A grant *de bonis non* is necessary to complete the administration.

Death of attorney

8.64 If the attorney dies before completing the administration of the estate, the grant ceases. A "cessate" grant may be made to another attorney appointed by the donor of the original power, or to the original donor himself if he applies for a grant. A grant made under Rule 31 to one of a number of attorneys appointed severally ceases upon his death, and another of the attorneys may take a "cessate" grant under the original power of attorney, provided that the power has not been revoked.

8.65 Where an attorney to whom a grant has been made has died, and there is a person equally entitled with the donor of the power to a grant, a *de bonis non* grant may be made to such person, provided that the consent of the donor of the power is obtained.

Renunciation through attorney

8.66 Under a power of attorney containing authorisation to that effect, an attorney may renounce the right to a grant on behalf of a person who is resident abroad (*Rosser* (1864) 3 Sw. & Tr. 490).

Oath leading to grant to attorney

8.67 The oath must set out all the particulars which would be required in the case of a direct grant to the donor of the power of attorney.

EXAMPLE FORMS OF OATH FOR ATTORNEY AND POWER OF ATTORNEY

(*Note*: At least two individuals should normally be appointed as attorneys, or a trust corporation appointed as attorney, where a beneficial minority or life interest arises in the estate.)

(1) *Oath for administration (with will) to attorney of executor*

[USUAL HEADING]

I, *E.F.* of , make oath and say as follows:

1. That *A.B.* of , deceased, died on the day of 19 , aged years, domiciled in England and Wales, having made and duly executed his last will and testament and thereof appointed *C.B.* sole executor.

2. That (no) minority (or) life interest arises in the estate.

3. That there was (no) land vested in the said deceased which was settled previously to his death (and not by his will) and which remained settled land notwithstanding his death.

4. That I believe the paper writing now produced to and marked by me to contain the true and original last will and testament of the said deceased.

5. That I am the lawful attorney of the said *C.B.*

6. That I will:

(i) collect, get in and administer according to law the real and personal estate of the said deceased for the use and benefit of the said *C.B.* until further representation be granted;

(ii) when required to do so by the Court, exhibit in the Court a full inventory of the said estate and render an account thereof to the Court; and

(iii) when required to do so by the High Court, deliver up to that Court the grant of letters of administration (with will).

7. That to the best of my knowledge, information and belief the gross estate passing under the grant does not exceed/amounts to £ and that the net estate does not exceed/amounts to £ [and this is not a case in which an Inland Revenue Account is required to be delivered].

Sworn, etc.

(2) *Oath for administration (with will) to attorney of executor to whom power has been reserved, the proving executors having died*

[USUAL HEADING]

I, *E.F.* of , make oath and say as follows:

1. That I believe the paper writing now produced to and marked by me to contain an official copy of the true and original last will and testament of *A.B.*, of , deceased, who died on the day of 19 , aged years, domiciled in England and Wales.

2. That on the day of 19 , probate of the said will was granted at the (Probate) Registry to *C.D.* and *G.H.*, two of the executors named therein, power being reserved of making the like grant to *K.P.*, the other executor named therein.

3. That the said *C.D.* and *G.H.* are both now dead.

4. (*Insert statements as to any minority or life interest*).

5. (*Insert statement as to settled land*).

6. That I am the lawful attorney of the said *K.P.*
7. That I will:

(i) collect, get in and administer according to law the real and personal estate of the said deceased for the use and benefit of the said *K.P.* until further representation be granted (*continue as in previous form*).

8. That to the best (*continue as in para. (7) of previous form*).

(3) *Oath for administration (with will) to attorney of residuary legatee and devisee*

[USUAL HEADING]

I, *A.B.* of , make oath and say as follows:

1. That I believe the paper writing now produced to and marked by me to contain the true and original last will and testament of *C.D.*, of , deceased, who died on the day of 19 , aged years domiciled in England and Wales.

2. That the said deceased did not in his said will name any executor (*or otherwise clear executor*).

3. That *E.F.* is the residuary legatee and devisee named in the said will.
4. (*Insert statements as to any minority or life interest*).
5. (*Insert statement as to settled land*).
6. That I am the lawful attorney of the said *E.F.*
7. That I will:

(i) collect, get in and administer according to law the real and personal estate of the said deceased for the use and benefit of the said *E.F.* and until further representation be granted (*continue as in form (1) above*).

8. That to the best (*continue as in para. (7) of form (1) above*).

(4) *Oath for administration (with will) to attorney in his representative capacity*

[USUAL HEADING]

I, *A.B.* of , make oath and say as follows:

1. That I believe the paper writing now produced to and marked by me to contain the true and original last will and testament of *C.D.*, of deceased, who died on the day of 19 , aged years, domiciled in England and Wales.

2. That the said deceased did not in his said will name any executor (*or otherwise clear executor*).

3. That *E.F.* (son of deceased) the residuary legatee and devisee named in the said will survived the said deceased and has since died without having taken upon himself letters of administration (with will) of the estate of the said deceased.

4. That the said *E.F.* died intestate a widower leaving *G.F.* his lawful son and only person entitled to his estate and letters of administration of the estate of the said *E.F.* were granted at the Registry on the day of 19 , to me as the lawful attorney of the said *G.F.* for his use and benefit and until (*as shown in the leading grant*).

5. (*Insert statement as to any minority or life interest*).

6. (*Insert statement as to settled land.*)
7. That I will:

(i) collect, get in and administer according to law the real and personal estate of the said deceased for the use and benefit of the said *G.F.* and until further representation be granted in the estate of the said *E.F.* deceased (*continue as in form (1) above*).

8. That to the best (*continue as in para. (7) of form (1) above*).

(5) *Oath for administration to attorney in his representative capacity*

[USUAL HEADING]

I, *A.B.* of , make oath and say as follows:

1. That *C.D.*, of , deceased, died on the day of 19 , aged years, domiciled in England and Wales, intestate, leaving *D.D.* his lawful widow and relict and only person entitled to his estate who has since died without taking upon herself letters of administration thereof.

2. That the said *D.D.* died intestate a widow, leaving *E.D.* her lawful son and only person entitled to her estate, and that letters of administration of the estate of the said *D.D.* were granted at the Probate Registry on the day of 19 , to me as the lawful attorney of the said *E.D.* for his use and benefit and until (*as shown in the leading grant*).

3. (*Insert statement as to any minority or life interest*).
4. (*Insert statement as to settled land*).
5. That I will:

(i) collect, get in and administer according to law the real and personal estate of the said deceased for the use and benefit of the said *E.D.* and until further representation be granted in the estate of the said *D.D.*;
(ii) when required to do so by the Court, exhibit in the Court a full inventory of the said estate and render an account thereof to the Court; and
(iii) when required to do so by the High Court, deliver up to that Court the letters of administration.

6. That to the best (*continue as in para. (7) of form (1) above*).

(6) *Oath for administration to attorney of person entitled*

[USUAL HEADING]

I, *A.B.* of , make oath and say as follows:

1. That *C.D.*, of , deceased, died on the day of 19 , aged years, domiciled in England and Wales, intestate, a widower leaving *E.D.*. his lawful* (*son*) and only person entitled to his estate:

2. (*Insert statement as to any minority or life interest*).
3. (*Insert statement as to settled land*).
4. That I am the lawful attorney of the said *E.D.*.

5. That I will:

   (i) collect, get in and administer according to law the real and personal estate of the said deceased for the use and benefit of the said *E.D.* until further representation be granted; (*complete as in form (5) above*).

6. That to the best (*continue as in para (7) of form (1) above*).

(*If the intestate died on or after 4th April 1988 it does not matter whether the relationship is lawful and the word "lawful" may be omitted.)

(7) *Executor's power of attorney*

[USUAL HEADING]

A.B. deceased,
of ,
died on the day of 19 ,
domiciled in England and Wales, having made and duly executed h last will and testament, [and codicil(s)] bearing date the day of 19 (and the day of 19) and therein appointed *C.D.* (and *E.F.*) executor(s).

I/we, the said *C.D.* (and *E.F.*)
of
do hereby nominate, constitute and appoint [*insert attorney's name, address and description* (*two grantees normally being required if a life or minority interest arises in the estate*)] to be my/our lawful Attorney(s) for the purpose of obtaining letters of administration (with the said will annexed) of the estate of the said *A.B.* deceased, to be granted to him/them for my/our use and benefit, and until further representation be granted;

And I/we hereby promise to ratify and confirm whatever my/our said Attorney(s) shall lawfully do or cause to be done in the premises.

IN WITNESS whereof have hereunto set hand and seal this day of 19

Signed, Sealed and Delivered by the said

in the presence of

SEAL

CHAPTER 9

Guarantees

9.01 Guarantees are *not* required on applications for grants or resealing of Colonial grants, proceeding under the current Rules.

9.02 Section 120 of the Supreme Court Act 1981 provides:

"(1) As a condition of granting administration to any person the High Court may, subject to the following provisions of this section and subject to and in accordance with probate rules, require one or more sureties to guarantee that they will make good, within any limit imposed by the court on the total liability of the surety or sureties, any loss which any person interested in the administration of the estate of the deceased may suffer in consequence of a breach by the administrator in his duties as such.
(2) A guarantee given in pursuance of any such requirement shall enure for the benefit of every person interested in the administration of the estate of the deceased as if contained in a contract under seal made by the surety or sureties with every such person and, where there are two or more sureties, as if they had bound themselves jointly and severally.
(3) No action shall be brought on any such guarantee without the leave of the High Court.
(4) Stamp duty shall not be chargeable on any such guarantee.
(5) This section does not apply where administration is granted to the Treasury Solicitor, the Official Solicitor, the Public Trustee, the Solicitor for the affairs of the Duchy of Lancaster or the Duchy of Cornwall or the Crown Solicitor for Northern Ireland, or to the consular officer of a foreign state to which section 1 of the Consular Conventions Act 1949 applies, or in such other cases as may be prescribed."

9.03 Similar provisions are made in Section 11 of the Administration of Estates Act 1971 in respect of Colonial grants being resealed in England and Wales under the Colonial Probates Acts 1892 and 1927.

9.04 Unlike the previous Non-Contentious Probate Rules the current Rules make no provision for guarantees and accordingly *no guarantee* is required on any application under the current Rules.

CHAPTER 10

Trust Corporations, Non-Trust Corporations and Settled Land

TRUST CORPORATIONS

10.01 The court has statutory authority to make grants of representation to trust corporations. A grant may be made to a trust corporation either alone or jointly with an individual (Section 114(2), Supreme Court Act 1981).

Definition

10.02 Section 128 of the Supreme Court Act 1981 defines a "trust corporation" as "the Public Trustee, or a corporation, either appointed by the court in any particular case to be a trustee or authorised by rules made under Section 4(3) of the Public Trustee Act 1906 to act as custodian trustee". Section 3 of the Law of Property (Amendment) Act 1926 (which is still effective to extend the definition in the Supreme Court Act 1981 although earlier in date) extends the definition of "trust corporation" to include the Treasury Solicitor, the Official Solicitor and various other persons and bodies. Section 3 should be referred to for further details. Rule 30 of the Public Trustee Rules 1912 (as amended) defines "custodian trustee" and reference should be made to the Rule in cases of doubt. Amongst others, the definition includes the holders of certain official positions (*e.g.* the Treasury Solicitor, the Official Solicitor); corporations authorised by the Lord Chancellor to act as trust corporations in relation to charitable, ecclesiastical and public trusts; Regional Health Authorities, Area Health Authorities and Special Health Authorities, and certain local authorities.

10.03 If a local or public authority seeks to obtain a grant for any other purpose (*e.g.* as a creditor of the deceased), it is regarded as a non-trust corporation and must apply for the grant through its nominee.

10.04 To obtain a grant in its corporate capacity, a trust corporation must:

(1) be constituted under the law of the United Kingdom or any part thereof, or under the law of any other Member State of the European Economic Community or any part thereof, and

(2) be empowered by its constitution to undertake trust business, and

(3) have one or more places of business in the United Kingdom.

10.05 A grant cannot be made to a foreign trust corporation as such (*Re Barlow* [1933] P. 184), but it may apply for a grant through its nominee or attorney. A trust corporation having its registered office in the Republic of Ireland cannot (save as below) take a grant of probate in England or Wales where its power to act as an executor has been obtained since the establishment of the Irish Free State, by reason that it is not a corporation constituted under the law of the United Kingdom, or any part thereof; but where power to act as an executor was obtained before the establishment of the Irish Free State, the corporation may take a grant in England. However, since the Republic of Ireland is now a Member State of the European Economic Community, a corporation which obtained its power to act as executor after the establishment of the Irish Free State may nevertheless act as a trust corporation provided it comes within the scope of Rule 30 of the Public Trustee Rules 1912 (*Re Bigger* [1977] 2 All E.R. 644; [1977] Fam. 203).

Trust corporation appointed executor

10.06 A trust coporation may be appointed as executor of a will, either to act alone or jointly with individuals. Where a branch of a bank which is a trust corporation is appointed executor, a grant is normally made to the bank itself (*Re J.C. White* (1924) Motion).

Renunciation by a trust corporation

10.07 A trust corporation may renounce its right to a grant by form of renunciation under seal or through an official of the corporation duly appointed for the purpose by resolution. In the latter case, a certified copy of the resolution (which may be in general terms) must be lodged with the renunciation signed by the official.

Grant to trust corporation by consent

10.08 Where a trust corporation applies for a grant otherwise than as executor, attorney, residuary legatee or devisee in trust or a beneficiary, the consents of all persons entitled to a grant, and of all persons interested in the residuary estate of the deceased, are normally required to be lodged. The registrar has a discretion to dispense with consents on such terms, if any, as he thinks fit (Rule 36(3)).

Administration with will annexed to trust corporation

10.09 Where there is no executor named in the will, or the executors are dead, or they are cleared off by renunciation or citation, a trust corporation named in the will as residuary legatee and devisee in trust is entitled to letters of administration with will annexed in its own right. If executors appointed by the will are of age and are also interested in the residuary estate, and wish a trust corporation to apply for a grant on their behalf, they must renounce probate of the will and (in their capacity as residuary legatees and devisees, or as the case may be) consent to the trust corporation taking the grant; the consent of any other person interested in the residue must also be filed. If one of the executors is a minor, and a trust corporation is applying for the grant alone, the grant will be limited until the minor obtains a grant.

10.10 If no executor is named in the will, or where the executors are dead or cleared off by renunciation or citation, a grant of letters of administration with will annexed may be made to a trust corporation upon the consent of all persons having an interest in the residuary estate of the testator. The grant may be made to a trust corporation alone, or jointly with a person having an interest in the residue. The signed consents of any residuary legatees or devisees in trust, residuary legatees or devisees for life, and ultimate residuary legatees and devisees and persons entitled to share in any residuary estate undisposed of by the will must, if possible, be obtained and filed. Where the consents of all persons interested in the residue cannot be obtained, the facts of the case should be referred to a registrar, who has a discretion to dispense with a consent on such terms, if any, as he thinks fit.

Administration (intestacy) to trust corporation

10.11 Similarly, on an intestacy, letters of administration may be granted to a trust corporation alone or jointly with an individual. A grant may be made to a trust corporation in its own right upon the request and with the consent of all the persons entitled to share in the estate of the intestate. Alternatively, such persons may request the corporation to join with them in taking a grant. Where a person entitled will not exercise his right to take or to join in taking a grant, and will not consent or renounce, the facts of the case should be referred to a registrar, who has a discretion to dispense with a consent upon such terms, if any, as he thinks fit.

All persons entitled to grant being minors

10.12 (1)(a) Where all persons entitled to administration are under the age of 18 years, a grant may issue as of right to a trust corporation on the consent of all persons who are entitled to a grant for the use and benefit of the minors under Rule 32(1).

(b) If there is no such person, the issue of a grant to a trust corporation is discretionary. The written refusal to act of the next of kin may be accepted as sufficient, but if next of kin are willing to act, consideration will be given to the alternative of assigning them as guardians for the purpose of taking a grant.

(c) In cases of foreign domicile, or where all the above persons are abroad, the matter should be referred to a registrar.

(d) A grant to a trust corporation under (a) or (b) above will be limited until one of the persons under 18 years of age shall obtain a grant.

(2)(a) Where the only persons entitled to probate as executors are under 18, a grant may be made to a trust corporation on the consent of the persons entitled to the residue. If the executors are also persons entitled to the residue, consents on their behalf may be accepted as under 1(a) above. If such consents are not given or if other persons entitled to the residue are not *sui juris*, the matter should be referred to a registrar.

(b) A grant under this paragraph will be limited until one of the executors attains the age of 18 years.

(3) When all persons entitled are minors and none of them is an executor, a grant will be made to a trust corporation in its own right and not for the use and benefit of the minors.

Minor—Assignment of trust corporation as guardian

10.13 With the consent of all persons who are entitled to a grant for the use and benefit of the minor under Rule 32, a trust corporation may apply to be assigned as guardian for the purpose of taking a grant for the use and benefit of a minor; but the procedure relating to minors as set out in the foregoing paragraphs is generally preferable as it obviates the necessity of obtaining an order before applying for the grant.

Incapable person—Grant to trust corporation by order

10.14 Application should be made to a registrar for an order under Rule 35 if it is desired that a trust corporation obtain a grant for the use and benefit of a person mentally incapable of managing his affairs. See para. 8.33 as to obtaining of the order.

Trust corporation as attorney

10.15 Provided that it has such powers under its constitution, a trust corporation may take a grant as the attorney of a person or of a company, and may take the grant alone notwithstanding life or minority interests. The grant is limited until further representation be granted or in such other way as the registrar may direct.

The Public Trustee as grantee

10.16 The Public Trustee has authority to accept, in his official name, a grant of probate or administration of any kind either as principal or as agent for any person (Public Trustee Rules 1912, Rule 6). Under Section 6(1) of the Public Trustee Act 1906, the Public Trustee is equally entitled to a grant of administration (with or without will) with any other person or class of persons who may be entitled, but as between the Public Trustee and the widow or widower, or persons entitled to share in the estate of the deceased, the widow or widower, or persons entitled to share in the estate are preferred, unless good cause is shown to the contrary.

10.17 The Public Trustee may renounce executorship, but a chain of executorship may continue through him if he takes a grant of probate.

Procedure on trust corporation applying for grant

10.18 Application for the grant must be made by a person appointed for that purpose by resolution of the corporation. A certified copy of the resolution is not required on each application where the corporation has already filed with the Senior Registrar at the Principal Registry a certified copy identifying the authorised person or persons by the position held and it is deposed in the oath that a certified copy of the resolution has been so filed with the Senior Registrar, that the officer is therein identified by the position he holds and that the resolution is still in force, or where the corporation is a person holding an official position if the person through whom the application is made is included in a list filed in the Principal Registry of persons authorised to make such applications. In all other cases a certified copy of the resolution must be filed with the oath leading to the grant (Rule 36(2)).

10.19 The oath leading to the grant must show:

(1) The address of the registered office of the trust corporation.

(2) That the corporation is a trust corporation as defined by Rule 2(1) of the Non-Contentious Probate Rules 1987, and that it is empowered by its constitution to accept the grant.

(3) How the corporation is authorised to apply, *e.g.* by reference to its appointment as executor or trustee of the will, or by showing that it is applying with the consent of the persons entitled to the grant and the persons interested in the residuary estate of the deceased (Rule 36(3)). Renunciation by executors and consents of persons entitled to the grant and of persons interested in the residuary estate must be recited in the oath and filed. If the corporation has been appointed executor on terms

and conditions specifically referred to as being in existence at the date of the will (or of its republication), then, provided that the oath contains a statement that nothing in those terms and conditions limits the corporation's power to take a full grant, it will not normally be necessary to produce them to the registry on the application.

(4) That the deponent is the person duly authorised by the corporation to apply on its behalf. The resolution by which he is appointed should be referred to by date.

(5) That the trust corporation (and not the deponent) will administer the estate according to law.

Example form of oath

Oath for grant of administration (with will annexed) to a trust corporation on consent of residuary legatees and devisees

[USUAL HEADING]

I, [*Insert the name, address (which may be the official address) and official position of the corporation's nominee. Any other deponent must give name, address and occupation or, if none, description.*]
of
in the employ of
whose registered office is situate at
make oath and say as follows:

1. *A.B.*
of
formerly of
deceased, died on the day of 19 ,
aged years, domiciled in England and Wales.

2. I believe the paper writing now produced to and marked by me to contain the true and original last will and testament of the deceased. That the deceased did not in his said will name any executor (*or state how executors named are cleared off*).

3. To the best of my knowledge, information and belief there was no land vested in the deceased which was settled previously to his death (and not by his said will) and which remained settled land notwithstanding such death.

4. That *B.B.* widow of the deceased the residuary legatee and devisee for life named in the said will, and *C.B., D.B.* and *E.B.*, children of the deceased the residuary legatees and devisees substituted in the said will, have consented that letters of administration with the said will annexed be granted to
Bank/Company/PLC.

5. That the said , by resolution dated the day of 19 (a certified copy of which is lodged herewith) appointed me for the purpose of applying for a grant of letters of administration with will annexed of the estate of the said deceased on its behalf, and that the said is a trust corporation as defined

by Rule 2(1) of the Non-Contentious Probate Rules 1987, and that it is empowered by its constitution to accept the grant now applied for.

6. That minority life interest arises in the estate.
7. That the said corporation will:
   (i) collect, get in and administer according to law the real and personal estate of the said deceased;
   (ii) when required to do so by the Court, exhibit in the Court a full inventory of the said estate and render an account thereof to the Court; and
   (iii) when required to do so by the High Court, deliver up to that Court the grant of letters of administration with will annexed.

8. That to the best of my knowledge, information and belief the gross estate passing under the grant does not exceed/amounts to £ and that the net estate does not exceed/amounts to £ [and that this is not a case in which an Inland Revenue Account is required to be delivered].

Sworn, etc.

CORPORATIONS (OTHER THAN TRUST CORPORATIONS)

10.20 Where a corporation (not being a trust corporation) would, if an individual, be entitled to a grant, administration for its use and benefit, limited until further representation is granted, may be granted to its nominee or to its lawfully constituted attorney (Rule 36(4)).

Non-trust corporation appointed as executor

10.21 If a corporation which is not a trust corporation under the laws of the United Kingdom is appointed as an executor, it cannot obtain a grant of probate. In such a case the appropriate form of grant is letters of administration with will annexed, to the nominee, or attorney of the corporation.

Non-trust corporation and individual appointed executors

10.22 If a non-trust corporation and an individual are appointed as executors, a joint grant cannot be made to them, because the individual is entitled to a grant of probate. Probate may be granted to the individual alone, if it is sworn in the oath leading to such grant that the corporation is not a trust corporation. If the individual renounces probate, letters of administration with will annexed may be granted to the nominee or attorney of the corporation. Where such a corporation and an individual are appointed as executors, letters of administration with will annexed may issue to their jointly constituted attorney.

Non-trust corporation renounces

10.23 Where a non-trust corporation wishes to renounce its right to a grant, it should by resolution appoint a nominee to renounce on its behalf. A sealed, or otherwise authenticated, copy of the resolution should be filed with the form of renunciation. A form of renunciation by the corporation under seal will, however, usually be accepted as sufficient.

Oath leading to grant on behalf of a non-trust corporation

10.24 The oath must show:

(1) that the corporation is not a trust corporation as defined by Rule 2(1) of the Non-Contentious Probate Rules 1987;
(2) whether or not a minority or life interest arises in the estate;
(3) the entitlement to the grant (*e.g.* that the corporation is the residuary legatee and devisee in trust named in the will);
(4) how the person applying for the grant on behalf of the corporation is authorised to do so; a resolution should be referred to by date, and a certified copy thereof under seal of the corporation (or otherwise authenticated to the satisfaction of the registrar) must be filed; if the grant is applied for by an attorney, the power of attorney under seal (or otherwise authenticated to the satisfaction of the registrar) must be filed;
(5) that the nominee or attorney will administer the estate of the deceased according to law for the use and benefit of the corporation and until further representation be granted.

The grant is made to the nominee or attorney by name and it ceases and expires upon his death; if a further grant is necessary it will be made to a new nominee or attorney.

Form of resolution of a non-trust corporation accepting a grant through its nominee

[USUAL HEADING]

Resolved that we (*name of corporate body*) accept the appointment of ourselves as (*sole executor, or as the case may be*) of the will of *A.B.* of , deceased, the said will bearing date the day of 19 , and that we hereby appoint *C.D.* of , the Secretary (*or other chief permanent official*) of the said (*corporate body*) the nominee of the said (*corporate body*) for the purpose of obtaining a grant of letters of administration with will annexed of the estate of the said deceased for the use and benefit of the said (*corporate body*) and until further representation be granted, and for the purpose of swearing the necessary papers and taking the necessary steps to obtain such grant.

Dated the day of 19 .
I hereby certify the foregoing to be a true copy.

(*Signature*)
Secretary (*or other chief permanent official*)

SETTLED LAND

10.25 A grant in respect of settled land is only required where land was vested in the deceased at the time of his death, which was settled previously to his death, and not by his will, and which remained settled land notwithstanding his death.

Definition of settled land

10.26 Settled land, within the meaning of Section 2 of the Settled Land Act 1925, is any kind of immovable property (including leaseholds) *not held upon an immediate and binding trust for sale*, which is, or is deemed to be, the subject of a settlement. This not only includes land which is limited in trust for any person by way of succession, but almost every case in which the interest of the beneficial owner of the property is in any way restrained, qualified or restricted. A settled land grant is necessary where a continuing trust which existed at the time of death of a tenant for life has since ceased, for the reason that at *the time of his death* the settlement had not come to an end.

10.27 Where some of the land has been sold, only the remaining land can form the basis for a settled land grant, and the sold portion represents "capital money". A grant can only be applied for in respect of the unsold portion, even though Inheritance Tax may be payable on the whole of the property. Should some of the "capital money" have been re-invested, it can only be included in the grant as settled "land" if it has been vested in the tenant for life.

Creation of settlements

10.28 Settlements may be created by a settlement *inter vivos* or by will. Section 4 of the Settled Land Act 1925 provides that, where the settlement is by deed, two documents are necessary, the main deed of settlement (known as a "trust instrument") and a vesting deed. The trust instrument sets out the trusts and appoints trustees, and the vesting deed describes the land, states that it is vested in the life tenant and gives the names of the trustees appointed by the trust instrument. By Section 6 of the Settled Land Act 1925, a will is a trust instrument for the purposes of the Act, and the personal representatives of the testator (*i.e.* the settlor) must, if and when required so to do, vest the legal estate in the life tenant by executing a vesting deed (or vesting assent) under Section 8(4).

When a grant in respect of settled land is required

10.29 A grant in respect of settled land is required, and can be made, provided that:

(1) the land is settled land within the meaning of the Settled Land Act 1925;
(2) there is no immediate and binding trust for sale of all the land;
(3) the land was effectively vested in the deceased tenant for life;
(4) the land did not cease to be settled land on and by reason of the death of the tenant for life.

It may be necessary to have more than one grant where the deceased was tenant for life under several settlements, because the trustees or persons entitled under one settlement are not necessarily entitled as regards another.

Order of priority of right to grant
10.30 The order of priority of right to a grant in respect of settled land (see Rule 29) is as follows:

(1) *Trustees of the settlement—special executors*: Where the tenant for life died testate, the persons who were trustees of the settlement (see Section 30 of the Settled Land Act 1925 for a definition of "trustees of a settlement") at the date of his death are deemed to be his "special executors" in respect of the settled land whether or not they were expressly appointed as special executors to the settled land by the will of the tenant for life (see Section 22 Administration of Estates Act 1925) and may apply for a grant of probate limited to the settled land.

(2) *Other trustees of the settlement*: If there were no trustees at the date of death of the tenant for life, or if the trustees at the date of his death have relinquished the trusts, trustees appointed after his death are entitled to a grant of letters of administration (with will) in his estate in respect of the settled land. Trustees appointed after the death of the tenant for life cannot join in a grant with a "special executor".

When the tenant for life died wholly intestate, trustees of the settlement may obtain a grant irrespective of whether they held office at the date of his death or have been appointed since.

(3) *Legal personal representatives of the deceased tenant for life*: Where there are no trustees of the settlement, or where such trustees are cleared off by renunciation or citation, a grant in respect of the settled land may be made to the duly constituted legal personal representatives of the tenant for life.

(4) *Persons interested in the conveyance of the settled land*: Where there is none of the above classes of persons, or when none of them is willing or

competent to apply, the grant may be made to the remainderman or to a person interested in the conveyance of the property. In these circumstances, an order under Section 116 of the Supreme Court Act 1981 must be obtained by way of *ex parte* application to a registrar.

Types of grant in respect of settled land

10.31

(1) *Grant "including settled land*": A general grant to include the free estate of the tenant for life and the settled land vested in him may be made only when a "save and except settled land" grant and a "limited to settled land" grant would, if made separately, be made to the same people and be of the same character, *e.g.* probate to special executors as to the land, and probate to testamentary executors; or administration to trustees (or others) who are not special executors, and administration to the residuary legatees or other persons entitled to the free estate. In any other case separate grants in respect of the free estate and the settled land are necessary.

A grant of "letters of administration (*with or without will, as the case may be*) including settled land" may be made to the persons entitled to administer the free estate of the deceased tenant for life where there are no trustees of the settlement, or where such trustees are cleared off by renunciation or citation.

(2) *Probate "limited to settled land":* Where the tenant for life died testate, the trustees of the settlement who held that office at the date of his death are his "special executors" in respect of the settled land (Section 22, Administration of Estates Act 1925) and in that capacity may obtain a grant of probate "limited to settled land".

There can be no chain of executorship through a special executor of settled land.

(3) *Letters of administration (with will) "limited to settled land"*: If the tenant for life died testate and there are no "special executors" as referred to above, or if such special executors are cleared off, the following classes of persons are entitled to letters of administration (with will) "limited to settled land" in the order of priority set out below. All persons in previous classes must be accounted for before a grant can be made to a person in a lower class:

(a) Trustees of the settlement at the time of application for the grant.

(b) The legal personal representatives of the deceased tenant for life.

Where there is none of the above classes of persons, or when none of them is willing or competent to apply, the grant may be made to the remainderman or to a person interested in the conveyance of the land. An order under Section 116 of the Supreme Court Act 1981 is necessary to lead to such grant and may be obtained on *ex parte* application to a registrar.

(4) *Letters of administration "limited to settled land"*: Where the tenant for life died wholly intestate, a grant of letters of administration "limited to settled land" may be made to trustees of the settlement at the time of application for the grant. If there are no trustees, or if none of them is willing or competent to apply, the grant may be made to persons in the same order of priority as for a grant of "letters of administration (with will) limited to settled land".

Renunciation by, or reserving of power to, special executors

10.32 A special executor may renounce his right to a grant in respect of settled land or power to take a grant may be reserved to him. If a special executor has renounced a grant limited to settled land, he cannot, as one of the general executors of the tenant for life, join in a grant of probate "including settled land".

Procedure on application for grant

10.33 A grant "limited to settled land" may be made to a single individual notwithstanding the existence of a life or minority interest in the land, because such interest arises under the settlement and not under the will or intestacy of the deceased tenant for life.

10.34 When application is made for a grant "save and except settled land" it is not necessary to recite details of the settlement in the oath, but it must be stated that there was settled land vested in the deceased which remained settled land notwithstanding his death. If a grant "limited to the settled land" has already issued, particulars thereof must be recited in the oath. Every oath leading to a grant in respect of settled land must recite the particulars of the settlement. If the settlement is by deed the date of it must be shown. If the settlement is by will (and/or codicil) the full name of the settlor, the date on which the will (and codicil) was proved, and the registry in which is was proved must be shown.

10.35 The oath must recite any former grant, and an office copy of the former grant must be lodged with the papers unless application for the further grant is made at the same registry.

10.36 The original disposition (probate or settlement), the vesting deed and deed of appointment of trustees, if any, must be produced for inspection on lodging the papers for the grant and they will be returned after examination.

10.37 If there is settled land passing under two or more settlements, and the trustees are the same under all, the grant in respect of settled land will embrace all the settlements if they are recited in the oath. Where a tenant for life has died having land vested in him under several settlements with different or varying trustees, the requisite number of grants will be made, each limited to the settled land under the settlement in question.

10.38 If there is settled land, and a grant has been taken in respect of the free estate without excluding such settled land for the operation of that grant, it will not be possible to obtain a grant in respect of the settled land until the original grant has been either amended or revoked according to the circumstances of the case.

10.39 Where the will of the deceased tenant for life has already been proved by general executors or other persons entitled, the applicants for a settled land grant are not required to identify and mark the will. If the will of the deceased tenant for life has not been proved, it must be lodged and sworn to by the applicants for the settled land grant and must be marked by them. If necessary, the validity of the will must be established by the applicants. Where, subsequently, a grant "save and except settled land" is sought, an office copy of the will (or a sealed and certified copy of it) may be marked by the applicants without leave of the registrar being required, or they may attend at the registry where the will was proved and mark the original.

10.40 A copy of the will is attached to the settled land grant in every case where the tenant for life died testate.

10.41 For forms of Inland Revenue Account to be lodged with the application for the grant, see paras. 6.10–15. Where the application is for a grant "limited to settled land", the Inland Revenue Account must be submitted to the Capital Taxes Office for assessment (see para. 6.19). For completion of the Inland Revenue Account see paras. 6.58–123 and for the settled land particulars see paras. 6.65–66, 6.70 and 6.105–107.

Forms

10.42 The following precedents relate only to cases in which there was settled land vested in a deceased tenant for life which remained settled land notwithstanding his death. Forms of oath to lead to grants "limited to settled land" and "including free estate and settled land" are given.

(1) *Oath for probate "limited to settled land" to special executor—Will already proved*

[USUAL HEADING]

I, *C.D.* of , make oath and say as follows:

1. That *E.F.*, of , deceased, died on the day of 19 , aged years, domiciled in England and Wales, having made and duly executed h last will and testament [and codicil(s)] which said will [and codicil(s)] w proved at the Registry on the day of 19 , in respect of the estate of the said deceased save and except settled land by *A* and *B* the executors named therein.

2. That there was land vested in the said deceased immediately before h death which was settled previously thereto and not by h will [and codicil(s)] and which remained settled land notwithstanding h death, namely under the will [and codicil(s)] of *G.H.*, deceased who died on the day of 19 and whose will [and codicil(s)] w proved at the Registry on the day of 19 , [*or as the case may be*].

3. That at the date of death of the said deceased I was (we were) the (sole surviving) trustee(s) of the said settled land and as such am (are) the special executor(s) as to the said settled land.

4. That I (we) will:

(i) collect, get in and administer according to the law the estate of the said deceased limited to the said settled land;
(ii) when required to do so by the Court exhibit in the Court a full inventory of the said settled land and render an account thereof to the Court; and
(iii) when required to do so by the High Court, deliver up to that Court the grant of probate.

5. That to the best of my (our) knowledge, information and belief the gross value of the estate limited to the said settled land amounts to £ and the net value of the estate so limited amounts to £ .

Sworn, etc.

(2) *Oath for probate "limited to settled land" to special executor—Will not proved previously*

[USUAL HEADING]

I, *A.B.* of make oath and say as follows:

1. That *C.D.*, of , deceased died on the day of 19 , aged years, domiciled in England and Wales having made and duly executed h last will and testament [and codicil(s)].

2. That I believe the paper writing now produced to and marked by me to contain the true and original last will and testament [and codicil(s)] of the said deceased.

3. That there was land vested in the said deceased immediately before h death which was settled previously thereto and not by h will [and codicil(s)] and which remained settled land notwithstanding his death, namely under the will [and codicil(s)] of *E.F.*, deceased proved at the Registry on the day of 19 [*or as the case may be*].

4. That at the date of death of the said deceased I was [we were] the [sole surviving] trustee(s) of the said settled land and as such am/are the special executor(s) as to the settled land.

5. That I will *etc.* (*continue as in clauses 4 and 5 of the preceding form*)

Sworn, etc.

(3) *Oath for administration "limited to settled land" to trustee of settlement*

[USUAL HEADING]

I, *A.B.* of ,
make oath and say as follows:

1. That *C.D.*, of , deceased, died on the day of 19 , aged years, domiciled in England and Wales and intestate.

2. [That on the day of 19 , letters of administration of the estate of the said deceased were granted by this Division at the Registry thereof save and except settled land to].

3. That there was land vested in the said deceased which was settled previously to h death and which remained settled land notwithstanding h death namely under the will [and codicil(s)] of *E.F.*, deceased, who died on the day of 19, and whose will w proved in this Division at the Registry thereof on the day of 19 , by [*or as the case may be*].

4. That I am [or we are] the [*sole surviving*] trustee(s) of the said settled land.

5. That will:

(i) collect, get in and administer according to the law the estate of the said deceased limited to the said settled land;
(ii) when required to do so by the Court, exhibit in the Court a full inventory of the said settled land and render an account thereof to the Court; and
(iii) when required to do so by the High Court, deliver up to that Court the letters of administration.

6. That to the best of my (our) knowledge, information and belief the gross value of the estate limited to the said settled land amounts to £ and the net estate so limited amounts to £ .

Sworn, etc.

(4) *Oath for probate "including settled land"—All the proving general executors being also special executors*

[USUAL HEADING]

We, *A.B.* of , and *C.D.*, of ,
make oath and say as follows:

1. That we believe the paper writing now produced to and marked by us to contain the true and original last will and testament [and codicil] of *E.F.*, of , deceased, who died on the day of 19 , aged years, domiciled in England and Wales.

2. That there was land vested in the said deceased immediately before his death which was settled previously thereto (and not by his will) which remained settled land notwithstanding his death, namely under the will of *G.H.*, deceased, proved at the Registry on the day of 19 .

3. That we were the trustees of such settled land at the date of death of the said deceased and that we are the executors named in the said will.

4. That we will:

(i) collect, get in and administer according to the law the real and personal estate of the said deceased including the said settled land;
(ii) when required to do so by the Court, exhibit in the Court a full inventory of the said estate and render an account thereof to the Court; and
(iii) when required to do so by the High Court, deliver up to that Court the grant of probate.

5. That to the best of our knowledge, information and belief the gross estate passing under the grant including the said settled land amounts to £ and that the net estate including the said settled land amounts to £ .

6. That the net value of the said settled land is £ .

Sworn, etc.

(5) *Oath for administration "including settled land"—No trustees*

[USUAL HEADING]

I, *A.B.* of , make oath and say as follows:

1. That *C.D.*, of , deceased, died on the day of 19 , aged years, domiciled in England and Wales, intestate [*clear off prior rights*].

2. That no (a) minority interest arises under the intestacy and that no (a) life interest arises under the intestacy.

3. That there was land vested in the said deceased immediately before h death which was settled previously thereto and which remained settled land notwithstanding his death, namely under the will [and codicil(s)] of *G.H.*, deceased proved at the Registry on the day of 19 , (*or as the case may be*).

4. That there is no trustee of the said settled land.

5. That [*Show right to grant under the intestacy*].

6. That I will:

(i) collect, get in and administer according to the law the real and personal estate of the said deceased including the said settled land;
(ii) when required to do so by the Court, exhibit in the Court a full inventory of the said estate and render an account thereof to the Court; and
(iii) when required to do so by the High Court, deliver up to that Court the grant of letters of administration;

7. That to the best of my knowledge, information and belief the gross estate passing under the grant including the said settled land amounts to £ and that the net estate including the said settled land amounts to £ .
8. That the net value of the said settled land is £ .

Sworn, etc.

(6)*Oath for administration "including settled land"—Person entitled to free estate also trustee of settlement*

[USUAL HEADING]

I, *A.B.* of , make oath and say as follows:
1. That *C.D.*, of , deceased died on the day of , 19 aged years, domiciled in England and Wales, a widow and intestate.
2. That I am the lawful* son and one of the persons entitled to share in the estate of the said deceased.
3. That (no) minority interest arises under the intestacy and that (no) life interest arises under the intestacy.
4. That there was land vested in the said deceased immediately before her death which was settled previously thereto and which remained settled land notwithstanding her death, namely under the will of *E.F.*, deceased, proved at the Registry on the day of , 19 .
5. That I am the sole surviving trustee of the said settled land.
6. That I will:

(i) collect, get in and administer *etc.* (*continue as in preceding form*).

Sworn, etc.

*If the intestate died on or after 4th April 1988 "lawful" is not relevant and may be omitted.

CHAPTER 11

Miscellaneous Grants

GRANTS "DE BONIS NON"

11.01 If persons who have taken a grant in their own right die without having completed the administration of the estate, and there is no chain of executorship a *de bonis non* grant may be made to a new representative for the purpose of completing the administration. (As to "chain of executorship", see paras. 3.16 ff). A grant *de bonis non* is also appropriate on the death of the donor of a power of attorney, or of a minor or incapable person for whose use and benefit the previous grant was made, and when a sole or sole surviving grantee has become mentally incapable of managing his affairs.

Entitlement to grant

11.02 The rules as to entitlement to an original grant of administration (with or without will annexed) also apply to a grant *de bonis non*, and such further administration is granted to the persons who had an equal or next right to that of the original grantee and living interests are preferred to those of the legal personal representatives of dead interests.

Where the sole or sole surviving grantee has become mentally incapable of managing his affairs, a grant *de bonis non* may be issued, for the use and benefit of the incapable person, to the person so entitled under Rule 35 (see paras. 8.40 ff). Where a sole proving executor becomes mentally incapable, an executor to whom power has been reserved may apply for double probate.

Resealed grants

11.03 Where a Colonial grant has been resealed in England and Wales, a grant *de bonis non* may be obtained in England and Wales on the death of the person to whom the grant was issued. The grant *de bonis non* is made in accordance with the appropriate rules and principles according to the place where the deceased died domiciled.

Administration (with will annexed) "de bonis non"

11.04 Where a sole or surviving proving executor has died and the chain of executorship has been broken, or where the former grant was of administration with will annexed, a *de bonis non* grant will be made to persons in the order of priority set out in Rule 20. The oath leading to the grant must show how any chain of executorship has been broken, and clear off any interests prior to that of the applicant.

Administration (intestacy) "de bonis non"

11.05 If the former grantee was the only person entitled to the estate of the intestate, the grant *de bonis non* is made to his or her legal personal representative.

11.06 Where other persons are entitled to share in the estate with the former grantee or grantees they are first entitled to the grant *de bonis non*. If all other persons entitled to share in the estate are dead, or if living they renounce or a registrar so directs under Rule 27(5), the grant will be made to the legal personal representative of any deceased person who was entitled to share in the estate. However, where the spouse of the intestate was one of the persons entitled to share in the estate, the personal representative of the spouse has a prior right to personal representatives of other persons who were entitled to share.

11.07 Where the former grant was made to the spouse of the intestate, the right to the grant *de bonis non* must be determined by the value of the estate at the time of payment or appropriation in respect of the statutory sum to which the surviving spouse was entitled. If the grant was made to the spouse alone on the basis that at the time of issue the whole of the estate devolved solely on the surviving spouse, the grant *de bonis non* is usually made to his or her personal representative. If additional estate has been discovered since the issue of the former grant, or if the estate at the time of issue of the former grant increased in value before payment or appropriation in respect of the statutory sum, the value of the estate at the date of such payment or appropriation must be considered in determining whether the next of kin of the intestate have a beneficial interest in the estate and are entitled to the grant *de bonis non* in preference to the personal representative of the spouse.

Application for grant (practice)

11.08 Application for the grant *de bonis non* may be made at any probate registry (including the Principal Registry) irrespective of where the original grant was extracted. If the deceased died testate, the applicant for the grant, when he swears the oath, must swear to and mark the will, and (unless the registrar gives leave for a facsimile copy to be marked) he may do so by:

(1) attending at the registry from which the first grant issued and marking the original will;
(2) marking an office copy of the will, issued by the registry in which the original is deposited or by the Principal Registry;
(3) marking the probate copy of the will in the previous grant. (However, the previous grant must afterwards remain in the registry, and therefore this method should not be used when the grant is needed for other purposes.)

Particulars of the former grant (or grants) must be recited in the oath. An office copy of the grant must be lodged with the papers if application is being made at a registry other than the one from which the original grant issued.

11.09 The oath must speak as to the existence or otherwise of minority and life interests. Where there is such an interest, the grant must normally be made to at least two (but not more than four) individuals or to a trust corporation with or without an individual. Where the deceased died on or after 1st January 1926, the oath must state whether or not there was settled land vested in him which remained settled land notwithstanding his death. Where the applicant for the *de bonis non* grant is the legal personal representative of a dead interest, the original grant (or an office copy) by which he or she was so constituted should be lodged for inspection with the papers to lead to the grant.

11.10 The grant issues in respect of the *unadministered* assets, and only these assets are to be brought into any necessary Inland Revenue Account and their gross amount given in the oath. Where the grant is required in respect of "nil" estate, the purpose for which the grant is required must be stated in the oath. For the appropriate form of any necessary Inland Revenue Account see para. 6.14.

Recovery of incapable grantee after de bonis non grant issued for his use and benefit

11.11 If the incapable grantee recovers his capacity, the temporary grant (and the original grant when it has not been impounded under the former practice) must be brought into, or sent by post to, the Record Keeper's Department of the Principal Registry, or the appropriate district probate registry, and upon evidence as to the grantee's recovery (*i.e.* a doctor's affidavit or where the temporary grant was made to a person authorised by the Court of Protection, the order of that court determining the proceedings) and the consent of the temporary grantee, the registrar will order that the temporary grant be noted as to its cessation (and that where the original grant had been impounded it be re-delivered to the original grantee). The temporary grant is also given out.

Death of executor grantee before recovery

11.12 If a sole or sole surviving executor grantee dies without having recovered his capacity, having made a will appointing executors who duly prove it, the grant, where impounded under the former practice, may be delivered to them, by order of a registrar, for the purpose of establishing a chain of executorship.

Example forms of oath

(1) *Oath for administration (with will) de bonis non*

[USUAL HEADING]

I, *A.B.* of
make oath and say as follows:

1. That I believe the paper writing now produced to and marked by me to contain an official copy of the true last will and testament [and codicil(s)] of *C.D.* of deceased who died on the day of 19 , aged years, domiciled in England and Wales.

[2. *The former grant or grants must be recited, as must be the death of the last grantee or the circumstances in which part of the estate is left unadministered, that part of the estate has been left unadministered, how any chain of executorship is broken, how every person with a prior right to a grant* de bonis non *is cleared off, and the capacity in which the applicant applies for the grant.*]

3. That no (*or* a) minority interest arises in the estate and that no (*or* a) life interest arises in the estate.

4. That to the best of my knowledge, information and belief, there was no land vested in the said deceased which was settled previously to his death and not by his will and which remained settled land notwithstanding his death.

5. That I will:

(i) collect, get in and administer according to the law the real and personal estate of the said deceased left unadministered;
(ii) when required to do so by the Court, exhibit in the Court a full inventory of the said estate left unadministered and render an account thereof to the Court; and
(iii) when required to do so by the High Court, deliver up to that Court the letters of administration (with will).

6. That to the best of my knowledge, information and belief the gross estate left unadministered passing under the grant amounts to £ and that the net estate left unadministered amounts to £ [and that this is not a case in which an Inland Revenue Account is required to be delivered].

Sworn, etc.

(2) *Oath for administrators de bonis non*

[USUAL HEADING]

I, *B.B.* of ,
make oath and say as follows:

1. That *A.B.* of , deceased, died on the day of 19 , aged years, domiciled in England and Wales intestate [*a widower without issue or spinster without issue or as the case may be*] without leaving any other person entitled in priority to share in h estate by virtue of any enactment;

2. [*The former grant or grants must be recited, as must be the death of the last grantee or the circumstances in which part of the estate is left unadministered, how every person with a prior right to a grant* de bonis non *is cleared off and the capacity in which the applicant applies for the grant.*]

3. That no (*or* a) minority interest arises under the intestacy and that no (*or* a) life interest arises under the intestacy.

4. That to the best of my knowledge, information and belief, there was no land vested in the said deceased which was settled previously to his death and which remained settled land notwithstanding his death.

5. That I will:

(i) collect, get in and administer according to the law the real and personal estate of the said deceased left unadministered [*where the grant sought is a limited one, e.g., as in the case where minors are beneficially entitled to the estate or the person entitled to the estate is mentally incapable, insert the limitation "for the use and benefit of .... etc".*]

(ii) when required to do so by the Court, exhibit in the Court a full inventory of the said unadministered estate and render an account thereof to the Court; and

(iii) when required to do so by the High Court, deliver up to that Court the letters of administration.

6. That to the best of my knowledge, information and belief the gross estate left unadministered passing under the grant amounts to £ and that the net estate left unadministered amounts to £ [and that this is not a case in which an Inland Revenue Account is required to be delivered].

Sworn, etc.

CESSATE GRANTS

11.13 A limited grant ceases to be operative when the necessity for the limitation ceases, or when the grantee dies or ceases to be competent. If the estate is not fully administered, it is necessary to obtain a "cessate" grant for the purpose of dealing with the unadministered estate.

11.14 Although the new grant is a full one and confers power over the whole estate of the deceased, it is only the value of the unadministered estate which is shown in the Inland Revenue Account and sworn to in the oath leading to the grant. For the appropriate form of any necessary Inland Revenue Account, see para 6.14.

11.15 The most common circumstances in which a "cessate" grant issues are:

(a) Probate has been granted to an executor appointed for a period of time (*e.g.* for life or widowhood). The grant ceases on the expiration of that period, and a "cessate" grant is made to the substituted executor (if any), or to residuary legatees and devisees, or other persons entitled thereto, as the case may be.
(b) Probate has been granted of a lost will as contained in a copy or reconstruction limited until the original or a more authentic copy is proved. The original will, or a more authentic copy, is found and is proved.
(c) Letters of administration (with or without will) have been granted to the attorney of a person entitled to a grant, or to a person on behalf of a person incapable of managing his own affairs, or to guardians of minors. When the person entitled to a grant applies for a direct grant to be made to him, or when the incapable person recovers his capacity, or when one of the minors attains 18 years of age, the grant ceases, and the appropriate type of "cessate" grant is made to such person.

Practice
11.16 The practice to be followed on applying for a "cessate" grant is similar to that which applies in obtaining a grant *de bonis non* (see paras. 11.08–09). The oath leading to the grant must recite the particulars of the previous grant and the reason why it has ceased. If the grant is sought by a person who has recovered from incapacity, evidence as to recovery must be furnished as in the case of the recovery of an incapable grantee.

Example forms of oath

(1) *Oath for cessate probate to a substituted executor*

[USUAL HEADING]

I, *C.D.* of ,
make oath and say as follows:

1. That *B.B.*, of ,
deceased, died on the day of
19 , aged years, domiciled in England and Wales, having made and duly

executed his last will and testament, and thereof appointed his son *A.B.* executor for life.

2. That on the day of 19 , the said *A.B.* duly proved the said will at the Registry, and has since died, on the day of 19 , whereby the said probate has ceased and expired.

3. That I believe the paper writing now produced to and marked by me, to contain an official copy of the last will and testament of the said testator.

4. That I am the nephew of the said testator and the executor substituted in his said will.

5. That there was (no) land vested in the said deceased immediately before his death which was settled previously thereto and not by his will and which remained settled land notwithstanding his death.

6. That I will:

(i) collect, get in and administer according to the law the real and personal estate of the said deceased;
(ii) when required to do so by the Court, exhibit in the Court a full inventory of the said estate and render an account thereof to the Court; and
(iii) when required to do so by the High Court, deliver up to that Court the grant of probate.

7. That to the best of my knowledge, information and belief the gross value of the estate left unadministered amounts to £ and the net value of the estate left unadministered amounts to £ [and that this is not a case in which an Inland Revenue Account is required to be delivered].

Sworn, etc.

(2) *Oath for cessate probate on finding will which had been lost*

[USUAL HEADING]

I, *A.B.* of , make oath and say as follows:

1. That *C.D.*, of , deceased, died on the day 19 , aged years, domiciled in England and Wales, having made and duly executed his last will and testament and thereof appointed me the sole executor.

2. That the said will was at the date of death of the said deceased whole and unrevoked and duly executed and in the same state as when executed but was after the death of the said deceased lost or mislaid.

3. That by a Registrar's Order made on the day of 19 , it was ordered that probate of the said will as contained in a (*copy*) thereof be granted to me this deponent limited until the original will or a more authentic copy thereof be proved.

4. That I believe the paper writing now produced to and marked by me to contain the said true and original last will and testament of the said deceased.

5. That I am the sole executor named in the said will.

6. That there was (no) land vested in the said deceased immediately before his death which was settled previously thereto and not by his will and which remained settled land notwithstanding his death.

7. That I will:

(i) collect, get in *etc.* (*Continue as in preceding form*)

Sworn, etc.

(3) *Oath for cessate probate on a minor (sole executor) attaining the age of 18*

[USUAL HEADING]

I, *A.B.* of ,
make oath and say as follows:

1. That *C.B.*, of , deceased, died on the day of 19 , aged years, domiciled in England and Wales, having made and duly executed his last will and testament, and thereof appointed me his son sole executor and residuary legatee. I was then a minor.

2. That on the day of 19 , letters of administration (with the said will annexed) of the estate of the said deceased were granted at the Registry to *X* and *Y* for my use and benefit and until I should attain the age of 18 years.

3. That on the day of 19 , I, the said *A.B.* attained the age of 18 years and the said letters of administration (with will annexed) have consequently ceased and expired.

4. That I am the sole executor named in the said will.

5. That I believe the paper writing now produced to and marked by me to contain an official copy of the last will and testament of the said deceased.

6. That there was (no) land vested in the said deceased immediately before his death which was settled previously thereto (and not by his will) and which remained settled land notwithstanding his death.

7. That I will:

(i) collect, get in *etc.* (*Continue as in form (1) above*)

Sworn, etc.

(4) *Oath for cessate probate to an executor whose attorney had obtained a grant*

[USUAL HEADING]

I, *A.B.* of ,
make oath and say as follows:

1. That *C.B.*, of , deceased, died on the day of 19 , aged years, domiciled in England and Wales, having made and duly executed his last will and testament, and thereof appointed me *A.B.* sole executor.

2. That on the day of 19 , letters of administration (with the said will annexed) of the estate of the said deceased were granted at the Registry to *E.F.*, my lawful attorney, for my use and benefit, and until I should obtain probate of the said will [*or* and until further representation be granted].

3. That I am the sole executor named in the said will.

4. That I believe the paper writing now produced to and marked by me to contain an official copy of the last will and testament of the said deceased.

5. That there was (no) land *etc.* (*Continue as in form (3) above*).

GRANTS LIMITED AS TO PROPERTY

11.17 Section 113 of the Supreme Court Act 1981 provides that:

> "(1) Subject to subsection (2), the High Court may grant probate or administration in respect of any part of the estate of a deceased person, limited in any way the court thinks fit.
> (2) Where the estate of a deceased person is known to be insolvent, the grant of representation to it shall not be severed under subsection (1) except as regards a trust estate in which he had no beneficial interest."

11.18 If a person entitled to a general grant wishes to obtain a grant as to only a part of the estate, an order under Rule 51 is required; but a person entitled only to a grant as to part of the estate has a right to such grant without an order. Where a grant as to part of the estate has been made by order under Rule 51, a grant in respect of the rest of the estate may issue without further order.

Application for order

11.19 Application for the order is made *ex parte* to a registrar. The application must be supported by an affidavit setting out the grounds of the application, giving details of the estate to be covered by the grant, stating whether the estate is known to be insolvent, and also showing how the persons entitled to a grant in respect of the whole estate in priority to the applicant have been cleared off. Renunciations and other necessary documents should be lodged with the affidavit. An *ex parte* application is made by leaving the affidavit and relative documents at the Principal Registry, or, if the application for the grant is to be made at a district registry, with the appropriate district probate registrar.

DISCRETIONARY GRANTS

11.20 Section 116 of the Supreme Court Act 1981 provides that:

> "(1) If by reason of any special circumstances it appears to the High Court to be necessary or expedient to appoint as administrator some person other

> than the person who, but for this section, would in accordance with probate rules have been entitled to a grant, the court may in its discretion appoint as administrator such person as it thinks expedient.
> (2) Any grant of administration under this section may be limited in any way the court thinks fit."

Minority or life interest

11.21 If a minority or life interest arises in the estate, application must normally be made for the appointment of two or more individuals, or of a trust corporation, with or without an individual, as administrators (Section 114(2), Supreme Court Act 1981).

Examples of "special circumstances"

11.22 An order to lead to a "discretionary" grant may be obtained:

(1) Where the persons entitled to a grant cannot be traced.
(2) Where the persons entitled are unfit to administer the estate (*e.g.* by reason of their bad character or bankruptcy).
(3) Where all the persons entitled agree to a grant being made to a stranger having no interest in the estate.
(4) Where a remainderman seeks to obtain a grant in respect of settled land by reason that the persons entitled to the grant cannot be traced, or are unwilling or incompetent to take a grant.
(5) Where there is no personal representative of a deceased person and a cause of action survives against his or her estate under Section 1 of the Law Reform (Miscellaneous Provisions) Act 1934, the court may order that a grant be made to the nominee of a party intending to prosecute the action (*In the Estate of Simpson* [1936] P. 40; *In the Estate of Gunning* [1936] P. 42). (The order to lead to the grant will specify the action and direct that the powers of the grantee be limited for the purpose of being a party to the action.)
(6) Where the person with a prior right to a grant is disqualified by reason of having been found guilty of the murder or manslaughter of the deceased.
(7) Where a trustee in bankruptcy of a person entitled under the will or on an intestacy requires a grant. (The order will direct that the grant be limited to such period as he shall hold office as trustee of the property of the person entitled.) Where a trustee under a deed of arrangement cannot establish that the whole interest of the person entitled has been assigned to him, he may apply for a similar order.

Application for order

11.23 Application for an order may be made *ex parte* to a registrar and must be supported by an affidavit setting out the facts of the case sworn to by the proposed grantee. Any other relevant document should be lodged with the affidavit [Rule 51(a)]. The application may be made at the Principal Registry, or, if the application for the grant is to be made to a district registry, to the appropriate district probate registrar.

Oath

11.24 The oath leading to the grant must follow the terms of the order and show that the applicants have been appointed to administer the estate by virtue of an order made by the registrar under Section 116 of the Act. The facts of the case having been set out in the affidavit leading to the order, there is no need to clear prior interests in the oath. The original order and documents which led to the making of it must be lodged with the papers leading to the grant.

GRANTS AD COLLIGENDA BONA

11.25 Where an estate may be endangered by delay in administering it, the court will not wait for the persons entitled to a grant under the rules to apply for it, but may grant letters of administration *ad colligenda bona* for the purpose of preserving the estate. Such a grant is of administration only, although the deceased may have died testate, and may be made by order to any person whom the court considers suitable (*e.g.* to entire strangers who have been brought into connection with the matter). The grant will be limited as necessary and ceases when the object for which the grant is given is completed. It is rare that circumstances necessitate such a grant and it is generally easier to apply for a full grant to be made under the discretionary powers of the court.

Application for order

11.26 The mode of application for an order to lead to a grant *ad colligenda bona*, under Rule 52(b), is the same as for a discretionary grant (see para. 11.23). The oath need not state whether the deceased died testate or intestate. The oath must recite the order by which the applicant is appointed administrator and quote the limitation imposed by the order. The grant will be limited as directed by the order. See paras. 6.10 ff for the appropriate form of any necessary Inland Revenue Account.

Life or minority interest

11.27 Where a life or minority interest arises in the estate of the deceased, application must normally be made for the appointment of two or more individuals, or of a trust corporation, with or without an individual, as administrators (Section 114(2), Supreme Court Act 1981).

Cessation of grant

11.28 When the object for which the grant was given is completed, the person or persons entitled may apply for a general grant without further order of the court. The oath must recite details of the former grant and, if application is made at the Principal Registry or at a district registry other than that from which the first grant issued, an office copy of that grant must be lodged with the papers.

ADMINISTRATION PENDING SUIT

11.29 Where there are any legal proceedings pending, concerning the validity of the will of a deceased person, or for obtaining, recalling or revoking any grant, the High Court may grant administration of the estate of the deceased to an administrator pending suit, who shall have the rights, duties and powers of a general administrator, other than the right of distributing the estate (unless the Court gives him leave to distribute). Such administrator shall be under the control of the court, and shall act under its direction (Section 117, Supreme Court Act 1981). The court must be satisfied that there is a necessity for the grant, *viz*, that there is something urgent to be done, and that there is no person empowered to do it. Application to be appointed as administrator pending suit is generally made by a party to the action, though any person having an interest in the estate may apply. An application by a creditor of the deceased would be considered.

Application for order appointing administrator

11.30 Application for an order appointing an administrator pending suit is made to a Master of the Chancery Division by way of summons. The court has power to appoint a sole administrator pending suit notwithstanding that there may be a life or minority interest arising in the estate (*Re Haslip* [1958] 2 All E.R. 275)

.

Application for grant

11.31 The grant is obtainable only at the Principal Registry. After the order appointing the administrator has been made, the administrator's oath, any necessary Inland Revenue Account (see paras. 6.10 ff), and an office copy of the order appointing the administrator should be lodged. The court fee appropriate to a full grant is payable, and also Inheritance Tax in respect of all the property of which the deceased was competent to dispose.

Subsequent application for full grant

11.32 A grant of administration pending an action ceases on the determination of the action, and application for the full grant is made in the usual way. The value of the whole estate must be sworn to in the oath and full details of the estate must be shown in a form of Inland Revenue Account appropriate to a first grant. Where Inheritance Tax has been paid the Capital Taxes Office will give a certificate to that effect on the Inland Revenue Account (see para. 6.25). The oath leading to the grant must recite particulars of the final order made in the action and an office copy of the final order must be obtained from the Chancery Division and lodged with the oath.

CHAPTER 12

Commorientes; Leave to Swear Death; Murder and Manslaughter

COMMORIENTES

12.01 Where two or more persons in immediate succession to each other (whether under a will or on intestacy) die in circumstances rendering it uncertain which of them survived the other or others, the question of survivorship must be considered by the registrar in determining the title to a grant in the estate of any such persons. In all cases (but see below) where two or more persons have died on or after 1st January 1926, in circumstances rendering it uncertain which of them survived the other or others, such deaths shall (subject to any order of the court), for all purposes affecting the title to property, be presumed to have occurred in order of seniority, and accordingly the younger is deemed to have survived the elder (Section 184, Law of Property Act 1925). The presumption applies only where there is uncertainty as to the order in which the deaths occurred (*Hickman v. Peacey* [1945] A.C. 304).

12.02 The presumption does not, however, apply when one of the persons has executed a will which provides for the contingency of deaths occurring in such circumstances. Where a testator declared in his will that if he and his wife should die in circumstances rendering it uncertain which of them survived the other, his wife should be deemed to have predeceased him, it was held that the terms of the will excluded the presumption (*Re Guggenheim* "The Times", 20th June 1941).

12.03 If no contrary provision is made by will, the presumption under Section 184 applies in all cases where there is no evidence of survivorship and, although it may appear that the deaths were simultaneous, it has been held that it is impossible to furnish proof of simultaneous death (*Hickman v. Peacey* [1945] A.C. 304). The intentions of the testator must be fully considered in construing a will which makes provision for "simultaneous deaths", by reason that the ordinary man would infer that deaths in such circumstances were simultaneous.

Death of husband and wife after 1952

12.04 The presumption under Section 184 has been modified by the Intestates' Estates Act 1952 so that in the case of a husband and wife dying on or after 1st Janaury 1953 in circumstances rendering it uncertain which of them survived the other and one or both of them died wholly or partially intestate, the presumption does not apply and the estate of the intestate devolves as if the other spouse did not survive.

12.05 If, however, a husband or wife leaves a will which effectively disposes of the whole estate, the presumption under Section 184 as to the deaths having occurred in order of seniority does not apply in respect of his or her estate; but if there is a partial intestacy the distribution of estate undisposed of by the will is governed by Section 46(3) of the Administration of Estates Act 1925 as in a complete intestacy.

Procedure on application for grant

12.06 In every case in which uncertainty as to survivorship arises, all the evidence of the circumstances which is readily available should be submitted to the registrar at the earliest opportunity in order that he may decide whether a grant of representation may issue on that evidence or whether further enquiries should be made. The sort of evidence which is commonly presented consists of an affidavit by the person who found the bodies and an affidavit by the doctor who examined them. Although the findings of a coroner's jury cannot be accepted as evidence, a copy of the notes of evidence, if available, may assist the registrar in some cases, but it is not necessary to delay applications or incur expense in obtaining copy notes of evidence before obtaining the registrar's directions.

12.07 If the registrar decides that the application may proceed on the basis of uncertainty of survivorship, the oath leading to the grant must state "That all possible enquiries as to survivorship have been made, but it appears that the said *A.* and *B.* died in circumstances rendering it uncertain which of them survived the other". The oath should also show that the applicant relies upon the statutory presumption to establish his title to the grant (*e.g.* "That the said   , being younger, is by virtue of Section 184 of the Law of Property Act 1925 deemed to have survived the said   ").

12.08 In the case of a husband and wife dying on or after 1st January 1953 on an intestacy, it is sufficient for the oath to state that the intestate and spouse died in circumstances rendering it uncertain which of them survived the other. The statutory provision need not be quoted.

Foreign domicile

12.09 Where the deceased persons died domiciled out of the jurisdiction of the English court, the distribution of the estates is determined by the law of the domicile (*Re Cohn* [1945] Ch. 5; 171 L.T. 377).

Example forms of oath for commorientes

(1) *Oath for administrator (commorientes spouses)—Death on or after 1st January 1953.*

[USUAL HEADING]

I, *C.B.* of ,
make oath and say as follows:

1. That *A.B.*, of deceased, died on the day of 19 , aged years, domiciled in England and Wales, intestate.
2. That all possible enquiries as to survivorship have been made, but it appears that the said *A.B.* and *B.B.* his lawful wife (her lawful husband) died in circumstances rendering it uncertain which of them survived the other.
3. That no (*or* a) minority or life interest arises under the intestacy.
4. That there was (no) land vested in the said deceased immediately before his death which was settled previously thereto and which remained settled land notwithstanding his death.
5. That I am the lawful* (*son*) and one of the persons entitled to share in the estate of the said intestate.
6. That I will:

    (i) collect, get in and administer etc. (*complete as in form after para. 5.49*).

Sworn, etc.

*If the intestate died on or after 4th April 1988 "lawful" is not relevant and may be omitted.

(2) *Oath for administration with will (commorientes)—Grant to legal personal representative*

[USUAL HEADING]

I, *C.B.* of ,
make oath and say as follows:

1. That I believe the paper writing now produced to and marked by me to contain the true and original last will and testament of *A.B.*, of , deceased, who died on the day of 19 , aged years, domiciled in England and Wales.
2. That all possible enquiries as to survivorship have been made but it appears that the said *A.B.* and *B.B.* brother of the deceased the sole executor and residuary legatee and devisee named in the said will, died in circumstances rendering it uncertain which of them survived the other.
3. That no (*or* a) minority or life interest arises in the estate of the said deceased.
4. That there was (no) land vested in the said deceased immediately before his death which was settled previously thereto (and not by his said will) and which remained settled land notwithstanding his death.
5. That the said *B.B.* being the younger, is by virtue of Section 184 of the Law of Property Act 1925 deemed to have survived the said *A.B.*.

6. That I am the sole executor of the will (*or* the administrator of the estate) of the said *B.B.*, probate (*or* letters of administration) thereof having been granted to me at the Registry on the day of 19 .

7. That I will:
   (i) collect, get in and administer etc. (*complete as in form after para. 4.45*).

Sworn, etc.

LEAVE TO SWEAR DEATH

12.10 The Family Division has no power to make an order presuming the death of any person but where a grant is sought in the estate of a person who is presumed to have died application may be made for an order giving the applicant for the grant leave to swear to the death. A decree of presumed death and of dissolution of marriage made under the Matrimonial Causes Act 1973 dissolves the marriage and is not sufficient for any other purpose in a non-contentious probate matter.

12.11 The court will not entertain an application for an order for leave to swear to the death of any person other than the person to whose estate a grant is sought. Where, after the issue of the grant, the person who was believed to be dead is found living, application must be made for revocation of the grant. The application for revocation should be supported by affidavit and should be made to the registry which sealed the original grant (Rule 41).

Application for order

12.12 An order giving leave to swear to death may be obtained by way of *ex parte* application to a registrar of the Principal Registry or to the district probate registrar at the registry at which application for the grant will subsequently be made. An order giving leave to swear to death is retained in the registry and cannot be given out, but it is available for inspection by the applicant's solicitor who may make a note of its contents for inclusion in the oath leading to the grant.

Affidavit evidence required

12.13 An affidavit sworn by the applicant is required, and where necessary it must be supported by other affidavits as mentioned below (Rule 53). Where the application is based upon the fact that the alleged deceased has not been heard of for several years or that he has suddenly disappeared, the evidence of the applicant should, if possible, be corroborated by an affidavit sworn by a disinterested person.

12.14 The affidavit of the applicant should state:

(1) The name and age of the alleged deceased, his last known address and occupation (or status) and when he was last known to be alive.
(2) That the applicant believes the alleged deceased to be dead and the facts relied upon to presume death.
(3) The efforts made to trace the alleged deceased, and whether any advertisements have been inserted. Copies of advertisements, if any, should be exhibited to the affidavit and it must be stated whether or not, and if so what, information was obtained as a result of the advertisements.
(4) Whether the alleged deceased died testate or intestate. If testate, the will must be produced with and identified in the affidavit.
(5) The names and relationships to the alleged deceased of all persons who are entitled to share in his estate in the event of an intestacy, and whether they are *sui juris*.
(6) Whether the life of the alleged deceased was insured. If so, particulars of all policies and the names of the insurance companies must be given, and it must be stated whether notice of the application has been given to the insurance companies. Replies, if any, from the insurance companies must be exhibited to the affidavit. If no replies have been received, an affidavit as to service of the notice is required. If a claim has been admitted by an insurance company, it should be so stated.
(7) Whether any letters have been received from the alleged deceased since his disappearance. If so, they should be exhibited to the affidavit.
(8) If the alleged deceased had a bank account, whether it has been operated since his disappearance.
(9) Details and value of the estate.
(10) That the applicant believes that the alleged deceased died on or since a particular date.
(11) If a body presumed to be that of the alleged deceased has been found, but not identified, particulars of the inquest held and the finding thereof.

12.15 Where the belief of death arises through the disappearance of a ship or loss of an aircraft, affidavit evidence as to the following is also required:

(1) That the alleged deceased was actually on board the ship or aircraft when it left the last port or airfield. The last letter, if any, written whilst on board, should be exhibited.
(2) The date and place when the ship or aircraft was last seen or in communication.

(3) The non-arrival, within a reasonable time, of the ship or aircraft at the port or airfield of destination.
(4) The absence of news of the ship or aircraft from the time when it was last seen or in communication.
(5) Whether the ship or aircraft was insured, and, if insured, whether the insurers have paid as for a total loss. If a certificate has been issued under the Merchant Shipping Act 1970, it must be produced.

A supporting affidavit from the owner of the ship or aircraft, or from an official representing the owners, speaking to the facts of the case within his knowledge may also be required.

12.16 A record is kept in the Principal Registry of various disasters in which two or more people die. Before applying for an order for leave to swear to the death of a person involved in such a disaster, an enquiry should be made of the Secretary of the Principal Registry whether any evidence is already available to the court.

Order to be recited in oath leading to grant

12.17 In the oath leading to the grant, the order must be recited along the following lines:

> "That by an order dated the day of 19 , made by one of the Registrars of the Principal Registry (*or* made by the district probate registrar of the district probate registry) leave was given to swear to the death of the above-named deceased as having occurred on or since the day of 19 ."

MURDER AND MANSLAUGHTER

12.18 On the grounds of public policy a person who unlawfully kills another forfeits any interest he may have (but see below), and also any right to a grant, in the estate of the person killed. This applies in the case of murder (*Crippen* [1911] P. 108; *Re Callaway, Callaway v. Treasury Solicitor* [1956] Ch. 559), and it has been held that such forfeiture should also apply to cases of manslaughter (*Re Hall* [1914] P.1), and manslaughter by reason of diminished responsibility (*Re Giles, Giles v. Giles* [1972] Ch. 544); but there is no forfeiture when a murderer is found to be insane at the time of the murder (*Re Pitts* [1931] 1 Ch. 546; 145 L.T. 116; *Re Houghton* [1915] 2 Ch. 173; *Re Battens Will Trusts* (1961) 105 S.J. 529.) No distinction is made between testacies and intestacies.

12.19 On production of a properly authenticated copy of the certificate of conviction, an application may be made for an order and grant under Section 116 of the Supreme Court Act 1981 passing over the unlawful killer or his legal personal representative. The affidavit in support of the application should also confirm, where appropriate (see below), that no application for modification of the forfeiture rule has been made under the Forfeiture Act 1982 and that the time for making any such application has expired.

12.20 *As from 13th October 1982*, application may be made to the court for modification of the forfeiture rule (Forfeiture Act 1982). The court is not able to make an order modifying the effect of the rule in respect of any interest in property which, in consequence of the rule, has been acquired before 13th October 1982 by a person other than the offender or a person claiming through him (Section 2(7)), but otherwise an order may be made whether the unlawful killing occurred before or after 13th October 1982 (Section 7(4)). Any application for modification of the rule must be made within three months of the conviction (Section 2(3)). No order can be made for modification if the conviction is for murder (Section 5).

12.21 A murderer's forfeited share in the estate passes to the other members of the class beneficially interested and not to the Crown as *bona vacantia* (*Re Callaway, Callaway v. Treasury Solicitor* [1956] Ch. 559; *Re Peacock, Midland Bank Executor and Trustee Co. Ltd v. Peacock and Another* [1957] 1 Ch. 310). Where a will contains a gift to a class (or group) of persons and a member is disqualified by public policy from taking his share, the share does not lapse but goes to increase the shares of the other members.

CHAPTER 13

Resealing

13.01 Grants issued by the court of the countries to which the Colonial Probates Acts 1892 and 1927 apply, may be resealed in any probate registry. Grants issued by the Principal or any of the district probate registries in England and Wales may be resealed in those countries. Resealing avoids the inconvenience and expense of obtaining multiple grants, but if so desired a separate grant may be applied for in any country in which estate of the deceased is situate. The resealing of a grant constitutes the grantees legal personal representatives as to the relevant estate of the deceased situate in the country in which the grant is resealed.

ADMINISTRATION OF ESTATES ACT 1971

Scotland and Northern Ireland

13.02 The Administration of Estates Act 1971 abolished the resealing of grants between England and Wales, Scotland and Northern Ireland. Section 1 provides that where a person dies domiciled in Scotland, a confirmation granted in respect of all or part of his estate and noting his Scottish domicile, and a certificate of confirmation noting his Scottish domicile and relating to one or more items of his estate shall, without being resealed, be treated for the purposes of the law of England and Wales as a grant of representation to the executors named in the confirmation or certificate.

13.03 Similarly, where a person dies domiciled in Northern Ireland, a grant of probate of his will or letters of administration (with or without will) in respect of his estate made by the High Court in Northern Ireland and noting his domicile there, shall, without being resealed, be treated for the purposes of the law of England and Wales as if it has been originally made by the High Court of England and Wales.

13.04 When a person dies domiciled in England and Wales, Scotland or Northern Ireland leaving estate in England and Wales, the usual procedure is for a grant to be extracted from the country of domicile. If the deceased was not domiciled in England and Wales and either there is no estate in the country of domicile or it is intended to deal with the estate that is situated in England and Wales first, application for a grant should be made in the appropriate manner and unless otherwise directed, the grant will be limited to the estate in England and Wales and until representation is granted in the county of domicile.

13.05 For the procedure concerning delivery of the Inland Revenue Account and payment of Inheritance Tax where more than one grant in the United Kingdom is required, see paras. 6.24–26.

RESEALING COLONIAL GRANTS IN ENGLAND AND WALES

13.06 The Colonial Probates Act 1892, as extended by the Colonial Probates (Protected States and Mandated Territories) Act 1927, governs the resealing of colonial grants in England and Wales. The term "colonial" is used for convenience in the following paragraphs, but the Act also provides for the resealing of grants issued by several former colonies and protectorates, etc., which have attained independence within the Commonwealth, and by the Republic of South Africa.

13.07 The Act provides that grants issued in a country or territory to which it has been applied by Order in Council may be resealed in the United Kingdom, and shall then be of the like force and effect, and have the same operation in the United Kingdom as if granted by the resealing court. When an Order in Council has applied the Act to a country or territory, grants issued in that country or territory may be resealed whether issued before or after the application of the Act.

Territories to which the Acts are applicable

13.08 The Colonial Probates Act Application Order 1965 (as amended) applies the Colonial Probates Acts to the specific territories listed below.

Aden (grants made after 30th November 1967 cannot be resealed)
Alberta
Antigua
Australian Capital Territory
Bahamas
Barbados
Basutoland (now Lesotho)
Belize (formerly British Honduras)
Bermuda
Botswana (formerly Bechuanaland)
British Antarctic Territory
British Columbia
British Guiana (now Guyana)
British Honduras (now Belize)
British Sovereign Base Areas in Cyprus
Brunei

Cayman Islands
Ceylon (now Sri Lanka)
Christmas Island (Australia)
Cocos (Keeling) Islands
Cyprus (Republic)
Dominica
Falkland Islands
Falkland Islands Dependencies
Fiji
Gambia
Ghana
Gibralter
Gilbert and Ellice Islands now Kiribati and Tuvalu respectively)
Grenada
Guyana (formerly British Guiana)
Hong Kong
Jamaica
Kenya
Kiribati
Lesotho (formerly Basutoland)
Malawi
Malaysia
Manitoba
Montserrat
New Brunswick
New Guinea
New Hebrides (grants made on or after 30th July 1980 cannot be resealed)
New South Wales
New Zealand
Newfoundland
Nigeria
Norfolk Island
Northern Territory of Australia
North-West Territories of Canada
Nova Scotia
Ontario
Papua (New Guinea)
Prince Edward Island
Queensland
St. Christopher (Kitts), Nevis and Anguilla
St. Helena
St. Lucia
St. Vincent
Saskatchewan
Seychelles (Republic)
Sierra Leone
Singapore
Solomon Islands
South Africa
South Australia
Southern Rhodesia (now Zimbabwe)
Sri Lanka (formerly Ceylon)
Swaziland
Tanzania
Tasmania
Tortola (formerly Virgin Islands)
Trinidad and Tobago (Republic)
Turks and Caicos Islands
Tuvala (formerly Ellice Islands)
Uganda
Victoria
Virgin Islands (now Tortola)
Western Australia
Zambia
Zimbabwe (formerly Southern Rhodesia)

Acceptance of grant for resealing

13.09 A grant is normally accepted for resealing without leave of a registrar if it is made:

(1) By the court having jurisdiction at the place where the deceased died domiciled, or

(2) To a person who is also entrusted with the administration of the estate by the court having jurisdiction at the place where the deceased died domiciled, or

(3) To a person who is also beneficially entitled to the estate according to the law of the place where the deceased died domiciled, or

(4) In respect of a will admissible to proof in England and Wales, to the executor named therein in the English or Welsh language, or whatever the language of the will, to a person named therein whose duties are sufficient to constitute him as executor according to the tenor.

In the case of either 2 or 3 above it must be evidenced that the grantee is such a person by production of the grant made to him by the court of the domicile, or by evidence of law showing that he is beneficially entitled to the estate by the law of the domicile. If the grantee does not fall within the terms of 1, 2, 3, or 4 above, leave of a registrar is required before the grant may be resealed (Rule 39(3)).

Limited or temporary grant

13.10 No limited or temporary grant may be resealed, except by leave of a registrar, although such leave is not required in the case of a grant expressed to relate to personal estate only.

A grant expressly limited to estate within the jurisdiction of the issuing court will not be resealed as the grantee(s) would not be authorised to deal with estate in England and Wales under the grant.

Nil estate in England and Wales

13.11 A grant may be resealed although the deceased possessed no estate in England and Wales, provided that a statement is lodged by the applicant giving sufficient reason for requiring the resealing.

Application for resealing

13.12 Rule 39 provides that an application for resealing under the Colonial Probates Acts shall be made by the person to whom the grant was made or by any person authorised in writing to apply on his behalf. All the grantees should join in the application or authorisation. If this cannot be done, the signed consents of those who do not apply should be lodged; failing this, an affidavit giving reasons may be required. If any of the grantees are dead, a statement setting out the facts and date of death should be filed, and the grant will be resealed in favour of the "now surviving" grantees. Where the colonial grant has been made to the attorney of the person entitled, it is not now necessary to lodge the original power of attorney or a copy thereof.

Resealing after appointment of additional grantee

13.13 If a grant which has been resealed in England and Wales is subsequently endorsed by the Colonial court to show that another grantee has been added or that a non-proving executor appointed by the will is deemed to be an executor to whom power was reserved and is deemed to be joint executor, it may be resealed again. A further fiat will be endorsed on the grant showing that it is resealed at the instance of the added grantee or joint executor. Where an exemplification contains copies of a probate and a double probate it may be resealed, provided that the application for resealing is at the instance of all parties. If a probate and double probate are lodged together, both may be resealed.

Duplicate Colonial Grants

13.14 No reason need be given for an application to reseal a duplicate grant. The fiat for resealing will bear the date on which it is signed, and no reference is made to the original resealing.

Application for resealing, procedure

13.15 The application may be made at any probate registry by the grantee, or by any person authorised in writing to apply on his behalf, or through a solicitor, by lodging the requisite documents with the Receiver of Papers in the Principal Registry or with the district probate registry. If desired, the grantee or person authorised by him may make application in person by attending at the Personal Application Department of the Principal Registry, but in that case additional fees are payable for preparation of papers by that department. An application by post from an address out of England and Wales is acceptable.

13.16 The following documents are required:

(1) The original grant, or a duplicate thereof, under seal of the Colonial court, or a copy thereof certified by or under the authority of the Colonial court, or an exemplification which contains all the essential parts of the grant and includes a copy of the will, if any.
(2) A plain copy of the grant, and plain copy of the will, if any. If desired, a copy of the will can be made at the registry for a fee.
(3) Where application is made by some person on behalf of the grantee, the document authorising such person to apply.
(4) An Inland Revenue Account. The Account should be submitted to the Capital Taxes Office for control prior to lodging the papers at the Registry (see para. 6.63).

RESEALING OF GRANTS MADE IN ENGLAND AND WALES IN COMMONWEALTH COUNTRIES AND COLONIES

13.17 Applications for the resealing of grants made in England and Wales in Commonwealth or Colonial courts cannot be made through a probate registry but must be made through an agent in the country concerned.

CHAPTER 14

Amendment, Notation, Revocation and Duplicate Grants

AMENDMENT OF ERRORS AND OMISSIONS IN GRANTS

14.01 If a registrar is satisfied that a grant should be amended or revoked he may make an order accordingly. Save in exceptional circumstances, no grant may be amended or revoked unless application is made by, or with the consent of, the person to whom the grant was made (Rule 41). It depends on the nature of the error or omission as to whether the registrar will allow the grant to be amended or order its revocation. Where the error or omission is of a minor nature or is non-vital to the grant the registrar will usually order amendment, but it is advisable to obtain the directions of the registrar before taking any steps in the matter.

14.02 The following paragraphs refer to errors and omissions of the most common type and show whether amendment of the grant may be allowed.

Surname of deceased

14.03 An error in the surname usually necessitates revocation of the grant, but amendment may be allowed in the case of a minor spelling error.

Forenames of deceased

14.04 If the first, or only, forename is wrong, the grant must normally be revoked, except where the correct name is of the same sound (*e.g.*"Marjorie" and "Marjory"), when an amendment is usually allowed. Errors in other forenames, or the omission of such names, may be rectified by amendment.

Alias

14.05 Provided that the grant shows the true name, an alias name may be inserted by way of amendment. A grant made in an alias name must be revoked; it may not be amended to show the true name.

Address of deceased

14.06 Amendment is allowed when there are minor errors or omissions in the address of the deceased, also when it is desired to insert an additional address.

Date of death

14.07 An error in the date of death may be rectified by amendment, provided that such correction does not affect the title to the grant.

Name of grantee

14.08 The practice as to an amendment in the name of a grantee follows that relating to an error in the name of the deceased. Where a person whose name is mis-recited in a will has used such incorrect name in obtaining a grant, an amendment may be allowed. In such a case proof of identity may be required.

Address of grantee

14.09 Minor errors in the address of a grantee may be rectified by amendment.

Limitations

14.10 An amendment to, or an insertion of, a limitation in a grant may be allowed.

Amendment as to settled land

14.11 A general grant may be amended by insertion of the limitation "save and except settled land", provided that the affidavit to lead to such an amendment states that the value of the settled land is not included in the gross amount of the estate shown in the grant. Where the value of the settled land has been included, the registrar has a discretion to either allow amendment of the grant or order its revocation. Similarly, a general grant may be amended by insertion of the words "including settled land", provided that the affidavit to lead to the amendment states that the value of the settled land is already included in the amount of estate shown in the grant, and that all the grantees are entitled to a grant of the same character in respect of the settled land. A grant made "save and except settled land" cannot be amended to include settled land. A separate grant "limited to settled land" must be obtained. A grant "limited to settled land" will not be amended to include free estate. A grant "save and except settled land" must be obtained in respect of the free estate.

Unauthorised alteration in grant

14.12 A grant must not be altered without authority. If an unauthorised amendment has been made, the grant must be lodged at the registry from which it issued. The grant will be retained in the registry, and a duplicate grant must be obtained. The duplicate may be altered after an order authorising amendment has been made. The grant will be revoked if the unauthorised alteration is of an extensive or serious character.

Official error in grant

14.13 Any grant which, after passing the seal, is found to be inaccurate or deficient by reason of official error and which is returned to the issuing registry for correction within fourteen days of its sealing, will be re-issued in a corrected form, provided it has not been registered. In all other cases correction must be made by registrar's order. Official errors are corrected without fee.

Application for amendment of grant, procedure

14.14 The grantee, or grantees, should swear an affidavit of facts, setting out the nature of the error and the proposed amendment. The affidavit and grant should be lodged in, or sent by post to, the registry from which the grant issued. If the grant issued out of the Principal Registry, the documents should be lodged with, or sent to, the Record Keeper of that Registry. If the registrar thinks fit he will make an order authorising amendment. The grant will be amended in the registry and a notation referring to the order will be made on it.

Affidavit to lead to amendment of grant

[USUAL HEADING]

I, *A.B.*, of ,
make oath and say as follows:

1. That on the day of 19 , letters of administration of the estate of *C.D.*, of , deceased, were granted at the Probate Registry to me the (lawful) (mother) and only person entitled to the estate of the deceased.

2. That in the said grant of administration the date of death of the deceased is stated to be the 10th day of April 1988, whereas the true date was the 20th day of April 1988, as appears by the certificate of death now produced to me and marked "A".

3. That the error arose by my not having observed when reading the oath to lead to the said grant that the wrong date, namely, "10th", had been inadvertently inserted in that document.

4. That I desire that the said grant of administration may be amended by substituting "20th" for "10th" as the date of death of the deceased.

Sworn, etc.

(*Note: The above form of affidavit may be adapted as required.*)

NOTATION OF GRANTS

Notation of appointment of additional administrator

14.15 When an order appointing an additional administrator has been obtained under Section 114(4) of the Supreme Court Act 1981, the order and grant should be lodged at the registry from which the grant issued (Record Keeper's Department in the case of a Principal Registry grant). The appointment of the additional administrator will be noted on the grant.

Notation of election to redeem life interest

14.16 A note is made on the grant after notice of election to redeem the life interest has been filed in the registry.

REVOCATION

14.17 Section 25(1)(b) of the Supreme Court Act 1981 gives the court authority to revoke grants of probate and letters of administration, and Section 121(1) of the same Act gives the court power of its own motion to revoke a grant where it appears that it ought not to have been granted, or if it contains an error. Although in the most common type of case an order for revocation of a grant is usually made by a registrar (under Rule 26(2) or Rule 41), a grant may be revoked by decree made in an action for revocation or by an order made by a judge in chambers or open court.

14.18 The most common grounds for revocation of a grant are as follows:

(1) When the grant contains an error which cannot be corrected by amendment.

(2) When a grant of administration has been obtained on the erroneous supposition that the deceased died intestate.

(3) When a later will is discovered after an earlier one has been proved.

(4) When a grant has been made to a person under 18 years of age.

(5) When a grant has been sealed after the death of the person, or of any of the persons, who applied for it. (There may be cases of doubt when the grantee died on the day of the date of the grant and it is difficult to establish whether he died before or after the actual sealing (*Re Seaford* [1968] P. 53). In such cases the registrar will normally require an affidavit of facts on which to make his decision.)

(6) When, after proof of a will, a codicil which revokes the will or alters the appointment of executors is discovered.

(7) When a revoked or forged will has been proved.

(8) When a grant of administration has been made to persons who claimed to be next of kin of the deceased, and others nearer of kin are discovered.

(9) When probate has been granted to two or more executors and one of them becomes incapable of managing his affairs. (A new grant is made to the capable executors, with power reserved to the incapable executor to obtain probate on recovering his capacity. If desired, the remaining grantee or grantees may furnish one affidavit to lead to revocation and to serve as the oath leading to the new grant.)

(10) When one of two or more administrators (with or without will) becomes incapable of managing his affairs. (A new grant is made to the capable administrators. If there is a subsisting life or minority interest in the estate, the further grant must normally be made to not less than two individuals, or to a trust corporation with or without an individual.)

(11) When it is discovered that a will which has been admitted to proof was not properly executed. (If satisfied with the evidence, the registrar will mark the will "probate refused" and order revocation of the grant.)

(12) When a grant has been made in the estate of a living person.

Application for revocation of grant procedure

14.19 Application for revocation of a grant should be made by the grantee, or by the person entitled to the new grant. In the latter case, the written consent of the grantee should, if possible, be obtained and lodged with the application.

14.20 An affidavit by the applicant is required, stating the details of the grant and the reason why it should be revoked, also the capacity in which a new grant is sought (forms of affidavit after para. 14.23.) The affidavit and the original grant must be lodged in, or sent by post to, the registry from which the grant issued (Record Keeper's Department in the case of a Principal Registry grant).

14.21 If the original grant has been lost or mislaid, or there is other good reason why it cannot be produced, an office copy of the grant should be lodged and the applicant may be required to file an undertaking to bring the original grant in to the registry if it should become available.

Combined application for revocation of probate and new grant

14.22 Where a grant of probate has been issued to two or more executors, one of whom subsequently becomes mentally incapable of managing his affairs, and it is proposed to revoke it and obtain a new grant of probate to the remaining grantee or grantees, one affidavit may be used both to lead to the order for revocation and to serve as the oath on which the new grant issues. The will may be referred to as that already proved and need not be re-marked, nor need a copy be annexed. No further Inland Revenue Account need be lodged.

Application for new grant

14.23 The person or persons entitled to the new grant cannot be sworn to the papers leading to it until the revocation of the former grant is complete. The oath leading to the grant must recite details of the previous grant and the order revoking it. If application is made at the Principal Registry a plain copy of the revoked grant bearing notation of revocation thereon must be lodged with the papers. For the appropriate form of any necessary Inland Revenue Account, see paras. 6.10–14.

Forms of affidavit to lead to revocation and of oath for substituted grant

(1) *Affidavit to lead to revocation of probate, a later will having been found*

[USUAL HEADING]

I, of ,
make oath and say as follows:

1. That of , deceased, died on the day of 19 , domiciled in England and Wales, having made and duly executed a will bearing date the day of 19 , whereof I the said was appointed sole executor.

2. I verily believed (until I had, as hereinafter deposed, ascertained to the contrary) that the said will was the last will and testament of the said deceased and I applied to this Division at the Registry thereof for and obtained on the day of 19 , a grant of probate of the said will on the basis that such will was the last will and testament of the said deceased.

3. That since the date last mentioned I have discovered [*state how*] a will made and executed by the said deceased, of a later date than the date of the above-mentioned will, namely, a will bearing date the day of 19 , whereof the said deceased appointed sole executor, and whereby the said deceased revoked all wills previously made by him.

4. That I am therefore desirous that the probate, heretofore granted to me, shall be revoked and declared null and void.

Sworn, etc.

(2) *Affidavit to lead to revocation of administration, a will having been found*

[USUAL HEADING]

I, of ,
make oath and say as follows:

1. That of ,
died on the day of 19 ,
domiciled in England and Wales.

2. That I verily believed (until I had, as hereinafter deposed, ascertained to the contrary) that the said deceased died intestate, and being the lawful* child and one of the persons entitled to share in the estate of the said deceased [*or as the case may be*] I applied to this Division at the Registry for, and, on the day of 19 , obtained letters of administration of the estate of the said deceased, on the basis that he died intestate a widower [*or as the case may be*].

3. That since the date last mentioned [*on looking through the papers and deeds of the said deceased, or as the case may be*] I found the original last will and testament of the said deceased, which said will is duly made and executed by the said deceased and bears date the day of 19 .

4. [*State why search was not made earlier or other reasons why the will was not discovered.*]

5. That I am therefore desirous that the letters of administration granted to me, as before stated, shall be revoked and declared null and void.

Sworn, etc.

*If the deceased died on or after 4th April 1988 "lawful" is not relevant and may be omitted.

(3) *Affidavit to lead to revocation of administration—Grantee not entitled*

[USUAL HEADING]

I, of ,
make oath and say as follows:

1. That of ,
died on the day of 19 ,
domiciled in England and Wales intestate, a bachelor without issue or parent or any other person entitled in priority to share in the estate by virtue of any enactment.

2. That I verily believed, (until I had, as hereinafter deposed, ascertained to the contrary) that the deceased died without a brother or sister of the whole blood or issue of such and being the lawful* brother of the half blood of the said deceased I applied to this Division at the Registry for and, on the day of 19 , obtained letters of administration of the estate of the said deceased on the basis that he died intestate, a bachelor without issue or parent or brother or sister of the whole blood or issue of such.

3. That since the date last mentioned I have discovered that the said deceased left surviving a lawful* brother of the whole blood, namely .

4. That the said had not been seen or heard of for a period of more than years, and although I had made frequent and constant enquiries for him I could not learn anything of his whereabouts until the day of 19 , when I received a communication from the said who is now living.

5. That I am therefore desirous that the letters of administration granted to me as before stated shall be revoked and declared null and void.

Sworn, etc.

*If the intestate died on or after 4th April 1988 "lawful" is not relevant and may be omitted.

(4) *Oath to lead to substituted grant—Probate*

[USUAL HEADING]

I, *C.B.* of , make oath and say as follows:

1. That *A.B.*, of , deceased, died on the day of 19 aged years, domiciled in England and Wales, having made and duly executed his last will and testament, bearing date the day of 19 , and thereof appointed me sole executor.

2. That notwithstanding the premises probate of an earlier will of the said testator, namely, a will dated the day of 19 , was on the day of 19 , granted at the Registry, to *E.F.*, the sole executor named therein.

3. That the said grant of probate has since been voluntarily brought in by the said *E.F.* and has been duly revoked and declared null and void.

4. That I believe the paper writing now produced to and marked by me to contain the true and original last will and testament of the said deceased.

5. That I am the sole executor named in the said will.

6. That there was (no) land vested in the deceased immediately before his death which was settled previously thereto and not by his will and which remained settled land notwithstanding his death.

7. That I will:

(i) collect, get in and administer etc. (*complete as in form after para. 3.27*).

Sworn, etc.

(5) *Oath to lead to substituted grant—Administration*

[USUAL HEADING]

I, *E.D.* of ,
make oath and say as follows:

1. That *A.D.*, of ,
deceased, died on the day of 19 ,
aged years, intestate, domiciled in England and Wales, a widower without issue or any other person entitled in priority to share in the estate by virtue of any enactment, leaving *C.D.*, his lawful* father, the only person entitled to his estate, who has since died without having taken upon himself letters of administration of the estate of the said intestate.

2. That letters of administration of the estate of the said deceased were on the day of 19 , granted at the Registry to *F.D.*, the lawful* brother of the whole blood of the said deceased, on the basis that the said deceased died a widower without issue or parent or any other person entitled in priority to share in the estate by virtue of any enactment.

3. That the said grant of administration has been since voluntarily brought in and has been duly revoked and declared null and void.

4. That I am the administrator of the estate of the said *C.D.*, deceased, letters of administration of his estate having been granted to me at the Registry on the day of 19 .

5. That no minority or life interest arises under the intestacy and that there was (no) land vested in the said deceased immediately before his death which was settled previously thereto and which remained settled land notwithstanding his death.

6. That I will:

(i) collect, get in and administer etc. (*complete as in form after para. 5.49*).

Sworn, etc.

*If the intestate died on or after 4th April 1988 "lawful" is not relevant and may be omitted.

DUPLICATE GRANTS

14.24 Duplicate grants of probate or administration may only issue on the application of the grantee or grantees, and can only be obtained at the registry from which the original grant issued. A duplicate may be obtained when the original grant issues or subsequently. Postal application is accepted. It is not the practice to issue a duplicate grant merely for the purpose of assisting with registration. An office copy of the original grant bearing a seal is obtainable for that purpose and any number of such copies may be obtained either on payment of 25p per page when the copies are requested with the application for the grant or on a personal attendance, or on payment of £2 for one copy and 25p per page for each additional copy when the copies are requested by post (other than with the grant application). The copies may be obtained at the registry from which the grant issued or from the Principal Registry.

14.25 A duplicate grant bears the same date as the original and is marked "Duplicate Grant" in the top margin, and the date of issue of the duplicate is shown in the right-hand margin. Any amendment or notation officially made on the original grant after its issue is shown on the duplicate.

Procedure

14.26 The following documents are required:

(1) A letter of request for the issue of the duplicate, giving the reason why the duplicate is required. The letter must be signed by the grantee or grantees, or by the extracting solicitor.
(2) Where application is subsequent to the date of issue of a grant obtained at the Principal Registry, the original grant or an office copy thereof.
(3) If the original grant was obtained at the Principal Registry before 1st January 1931, an engrossment of the testamentary documents admitted to proof (if any) may be required. This also applies where the original grant was obtained at a district probate registry before the photographic method was introduced at that registry.
(4) Where the original grant was obtained at the Principal Registry before 1934, or at a district probate registry before 1st May 1934, a certificate from the Capital Taxes Office as to the amount of Estate Duty paid.

CHAPTER 15

Applications to the Court and Citations

EX PARTE APPLICATIONS

Application at the Principal Registry or at a district probate registry

15.01 Where an *ex parte* application is necessary in connection with a grant which is to be obtained at, or which has issued from, the Principal Registry, the affidavits setting out the facts of the case, and any other necessary documents, should be lodged at the Probate Department of the Principal Registry. Where an *ex parte* application is necessary in connection with a grant which is to be obtained at, or which has issued from, a district probate registry, such application should be made to the district probate registrar of that registry by lodging the affidavits setting out the facts of the case, and any other necessary documents, at the district probate registry.

If the registrar rejects the application or is not satisfied with the evidence, the documents will be returned to the practitioner with a note as to the points to be dealt with. If an order is made it is usually sent, by post, a few days after the application is lodged.

Order to be filed

15.02 The order, together with the affidavits and any other document used in support of the application, must subsequently be filed in the registry, and where appropriate with the papers to lead to the grant. It should, however, be noted that an order giving leave to swear death is not handed out, but remains in the registry at which it is obtained.

Orders obtainable on ex parte *application to a registrar*

15.03

(1) An order for a grant under Section 116 of the Supreme Court Act 1981 (see paras. 11.20ff).

(2) An order for a grant as to only part of an estate pursuant to Section 113 of the Supreme Court Act 1981 (see paras. 11.17ff).

(3) An order for a grant *ad colligenda bona* (see paras. 11.25ff).

(4) An order for leave to swear to the death of a missing person (see paras. 12.10ff).

(5) An order for a grant under Rule 30, where the deceased died domiciled outside England and Wales (see paras. 7.25ff).
(6) An order for the assignment of a guardian to a minor (see paras. 8.15ff).
(7) An order for a grant for the use and benefit of a person mentally incapable of managing his own affairs (see paras. 8.25ff).
(8) An order admitting to proof a copy or reconstruction of a lost or destroyed testamentary document (see paras. 2.144ff).
(9) An order to join with a person entitled to a grant of administration a person entitled in a lower degree or a person having no right to a grant (see para. 5.09).
(10) An order appointing an additional administrator after a grant has been made (see para. 5.10).
(11) An order giving leave to retract a renunciation (see paras. 17.14–17).
(12) An order for the issue of a grant after citation of persons with a prior right (see paras. 15.37 ff).
(13) An order that a will be rectified where the application is unopposed (see paras. 2.58 ff).
(14) An order for the amendment or revocation of a grant (see paras. 14.01–14 and 14.17–22).

SUMMONSES

15.04 A summons for hearing by a registrar must be issued out of the registry in which it is to be heard (Rule 61(3)). Some summonses may only be heard by a registrar of the Principal Registry. A summons to be heard by a judge must be issued out of the Principal Registry (Rule 61(4)).

Issue of summons

15.05 The summons must be drawn in duplicate and must clearly set out the nature of the application and bear the name and address of the issuing practitioner. After the issuing clerk has inserted a day and time of hearing in both copies, one copy is retained in the registry and the other copy is sealed as the original summons and returned to the practitioner.

Service of summons

15.06 Service is effected by leaving a copy of the summons at, or sending it by prepaid ordinary or registered post or by recorded delivery to, the address for service of the party to whom it is addressed, or if there is no address for service the usual or last known address of that party or, if the address for service or usual or last known address includes a numbered box at a document exchange approved for the time being by the Lord Chancellor, leaving the copy summons at that document exchange or at a document exchange which transmits documents every business day to that document exchange (Order 65, Rule 5, R.S.C. applied by Rule 67, N.C.P.R). A copy of each affidavit to be used at the hearing should accompany the copy summons. Service must be effected at least two clear days before the return day, unless a judge or registrar of the relevant registry, at or before the hearing, dispenses with service on such terms, if any, as he may think fit (Rule 66(2)).

Hearing of summons

15.07 On the day and at the time fixed, the party who issued the summons must attend with the original summons at the place appointed for the hearing. If any party to the summons fails to appear within a reasonable time after the time fixed for the hearing, the judge or registrar may proceed in his absence. If a party served with a summons fails to appear, sufficient evidence as to service, or a written acknowledgement of service by such party, must be produced.

15.08 When the hearing of a summons has been adjourned, either to a specific date or generally, the practitioner must restore it to the list for hearing by completing an "adjourned summons" form obtainable in the registry; it must be lodged there, and notice as to the date and time of the adjourned hearing must be given to all other parties.

Consent summons

15.09 Where the parties are agreed as to the terms of the order sought and their consent to the same is endorsed on the summons when it is issued, the registrar will normally deal with the summons without requiring any attendance on it.

Order made on summons

15.10 A copy of the order made on the summons is sent by post from the registry to every party concerned.

Appeals from registrars

15.11 Any person aggrieved by a decision or requirement of a registrar may appeal by summons to a judge. If any person besides the appellant appeared or was represented before the registrar, the summons must be issued within seven days of the decision or requirement complained of, for hearing on the first available day, and must be served on every such person as aforesaid (Rule 65). In accordance with the Registrar's Direction of 21st February 1985, if either party wishes to bespeak a copy of the registrar's notes of evidence, the appellant's solicitor (or the respondent's solicitor, if the appellant is acting in person) must within twenty-one days from the date the appeal is lodged (or after service of the appeal, in the case of the respondent's solicitor) certify that either the appellant or the respondent considers that notes of evidence taken before the registrar are necessary for the purpose of the appeal and that notes of evidence will be lodged. Where such a certificate has been given the certifying solicitor must, unless otherwise directed, not less than twenty-one days prior to the hearing of the appeal, lodge a copy of the notes of evidence (which can be bespoken from the registrar) and of judgement (being notes prepared by the certifying solicitor, agreed by the respondent's legal advisers where the respondent is represented, and approved by the registrar). Where either party is represented but neither wishes to bespeak a copy of the registrar's notes of evidence, a copy of the notes of judgement must either be prepared by the appellant's solicitor and, if the respondent is represented, agreed by his solicitor, or be prepared by the respondent's solicitor, if the appellant is not represented. In any case the notes must be approved by the registrar and not less than twenty-one days prior to the hearing a copy of the notes must be lodged by the solicitor who prepared them. If both parties are acting in person the appellant must notify the registrar of the appeal and the registrar must, where possible, make a note for the assistance of the judge hearing the appeal. It is the practice for a copy of the Registrar's Direction of 21st February 1985 to be given out to anyone issuing a summons appealing from a registrar's decision or requirement.

MOTIONS FOR COMMITTAL

15.12 The Non-Contentious Probate Rules 1987 contain no provision for any application to be made by way of motion. However, an application for committal is made by motion to a judge—Order 52, Rule 4(1), R.S.C. For the purpose of making an application to the court on motion, a notice of motion, the affidavit(s) in support of the application and any other relevant documents must be filed in the Probate Department of the Principal Registry.

15.13 The notice of motion should set out the date, time and place of the hearing (obtained in the Probate Department of the Principal Registry in the same way as a summons—see paras. 15.04 and 15.05), the grounds of the application and the nature of the order which is sought. Copies of the notice and of all documents to be used in support of the application must be served personally on the person whose committal is sought unless such service is dispensed with or unless some manner of substituted service is ordered (see Order 52, Rule 4(2) and (3), R.S.C.)

15.14 Service of the notice must be effected at least two clear days before the day of hearing.

15.15 Appeal from an order for committal is to the Court of Appeal. Notice of appeal must be served on all other parties within four weeks of the perfection of the order, unless that time is extended by the judge or the Court of Appeal. The appeal must be set down within seven days after the service of the notice of appeal or the perfection of the order, whichever is the later, and within four days after setting down notice thereof must be given to all parties served with notice of appeal (Order 59, R.S.C.)

ORDER TO ATTEND FOR EXAMINATION

15.16 Where it appears that there are reasonable grounds for believing that any person has knowledge of any document which is or purports to be a testamentary document, that person may be ordered to attend for the purpose of being examined in open court (Section 122, Supreme Court Act 1981).

15.17 Provided that a probate action has not been commenced, the application for the order to attend is made to a registrar on summons, the summons being served on the person against whom the order is sought (Rule 50(1)).

15.18 If an order is made on the summons for the person to attend for examination in open court, an appointment is fixed before a judge. A copy of the order with notice of the appointment (endorsed with the appropriate penal notice) is served personally on the person ordered to attend.

15.19 The judge may require the person to answer any question relating to the document concerned and may order him to bring in the document in such manner as the court may direct. A person who fails to attend for examination, answer any question or bring in any document is guilty of contempt of court.

SUBPOENA TO BRING IN WILL

15.20 When a person who is shown to have a testamentary document in his possession, custody or power, refuses to deliver it up, he may be compelled to bring it into a probate registry.

15.21 A registrar is empowered to issue a subpoena to bring in the document under Section 123 of the Supreme Court Act 1981 (Rule 50(2)). Application for the issue of the subpoena is made by lodging in the registry an affidavit of the facts to support the application for the issue of the subpoena, together with two forms of subpoena. When applying, it should be stated whether the document is required to be brought into the Principal Registry or a particular district probate registry. The sealed subpoena is returned to the solicitor. The subpoena, endorsed with the appropriate penal notice, must be personally served. It is enforceable by committal. If the testamentary document is in the possession of the person served, he may bring it into, or at his risk send it by post to, the registry specified in the subpoena. If he denies that the document is in his possession or control, he may file an affidavit to that effect in the registry from which the subpoena issued.

CITATIONS

15.22 A citation is an instrument issued under the seal of the court at the instance of a person having an interest in an estate, whereby all other persons having interests may be called upon to enter an appearance in the matter and either proceed themselves or show cause why the order asked for by the citor should not be made. The citation must set out all the relevant facts of the case and the nature of the order the court is asked to make. Citations may issue from the Principal Registry or any district probate registry.

Citation to accept or refuse a grant

15.23 This citation is issued when persons having a prior right to take a grant delay or decline to do so and will not renounce their right; it compels such persons to decide whether or not to take a grant and, in the event of refusal by them, enables an order to be made for the issue of a grant to the citor (Rule 47(1)). (For form of citation and supporting affidavit see forms (1) and (2) after para. 15.30.) Where power to take probate has been reserved to an executor, he may be called upon to accept or refuse a grant by citation issued at the instance of executors who have already proved the will or the survivor of them, or of the executors of the last survivor of deceased executors who proved the will, so that the chain of executorship, if any, may continue without risk of its being broken subsequently (Rule 47(2)). (For form of citation and supporting affidavit see forms (3) and (4) after para. 15.30.)

Citation to take probate

15.24 If an executor has intermeddled in the estate of his testator and has not proved the will within six months from the date of death of the testator, he can after that period be cited to take probate (*not* to accept or refuse) by any person having an interest in the estate, provided that no proceedings as to the validity of the will are pending (Rule 47(3)). (For form of citation and supporting affidavit see forms (5) and (6) after para. 15.30).

Citation to propound a testamentary document

15.25 This citation is appropriate when a person has knowledge of the existence of a testamentary document or puported testamentary document which adversely affects his interest under an intestacy, or under an earlier will. The citation calls upon the executor and beneficiaries under such document to propound it (i.e. to have it pronounced for in solemn form in a probate action (Rule 48(1)). (For form of citation and supporting affidavit see forms (7) and (8) after para. 15.30.)

Persons to be cited

15.26 A citation to accept or refuse a grant must call upon each and every person with a right to a grant, prior to that of the citor, to appear and take the grant. Where there is a will and a residuary legatee or devise desires to take a grant, he must cite each and every executor and residuary legatees and devisees of a higher class than himself; legatees, devisees or creditors wishing to take a grant must cite the executors and residuary legatees and devisees of all classes, or, if the residuary estate is not wholly disposed of, the persons entitled to such undisposed of estate as on an intestacy.

15.27 In the case of intestacy, a person having a beneficial interest in the estate must cite all persons with a prior right to a grant. A creditor of the deceased must similarly cite all such persons. If the deceased died without known relations, a creditor must cite "the kin (if any) who are entitled to share and all other persons having or claiming to have an interest in the estate", and notice must be given to the Treasury Solicitor, or as the case may be (Rule 38), by delivering or sending a copy of the citation to him.

Will must be lodged

15.28 When a citation refers to a will it is normally necessary that the will be lodged in the registry before the citation issues. The registrar is empowered to dispense with the lodging of the will if the will is not in the citor's possession and if the registrar is satisfied that it is impracticable to require it to be lodged (Rule 46(5)), but if it is in the possession of a person who refuses to part with it he will normally require such person to be served with a subpoena to bring the will into the registry.

Extracting a citation, procedure

15.29 A citor is required to enter a caveat before issuing a citation (Rule 46(3)), and every citation must contain an address for service within England and Wales (Rule 49). For the purpose of extracting a citation, a draft of it must be prepared and lodged in the Probate Department of the Principal Registry or in a district probate registry, for settlement together with the will (if any) and any other relevant papers, including a draft affidavit in verification of all the facts contained in the citation. The affidavit should not be sworn until the draft citation has been settled by the registrar.

15.30 When the draft citation has been settled, the papers (except original testamentary documents) will be returned to the solicitor who should enter a caveat if he has not already done so. The draft and sworn affidavit, the settled draft and engrossed citation should be returned to the registry for the citation to be issued.

Example forms of citations and verifying affidavits

(1) *Citation to accept or refuse probate and letters of administration with will—By a legatee against executor, residuary legatee and devisee in trust and residuary legatee and devisee*

[USUAL HEADING]

Elizabeth the Second, by the grace of God, of the United Kingdom of Great Britain and Northern Ireland and of our other realms and territories, Queen, Head of the Commonwealth, Defender of the Faith:

To *A.B.* of   and to *C.D.* of   .

In an affidavit sworn on the   day of   19   *E.F.* has sworn that *G.H.* of   deceased died on the   day of   19   domiciled in England and Wales having made and duly executed his last will and testament dated the   day of   19   (now lodged in the   Registry); that you the said *A.B.* are appointed sole executor and residuary legatee and devisee in trust in the said will; that you the said *C.D.* are named as the residuary legatee and devisee in the said will; and that the said *E.F.* is a legatee named in the said will.

This is to command you the said *A.B.* that within eight days after service hereof on you, inclusive of the day of such service, you do cause an appearance to be entered in the   Registry at   and accept or refuse probate of the said will or letters of administration, with the said will annexed, of all the estate which by law devolves to and vests in the personal representative of the said deceased or show cause why such letters of administration, with the said will annexed, should not be granted to the said *E.F.*

And this is to command you the said *C.D.* that within eight days of service hereof on you, inclusive of the day of such service, you do cause an appearance to be entered in the Registry at and accept or refuse letters of administration, with the said will annexed, of all the estate which by law devolves to and vests in the personal representative of the said deceased or show cause why such letters of administration, with the said will annexed, should not be granted to the said *E.F.*.

And take notice that in default of you the said *A.B.* appearing, accepting and extracting probate or letters of administration, with will, as aforesaid, or you the said *C.D.* appearing, accepting and extracting letters of administration, with will, as aforesaid, our said court will proceed to grant letters of administration, with will, of the estate of the said deceased to the said *E.F.* notwithstanding your absence.

Dated at this day of 19

Citation extracted
by
of Registrar
Solicitors

(2) *Affidavit verifying averments in, and in support of, citation to accept or refuse probate and letters of administration with will by a legatee.*

[USUAL HEADING]

I, *E.F.* of make oath and say as follows:

1. That *G.H.* of deceased died on the day of 19 domiciled in England and Wales having made and duly executed his last will and testament dated the day of 19 (now lodged in the Registry).

2. That *A.B.* of is the sole executor and residuary legatee and devisee in trust appointed in the said will.

3. That *C.D.* of is the residuary legatee and devisee named in the said will.

4. That the said *A.B.* has not yet taken probate of the said will or letters of administration, with the said will annexed, of the estate of the said deceased and the said *C.D.* has not yet taken letters of administration, with the said will annexed, of the said estate.

5. That I am a legatee named in the said will and wish to obtain letters of administration, with the said will annexed, of the said estate.

6. That no life or minority interest arises under the said will.

7. That to the best of my knowledge, information and belief, there was no land vested in the deceased which was settled previously to his death and not by his said will and which remained settled land notwithstanding his death.

Sworn, etc.

(3) *Citation to accept or refuse probate—By executor of last surviving proving executor against executor to whom power was reserved*

[USUAL HEADING]

Elizabeth the Second (*Continue as in form (1) above.*)

To *A.B.* of .

In an affidavit sworn on the day of 19 *C.D.* has sworn that probate of the last will of *E.F.* of deceased who died on the day of 19 domiciled in England and Wales was granted at the Registry on the day of 19 to *G.H.* and *I.J.*, two of the executors named in the said will, with power being reserved to you the said *A.B.*, the other executor named in the said will, to take probate; that the said *G.H.* survived the said *I.J.* and died on the day of 19 leaving part of the estate of the said *E.F.* deceased unadministered; that probate of the last will of the said *G.H.* deceased was granted at the Registry on the day of 19 to the said *C.D.* the sole executor named in the said will of the said *G.H.* deceased.

This is to command you the said *A.B.* that within eight days after service hereof on you, inclusive of the day of such service, you do cause an appearance to be entered in the Registry at and accept or refuse probate of the said will of the said *E.F.* deceased.

And take notice that in default of you the said *A.B.* appearing, accepting and extracting probate of the said will, all your rights in respect of the executorship will wholly cease.

Dated at this day of 19 .

Citation extracted
by
of Registrar
Solicitors

(4) *Affidavit verifying averments in, and in support of, citation to accept or refuse probate against executor to whom power was reserved, by executor of last surviving proving executor*

[USUAL HEADING]

I, *C.D.* of , make oath and say as follows:

1. That probate of the last will of *E.F.* of deceased who died on the day of 19 , domiciled in England and Wales was granted at the Registry on the day of 19 to *G.H.* and *I.J.* two of the executors named in the said will, with power being reserved to *A.B.* of the other executor named in the said will.

2. That the said *G.H.* survived the said *I.J.* and died on the day of 19 leaving part of the estate of the said *E.F.* deceased unadministered.

3. That the said *A.B.* has not yet taken probate of the said will of *E.F.* deceased.

4. That I was granted probate of the last will of the said *G.H.* deceased at the Registry on the day of 19 as the sole executor named in the said will.

5. That I wish to act as executor, by chain of representation, of the said will of *E.F.* deceased.

6. That the gross value of the estate of the said *E.F.* deceased left unadministered is £ .

Sworn, etc.

(5) *Citation to take probate—By a person interested in the estate against an executor who has intermeddled*

[USUAL HEADING]

Elizabeth the Second (*Continue as in form (1) above*)

To *A.B.* of

In an affidavit sworn on the day of 19 *C.D.* has sworn that *E.F.* of deceased died on the day of 19 domiciled in England and Wales having made and duly executed his last will dated the day of 19 (now lodged in the Registry); that you the said *A.B.* are the sole executor named in the said will and have intermeddled in the estate of the said *E.F.* deceased; and that the said *C.D.* is interested in the estate of the said *E.F.* deceased.

This is to command you the said *A.B.* that within eight days after service hereof on you, inclusive of the day of such service, you do cause an appearance to be entered in the Registry at and show cause why you should not be ordered to take probate of the said will.

Dated at this day of 19

Citation extracted
by
of Registrar
Solicitors

(6) *Affidavit verifying averments in, and in support of, citation to take probate, by a person interested in the estate against an executor who has intermeddled*

[USUAL HEADING]

I, *C.D.* of make oath and say as follows:

1. That *E.F.* of deceased died on the day of 19 domiciled in England and Wales having made and duly executed his last will dated the day of 19 (now lodged in the Registry).

2. That *A.B.* of is appointed sole executor in the said will.

3. That more than six calendar months have expired since the death of the said deceased and no proceedings are pending as to the validity of the said will but the said *A.B.* has not yet proved it.

4. That the said *A.B.* has intermeddled in the estate of the said deceased by (*Set out sufficient details of the said intermeddling, e.g.* selling the freehold property at which was registered in the name of the said deceased).

5. That I am the residuary legatee and devisee named in the said will and I seek an order that the said *A.B.* take probate of the said will.

Sworn, etc.

(7) *Citation to propound a will—By a person interested under an earlier will (or by a person interested on intestacy) against the executor and persons interested under the will*

[USUAL HEADING]

Elizabeth the Second (*continue as in form (1) above.*)

To *A.B.* of ,
C.D. of ,
and to *E.F.* of .

In an affidavit sworn on the day of 19 *G.H.* has sworn that *I.J.* of deceased died on the day of 19 domiciled in England and Wales having made and duly executed his last will dated the day of 19 (now lodged in the Registry) in which the said *G.H.* is named as an executor and a legatee (*or* intestate leaving the said *G.H.* his lawful widow, the only person entitled to his estate); and that the said deceased left a paper writing dated the day of 19 (now lodged in the Registry) purporting to be a will, in which you the said *A.B.* are appointed sole executor, you the said *C.D.* are named as the sole residuary legatee and devisee and you the said *E.F.* are named as the sole legatee.

This is to command you the said *A.B.*, *C.D.* and *E.F.* that within eight days of service hereof on you, inclusive of the day of such service, you do cause an appearance to be entered in the Registry at and propound the said will dated the day of 19 if you consider it for your interest to do so, or show cause why probate of the said will dated the day of 19 should not be granted to the said *G.H.* (*or* why letters of administration of all the estate which by law devolves to and vests in the personal representative of the said deceased should not be granted to the said *G.H.*)

And take notice that in default of one or more of you, the said *A.B.*, *C.D.* and *E.F.*, appearing and doing as aforesaid, our said court will proceed to issue a grant of representation of the estate of the said deceased as if the said will dated the day of 19 were invalid, notwithstanding your absence.

Dated at this day of 19 .

Citation extracted
by
of Registrar
Solicitors.

(8) *Affidavit verifying averments in, and in support of, citation to propound a will—By a person interested under an earlier will (or by a person interested on intestacy) against the executor and persons interested under the will*

[USUAL HEADING]

I, *G.H.* of , make oath and say as follows:

1. That *I.J.* of deceased died on the day of 19 , domiciled in England and Wales having made and duly executed his last will dated the day of 19 (now lodged in the Registry) in which I am named as an executor and a legatee (*or* intestate leaving me his lawful widow the only person entitled to his estate).

2. That the said deceased left a paper writing dated the day of 19 (now lodged in the Registry) purporting to be a will, in which *A.B.* of is appointed sole executor, *C.D.* of is named as the sole residuary legatee and devisee and *E.F.* of is named as the sole legatee.

3. That I wish to issue a citation against the said *A.B.*, *C.D.* and *E.F.* to propound the said purported will dated the day of 19 if they, or any of them, consider it for their interest to do so and that in default probate of the said will dated the day of 19 (*or* letters of administration of the estate of the said deceased) be granted to me.

Sworn, etc.

Service of citation

15.31 A citation must be personally served on the person cited unless the registrar, on cause being shown by affidavit, directs some other mode of service, which may include notice by advertisement (Rule 46(4)). Service is effected by leaving a copy of the citation with the citee, and producing the original to him if requested. A certificate of service should be endorsed on the citation after service.

15.32 Where personal service cannot be effected, application may be made to the registrar to substitute another mode of service. The registrar will require an affidavit stating why personal service is not possible and what efforts (if any) have been made to effect such service. If satisfied, the registrar will usually direct service by advertisement. If, when applying for the issue of the citation, it is known that personal service cannot be effected, application for substituted service may be made then by stating the facts in the affidavit to lead the citation. If the registrar directs service by advertisement, the sealed copy of the citation must be lodged, with a draft of the advertisement, at the registry. The registrar will settle the draft abstract and will give directions as to the number of insertions and in what newspapers they are to appear, and the time for appearance by the citee.

Service on persons under disability

15.33 Service on a minor who is not also mentally incapacitated should be effected on his father or guardian, or if he has no father or guardian on the person with whom he is residing or in whose care he is at the time (Order 80 of R.S.C. as applied by Rule 3). Service on a mentally incapacitated person is effected by serving the person authorised by the Court of Protection to take proceedings on his behalf. If there is no person so authorised, service should be effected on the person with whom the incapable person resides or in whose care he is.

Appearance to citation

Entry of appearance

15.34 Appearances to citations are entered in the registry from which the citation issued; at the Probate Department if in the Principal Registry. The form of appearance to a citation (Form 5, 1st Schedule to Rules (Appendix 1)) may be obtained in the registry and the following particulars must be entered: caveat number and date of entry; date of citation; the full names and address of the deceased; the full names, address and interest in the estate, of the citor; the full names, address and interest in the estate, of the party entering the appearance and his address for service within England and Wales.

15.35 If the interest claimed is under a will or codicil, the date thereof must be given. When the interest arises under an intestacy the exact relationship to the intestate must be stated, unless the person appearing does so as a creditor only. After filing the form of appearance the citee must forthwith serve a sealed copy of the form on the citor by leaving it at, or sending it by prepaid ordinary or registered post or by recorded delivery to, the citor's address for service. If that address includes a numbered box at a document exchange approved by the Lord Chancellor, service may also be effected by leaving the sealed copy at that document exchange or at a document exchange which transmits documents every business day to that document exchange (Order 65, Rule 5, R.S.C. as applied by Rule 67, N.C.P.R.). The appearance must be entered within the time prescribed in the citation, or at any time thereafter if the citor has taken no step in default (Rule 46(6)).

Default of appearance by a person under disability

15.36 If the person cited is under disability and no appearance has been entered on his behalf, application should be made to the registrar of the registry where the citation issued for the appointment of a guardian to be considered (Order 80, Rule 6 R.S.C., as applied by Rule 3 N.C.P.R.).

Subsequent procedure

(1) *Citation to accept or refuse a grant*

15.37 If the time allowed for appearance has expired and the person cited has not entered an appearance, the citor may apply *ex parte* to a registrar (at the registry where the citation issued) for an order that a grant be made to himself (Rule 47(5)(a)), except where the citee is an executor to whom power was reserved. In the latter case, the citor may apply *ex parte* to the registrar for an order that a note be made on the grant that such executor has been duly cited and has not appeared and that all his rights in respect of the executorship have wholly ceased (Rule 47(5)(b)). The application for an order must be supported by an affidavit showing that the citation was duly served and the original citation endorsed with a certificate of service should be exhibited to the affidavit. If the citation was served by advertisement, copies of the newspapers, the settled draft abstract and the original citation must be filed.

15.38 When the person cited has entered an appearance and wishes to take a grant, he may make an *ex parte* application to the appropriate registrar for an order giving him leave to apply for the grant. Application is made by lodging at the Probate Department of the Principal Registry or at the district probate registry, as appropriate, an affidavit stating that the applicant has been cited and has appeared and is willing to take a grant (Rule 47(4)).

15.39 If the person cited has entered an appearance but has not applied for a grant as indicated above or does not prosecute his application with reasonable diligence, the citor may apply by summons to the appropriate registrar for an order that a grant be made to himself (Rule 47(7)(a)). If the person cited is an executor to whom power was reserved, the citor may apply by summons to the appropriate registrar for an order striking out the appearance and that the grant be noted to the effect that such executor has been duly cited and has not appeared, and that all his rights in respect of the executorship have wholly ceased (Rule 47(7)(b)). The summons must be served on the citee.

(2) *Citation to take probate*

15.40 If the time allowed for appearance has expired and the person cited has not entered an appearance, the citor may apply by way of summons to the appropriate registrar for an order requiring the person cited to take a grant within a specified time or for a grant to himself or to some other person specified in the summons (Rule 47(5)(c)). The summons must be served on the person cited, and must be supported by an affidavit as to service of the citation (Rule 47(6)).

15.41 If the person cited has entered an appearance and is willing to take a grant, he may make an *ex parte* application to the appropriate registrar for an order that a grant be made to himself. Such application is made by filing an affidavit showing that he has entered an appearance and is willing to take the grant (Rule 47(4)).

15.42 If the person cited has entered an appearance but has not applied for a grant, or does not prosecute his application with reasonable diligence, the citor may apply by way of summons to the appropriate registrar for an order requiring the person cited to take a grant within a specified time or for a grant to himself or to some other person specified in the summons (Rule 47(7)(c)).

Failure to comply with an order to take probate renders the executor so ordered liable to committal.

(3) *Citation to propound a testamentary document*

15.43 If the time allowed for appearance has expired and no appearance has been entered by the person cited, the citor may apply *ex parte* to a registrar for an order for a grant as if the will (or codicil) were invalid. The application must be supported by an affidavit showing that the citation was duly served (Rule 48(2)(a)). If an appearance has been entered but no appearer proceeds with reasonable diligence to propound the will (or codicil), the citor may apply by summons to a registrar for such an order for a grant as if the will (or codicil) where invalid (Rule 48(2)(b)). If the person cited enters an appearance and wishes to commence a probate action, he should issue a writ in the Chancery Division against the citor (or, if appropriate, take proceedings in the relevant County Court).

CHAPTER 16

Standing Searches and Caveats

STANDING SEARCHES

16.01 It is possible to apply to the Principal Registry for a "standing search" to be made (Rule 43). This service is of especial assistance to persons who require to know when a personal representative is constituted, *e.g.* if an application under the Inheritance (Provision for Family and Dependants) Act 1975 is contemplated. A person who applies for a standing search will be sent, without further application, an office copy of any grant which corresponds with the particulars given and which either issued not more than twelve months before the entry of the standing search or issues within a period of six months thereafter. Application is made by notice in Form 2, 1st Schedule to Rules (Appendix 1) to the Record Keeper of the Principal Registry giving the full name of the deceased, any alternative or alias name, full address of the deceased, and the exact date of death together with the appropriate fee (currently £2).

16.02 A standing search may be extended for further six monthly periods on application and payment of a further fee. The application for extension must be made by the applicant or his solicitor in writing and must be lodged, or received by post, in the Principal Registry, within the last month of the existing six monthly period.

CAVEATS

Entry, duration, withdrawal and extension of caveat

16.03 Any person who wishes to show cause against the sealing (or resealing) of a grant without notice to himself, may enter a caveat in the Principal Registry or in any district probate registry or sub-registry (Rule 44(1)). The registrar will not allow any grant (other than a grant *ad colligenda bona* or a grant pending suit) to be sealed (or resealed) if he has knowledge of an effective caveat, but a caveat does not operate to prevent the sealing of a grant on the day on which the caveat is entered (proviso to Rule 44(1)). A grant which has been sealed remains operative unless and until the court orders its revocation. A caveat is not effective to prevent the issue of a grant to the caveator. It is therefore never necessary for an applicant for a grant to withdraw or clear any caveat by or on behalf of himself.

Entry of caveat

16.04 Any person may enter a caveat, either by himself or by a solicitor acting on his behalf. A person wishing to enter a caveat may do so by attending at any probate registry or sub-registry and completing the prescribed form (see Form 3, 1st Schedule to Rules, Appendix 1) in the caveat book, or by sending through the post, at his own risk, a notice in the prescribed form (Rule 44(2)).

16.05 The following details must be entered in the form of caveat:
(1) The full names (with alias names, if any) and last known address of the deceased, and the date of death.
(2) The full names of the caveator and his address for service of documents, which must be within England and Wales (Rule 49).
(3) If the caveat is entered by a solicitor on behalf of the caveator, the name of the caveator must be stated.
(4) The date of entry and the signature of the caveator or his solicitor.
The registry maintaining the index of all caveats entered is immediately notified of the entry of a caveat in another registry, and a copy of the caveat is also sent to the index registry. A receipt is given upon entry of a caveat, and it must be produced if the caveat is to be withdrawn. (The caveat index is currently maintained at the Leeds District Probate Registry; see para. 1.06.)

Duration of caveat

16.06 Except as otherwise provided by Rule 44 (see the following paragraph), Rule 45 (see para. 16.08) and Rule 46 (see para. 16.09), a caveat remains in force for six months from the date on which it is entered (Rule 44(3)(a)).

16.07 Under Rule 44 a caveat may be extended (see para 16.10), kept in force by a summons for directions by a person without a contrary interest whose caveat has been warned (see para. 16.20), kept in force by an appearance to a warning by a person with a contrary interest (see paras. 16.18 ff), withdrawn by the caveator if no appearance has been entered to a warning (see para. 16.11), be removed on filing an affidavit as to service of a warning if no appearance has been entered or summons for directions has been issued (see para. 16.25) or directed to cease to have effect by a registrar on the hearing of a summons for directions issued by a person without a contrary interest whose caveat has been warned (see para. 16.20).

16.08 Under Rule 45, unless a registrar of the Principal Registry by order made on summons otherwise directs, the commencement of a probate action operates to prevent the sealing of a grant (other than one pending suit), whether or not a caveat has been entered, until application is made for a grant by the person shown to be entitled thereto by the decision of the court in the action. Upon being advised by the court concerned of the commencement of a probate action, the Senior Registrar is required to give notice of the existence of the action to any caveator (other than the plaintiff in the action) in respect of each caveat then in force and to give notice of the existence of the action to any subsequent caveator. When the application is made for the grant by the person shown to be entitled to it by the decision of the court in the action, any caveat entered by the plaintiff in the action and any caveat in respect of which notice has been given, ceases to have effect.

16.09 Under Rule 46, unless a registrar of the Principal Registry by order made on summons otherwise directs, any caveat in force at the commencement of citation proceedings, unless withdrawn by the caveator (see para. 16.11) remains in force until application for a grant is made by the person entitled to it by the decision of the court in the citation proceedings. On the application for the grant by that person any caveat entered by a party who had notice of the proceedings ceases to have effect.

Extension of caveat

16.10 Rule 44(3)(a) provides that a caveat may be extended. Application must be made within the last month before expiry of the caveat and must be made in writing to the registry or sub-registry in which the caveat was entered. There is no limit to the number of times that a caveat may be extended.

Withdrawal of caveat

16.11 A caveator who has not entered an appearance to a warning may at any time withdraw his caveat by giving notice at the registry or sub-registry at which it was entered. If the caveat has been warned, the caveator must forthwith give notice of withdrawal of the caveat to the person who warned it (Rule 44(11)). Withdrawal may be made by personal attendance at the registry or sub-registry at which the caveat was entered, or by post and the original receipt given at the time of entry of the caveat must be produced on withdrawal. Notice of withdrawal of a caveat is sent to the registry maintaining the central index by the registrar of another registry.

16.12 Upon the withdrawal of a caveat which is stopping the issue of a grant, notice of the withdrawal is given to the extracting solicitor or the personal applicant, by the registry at which the grant is sought, with a request for information as to whether the application for the grant should proceed.

Death of caveator

16.13 Application must be made by way of summons to a registrar in order to remove a subsisting caveat entered by a caveator who has since died. The summons should be served on the caveator's personal representative.

Restraint as to entry of further caveat

16.14 Unless leave is obtained from a registrar of the Principal Registry, no further caveat may be entered by or on behalf of any caveator whose caveat is either in force or has ceased to have effect:
(1) by direction of a registrar on the hearing of a summons for directions (under Rule 44(6)), or
(2) by reason that the caveator failed to either appear to a warning or issue a summons for directions under Rule 44(6), or
(3) following the decision of the court in proceedings by way of citation or in a probate action, the caveator having had notice of such proceedings or action (Rule 45(14)).

Warning caveat (Rule 44(5))

16.15 Any person claiming an interest in the estate may issue a warning by completing the required form (Form 4, 1st Schedule to Rules (Appendix 1)) and issuing it from the registry where the caveat index is maintained. Caveats may only be warned from that registry. The warning is a notice to the caveator to enter an apperance at the registry where the caveat index is maintained within eight days, inclusive of the day of service, setting out his interest in the estate of the deceased, or if he has no contrary interest but still wishes to show cause against the sealing of a grant, to issue a summons for directions for hearing by a registrar. The caveat index is currently maintained at the Leeds District Probate Registry (see Para. 1.06).

16.16 The person warning the caveat must set out his exact interest in the form of warning. If claiming under a will or codicil, the date thereof and his interest thereunder must be clearly shown. If claiming to be entitled under an intestacy, his relationship to the deceased and interest in the estate must be stated. An address in England and Wales for service of documents must be given (Rule 49).

Service of warning

16.17 A warning is served by leaving it or a copy thereof at the address for service given in the caveat, or by sending a copy by prepaid ordinary or registered post or by recorded delivery to that address. If the address for service includes a numbered box at a document exchange approved by the Lord Chancellor, service may also be effected by leaving the warning or copy warning at that document exchange or at a document exchange which transmits documents every business day to that document exchange (Order 65, Rule 5, R.S.C. applied by Rule 67, N.C.P.R.).

Appearance to warning (Rule 44(10))

16.18 The caveator may, within the time specified in the warning, or at any time thereafter provided that no step in default has been taken, enter an appearance at the registry where the caveat index is maintained. Personal attendance by the caveator or his solicitor is necessary and the appearance is entered by completing the prescribed form (Form 5, 1st Schedule to Rules, Appendix 1), and making an entry in the appearance book. The person appearing must show his full name and address and set out his interest and give an address for service within England and Wales (Rule 49). A sealed copy of the appearance must forthwith be served on the person who has issued the warning. It is served at the address for service given in the warning and may be served in the same way as a warning (see para. 16.17). The caveat index is currently maintained at the Leeds District Probate Registry (see para. 1.06).

16.19 The person wishing to enter the appearance must have an interest contrary to that of the person who issued the warning. If claiming under a will or codicil, the date thereof and the nature of the interest (*e.g.* executor, residuary legatee or devisee) must be stated. If claiming under an intestacy, the relationship to the deceased must be shown.

Summons for directions (Rule 44(6))

16.20 A caveator who has no interest contrary to that of the person who issued the warning, but who wishes to show cause against the issue of a grant to that person may, within eight days after service of the warning (inclusive of the day of service) or at any time thereafter provided that no step in default has been taken, issue and serve a summons for directions returnable before a registrar (Rule 44(6)). The registrar has express power to direct, on the hearing, that the caveat cease to have effect, if he considers that an appropriate direction to give (Rule 44(7)).

16.21 It is also provided by Rule 27(6) that a dispute between persons equally entitled to a grant is to be brought by summons before a registrar.

16.22 An appearance on behalf of a minor or other person under disability may be entered only by a person duly qualified or appointed to act as his guardian.

16.23 If the caveator has entered an appearance to the warning, a grant cannot issue (except to the caveator himself) without a decree or order of the court. A decree or an order on summons may clear off the caveat, but a caveat is not normally cleared off unless it is expressly referred to in the decree or order, or unless it is clear from the proceedings, or is certified by the solicitor, that all caveators had notice of the proceedings. Where such a certificate is necessary, it should, if possible, be given on the back of the oath leading to the grant.

Procedure subsequent to entry of appearance

16.24 If, after an appearance has been entered, the parties come to an agreement or opposition is abandoned, a summons for discontinuance of proceedings may be taken out before a registrar of the Principal Registry, and an order removing the caveat and allowing the issue of a grant may be made. Where there is no such agreement or abandonment of opposition, a writ of summons is usually issued out of the Chancery Division (or proceedings issued in the relevant county court, if appropriate) by the party who warned the caveat, thus commencing an action.

Non-appearance to warning

16.25 Where no appearance has been entered to a warning, nor any summons for directions issued, by or on behalf of the caveator within the period of eight days allowed, the caveat may be cleared off, upon the applicant filing at the registry where the caveat index is maintained an affidavit showing that the warning was duly served (Rule 44(12)). The search for appearance and for any pending summons is made by a registry official and, subject to there being no appearance or summons for directions pending and that the time for appearance or issue of such a summons has elasped, a note of the time and date of the search is made on the affidavit which is then filed and the caveat removed.

Form of affidavit of service of warning:

[USUAL HEADING]

I, *A.B.*, of ,
clerk to Messrs. *C.* and *D.* solicitors, of ,
make oath and say as follows:

That I duly served Messrs. *E* and *F.*, of solicitors for , with a true copy of the warning now produced to me and marked "A" by delivering to and leaving the said copy with a clerk of the said Messrs. *E.* and *F.*, at their office aforesaid (*or* by leaving the said copy at their office aforesaid) before the hour of four in the afternoon on the day of 19 (*or* by sending the said copy by pre-paid first class post (*or as the case may be*), which was sent on the day of 19 , to their office aforesaid).

Sworn, etc.

CHAPTER 17

Renunciation and Retraction

RENUNCIATION

17.01 By the act of renunciation a person may formally abandon any right he may have to take a grant of probate or administration. However, any beneficial interest which the renunciant may have in the estate is not affected by his renunciation. A renunciation must be absolute and without reservation. Although it is effective from the day of its date, it does not become final until (and may be withdrawn at any time before) it is filed. It is deemed to be filed when the relevant grant has passed the seal and it remains effective should it become necessary to obtain further representation in the same matter, but on good cause being shown the court may allow it to be retracted.

Form of renunciation

17.02 The appropriate form should be used (see forms (1)–(3) after para. 17.13). Several persons may execute the same form provided that the capacity in which each renounces is clearly shown. The signature of each renunciant must be separately witnessed by a disinterested person. The document need not be under seal.

17.03 A renunciation in the English language and executed in a non-English speaking country is not accepted unless it was executed in the presence of a Notary Public or British Consul, or there is satisfactory indication that the renunciant understood the purport of the document. An authenticated translation must be filed with a renunciation in a foreign language.

17.04 For renunciations by trust corporations and non-trust corportions, see paras. 10.07 and 10.23.

Renunciation by executor

17.05 The court will not accept the renunciation of an executor who has intermeddled in the estate of the deceased. The form of renunciation must, therefore, state the fact that he has not intermeddled. However, the court has power to pass over an executor notwithstanding that he has intermeddled in the estate. In renouncing probate of the will of his testator, an executor also renounces executorship of any will of which that testator was a proving executor.

17.06 An executor who proves the will of his testator accepts the duties of executor of any will of which that testator was a proving executor (including any by chain of executorship), and cannot therefore renounce those duties (*In the Goods of Perry* (1840) 2 Curt. 655).

17.07 It is provided by Rule 37(1) that renunciation of probate by an executor does not operate as a renunciation of any right he may have to a grant of administration (*e.g.* to letters of administration (with will) as "a residuary legatee and devisee in trust") unless he expressly renounces such right. The form of renunciation by an executor who is also entitled in another capacity must, therefore, include also a renunciation of his right to letters of administration (with will) if a grant to some person with a lower title is sought. A minor executor's right to probate on attaining the age of 18 years cannot be renounced by any person on his behalf (Rule 34(1)).

Renunciation by person entitled to administration (with or without will)

17.08 The instrument of renunciation must set out the exact capacity in which the renunciant would be entitled to take a grant.

Renunciations by legal personal representatives and persons with potential rights

17.09 Executors or administrators (with or without will) may renounce the right to any grant to which they may be entitled in their represent- ative capacity. If the renunciant is not the sole personal representative of his deceased, the other representatives must be cleared off by renunciation or citation before a grant can be made to a person entitled in a lower capacity. If there is no duly constituted legal personal representative of the deceased, the persons entitled to be constituted as his representatives may, in that potential capacity, renounce their rights to any grant of a representative nature to which they would be entitled if so constituted.

Attorney

17.10 An attorney expressly appointed for that purpose may renounce on behalf of a person resident out of England and Wales (*Rosser* (1864) 3 Sw & Tr. 490).

On behalf of person mentally incapable

17.11 Provided that a mentally incapacitated person it not a minor executor (Rule 34(1)), a renunciation on his behalf will be accepted but only from a person specially authorised so to do by an order made by the Court of Protection.

Renunciation of administration on behalf of minors

17.12 Rule 34(2) provides that a minor's right to administration (with or without will) may be renounced only by a person assigned as guardian under Rule 32(2) and authorised to renounce by a registrar.

When renunciation may be made and filed

17.13

(1) *At time of application for grant*: The usual practice is to obtain the renunciation and file the instrument at the time of making application for a grant to some other person.

(2) *Before application for grant*: An executor may renounce probate, or, where no executor is appointed, a residuary legatee and devisee may renounce the right to proof of the will, at any time after the death of the testator and before application is made for a grant. Provided that it is accompanied by the original will (and codicils, if any), the renunciation may be deposited at the Principal Registry or at a district probate registry. Upon application for a grant the applicant may be required to attend the registry for the purpose of being sworn to the oath and marking the will (if necessary the documents will be transmittted to a registry which is the most convenient for that purpose) but the registrar has a discretion to allow a facsimile copy to be marked instead (Rule 10(2)).

(3) *Subsequent to grant, by executor to whom power was reserved*: An executor to whom power has been reserved may renounce after probate has been granted. The renunciation may be filed either in the Principal Registry or in the district probate registry from which the grant issued.

Example forms of renunciation

(1) *Form of renunciation of probate*

[USUAL HEADING]

A.B. of ,
deceased, died on the day of 19 ,
having made and duly executed h last will and testament [and codicil(s)]
bearing date(s) the day of 19 , and thereof
appointed *C.D.*, of executor.

I the said *C.D.*, do hereby declare that I have not intermeddled in the estate of the said deceased and will not hereafter intermeddle therein with intent to defraud creditors, and I hereby renounce all my right and title to probate and execution of the said will [and codicil(s)].

Signed by the said
this day of 19 }
in the presence of:
(*One disinterested witness who should add his residence and occupation to his signature.*)

(2) *Renunciation of administration (will)*

[USUAL HEADING]

A.B. of ,
deceased died on the day of 19 ,
having made and duly executed h last will and testament [and codicil(s)] bearing date the day of 19

[*Recite that no executor appointed, or as the case may be, and show right of renunciant.*]

I the said of
do hereby renounce all my right and title to letters of administration with the said will annexed, of the estate of the said deceased.

Signed by the said
this day of 19 }
in the presence of:

(*One disinterested witness is sufficient who should add his residential address as well as his signature.*)
Signature of Witness
Address

(3) *Renunciation of administration*

[USUAL HEADING]

A.B. of ,
deceased, died on the day of 19 ,
intestate a widower [*or* spinster *or as the case may be*] leaving [*insert name of renunciant*] his child [or *as the case may be*]. (*In all cases add* "one of the persons entitled to share in the estate" *or* "the only person entitled to the estate," [*or as the case may be*].)

I the said of
do hereby renounce all my right and title to letters of administration of the estate of the said deceased.

Signed by the said
this day of 19 }
in the presence of:

Witness
Address

RETRACTION

17.14 A renunciation is regarded as being absolute and final and the court will only allow retraction if good cause is shown. Rule 37(3) provides :

> "A renunciation of probate or administration may be retracted at any time with the leave of a registrar; provided that only in exceptional circumstances may leave be given to an executor to retract a renunciation of probate after a grant has been made to some other person entitled in a lower degree."

Retraction of renunciation by executor

17.15 Permission to retract is given only in exceptional circumstances having regard to Section 5 of the Administration of Estates Act 1925, which provides that where an executor renounces probate of the will his rights in respect of the executorship shall wholly cease and representation to the estate of the testator will be given as if the renunciant had not been appointed executor. An executor who wishes to retract is required to show that retraction is for the benefit of the estate, or for the benefit of persons interested in the estate.

Retraction of renunciation by persons other than executors

17.16 Where a person other than an executor wishes to retract his renunciation, good reason must be given to show that retraction is necessary (*e.g.*, that there is no other person able and willing to complete the administration of the estate of the deceased).

Application for order giving leave to retract

17.17 Application for an order giving leave to retract a renunciation may be made *ex parte* either to the district probate registrar of the registry where the renunciation is filed or to the Principal Registry (Rule 37(4)). The application is made by lodging an affidavit of the facts showing why retraction is necessary, together with the previous grant or an office copy of it. If leave to retract is granted, a form of retraction should be executed and lodged with the order and affidavit and papers leading to the further grant.

Form of retraction

[USUAL HEADING]

A.B. of ,
deceased, died on the day of 19 ,
having made and duly executed his last will and testament, bearing date

the day of 19 , and therein appointed *C.D.* sole executor and me, the undersigned *E.F.*, residuary legatee and devisee.

The said *C.D.* renounced probate and execution of the said will, and I, the said *E.F.*, also renounced letters of administration (with will annexed) of the estate of the said deceased.

Letters of administration (with will annexed) of the said estate were on the day of 19 , granted at the Registry to *G.H.* a creditor of the said deceased.

The said *G.H.* died on the day of 19 , leaving part of the said estate unadministered.

By order of the Registrar dated the day of 19 , I was given leave to retract my said renunciation.

I hereby declare that I retract my said renunciation of letters of administration (with will annexed) of the estate of the said *A.B.*, deceased.

Signed by the said *E.F.*
this day of 19 }
in the presence of

(Signature and address of witness)

APPENDIX 1

Rules

THE NON-CONTENTIOUS PROBATE RULES 1987

(S.I. 1987 No. 2024 (L. 10))

Arrangement of rules

Rule

SCHEDULES

Citation and commencement

1. These Rules may be cited as the Non-Contentious Probate Rules 1987 and shall come into force on 1st January 1988.

Interpretation

2.—(1) In these Rules, unless the context otherwise requires—

"the Act" means the Supreme Court Act 1981;

"authorised officer" means any officer of a registry who is for the time being authorised by the President to administer any oath or to take any affidavit required for any purpose connected with his duties;

"the Crown" includes the Crown in right of the Duchy of Lancaster and the Duke of Cornwall for the time being;

"grant" means a grant of probate or administration and includes, where the context so admits, the resealing of such a grant under the Colonial Probates Acts 1892 and 1927;

"gross value" in relation to any estate means the value of the estate without deduction for debts, incumbrances, funeral expenses or inheritance tax (or other capital tax payable out of the estate);

"oath" means the oath required by rule 8 to be sworn by every applicant for a grant;

"personal applicant" means a person other than a trust corporation who seeks to obtain a grant without employing a solicitor, and "personal application" has a corresponding meaning;

"registrar" means a registrar of the Principal Registry and includes—

(a) in relation to an application for a grant made or proposed to be made at a district probate registry, and
(b) in rules 26, 41 and 61(2) in relation to a grant issued from a district probate registry, and
(c) in relation to rules 46, 47 and 48,

the registrar of that district probate registry;

"registry" means the Principal Registry or a district probate registry;

"the Senior Registrar" means the Senior Registrar of the Family Division or, in his absence, the senior of the registrars in attendance at the Principal Registry;

"statutory guardian" means a surviving parent of a minor who is the guardian of the minor by virtue of section 3 of the Guardianship of Minors Act 1971;

"testamentary guardian" means a person appointed by deed or will to be guardian of a minor under the power conferred by section 4 of the Guardianship of Minors Act 1971;

"the Treasury Solicitor" means the solicitor for the affairs of Her Majesty's Treasury and includes the solicitor for the affairs of the Duchy of Lancaster and the solicitor of the Duchy of Cornwall;

"trust corporation" means a corporation within the meaning of section 128 of the Act as extended by section 3 of the Law of Property (Amendment) Act 1926.

(2) A form referred to by number means the form so numbered in the First Schedule; and such forms shall be used wherever applicable, with such variation as a registrar may in any particular case direct or approve.

Application of other rules

3. Subject to the provisions of these Rules and to any enactment, the Rules of the Supreme Court 1965 shall apply, with the necessary modifications, to non-contentious probate matters, save that nothing in Order 3 shall prevent time from running in the Long Vacation.

Application for grants through solicitors

4.—(1) A person applying for a grant through a solicitor may apply at any registry or sub-registry.

(2) Every solicitor through whom an application for a grant is made shall give the address of his place of business within England and Wales.

Personal applications

5.—(1) A personal applicant may apply for a grant at any registry or sub-registry.

(2) Save as provided for by rule 39 a personal applicant may not apply through an agent, whether paid or unpaid, and may not be attended by any person acting or appearing to act as his adviser.

(3) No personal application shall be proceeded with if—

(a) it becomes necessary to bring the matter before the court by action or summons;
(b) an application has already been made by a solicitor on behalf of the applicant and has not been withdrawn; or
(c) the registrar so directs.

(4) After a will has been deposited in a registry by a personal applicant, it may not be delivered to the applicant or to any other person unless in special circumstances the registrar so directs.

(5) A personal applicant shall produce a certificate of the death of the deceased or such other evidence of the death as the registrar may approve.

(6) A personal applicant shall supply all information necessary to enable the papers leading to the grant to be prepared in the registry.

(7) Unless the registrar otherwise directs, every oath or affidavit required on a personal application shall be sworn or executed by all the deponents before an authorised officer.

(8) No legal advice shall be given to a personal applicant by an officer of a registry and every such officer shall be responsible only for embodying in proper form the applicant's instructions for the grant.

Duty of registrar on receiving application for grant

6.—(1) A registrar shall not allow any grant to issue until all inquiries which he may see fit to make have been answered to his satisfaction.

(2) Except with the leave of a registrar, no grant of probate or of administration with the will annexed shall issue within seven days of the death of the deceased and no grant of administration shall issue within fourteen days thereof.

Grants by district probate registrars

7.—(1) No grant shall be made by a district probate registrar—

(a) in any case in which there is contention, until the contention is disposed of; or
(b) in any case in which it appears to him that a grant ought not to be made without the directions of a judge or a registrar of the Principal Registry.

(2) In any case in which paragraph (1)(b) applies, the district probate registrar shall send a statement of the matter in question to the Principal Registry for directions.

(3) A registrar of the Principal Registry may either confirm that the matter be referred to a judge and give directions accordingly or may direct the district probate registrar to proceed with the matter in accordance with such instructions as are deemed necessary, which may include a direction to take no further action in relation to the matter.

Oath in support of grant

8.—(1) Every application for a grant other than one to which rule 39 applies shall be supported by an oath by the applicant in the form applicable to the circumstances of the case, and by such other papers as the registrar may require.

(2) Unless otherwise directed by a registrar, the oath shall state where the deceased died domiciled.

(3) Where the deceased died on or after 1st January 1926, the oath shall state whether or not, to the best of the applicant's knowledge, information and belief, there was land vested in the deceased which was settled previously to his death and not by his will and which remained settled land notwithstanding his death.

(4) On an application for a grant of administration the oath shall state in what manner all persons having a prior right to a grant have been cleared off and whether any minority or life interest arises under the will or intestacy.

Grant in additional name

9. Where it is sought to describe the deceased in a grant by some name in addition to his true name, the applicant shall depose to the true name of the deceased and shall specify some part of the estate which was held in the other name, or give any other reason for the inclusion of the other name in the grant.

Marking of wills

10.—(1) Subject to paragraph (2) below, every will in respect of which an application for a grant is made—

(a) shall be marked by the signatures of the applicant and the person before whom the oath is sworn; and

(b) shall be exhibited to any affidavit which may be required under these Rules as to the validity, terms, condition or date of execution of the will.

(2) The registrar may allow a facsimile copy of a will to be marked or exhibited in lieu of the original document.

Engrossments for purposes of record

11.—(1) Where the registrar considers that in any particular case a facsimile copy of the original will would not be satisfactory for purposes of record, he may require an engrossment suitable for facsimile reproduction to be lodged.

(2) Where a will—

(a) contains alterations which are not to be admitted to proof; or

(b) has been ordered to be rectified by virtue of section 20(1) of the Administration of Justice Act 1982, there shall be lodged an engrossment of the will in the form in which it is to be proved.

(3) Any engrossment lodged under this rule shall reproduce the punctuation, spacing and division into paragraphs of the will and shall follow continuously from page to page on both sides of the paper.

Evidence as to due execution of will

12.—(1) Subject to paragraphs (2) and (3) below, where a will contains no attestation clause or the attestation clause is insufficient, or where it appears to the registrar that there is doubt about the due execution of the will, he shall before admitting it to proof require an affidavit as to due execution from one or more of the attesting witnesses or, if no attesting witness is conveniently available, from any other person who was present when the will was executed; and if the registrar, after considering the evidence, is satisfied that the will was not duly executed, he shall refuse probate and mark the will accordingly.

(2) If no affidavit can be obtained in accordance with paragraph (1) above, the registrar may accept evidence on affidavit from any person he may think fit to show that the signature on the will is in the handwriting of the deceased, or of any other matter which may raise a presumption in favour of due execution of the will, and may if he thinks fit require that notice of the application be given to any person who may be prejudiced by the will.

(3) A registrar may accept a will for proof without evidence as aforesaid if he is satisfied that the distribution of the estate is not thereby affected.

Execution of will of blind or illiterate testator

13. Before admitting to proof a will which appears to have been signed by a blind or illiterate testator or by another person by direction of the testator, or which for any other reason raises doubt as to the testator having had knowledge of the contents of the will at the time of its execution, the registrar shall satisfy himself that the testator had such knowledge.

Evidence as to terms, condition and date of execution of will

14.—(1) Subject to paragraph (2) below, where there appears in a will any obliteration, interlineation, or other alteration which is not authenticated in the manner prescribed by section 21 of the Wills Act 1837, or by the re-execution of the will or by the execution of a codicil, the registrar shall require evidence to show whether the alteration was present at the time the will was executed and shall give directions as to the form in which the will is to be proved.

(2) The provisions of paragraph (1) above shall not apply to any alteration which appears to the registrar to be of no practical importance.

(3) If a will contains any reference to another document in such terms as to suggest that it ought to be incorporated in the will, the registrar shall require the document to be produced and may call for such evidence in regard to the incorporation of the document as he may think fit.

(4) Where there is a doubt as to the date on which a will was executed, the registrar may require such evidence as he thinks necessary to establish the date.

Attempted revocation of will

15. Any appearance of attempted revocation of a will by burning, tearing, or otherwise destroying and every other circumstance leading to a presumption of revocation by the testator, shall be accounted for to the registrar's satisfaction.

Affidavit as to due execution, terms, etc., of will

16. A registrar may require an affidavit from any person he may think fit for the purpose of satisfying himself as to any of the matters referred to in rules 13, 14 and 15, and in any such affidavit sworn by an attesting witness or other person present at the time of the execution of a will the deponent shall depose to the manner in which the will was executed.

Wills proved otherwise than under section 9 of the Wills Act 1837

17.—(1) Rules 12 to 15 shall apply only to a will that is to be established by reference to section 9 of the Wills Act 1837 (signing and attestation of wills).

(2) A will that is to be established otherwise than as described in paragraph (1) of this rule may be so established upon the registrar being satisfied as to its terms and validity, and includes (without prejudice to the generality of the foregoing)—

(a) any will to which rule 18 applies; and
(b) any will which, by virtue of the Wills Act 1963, is to be treated as properly executed if executed according to the internal law of the territory or state referred to in section 1 of that Act.

Wills of persons on military service and seamen

18. Where the deceased died domiciled in England and Wales and it appears to the registrar that there is prima facie evidence that a will is one to which section 11 of the Wills Act 1837 applies, the will may be admitted to proof if the registrar is satisfied that it was signed by the testator or, if unsigned, that it is in the testator's handwriting.

Evidence of foreign law

19. Where evidence as to the law of any country or territory outside England and Wales is required on any application for a grant, the registrar may accept—
(a) an affidavit from any person whom, having regard to the particulars of his knowledge or experience given in the affidavit, he regards as suitably qualified to give expert evidence of the law in question; or
(b) a certificate by, or an act before, a notary practising in the country or territory concerned.

Order of priority for grant where deceased left a will

20. Where the deceased died on or after 1 January 1926 the person or persons entitled to a grant in respect of a will shall be determined in accordance with the following order of priority, namely—

(a) the executor (but subject to rule 36(4)(d) below);
(b) any residuary legatee or devisee holding in trust for any other person;
(c) any other residuary legatee or devisee (including one for life) or where the residue is not wholly disposed of by the will, any person entitled to share in the undisposed of residue (including the Treasury Solicitor when claiming bona vacantia on behalf of the Crown), provided that—

(i) unless a registrar otherwise directs, a residuary legatee or devisee whose legacy or devise is vested in interest shall be preferred to one entitled on the happening of a contingency, and

(ii) where the residue is not in terms wholly disposed of, the registrar may, if he is satisfied that the testator has nevertheless disposed of the whole or substantially the whole of the known estate, allow a grant to be made to any legatee or devisee entitled to, or to share in, the estate so disposed of, without regard to the persons entitled to share in any residue not disposed of by the will;

(d) the personal representative of any residuary legatee or devisee (but not one for life, or one holding in trust for any other person), or of any person entitled to share in any residue not disposed of by the will;

(e) any other legatee or devisee (including one for life or one holding in trust for any other person) or any creditor of the deceased, provided that, unless a registrar otherwise directs, a legatee or devisee whose legacy or devise is vested in interest shall be preferred to one entitled on the happening of a contingency;

(f) the personal representative of any other legatee or devisee (but not one for life or one holding in trust for any other person) or of any creditor of the deceased.

Grants to attesting witnesses, etc

21. Where a gift to any person fails by reason of section 15 of the Wills Act 1837, such person shall not have any right to a grant as a beneficiary named in the will, without prejudice to his right to a grant in any other capacity.

Order of priority for grant in case of intestacy

22.—(1) Where the deceased died on or after 1st January 1926, wholly intestate, the person or persons having a beneficial interest in the estate shall be entitled to a grant of administration in the following classes in order of priority, namely—

(a) the surviving husband or wife;

(b) the children of the deceased and the issue of any deceased child who died before the deceased;

(c) the father and mother of the deceased;

(d) brothers and sisters of the whole blood and the issue of any deceased brother or sister of the whole blood who died before the deceased;

(e) brothers and sisters of the half blood and the issue of any deceased brother or sister of the half blood who died before the deceased;

(f) grandparents;

(g) uncles and aunts of the whole blood and the issue of any deceased uncle or aunt of the whole blood who died before the deceased;

(h) uncles and aunts of the half blood and the issue of any deceased uncle or aunt of the half blood who died before the deceased.

(2) In default of any person having a beneficial interest in the estate, the Treasury Solicitor shall be entitled to a grant if he claims bona vacantia on behalf of the Crown.

(3) If all persons entitled to a grant under the foregoing provisions of this rule have been cleared off, a grant may be made to a creditor of the deceased or to any person who, notwithstanding that he has no immediate beneficial interest in the estate, may have a beneficial interest in the event of an accretion thereto.

(4) Subject to paragraph (5) of rule 27, the personal representative of a person in any of the classes mentioned in paragraph (1) of this rule or the personal representative of a creditor of the deceased shall have the same right to a grant as the person whom he represents provided that the persons mentioned in sub-paragraphs (b) to (h) of paragraph (1) above shall be preferred to the personal representative of a spouse who has died without taking a beneficial interest in the whole estate of the deceased as ascertained at the time of the application for the grant.

Order of priority for grant in pre-1926 cases

23. Where the deceased died before 1st January 1926, the person or persons entitled to a grant shall, subject to the provisions of any enactment, be determined in accordance with the principles and rules under which the court would have acted at the date of death.

Right of assignee to a grant

24.—(1) Where all the persons entitled to the estate of the deceased (whether under a will or on intestacy) have assigned their whole interest in the estate to one or more persons, the assignee or assignees shall replace, in the order of priority for a grant of administration, the assignor or, if there are two or more assignors, the assignor with the highest priority.

(2) Where there are two or more assignees, administration may be granted with the consent of the others to any one or more (not exceeding four) of them.

(3) In any case where administration is applied for by an assignee the original instrument of assignment shall be produced and a copy of the same lodged in the registry.

Joinder of administrator

25.—(1) A person entitled in priority to a grant of administration may, without leave, apply for a grant with a person entitled in a lower degree, provided that there is no other person entitled in a higher degree to the person to be joined, unless every other such person has renounced.

(2) Subject to paragraph (3) below, an application for leave to join with a person entitled in priority to a grant of administration a person having no right or no immediate right thereto shall be made to a registrar, and shall be supported by an affidavit by the person entitled in priority, the consent of the person proposed to be joined as administrator and such other evidence as the registrar may direct.

(3) Unless a registrar otherwise directs, there may without any such application be joined with a person entitled in priority to administration—

(a) any person who is nominated under paragraph (3) of rule 32 or paragraph (3) of rule 35;
(b) a trust corporation.

Additional personal representatives

26.—(1) An application under section 114(4) of the Act to add a personal representative shall be made to a registrar and shall be supported by an affidavit by the applicant, the consent of the person proposed to be added as personal representative and such other evidence as the registrar may require.

(2) On any such application the registrar may direct that a note shall be made on the original grant of the addition of a further personal representative, or he may impound or revoke the grant or make such other order as the circumstances of the case may require.

Grants where two or more persons entitled in same degree

27.—(1) Subject to paragraphs (2) and (3) below, where, on an application for probate, power to apply for a like grant is to be reserved to such other of the executors as have not renounced probate, the oath shall state that notice of the application has been given to the executor or executors to whom power is to be reserved.

(2) Where power is to be reserved to partners of a firm, notice for the purposes of paragraph (1) above may be given to the partners by sending it to the firm at its principal or last known place of business.

(3) A registrar may dispense with the giving of notice under paragraph (1) above if he is satisfied that the giving of such a notice is impracticable or would result in unreasonable delay or expense.

(4) A grant of administration may be made to any person entitled thereto without notice to other persons entitled in the same degree.

(5) Unless a registrar otherwise directs, administration shall be granted to a person of full age entitled thereto in preference to a guardian of a minor, and to a living person entitled thereto in preference to the personal representative of a deceased person.

(6) A dispute between persons entitled to a grant in the same degree shall be brought by summons before a registrar.

(7) The issue of a summons under this rule in a district probate registry shall be notified forthwith to the registry in which the index of pending grant applications is maintained.

(8) If the issue of a summons under this rule is known to the registrar, he shall not allow any grant to be sealed until such summons is finally disposed of.

Exceptions to rules as to priority

28.—(1) Any person to whom a grant may or is required to be made under any enactment shall not be prevented from obtaining such a grant notwithstanding the operation of rules 20, 22, 25 or 27.

(2) Where the deceased died domiciled outside England and Wales rules 20, 22, 25 or 27 shall not apply except in a case to which paragraph (3) of rule 30 applies.

Grants in respect of settled land

29.—(1) In this rule "settled land" means land vested in the deceased which was settled previously to his death and not by his will and which remained settled land notwithstanding his death.

(2) The special executors in regard to settled land constituted by section 22 of the Administration of Estates Act 1925 shall have a prior right to a grant of probate limited to settled land.

(3) The person or persons entitled to a grant of administration limited to settled land shall be determined in accordance with the following order of priority, namely—

(i) the trustees of the settlement at the time of the application for the grant;

(ii) the personal representatives of the deceased.

(4) Where the persons entitled to a grant in respect of the free estate are also entitled to a grant of the same nature in respect of settled land, a grant expressly including the settled land may issue to them.

(5) Where there is settled land and a grant is made in respect of the free estate only, the grant shall expressly exclude the settled land.

Grants where deceased died domiciled outside England and Wales

30.—(1) Subject to paragraph (3) below, where the deceased died domiciled outside England and Wales, a registrar may order that a grant do issue to any of the following persons—

(a) to the person entrusted with the administration of the estate by the court having jurisdiction at the place where the deceased died domiciled; or

(b) where there is no person so entrusted, to the person beneficially entitled to the estate by the law of the place where the deceased died domiciled or, if there is more than one person so entitled, to such of them as the registrar may direct; or

(c) if in the opinion of the registrar the circumstances so require, to such person as the registrar may direct.

(2) A grant made under paragraph (1)(a) or (b) above may be issued jointly with such person as the registrar may direct if the grant is required to be made to not less than two administrators.

(3) Without any order made under paragraph (1) above—

(a) probate of any will which is admissible to proof may be granted—

(i) if the will is in the English or Welsh language, to the executor named therein; or

(ii) if the will describes the duties of a named person in terms sufficient to constitute him executor according to the tenor of the will, to that person; and

(b) where the whole or substantially the whole of the estate in England and Wales consists of immovable property, a grant in respect of the whole estate may be made in accordance with the law which would have been applicable if the deceased had died domiciled in England and Wales.

Grants to attorneys

31.—(1) Subject to paragraphs (2) and (3) below, the lawfully constituted attorney of a person entitled to a grant may apply for administration for the use and benefit of the donor, and such grant shall be limited until further representation be granted, or in such other way as the registrar may direct.

(2) Where the donor referred to in paragraph (1) above is an executor, notice of the application shall be given to any other executor unless such notice is dispensed with by the registrar.

(3) Where the donor referred to in paragraph (1) above is mentally incapable and the attorney is acting under an enduring power of attorney, the application shall be made in accordance with rule 35.

Grants on behalf of minors

32.—(1) Where a person to whom a grant would otherwise be made is a minor, administration for his use and benefit, limited until he attains the age of eighteen years, shall, unless otherwise directed, and subject to paragraph (2) of this rule, be granted to the parents of the minor jointly, or to the statutory or testamentary guardian, or to any guardian appointed by a court of competent jurisdiction; provided that where the minor is sole executor and has no interest in the residuary estate of the deceased, administration for the use and benefit of the minor limited as aforesaid, shall, unless a registrar otherwise directs, be granted to the person entitled to the residuary estate.

(2) A registrar may by order assign any person as guardian of the minor, and such assigned guardian may obtain administration for the use and benefit of the minor, limited as aforesaid, in default of, or jointly with, or to the exclusion of, any person mentioned in paragraph (1) of this rule; and the intended guardian shall file an affidavit in support of his application to be assigned.

(3) Where there is only one person competent and willing to take a grant under the foregoing provisions of this rule, such person may, unless a registrar otherwise directs, nominate any fit and proper person to act jointly with him in taking the grant.

Grants where a minor is a co-executor

33.—(1) Where a minor is appointed executor jointly with one or more other executors, probate may be granted to the executor or executors not under disability with power reserved to the minor executor, and the minor executor shall be entitled to apply for probate on attaining the age of eighteen years.

(2) Administration for the use and benefit of a minor executor until he attains the age of eighteen years may be granted under rule 32 if, and only if, the executors who are not under disability renounce or, on being cited to accept or refuse a grant, fail to make an effective application therefor.

Renunciation of the right of a minor to a grant

34.—(1) The right of a minor executor to probate on attaining the age of eighteen years may not be renounced by any person on his behalf.

(2) The right of a minor to administration may be renounced only by a person assigned as guardian under paragraph (2) of rule 32, and authorised by the registrar to renounce on behalf of the minor.

Grants in case of mental incapacity

35.—(1) Unless a registrar otherwise directs, no grant shall be made under this rule unless all persons entitled in the same degree as the incapable person referred to in paragraph (2) below have been cleared off.

(2) Where a registrar is satisfied that a person entitled to a grant is by reason of mental incapacity incapable of managing his affairs, administration for his use and benefit, limited until further representation be granted or in such other way as the registrar may direct, may be granted in the following order of priority—

(a) to the person authorised by the Court of Protection to apply for a grant;
(b) where there is no person so authorised, to the lawful attorney of the incapable person acting under a registered enduring power of attorney;
(c) where there is no such attorney entitled to act, or if the attorney shall renounce administration for the use and benefit of the incapable person, to the person entitled to the residuary estate of the deceased.

(3) Where a grant is required to be made to not less than two administrators, and there is only one person competent and willing to take a grant under the foregoing provisions of this rule, administration may, unless a registrar otherwise directs, be granted to such person jointly with any other person nominated by him.

(4) Notwithstanding the foregoing provisions of this rule, administration for the use and benefit of the incapable person may be granted to such two or more other persons as the registrar may by order direct.

(5) Notice of an intended application under this rule shall be given to the Court of Protection.

Grants to trust corporations and other corporate bodies

36.—(1) An application for a grant to a trust corporation shall be made through one of its officers, and such officer shall depose in the oath that the corporation is a trust corporation as defined by these Rules and that it has power to accept a grant.

(2)(a) Where the trust corporation is the holder of an official position, any officer whose name is included on a list filed with the Senior Registrar of persons authorised to make affidavits and sign documents on behalf of the office holder may act as the officer through whom the holder of that official position applies for the grant.

(b) In all other cases a certified copy of the resolution of the trust corporation authorising the officer to make the application shall be lodged, or it shall be deposed in the oath that such certified copy has been filed with the Senior Registrar, that the officer is therein identified by the position he holds, and that such resolution is still in force.

(3) A trust corporation may apply for administration otherwise than as a beneficiary or the attorney of some person, and on any such application there shall be lodged the consents of all persons entitled to a grant and of all persons interested in the residuary estate of the deceased save that the registrar may dispense with any such consents as aforesaid on such terms, if any, as he may think fit.

(4)(a) Subject to sub-paragraph (d) below, where a corporate body would, if an individual, be entitled to a grant but is not a trust corporation as defined by these Rules, administration for its use and benefit, limited until further representation be granted, may be made to its nominee or to its lawfully constituted attorney.

(b) A copy of the resolution appointing the nominee or the power of attorney (whichever is appropriate) shall be lodged, and such resolution or power of attorney shall be sealed by the corporate body, or be otherwise authenticated to the registrar's satisfaction.

(c) The nominee or attorney shall depose in the oath that the corporate body is not a trust corporation as defined by these Rules.

(d) The provisions of paragraph (4)(a) above shall not apply where a corporate body is appointed executor jointly with an individual unless the right of the individual has been cleared off.

Renunciation of probate and administration

37.—(1) Renunciation of probate by an executor shall not operate as renunciation of any right which he may have to a grant of administration in some other capacity unless he expressly renounces such right.

(2) Unless a registrar otherwise directs, no person who has renounced administration in one capacity may obtain a grant thereof in some other capacity.

(3) A renunciation of probate or administration may be retracted at any time with the leave of a registrar; provided that only in exceptional circumstances may leave be given to an executor to retract a renunciation of probate after a grant has been made to some other person entitled in a lower degree.

(4) A direction or order giving leave under this rule may be made either by the registrar of a district probate registry where the renunciation is filed or by a registrar of the Principal Registry.

Notice to Crown of intended application for grant

38. In any case in which it appears that the Crown is or may be beneficially interested in the estate of a deceased person, notice of intended application for a grant shall be given by the applicant to the Treasury Solicitor, and the registrar may direct that no grant shall issue within 28 days after the notice has been given.

Resealing under Colonial Probates Acts 1892 and 1927

39.—(1) An application under the Colonial Probates Acts 1892 and 1927 for the resealing of probate or administration granted by the court of a country to which those Acts apply may be made by the person to whom the grant was made or by any person authorised in writing to apply on his behalf.

(2) On any such application an Inland Revenue affidavit or account shall be lodged.

(3) Except by leave of a registrar, no grant shall be resealed unless it was made to such a person as is mentioned in sub-paragraph (a) or (b) of paragraph (1) of rule 30 or to a person to whom a grant could be made under sub-paragraph (a) of paragraph (3) of that rule.

(4) No limited or temporary grant shall be resealed except by leave of a registrar.

(5) Every grant lodged for resealing shall include a copy of any will to which the grant relates or shall be accompanied by a copy thereof certified as correct by or under the authority of the court by which the grant was made, and where the copy of the grant required to be deposited under subsection (1) of section 2 of the

Colonial Probates Act 1892 does not include a copy of the will, a copy thereof shall be deposited in the registry before the grant is resealed.

(6) The registrar shall send notice of the resealing to the court which made the grant.

(7) Where notice is received in the Principal Registry of the resealing of a grant issued in England and Wales, notice of any amendment or revocation of the grant shall be sent to the court by which it was resealed.

Application for leave to sue on guarantee

40. An application for leave under section 120(3) of the Act or under section 11(5) of the Administration of Estates Act 1971 to sue a surety on a guarantee given for the purposes of either of those sections shall, unless the registrar otherwise directs under rule 61, be made by summons to a registrar and notice of the application shall be served on the administrator, the surety and any co-surety.

Amendment and revocation of grant

41.—(1) Subject to paragraph (2) below, if a registrar is satisfied that a grant should be amended or revoked he may make an order accordingly.

(2) Except on the application or with the consent of the person to whom the grant was made, the power conferred in paragraph (1) above shall be exercised only in exceptional circumstances.

Certificate of delivery of Inland Revenue affidavit

42. Where the deceased died before 13th March 1975 the certificate of delivery of an Inland Revenue affidavit required by section 30 of the Customs and Inland Revenue Act 1881 to be borne by every grant shall be in Form 1.

Standing searches

43.—(1) Any person who wishes to be notified of the issue of a grant may enter a standing search for the grant by lodging with the Senior Registrar, or sending to him by post, a notice in Form 2.

(2) A person who has entered a standing search will be sent an office copy of any grant which corresponds with the particulars given on the completed Form 2 and which—

(a) issued not more than twelve months before the entry of the standing search; or

(b) issues within a period of six months after the entry of the standing search.

(3) (a) Where an applicant wishes to extend the said period of six months, he or his solicitor may lodge at, or send by post to, the Principal Registry written application for extension.

(b) An application for extension as aforesaid must be lodged, or received by post, within the last month of the said period of six months, and the standing search shall thereupon be effective for an additional period of six months from the date on which it was due to expire.

(c) A standing search which has been extended as above may be further extended by the filing of a further application for extension subject to the same conditions as set out in sub-paragraph (b) above.

Caveats

44.—(1) Any person who wishes to show cause against the sealing of a grant may enter a caveat in any registry or sub-registry, and the registrar shall not allow any grant to be sealed (other than a grant ad colligenda bona or a grant under section 117 of the Act) if he has knowledge of an effective caveat; provided that no caveat shall prevent the sealing of a grant on the day on which the caveat is entered.

(2) Any person wishing to enter a caveat (in these Rules called "the caveator"), or a solicitor on his behalf, may effect entry of a caveat—

(a) by completing Form 3 in the appropriate book at any registry or sub-registry; or
(b) by sending by post at his own risk a notice in Form 3 to any registry or sub-registry and the proper officer shall provide an acknowledgement of the entry of the caveat.

(3) (a) Except as otherwise provided by this rule or by rules 45 or 46, a caveat shall be effective for a period of six months from the date of entry thereof, and where a caveator wishes to extend the said period of six months, he or his solicitor may lodge at, or send by post to, the registry or sub-registry at which the caveat was entered a written application for extension.
(b) An application for extension as aforesaid must be lodged, or received by post, within the last month of the said period of six months, and the caveat shall thereupon (save as otherwise provided by this rule) be effective for an additional period of six months from the date on which it was due to expire.
(c) A caveat which has been extended as above may be further extended by the filing of a further application for extension subject to the same conditions as set out in sub-paragraph (b) above.

(4) An index of caveats entered in any registry or sub-registry shall be maintained at the same registry in which the index of pending grant applications is maintained, and a search of the caveat index shall be made—

(a) on receipt of an application for a grant at that registry; and
(b) on receipt of a notice of an application for a grant made in any other registry,

and the appropriate registrar shall be notified of the entry of a caveat against the sealing of a grant for which application has been made in that other registry.

(5) Any person claiming to have an interest in the estate may cause to be issued from the registry in which the caveat index is maintained a warning in Form 4 against the caveat, and the person warning shall state his interest in the estate of the deceased and shall require the caveator to give particulars of any contrary interest in the estate; and the warning or a copy thereof shall be served on the caveator forthwith.

(6) A caveator who has no interest contrary to that of the person warning, but who wishes to show cause against the sealing of a grant to that person, may within eight days of service of the warning upon him (inclusive of the day of such service), or at any time thereafter if no affidavit has been filed under paragraph (12) below, issue and serve a summons for directions.

(7) On the hearing of any summons for directions under paragraph (6) above the registrar may give a direction for the caveat to cease to have effect.

(8) Any caveat in force when a summons for directions is issued shall remain in force until the summons has been disposed of unless a direction has been given under paragraph (7) above.

(9) The issue of a summons under this rule shall be notified forthwith to the registry in which the caveat index is maintained.

(10) A caveator having an interest contrary to that of the person warning may within eight days of service of the warning upon him (inclusive of the day of such service) or at any time thereafter if no affidavit has been filed under paragraph (12) below, enter an appearance in the registry in which the caveat index is maintained by filing Form 5 and making an entry in the appropriate book; and he shall serve forthwith on the person warning a copy of Form 5 sealed with the seal of the court.

(11) A caveator who has not entered an appearance to a warning may at any time withdraw his caveat by giving notice at the registry or sub-registry at which it was entered, and the caveat shall thereupon cease to have effect; and, where the caveat has been so withdrawn, the caveator shall forthwith give notice of withdrawal to the person warning.

(12) If no appearance has been entered by the caveator or no summons has been issued by him under paragraph (6) of this rule, the person warning may at any time after eight days of service of the warning upon the caveator (inclusive of the day of such service) file an affidavit in the registry in which the caveat index is maintained as to such service and the caveat shall thereupon cease to have effect provided that there is no pending summons under paragraph (6) of this rule.

(13) Unless a registrar of the Principal Registry by order made on summons otherwise directs, any caveat in respect of which an appearance to a warning has been entered shall remain in force until the commencement of a probate action.

(14) Except with the leave of a registrar of the Principal Registry, no further caveat may be entered by or on behalf of any caveator whose caveat is either in force or has ceased to have effect under paragraphs (7) or (12) of this rule or under rule 45(4) or rule 46(3).

Probate actions

45.—(1) Upon being advised by the court concerned of the commencement of a probate action the Senior Registrar shall give notice of the action to every caveator other than the plaintiff in the action in respect of each caveat that is in force.

(2) In respect of any caveat entered subsequent to the commencement of a probate action the Senior Registrar shall give notice to that caveator of the existence of the action.

(3) Unless a registrar of the Principal Registry by order made on summons otherwise directs, the commencement of a probate action shall operate to prevent the sealing of a grant (other than a grant under section 117 of the Act) until application for a grant is made by the person shown to be entitled thereto by the decision of the court in such action.

(4) Upon such application for a grant, any caveat entered by the plaintiff in the action, and any caveat in respect of which notice of the action has been given, shall cease to have effect.

Citations

46.—(1) Any citation may issue from the Principal Registry or a district probate registry and shall be settled by a registrar before being issued.

(2) Every averment in a citation, and such other information as the registrar may require, shall be verified by an affidavit sworn by the person issuing the citation (in these Rules called the "citor"), provided that the registrar may in special circumstances accept an affidavit sworn by the citor's solicitor.

(3) The citor shall enter a caveat before issuing a citation and, unless a registrar of the Principal Registry by order made on summons otherwise directs, any caveat in force at the commencement of the citation proceedings shall, unless withdrawn pursuant to paragraph (11) of rule 44, remain in force until application for a grant is made by the person shown to be entitled thereto by the decision of the court in such proceedings, and upon such application any caveat entered by a party who had notice of the proceedings shall cease to have effect.

(4) Every citation shall be served personally on the person cited unless the registrar, on cause shown by affidavit, directs some other mode of service, which may include notice by advertisement.

(5) Every will referred to in a citation shall be lodged in a registry before the citation is issued, except where the will is not in the citor's possession and the registrar is satisfied that it is impracticable to require it to be lodged.

(6) A person who has been cited to appear may, within eight days of service of the citation upon him (inclusive of the day of such service), or at any time thereafter if no application has been made by the citor under paragraph (5) of rule 47 or paragraph (2) of rule 48, enter an appearance in the registry from which the citation issued by filing Form 5 and shall forthwith thereafter serve on the citor a copy of Form 5 sealed with the seal of the registry.

Citation to accept or refuse or to take a grant

47.—(1) A citation to accept or refuse a grant may be issued at the instance of any person who would himself be entitled to a grant in the event of the person cited renouncing his right thereto.

(2) Where power to make a grant to an executor has been reserved, a citation calling on him to accept or refuse a grant may be issued at the instance of the executors who have proved the will or the survivor of them or of the executors of the last survivor of deceased executors who have proved.

(3) A citation calling on an executor who has intermeddled in the estate of the deceased to show cause why he should not be ordered to take a grant may be issued at the instance of any person interested in the estate at any time after the expiration of six months from the death of the deceased, provided that no citation to take a grant shall issue while proceedings as to the validity of the will are pending.

(4) A person cited who is willing to accept or take a grant may, after entering an appearance, apply ex parte by affidavit to a registrar for an order for a grant to himself.

(5) If the time limited for appearance has expired and the person cited has not entered an appearance, the citor may—

(a) in the case of a citation under paragraph (1) of this rule, apply to a registrar for an order for a grant to himself;

(b) in the case of a citation under paragraph (2) of this rule, apply to a registrar for an order that a note be made on the grant that the executor in respect of whom power was reserved has been duly cited and has not appeared and that all his rights in respect of the executorship have wholly ceased; or

(c) in the case of a citation under paragraph (3) of this rule, apply to a registrar by summons (which shall be served on the person cited) for an order requiring such person to take a grant within a specified time or for a grant to himself or to some other person specified in the summons.

(6) An application under the last foregoing paragraph shall be supported by an affidavit showing that the citation was duly served.

(7) If the person cited has entered an appearance but has not applied for a grant under paragraph (4) of this rule, or has failed to prosecute his application with reasonable diligence, the citor may—

(a) in the case of a citation under paragraph (1) of this rule, apply by summons to a registrar for an order for a grant to himself;
(b) in the case of a citation under paragraph (2) of this rule, apply by summons to a registrar for an order striking out the appearance and for the endorsement on the grant of such a note as is mentioned in sub-paragraph (b) of paragraph (5) of this rule; or
(c) in the case of a citation under paragraph (3) of this rule, apply by summons to a registrar for an order requiring the person cited to take a grant within a specified time or for a grant to himself or to some other person specified in the summons;

and the summons shall be served on the person cited.

Citation to propound a will

48.—(1) A citation to propound a will shall be directed to the executors named in the will and to all persons interested thereunder, and may be issued at the instance of any citor having an interest contrary to that of the executors or such other persons.

(2) If the time limited for appearance has expired, the citor may—

(a) in the case where no person has entered an appearance, apply to a registrar for an order for a grant as if the will were invalid and such application shall be supported by an affidavit showing that the citation was duly served; or
(b) in the case where no person who has entered an appearance proceeds with reasonable diligence to propound the will, apply to a registrar by summons, which shall be served on every person cited who has entered an appearance, for such an order as is mentioned in paragraph (a) above.

Address for service

49. All caveats, citations, warnings and appearances shall contain an address for service in England and Wales.

Application for order to attend for examination or for subpoena to bring in a will

50.—(1) An application under section 122 of the Act for an order requiring a person to attend for examination may, unless a probate action has been commenced, be made to a registrar by summons which shall be served on every such person as aforesaid.

(2) An application under section 123 of the Act for the issue by a registrar of a subpoena to bring in a will shall be supported by an affidavit setting out the

grounds of the application, and if any person served with the subpoena denies that the will is in his possession or control he may file an affidavit to that effect in the registry from which the subpoena issued.

Grants to part of an estate under section 113 of the Act

51. An application for an order for a grant under section 113 of the Act to part of an estate may be made to a registrar, and shall be supported by an affidavit setting out the grounds of the application, and

(a) stating whether the estate of the deceased is known to be insolvent; and
(b) showing how any person entitled to a grant in respect of the whole estate in priority to the applicant has been cleared off.

Grants of administration under discretionary powers of court, and grants ad colligenda bona

52. An application for an order for—

(a) a grant of administration under section 116 of the Act; or
(b) a grant of administration ad colligenda bona,

may be made to a registrar and shall be supported by an affidavit setting out the grounds of the application.

Applications for leave to swear to death

53. An application for leave to swear to the death of a person in whose estate a grant is sought may be made to a registrar, and shall be supported by an affidavit setting out the grounds of the application and containing particulars of any policies of insurance effected on the life of the presumed deceased together with such further evidence as the registrar may require.

Grants in respect of nuncupative wills and copies of wills

54.—(1) Subject to paragraph (2) below, an application for an order admitting to proof a nuncupative will, or a will contained in a copy or reconstruction thereof where the original is not available, shall be made to a registrar.

(2) In any case where a will is not available owing to its being retained in the custody of a foreign court or official, a duly authenticated copy of the will may be admitted to proof without the order referred to in paragraph (1) above.

(3) An application under paragraph (1) above shall be supported by an affidavit setting out the grounds of the application, and by such evidence on affidavit as the applicant can adduce as to—

(a) the will's existence after the death of the testator or, where there is no such evidence, the facts on which the applicant relies to rebut the presumption that the will has been revoked by destruction;
(b) in respect of a nuncupative will, the contents of that will; and
(c) in respect of a reconstruction of a will, the accuracy of that reconstruction.

(4) The registrar may require additional evidence in the circumstances of a particular case as to due execution of the will or as to the accuracy of the copy will, and may direct that notice be given to persons who would be prejudiced by the application.

Application for rectification of a will

55.—(1) An application for an order that a will be rectified by virtue of section 20(1) of the Administration of Justice Act 1982 may be made to a registrar, unless a probate action has been commenced.

(2) The application shall be supported by an affidavit, setting out the grounds of the application, together with such evidence as can be adduced as to the testator's intentions and as to whichever of the following matters as are in issue:—

(a) in what respects the testator's intentions were not understood; or

(b) the nature of any alleged clerical error.

(3) Unless otherwise directed, notice of the application shall be given to every person having an interest under the will whose interest might be prejudiced by the rectification applied for and any comments in writing by any such person shall be exhibited to the affidavit in support of the application.

(4) If the registrar is satisfied that, subject to any direction to the contrary, notice has been given to every person mentioned in paragraph (3) above, and that the application is unopposed, he may order that the will be rectified accordingly.

Notice of election by surviving spouse to redeem life interest

56.—(1) Where a surviving spouse who is the sole or sole surviving personal representative of the deceased is entitled to a life interest in part of the residuary estate and elects under section 47A of the Administration of Estates Act 1925 to have the life interest redeemed, he may give written notice of the election to the Senior Registrar in pursuance of subsection (7) of that section by filing a notice in Form 6 in the Principal Registry or in the district probate registry from which the grant issued.

(2) Where the grant issued from a district probate registry, the notice shall be filed in duplicate.

(3) A notice filed under this rule shall be noted on the grant and the record and shall be open to inspection.

Index of grant applications

57.—(1) The Senior Registrar shall maintain an index of every pending application for a grant made in any registry.

(2) Notice of every application for a grant shall be sent by the registry in which the application is made to the registry in which the index is maintained and shall be in the form of a document stating the full name of the deceased and the date of his death.

(3) On receipt of the notice referred to in paragraph (2) above, the registry shall search its current index and shall give a certificate as to the result of that search to the registry which sent the notice.

(4) The requirements of paragraph (2) above shall not apply in any case in which the application for a grant is made in the registry in which the index is maintained.

(5) In this rule "registry" includes a sub-registry.

Inspection of copies of original wills and other documents

58. An original will or other document referred to in section 124 of the Act shall not be open to inspection if, in the opinion of a registrar, such inspection would be undesirable or otherwise inappropriate.

Issue of copies of original wills and other documents

59. Where copies are required of original wills or other documents deposited under section 124 of the Act, such copies may be facsimile copies scaled with the seal of the court and issued either as office copies or certified under the hand of a registrar to be true copies.

Taxation of costs

60. Every bill of costs, other than a bill delivered by a solicitor to his client which falls to be taxed under the Solicitors Act 1974 shall be referred to a registrar of the Principal Registry for taxation and may be taxed by him or such other taxing officer in the Principal Registry as the President may appoint.

Power to require applications to be made by summons

61.—(1) A registrar may require any application to be made by summons to a registrar in chambers or a judge in chambers or open court.

(2) An application for an inventory and account shall be made by summons to a registrar.

(3) A summons for hearing by a registrar shall be issued out of the registry in which it is to be heard.

(4) A summons to be heard by a judge shall be issued out of the Principal Registry.

Transfer of applications

62. A registrar to whom any application is made under these Rules may order the transfer of the application to another registrar having jurisdiction.

Power to make orders for costs

63. On any application dealt with by him on summons, the district probate registrar shall have full power to determine by whom and to what extent the costs are to be paid.

Exercise of powers of judge during Long Vacation

64. All powers exercisable under these Rules by a judge in chambers may be exercised during the Long Vacation by a registrar of the Principal Registry.

Appeals from registrars

65.—(1) An appeal against a decision or requirement of a registrar shall be made by summons to a judge.

(2) If, in the case of an appeal under the last foregoing paragraph, any person besides the appellant appeared or was represented before the registrar from whose decision or requirement the appeal is brought, the summons shall be issued within seven days thereof for hearing on the first available day and shall be served on every such person as aforesaid.

Service of summons

66.—(1) A judge or registrar of the Principal Registry or, where the application is to be made to a district probate registrar, that registrar, may direct that a summons for the service of which no other provision is made by these Rules shall be served on such person or persons as the judge or registrar may direct.

(2) Where by these Rules or by any direction given under the last foregoing paragraph a summons is required to be served on any person, it shall be served not less than two clear days before the day appointed for the hearing, unless a judge or registrar at or before the hearing dispenses with service on such terms, if any, as he may think fit.

Notices, etc.

67. Unless a registrar otherwise directs or these Rules otherwise provide, any notice or other document required to be given to or served on any person may be given or served in the manner prescribed by Order 65 Rule 5 of the Rules of the Supreme Court 1965.

Application to pending proceedings

68. Subject in any particular case to any direction given by a judge or registrar, these Rules shall apply to any proceedings which are pending on the date on which they come into force as well as to any proceedings commenced on or after that date.

Revocation of previous rules

69.—(1) Subject to paragraph (2) below, the rules set out in the Second Schedule are hereby revoked.

(2) The rules set out in the Second Schedule shall continue to apply to such extent as may be necessary for giving effect to a direction under rule 68.

FIRST SCHEDULE

FORMS

FORM 1 (Rule 42)

CERTIFICATE OF DELIVERY OF INLAND REVENUE AFFIDAVIT

And it is hereby certified that an Inland Revenue affidavit has been delivered wherein it is shown that the gross value of the said estate in the United Kingdom (exclusive of what the said deceased may have been possessed of or entitled to as a trustee and not beneficially) amounts to £.............. and that the net value of the estate amounts to £..............

And it is further certified that it appears by a receipt signed by an Inland Revenue officer on the said affidavit that £.............. on account of estate duty and interest on such duty has been paid.

FORM 2 (Rule 43(1))

STANDING SEARCH

In the High Court of Justice
Family Division
The Principal Registry

I/We apply for the entry of a standing search so that there shall be sent to me/us an office copy of every grant of representation in England and Wales in the estate of—
Full name of deceased: ....
Full address: ....
Alternative or alias names: ....
Exact date of death:..
which either has issued not more than 12 months before the entry of this application or issues within 6 months thereafter.
Signed ....
Name in block letters..
Full address ....
Reference No. (if any) ....

FORM 3 (Rule 44(2))

CAVEAT

In the High Court of Justice
Family Division
The Principal [*or* .... District Probate] Registry.

Let no grant be sealed in the estate of (*full name and address*) deceased, who died on the .... day of .... 19 ..... without notice to (*name of party by whom or on whose behalf the caveat is entered*).

Dated this................ day of .... 19 ....

(*Signed*) (*to be signed by the caveator's solicitor or by the caveator if acting in person*)

whose address for service is: ....
Solicitor for the said .... (*If the caveator is acting in person, substitute "In person".*)

FORM 4 (Rule 44(5))

WARNING TO CAVEATOR

In the High Court of Justice
Family Division
[*The Registry in which the caveat index is maintained*]

To .... of .... a party who has entered a caveat in the estate of .... deceased.

You have eight days (starting with the day on which this warning was served on you):

(i) to enter an appearance either in person or by your solicitor, at the [*name and address of the registry in which the caveat index is maintained*] setting out what interest you have in the estate of the above-named .... of .... deceased contrary to that of the party at whose instance this warning is issued; or

(ii) if you have no contrary interest but wish to show cause against the sealing of a grant to such party, to issue and serve a summons for directions by a registrar of the Principal Registry or a district probate registry.

If you fail to do either of these, the court may proceed to issue a grant of probate or administration in the said estate notwithstanding your caveat.

Dated the .... day of .... 19 ....

Issued at the instance of ....

[*Here set out the name and interest (including the date of the will, if any, under which the interest arises) of the party warning, the name of his solicitor and the address for service. If the party warning is acting in person, this must be stated.*]

Registrar

FORM 5 (Rules 44(10), 46(6))

APPEARANCE TO WARNING OR CITATION

In the High Court of Justice
Family Division
The Principal [*or* .... District Probate] Registry
Caveat No. .... dated the .... day of .... 19 ......
[Citation dated the .... day of .... 19 ....]
Full name and address of deceased: ....
Full name and address of person warning [*or* citor]: ....
(*Here set out the interest of the person warning, or citor, as shown in warning or citation.*)
Full name and address of caveator [or person cited].
(*Here set out the interest of the caveator or person cited, stating the date of the will (if any) under which such interest arises.*)
Enter an appearance for the above-named caveator [*or* person cited] in this matter.
Dated the .... day of .... 19 ... .

(*Signed*)

whose address for service is:

Solicitor (or "In person").

FORM 6 (Rule 56)

NOTICE OF ELECTION TO REDEEM LIFE INTEREST

In the High Court of Justice
Family Division
The Principal [*or* .... District Probate] Registry
In the estate of .... deceased.
Whereas .... of .... died on the .... day of .... 19 ......
wholly/partially intestate leaving his/her/lawful wife/husband and ....
lawful issue of the said deceased;

And whereas Probate/Letters of Administration of the estate of the said .... were granted to me, the said .... [and to .... of ....] at the Probate Registry on the .... day of .... 19 ....;

And whereas [the said .... has ceased to be a personal representative because ....] and I am [now] the sole personal representative;

Now I, the said .... hereby give notice in accordance with section 47A of the Administration of Estates Act 1925 that I elect to redeem the life interest to which I am entitled in the estate of the late .... by retaining £..................... its capital value, and £ .... the costs of the transaction.
Dated the .... day of .... 19 ....
(Signed)

To the Senior Registrar of the Family Division.

SECOND SCHEDULE

(The Rules revoked by Rule 69 are not listed in this book.)

APPENDIX 2

Fees

THE NON-CONTENTIOUS PROBATE FEES ORDER 1981

(as amended by S.I.s 1103 of 1981, 1180 of 1983, 705 of 1986, 2185 of 1986 and 1176 of 1987)

Citation and commencement

1.—This Order may be cited as the Non-Contentious Probate Fees Order 1981 and shall come into operation on 3rd August 1981.

Interpretation

2.—(1) In this Order, unless the context otherwise requires—

"assessed value" means the value of the net real and personal estate (excluding settled land if any) passing under the grant as shown—

(i) in the Inland Revenue affidavit (for a death occurring before 13th March 1975), or

(ii) in the Inland Revenue account (for a death occurring on or after 13th March 1975), or

(iii) in a case in which, in accordance with arrangements made between the President of the Family Division and the Commissioners of Inland Revenue or regulations made under section 94(1)(a) of the Finance Act 1980 and from time to time in force, no such affidavit or account is required to be delivered, in the oath which is sworn to lead to the grant;

and in the case of an application to reseal a grant means the said value, as so shown, passing under the grant upon its being resealed;

"authorised place of deposit" means any place in which, by virtue of a direction given under section 170 of the Supreme Court of Judicature (Consolidation) Act 1925 original wills and other documents under the control of the High Court (either in the principal registry or in any district registry) are deposited and preserved;

"grant" means a grant of probate or letters of administration;

"district registry" includes the probate registry of Wales, any district probate registry and any sub-registry attached thereto;

"the principal registry" means the Principal Registry of the Family Division and any sub-registry attached thereto.

(2) A fee referred to by number means the fee so numbered in the Schedule to this Order.

Taking of fees

3.—(1) The fees set out in column 2 of the Schedule to this Order shall be taken in the principal registry and in each district registry in respect of the items set out opposite thereto in column 1.

(2) The fees prescribed by this Order shall be taken in cash.

Exclusion of certain death gratuities

4.—In determining the value of any personal estate for the purpose of this Order there shall be excluded the value of a death gratuity payable under section 17(2) of the Judicial Pensions Act 1981 or payable to the personal representatives of a deceased civil servant by virtue of a scheme made under section 1 of the Superannuation Act 1972.

Reduction, remission and exemption

5.—(1) Where it appears to the Lord Chancellor that the payment of any fee specified in the Schedule would, owing to the exceptional circumstances of the particular case, involve undue hardship, the Lord Chancellor may reduce or remit the fee in that case.

(2) Where by any convention entered into by Her Majesty with any foreign power it is provided that no fee shall be required to be paid in respect of any proceedings, the fees specified in this Order shall not be taken in respect of those proceedings.

(3) Where any application for a grant is withdrawn before the issue of the grant, a registrar may reduce or remit a fee.

(4) Where, on application for a grant by a personal applicant, the papers leading to the grant are prepared by the applicant himself, a registrar may remit up to one-half of the fee prescribed by fee no. 2.

(5) Fee no. 7 shall not be taken where a search is made for research or similar purposes by permission of the President of the Family Division for a document over 100 years old filed in the principal registry or a district registry or another authorised place of deposit.

Revocation of orders

6.—The Supreme Court (Non-Contentious Probate) Fees Order 1975, the Supreme Court (Non-Contentious Probate) Fees (Amendment) Order 1976, the Supreme Court (Non-Contentious Probate) Fees (Amendment) Order 1978 and the Supreme Court (Non-Contentious Probate) Fees (Amendment) Order 1980 are hereby revoked.

SCHEDULE

Column 1 Item	*Column* 2 Fee £
Application for grant: general	
1. On an application for a grant (or for resealing a grant) other than an application to which fee No. 3 applies:—	
(a) if the assessed value	
does not exceed £10,000	No fee
exceeds £10,000 but does not exceed £25,000	40.00
exceeds £25,000 but does not exceed £40,000	80.00
exceeds £40,000 but does not exceed £70,000	150.00
exceeds £70,000 but does not exceed £100,000	2.50 per £1000 or part thereof
(b) if the assessed value exceeds £100,000	250.00
and for every additional £100,000 or part thereof, a further fee of	50.00
Personal application fee	
2. On application for a grant by a personal applicant (or for resealing such a grant if the application is prepared in the registry) save where fee no. 3(a) is payable, in addition to any other fee:	
(a) if the assessed value does not exceed £500	1.00
exceeds £500 but does not exceed £1,000	2.00
exceeds £1,000 but does not exceed £5,000	5.00
(b) if the assessed value exceeds £5,000, for each £1,000 or part thereof	1.00
Special applications	
3. On an application for:—	
(a) a grant in respect of an estate exempt from estate duty by virtue of section 71 of the Finance Act 1952 or from capital transfer tax by virtue of paragraph 1 of Schedule 7 to the Finance Act 1975 (exemption for members of the armed forces, etc.);	
(b) a grant limited to settled land;	
(c) a grant limited to trust property;	
(d) a duplicate grant;	
(e) any second or subsequent grant (including one following a revoked grant) in respect of the same deceased person, other than a grant preceded only by a grant limited to settled land, to trust property or to a part of the estate	2.00

Column 1 Item	Column 2 Fee £
Caveats	
4. For the entry or the extension of a caveat	4.00
Search	
5. On an application for a standing search to be carried out in an estate, for each search period of six months	2.00
Deposit of wills	
6. On depositing a will for safe custody in the principal registry or a district registry	1.00
Inspection	
7. On inspection of an original will or any other document including a copy of a will	0.25
Copies of documents—Personal attendance or on application for grant	
8.(a) For a copy of all or part of any document, whether or not issued as an office copy, for each page	0.25
(b) For a sealed and certified copy of any document	1.00
and for each page after the first, a further fee of	0.25
(c) For an exemplification of a copy signed by a registrar and countersigned by the President of the Family Division, including the fees for preparing the necessary documents	5.00
Copies of documents—Postal applications other than on application for grant	
9. For handling a postal application, in respect of each estate, and where appropriate supplying,—	
(a) a copy of any will or grant or other document, whether or not issued as an office copy	2.00
(b) a sealed and certified copy of any will or grant. Only one fee shall be charged for the purposes of sub-paragraph (a) or (b) on a request for a copy of a will and a grant.	3.00
(c) an additional sealed and certified copy of any will or grant	1.00
and for each page after the first a further fee of	0.25

Column 1	*Column* 2
Item	Fee £
(d) an exemplification of a copy signed by a registrar and countersigned by the President of the Family Division, including the preparation of the necessary documents	6.00
(e) an additional copy of any document, other than a sealed and certified copy, for each page	0.25
Oaths and guarantees	
10. Save on a personal application for a grant:—	
(a) for administering an oath, for each deponent to each affidavit	2.00
(b) for marking each exhibit	0.50
(c) for superintending and attesting execution of a guarantee, for each surety	1.00
Taxation of costs	
11. For taxing a bill of costs in the principal registry inclusive of the registrar's certificate	The same fees as are payable in an action.
Settling documents	
12. For perusing and settling citations, advertisements, oaths, affidavits or other documents, for each document settled	5.00

APPENDIX 3

Distribution Tables

TABLES SHOWING DISTRIBUTION OF ESTATE AND PERSONS ENTITLED TO A GRANT IN THE CASE OF INTESTACY

Death on or after 1st June 1987, leaving a spouse surviving (See para. 5.13 for details of variations where deceased died before 1st June 1987)

Intestate leaves	*Distribution of estate*	*Entitled to grant*
1. Husband or widow without issue or parent or brother or sister of the whole blood or their issue (whatever the amount of the estate)	Husband or widow	Husband or widow
2. Husband or widow and issue (net estate not exceeding £75,000)	Husband or widow	Husband or widow
3. Husband or widow and issue (net estate exceeding £75,000)	Husband or widow takes personal chattels, £75,000 (free of costs and tax) with interest at the appropriate rate (a). Life interest in half remainder of estate, with reversion to issue, and as to the other half, to the issue absolutely.	Husband or widow and a child (b)
4. Husband or widow without issue (net estate not exceeding £125,000)	Husband or widow	Husband or widow

5. Husband or widow without issue (net estate exceeding £125,000)	Husband or widow takes personal chattels, £125,000 (free of costs and tax) with interest at the appropriate rate (a), and half remainder of estate absolutely. As to the other half where there are parents, to the parents absolutely. Where there are no parents, to the brothers and sisters of the whole blood absolutely in equal shares, the issue of such as have predeceased the intestate taking the share to which their parent would have been entitled *per stirpes*	Husband or widow

(a) The current rate is 6 per cent but it is liable to variation.

(b) If a minority or life interest arises in the estate the grant must normally be made to not less than two individuals, or to a trust corporation with or without an individual.

Death on or at any time after 1st January 1926. No surviving spouse.

Intestate leaves	*Distribution of estate*	*Entitled to grant*
1. Issue only	Issue (including illegitimate children where death on or after 1st Jan. 1970) who attain 18 years or marry under 18 take equally (children of predeceasing children take their parents' share, *per stirpes*)	*Issue
2. Father or mother	Father or mother (including the natural mother of an illegitimate child where the child died on or after 1 Jan. 1927 and the natural father or mother of an illegitimate child where the child died on or after 1 Jan. 1970)**	Father or mother
3. Father and mother	Father and mother in equal shares (including the natural father and mother of an illegitimate child where the deceased died on or after 1 Jan. 1970, but only the natural mother where the child died before that date but on or after 1 Jan. 1927)**	Either or both

4. Brothers and sisters of the whole blood, and issue of such as predeceased the intestate	Brothers and sisters of the whole blood in equal shares, the issue of such as have predeceased the intestate taking their parents' share, *per stirpes***	*A person or persons entitled to share in the estate
5. Brothers and sisters of the half blood and issue of such as predeceased the intestate	Brothers and sisters of the half blood in equal shares and issue as in 4**	*A person or persons entitled to share in the estate
6. Grandparents	Grandparents in equal shares**	Grandparent (one or more)
7. Uncles and aunts of the whole blood, and issue of such as predeceased the intestate	Uncles and aunts of the whole blood and issue as in 4**	*A person or persons entitled to share in the estate
8. Uncles and aunts of the half blood and issue of such as predeceased the intestate	Uncles and aunts of the half blood and issue as in 4**	*A person or persons entitled to share in the estate
9. No blood relation taking an interest as above	The Crown (Duchy of Lancaster, Duchy of Cornwall)	Treasury Solicitor for the use of Her Majesty (Solicitor for the Duchy)

*If a minority or life interest arises in the estate the grant must normally be made to not less than two individuals, or to a trust corporation with or without an individual.

**Where the deceased died on or after 4th April 1988 the relationship need not be lawful.

Index